Film and Television Locations

ALSO BY DOUG GELBERT
AND FROM MCFARLAND

*American Revolutionary War Sites, Memorials, Museums and
Library Collections: A State-by-State Guidebook
to Places Open to the Public* (1998)

*Civil War Sites, Memorials, Museums and Library
Collections: A State-by-State Guidebook to
Places Open to the Public* (1997)

*Company Museums, Industry Museums and Industrial Tours:
A Guidebook of Sites in the United
States That Are Open to the Public* (1994)

*Sports Halls of Fame:
A Directory of Over 100 Sports
Museums in the United States* (1992)

FILM AND TELEVISION LOCATIONS

A State-by-State Guidebook to Moviemaking Sites, Excluding Los Angeles

DOUG GELBERT

McFarland & Company, Inc., Publishers
Jefferson, North Carolina, and London

Library of Congress Cataloguing-in-Publication Data

Gelbert, Doug.
    Film and television locations : a state-by-state guidebook to moviemaking sites, excluding Los Angeles / Doug Gelbert.
        p.   cm.
    Includes index.
    ISBN 0-7864-1293-3 (softcover : 50# alkaline paper) ∞
    1. Motion picture locations— United States— Guidebooks.
    2. Television program locations— United States— Guidebooks.
I. Title.
PN1995.67.U6G45   2002
384'.8'0973 — dc21   2002010927

British Library cataloguing data are available

©2002 Doug Gelbert. All rights reserved

No part of this book may be reproduced or transmitted in any form or by any means, electronic or mechanical, including photocopying or recording, or by any information storage and retrieval system, without permission in writing from the publisher.

On the covers: Oak Alley Plantation, Vacherie, Louisiana
    (*Interview with a Vampire*)

Manufactured in the United States of America

McFarland & Company, Inc., Publishers
    Box 611, Jefferson, North Carolina 28640
        www.mcfarlandpub.com

CONTENTS

Introduction   1

Alabama	3	Massachusetts	106
Alaska	5	Michigan	114
Arizona	7	Minnesota	118
Arkansas	13	Mississippi	123
California	16	Missouri	125
Colorado	40	Montana	127
Connecticut	45	Nebraska	128
Delaware	47	Nevada	129
District of Columbia	48	New Hampshire	138
Florida	53	New Jersey	139
Georgia	65	New Mexico	144
Hawaii	73	New York	148
Idaho	75	North Carolina	173
Illinois	75	North Dakota	179
Indiana	88	Ohio	180
Iowa	90	Oklahoma	184
Kansas	92	Oregon	185
Kentucky	93	Pennsylvania	189
Louisiana	95	Rhode Island	197
Maine	101	South Carolina	199
Maryland	102	South Dakota	203

CONTENTS

Tennessee	203	Washington	233
Texas	207	West Virginia	239
Utah	223	Wisconsin	240
Vermont	227	Wyoming	241
Virginia	230		

Appendix: Locations Listed by Type   245
Actor and Director Index   263
Movie and Television Show Index   272

INTRODUCTION

Perhaps the boom began with a single traveler from New York. While driving leisurely across the country a movie fan who had recently seen *Field of Dreams* decided to seek out the baseball field built out of a cornfield in Iowa. He found it in Dyersville, looked around, walked on the field and drove on. But his visit had a profound effect on movie tourism.

Farm owner Don Lansing's plan had been to replant the 2½ acres of his 100-acre field in time for the next harvest. The New Yorker's visit got him to thinking otherwise. Lansing decided to keep the "Field of Dreams" and placed a bag of balls and some bats in the grass for anyone who wanted to play on the field. Some came to run the base paths and others to play catch. Many just sat in the bleachers. His neighbor, upon whose land the leftfield area was built, did indeed plow up the field, but the crush of visitors soon convinced him to restore the movie playing area to its original dimensions—290 feet to the stalks in left, 320 to center and 270 to rightfield.

Dyersville, whose previous claim to fame was intertwined with toy tractors, was now a tourist destination for tens of thousands of movie fans each year.

Municipalities across the country began to recognize the incalculable free publicity and residual benefits to having a hit movie or television show filmed in town. Hundreds of film commissions were established to lure production companies.

Local governments were finally catching up, not only with the trend of location shooting in movie and television production, but with fans' urge to make pilgrimages to honor their favorite entertainments. In 1962, when location shooting was the exception rather than the norm, producers for *To Kill a Mockingbird*

INTRODUCTION

traveled to Monroeville, Alabama, where the story was set — not to film the movie, but to make sketches of the town, which they recreated in minute detail on a Hollywood soundstage. Still, after the Academy Award–winning movie was released, thousands of fans went to Monroeville to see the real Old Monroe County Courthouse, believing it to be where the movie was filmed.

This book identifies real-life locations (excluding Los Angeles) where movies and television shows were shot. Every attempt has been made to insure that the sites listed still exist. However, to everyone but fans, movie locations are anything but sacrosanct. Businesses change hands overnight: buildings are torn down and open spaces plowed over. Inevitably, some of the sites listed in this book will disappear over time.

The entries are organized by state, then alphabetically by movie or television show title. Each listing includes the year of release, the two main stars, and a plot line before describing the film's location or locations. Some states have popular movie and television locations that have hosted dozens of productions. Where such locations exist, they are noted at the end of the state's section, following the listings for individual films and television shows. Indices are available to quickly locate a favorite actor, favorite movie, or television show or favorite location.

ALABAMA

Blue Sky

(1994). Jessica Lange, Tommy Lee Jones. Wife's free spirit causes problems for somber military man.

Much of the movie was filmed on Craig Field in Selma. During filming in Selma, Jessica Lange lived in the 1892 Lanford-Portis-Smith House on Church Street.

Body Snatchers

(1993). Terry Kinney, Meg Tilly. Family moves to military base with eerie consequences.

The setting for the army base was Craig Field, a former army base turned into an industrial park. Here it was converted back into the fictional Fort Daly.

Cobb

(1994). Tommy Lee Jones, Robert Wuhl. Reporter hired to write official biography of Ty Cobb meets the irascible baseball legend in his final days.

The oldest active ballpark in the country, Rickwood Field (1137 Second Avenue West, Birmingham) played the role of Tiger Stadium in Detroit, Shibe Park in Philadelphia and Forbes Field in Pittsburgh. Rickwood Field, opened in 1910, was refurbished before the filming of the movie. Jones replicates Cobb's famous high spikes steal of home here. Jones' home at the end of his life is the Ehrman Mansion in Sugar Pine Point State Park at Lake Tahoe, California. While filming in Nevada, older buildings in Reno on Fourth Street were dressed up with neon to appear as they might have in the 1940s, including the old Reno arch, which was returned from a damp warehouse. Town officials liked the rebirth of the rusty landmark and moved it to 10 Lake Street South, next to the National Automobile Museum.

The Heart Is a Lonely Hunter

(1968). Alan Arkin, Sandra Locke. Young man's life is changed when he is drawn into the world of a deaf-mute who rents a room in his house.

Scenes were shot in the Walker-Plant House (725 Dallas Avenue, Selma), a rare Georgian home built in 1915. Footage from the 1830s Old Live Oak Cemetery, also on Dallas Avenue, was used as well. Arkin's home was a private house on 620 Mabry Street.

Mississippi Burning

(1988). Gene Hackman, Willem Dafoe. FBI agents investigate the disappearance of civil rights activists in 1964 Deep South.

The production was filmed at dozens of locations around Alabama. The courthouse in the movie is the Chambers County Courthouse (Courthouse Square, LaFayette). Built in 1899, the two-story brick building with palladium windows dominates the town square.

Norma Rae

(1979). Sally Field, Rob Leibman. Jewish union leader recruits young single mother to organize workers in textile mill.

Although the textile plant in the movie was in Georgia, the state did not allow any of its mills to be used in filming. The mill that was finally selected was a textile mill in Opelika, which was already unionized. The hotel where Leibman urges workers to come pick up union cards is the Golden Cherry Motel (1010 2nd Av-

Stephen Seagal battled terrorists aboard the USS *Alabama* in *Under Siege*.

enue, Opelika), Room 207. The lake scene was lensed in Waverly.

Soul of the Game

(1996). Edward Herrmann, Delroy Lindo. Events surrounding the signing of Jackie Robinson with the Brooklyn Dodgers.

Baseball sequences were filmed at Rickwood Field (1137 Second Avenue West, Birmingham), standing in for period ballparks of the 1940s.

Space Camp

(1986). Kate Capshaw, Lea Thompson. Youngsters attending a space camp are accidentally launched into space.

Filmed at the United States Space and Rocket Center (One Tranquility Base off I-565, Huntsville), this was the first movie to use actual NASA launch footage. The youngsters were attending camp at this exposition center which houses one of the world's largest collection of space rockets. Regularly scheduled bus tours of the facility are available.

Stroker Ace

(1983). Burt Reynolds, Loni Anderson. Star NASCAR driver clashes off the track with his self-promoting sponsor.

Among the race tracks featured are the Talladega Superspeedway (Speedway Boulevard, Talladega); Daytona International Speedway (1801 W. International Speedway Boulevard, Daytona Beach); the Atlanta Motor Speedway (US 19/41 junction, Hampton), where tours of the raceway allow visitors to ride on the track, visit the garage and walk in victory lane; Lowe's Motor Speedway at Charlotte (US 29), where the guided tours include a van ride around the oval; and Darlington Raceway (Harry Byrd Highway) in Darlington, South Carolina.

Under Siege

(1992). Steven Seagal, Tommy Lee Jones. A cook does battle with a gang of terrorists who seize a United States Navy battleship.

Although set aboard the USS *Missouri*, which was used for underway shots, all interior sequences were filmed aboard the USS *Alabama* (2703 Battleship Parkway, Mobile). Decommissioned in 1947 after playing a dominant role in the occupation of Japan after World War II, the 680-foot battleship opened to the public in 1965. Many areas of the battleship are open to tourists, including the mess, bridge, decks, berths, turrets and captain's deck.

ALASKA

Ice Palace

(1960). Richard Burton, Robert Ryan. Multi-generational struggle played out against Alaska's impending statehood.

The parade celebrating statehood for Alaska was recreated on 2nd

Street in Anchorage but did not make the final cut of the movie. Brief scenes can be seen of Fairbanks as it looked at the time of statehood.

On Deadly Ground

(1994). Stephen Seagal, Michael Caine. Eskimos choose a disgruntled employee to battle exploitive oil company.

Seagal hides from the thugs of the polluting oil company in the native village at Worthington Glacier. The bar that Seagal clears out in the village of Valdez is called Acres, just outside of the downtown area, and huts, bones and beartraps from the movie can be seen here at Orca Bay Trading Post (137 Galena Drive).

Runaway Train

(1985). Jon Voight, Eric Roberts. Escaped convicts find themselves on a train with no brakes and no engineer.

The locomotive escaped convicts Voight and Roberts sneak onto is from the Whittier Branch of Alaska Railroad's southbound excursion between Girdwood and Whittier. It was a rare winter lacking in snow in Alaska, so additional railroad scenes were shot in Montana near Butte and at the old Montana Territorial Prison in Deer Lodge.

Star Trek VI: The Undiscovered Country

(1991). William Shatner, Leonard Nimoy. Enterprise crew tries to preserve peace treaty between Klingon Empire and Federation.

Shatner and De Forest Kelley escape from a penal colony on the ice planet Rura Penthe which was created on the Knik Glacier in Chugach State Park, east of Anchorage on Glenn Highway. The glacier, 28 miles long and 1000 feet thick, must be viewed

The 1890s mining town of Dalton City was built as a movie set for *White Fang* and now serves Haines, Alaska, as a tourist attraction. (City of Haines, Alaska)

by a helicopter tour. Many outfitters offer such tours between April and October.

White Fang

(1991). Ethan Hawke, Klaus Maria Brandauer. Friendship develops between a Yukon gold hunter and the mixed dog-wolf he rescues.

The 1890s mining town of Dalton City was built for the movie on a bluff overlooking Haines. When the filming was complete the town set was donated to the town and moved to Southeast Alaska Fairgrounds where it stands as a tourist attraction with operating businesses.

ARIZONA

Bill and Ted's Excellent Adventure

(1989). Keanu Reeves, Alex Winter. Time machine helps teens with fuzzy notions of history on school project.

The favorite place for kids to spend money in the movie was the Metrocenter Mall (9617 Metro Center Parkway West, Phoenix). San Dimas High School, where Reeves and Winter went to class, was Coronado High School (2501 N. 74th Street, Scottsdale).

Billy Jack

(1971). Tom Laughlin, Delores Taylor. Ex–Green Beret karate expert detests violence but is drawn into conflict in his travels.

The Courthouse Plaza in Prescott is a focal point of action in the movie. Laughlin is beat up at the corner of Gurley and Montezuma, and bullies douse Indians with flour in front of Kendall's Famous Burgers at 113 South Cortez.

Broken Arrow

(1996). John Travolta, Christian Slater. Rogue Army pilot steals two nuclear missiles and is chased by co-pilot and park ranger.

After being ejected from his stealth bomber, Slater parachutes to earth in Glen Canyon, along SR 230, north of Big Water. Slater and Samantha Mathis search for the downed plane in Marble Canyon near Lees Ferry. Slater and Travolta fight near the Bee Hive formations a half mile west of the dam, south of US 89. The final scenes on the freight train were staged on the Central Montana Railroad near Denton, Montana.

Bus Stop

(1956). Marilyn Monroe, Don Murray. Naive cowboy falls for a saloon singer and is determined to marry her.

All the interiors for this breakthough movie for Marilyn Monroe were shot in Hollywood. The original bus terminal, however, was shot at the corner of Central and Van Buren in Phoenix.

Can't Buy Me Love

(1987). Patrick Dempsey, Amanda Peterson. High schooler hires the prettiest cheerleader in school to pose as his girlfriend.

The school where Dempsey executes his scheme to achieve popularity was Tucson High School (Sixth Street, Tucson). Mall scenes were filmed at the Tucson Mall (4500 North Oracle Road, Tucson), and Dempsey's favorite place to go was the Pima Air Museum (6000 East Valencia Road, Tucson). More than 200 vintage aircraft are scattered about the grounds.

Casablanca

(1942). Humphrey Bogart, Ingrid Bergman. Cynical nightclub owner is drawn into the Resistance during World War II when an old love appears.

When this relatively low budget film was shooting a scene at the Hotel Monte Vista (100 N. San Francisco Street, Flagstaff), it was thought the movie would be a box-office bomb and would disappear quickly. The Monte Vista, on the National Register of Historic Places, opened in 1927 and was a favorite resting place for many Hollywood stars. Several of the 50 rooms are named for famous guests, and visitors can stay in the room where Casablanca was shot.

Days of Thunder

(1990). Tom Cruise, Robert Duvall. A local hot-shot race driver gets his shot on the big league circuit.

Cruise wanted to do his own driving in the film but the insurance company underwriting the movie would not allow it. At the Phoenix International Raceway (1313 North Second Street, Phoenix) Bobby Hamilton, driving in his first ever NASCAR Winston Cup competition, qualified fifth in the movie car. During the race, Hamilton actually took the lead and was among the leaders when NASCAR officials forced him to park the car. The scene with the car driven on the beach, plowing through a flock of seagulls and annoying the locals, was filmed on Daytona Beach, Florida, north of Main Street Pier. Also featured in Florida is Sophie Kay's Restaurant (3516 South Atlantic Beach, Daytona) and Tom's Pizza (140 E. Rich Avenue, DeLand). Cruise wins his first big race at Darlington Raceway in Darlington, South Carolina.

The Gauntlet

(1977). Clint Eastwood, Sandra Locke. Cop discovers who his real enemies are while transporting a mob witness.

The finale was staged at Phoenix Civic Plaza in downtown Phoenix as Eastwood drove an armored bus through hundreds of police marksmen.

Grand Canyon

(1991). Danny Glover, Kevin Kline. Unrelated lives intersect in Los Angeles.

The Grand Canyon is used mostly as a metaphor throughout the film but all the characters do get together on the canyon rim at the end of the story.

The Grifters

(1990). Angelica Huston, John Cusack. Mother and son con artists fall onto hard times while working a game.

Huston works a horse racing scam at the Turf Paradise Race Track (19th Avenue and Bell Road, Phoenix). Airport scenes were filmed at the Sky Harbor Airport in Phoenix.

Jerry Maguire

(1996). Tom Cruise, Renee Zellweger. A successful sports agent rediscovers ethics and loses all his clients but one.

Cuba Gooding makes his career-revitalizing catch in Sun Devil Stadium (Mill and 5th Streets, Tempe). The stands were filled with 25,000 extras for the shooting.

Junior Bonner

(1972). Steve McQueen, Robert Preston. Washed-up rodeo champion returns to hometown to discover his family in disarray.

One of the places McQueen drinks is the Palace Bar (120 South Montezuma, Prescott). Opened in 1877, the Palace is the oldest frontier saloon in Arizona. When a fire swept across Whiskey Row in 1900, patrons carried the ornate Brunswick Bar across the street to safety. It is still in use today.

Just One of the Guys

(1985). Joyce Hyser, Clayton Rohner. High school girl tries to get teachers to take her seriously by posing as a boy.

Scottsdale High School, which was used in the movie, is no longer standing, but other recognizable locations include historic Encanto in Phoenix, Big Surf (1500 McClintock Road, Tempe) and Hole-in-the-Rock in Patago Park (junction of Galvin Parkway and Van Buren Street, Phoenix).

Major League

(1989). Tom Berenger, Charlie Sheen. Scheming owner tries to get out of stadium lease by building a team guaranteed to lose.

Although this baseball saga is about the Cleveland Indians, nothing was filmed in Cleveland. The opening scenes were shot at Hi Corbett Field (3400 East Camino in Randolph Park, Tucson), built in the 1920s and then the spring training home of the Indians. The now demolished County Stadium (201 South 46th Street, Milwaukee, Wisconsin) played the home ballpark in Cleveland during the regular season.

Maverick

(1994). Mel Gibson, James Garner. Western gambler struggles to get money for poker tournament.

Filmmakers spent one million dollars to build an entire western town on the shore of Lake Powell at the mouth of Crosby Canyon. When filming was completed the town was taken down, leaving no trace.

Murphy's Romance

(1985). James Garner, Sally Field. Divorcee relocates to small desert town to train horses on a run-down farm and catches the eye of the town pharmacist.

Murphy's Drugstore, the primary setting for the romance, was an actual drugstore (310 North Main Street, Florence) in the 1930s but was a storage building at the time of the shoot. Rejuvenated, it is today a restaurant known as Murphy's Soup and Salad.

National Lampoon's Vacation

(1983). Chevy Chase, Beverly D'Angelo. Misadventures on the road during an annual family trip.

Chase is photographed in front of the wide steps of the low-slung El Tovar Hotel, a Registered National Historic Landmark on the south rim of the Grand Canyon. The historic lodge was constructed in 1905.

Nurse Betty

(2000). Renee Zellweger, Morgan Freeman. Waitress suffers a mental breakdown after husband's death and believes she is the real-life love of her favorite soap-opera star.

The fantasy dance sequence was filmed at the edge of the Grand Canyon in Grand Canyon National Park.

Raising Arizona

(1987). Nicolas Cage, Holly Hunter. Childless couple help themselves to one of another family's quintuplets.

A Home Depot (Cave Creek and Cactus, Phoenix) stood in for the Unpainted Arizona furniture store where Cage and Hunter kidnap Try Wilson's son. The City of Phoenix Squaw Peak Water Treatment plant (20th and Maryland, Phoenix) was the prison that is the scene of a jail break. Also used in Phoenix was the Jokake Inn at the Phoenician Resort (6000 East Camelback Road), which contributed interiors for Cage and Hunter's house. John Goodman and William Forsythe rob a bank played by the Reata Pass Steakhouse (27500 North Alma School Parkway, Scottsdale).

Revenge of the Nerds

(1984). Robert Carradine, Anthony Edwards. Group of college misfits finally fight back for their dignity.

The shenanigans on film were created at various locales at the University of Arizona campus in Tucson. Many of the students were used as extras.

Starman

(1984). Jeff Bridges, Karen Allen. A spaceman comes to earth as a young woman's husband.

Stranded spaceman Bridges arranges a rendezvous with his spaceship at Meteor Crater, 19 miles west of Winslow. The crater is the first confirmed meteor crater on earth, with a hole 540 feet deep and almost one mile wide. Earlier, Bridges had exercised his power over mechanical devices to win a slot machine jackpot at Binion's Horseshoe (128 E. Fremont Street, Las Vegas).

Three Kings

(1999). George Clooney, Mark Wahlberg. As the Gulf War winds down, American soldiers set out to steal gold stolen from Kuwait.

Much of the action, including oil fires, was shot in the Sacaton Mine, an abandoned open pit copper mine 40 miles south of Phoenix. The Iraqi desert fortress movie set still stands on the mine tailings.

Tin Cup

(1996). Kevin Costner, Rene Russo. Washed-up golf pro tries to win the United States Open and runs into an old rival.

Golf scenes were shot in west Texas, where the movie is set, and south of Tucson at the Tubac Golf resort (1 Otero Road, Tubac). On the climactic hole the script called for a water hazard, but #16, where the scene was shot, did not have a pond. A water hazard, dubbed Tin Cup Lake, was built, and today players at this public resort can attempt the same carry-over that Costner needed to execute to defeat Don Johnson. The flirting scenes between Costner and Russo were filmed along the Santa Cruz River near the golf course. In Houston, Texas, the Northgate Country Club stood in for North Carolina's Pine Hills Country Club.

Used Cars

(1980). Kurt Russell, Jack Warden. Brothers are competing used car dealers with differing philosophies.

Filmed around Main Street in Mesa, the scene with all the cars driving into the desert was filmed with local kids driving their own cars. The City Courthouse (Washington Street, Phoenix) also makes an appearance. A brief scene was shot on the 28-mile Magma Arizona Railroad, east of Phoenix. The line was the last steam-powered standard gauge railroad to operate in the western United States.

Waiting to Exhale

(1995). Whitney Houston, Angela Bassett. Four successful women try to make sense of the men in their lives.

Among the posh locales around Phoenix used here was the Hermosa Inn (5532 North Palo Cristi Road, Paradise Valley). Other filming sites included Fountain Hills and Moon Valley.

Popular Arizona Locations

MONUMENT VALLEY

One evening in 1938 Harry Goulding heard an announcement on the radio: United Artists in Hollywood was looking for a location to shoot a new western movie. Goulding lived in the Monument Valley region of northern Arizona and southern

The Hermosa Inn in Phoenix, Arizona, was used in the shooting of the drama *Waiting to Exhale*. (Hermosa Inn)

Utah. It is a stark land of towering buttes, isolated mesas and breathtaking spires. Life was hard there. When the government opened the region to homesteading in 1923, Goulding came as a young sheepherder with plans to open a trading post. He paid $320 for a 640-acre parcel. By the Depression most settlers were gone and the entire region, save for Goulding's solitary trading post, became part of the Navajo Reservation.

A movie might just bring some money into the area, he thought. Not knowing anyone and bereft of connections, Goulding loaded up a large portfolio of photographs of Monument Valley and headed down Route 66 to Hollywood. Stonewalled by a United Artists receptionist, Goulding stubbornly persisted until he was able to get his pictures in the hands of a production scout. Within an hour, director John Ford was making plans to visit Monument Valley the next day. Three days later crews began arriving to film *Stagecoach*, starring John Wayne and Claire Trevor.

Stagecoach would make Wayne a star and elevate the Western from B-movie status into the most popular form of American cinema. The Stagecoach scenes were shot in open desert country today known as Stagecoach Wash on Route 163 south of Redlands Pass. The stagecoach path is a dirt road parallel with the regular road. Filming also took place in the vicinity of the Mitten Buttes, which is the first stop on the 17-mile auto tour.

The success of *Stagecoach* quickly lured other filmmakers to Monument Valley. Ford and Wayne returned many times. In *The*

Searchers, shot mostly in the area near the present-day Visitors Center, Wayne captures Natalie Wood in the sand dunes south of the Sand Spring. In *She Wore a Yellow Ribbon*, Wayne's cavalry officer kept his headquarters in a small cabin behind Goulding's trading post at the base of Rock Door Mesa. Today the cabin, with the nameplate of Wayne's Captain Nathan Brittles still on the front door, is maintained as a museum to moviemaking in Monument Valley.

Also on the long roster of movies using the dramatic Monument Valley backdrop are *My Darling Clementine* (Henry Fonda, Victor Mature), *Fort Apache* (John Wayne, Henry Fonda) and *Sergeant Rutledge* (Woody Strode, Jeffrey Hunter). In the last, the massacre takes place at Spindle Station at the base of the Mitten Buttes, and the body of Chris Hubble is found just south of the North Window, the last stop on the auto tour.

OLD TUCSON STUDIOS

In 1939 Columbia Pictures sought a real-life backdrop for its big budget ($2.5 million) epic *Arizona*, to star William Holden and Jean Arthur. They chose a county-owned site south of Tucson and, after referring to historical records, began to build a clay facsimile of 1860s Tucson. Without benefit of running water in the area, local builders erected more than 50 buildings, using 350,000 adobe bricks. When the movie wrapped, the sets were deserted and the buildings abandoned in the desert.

When the television era arrived and the Western became its most popular genre, Hollywood remembered the Old Tucson Studios and made it a favorite location. More than 70 films were shot here, including *Gunfight at the OK Corral* (Kirk Douglas, Burt Lancaster), *Rio Bravo* (John Wayne, Dean Martin), *Outlaw Josie Wales* (Clint Eastwood, Sandra Locke) and *Three Amigos* (Chevy Chase, Steve Martin). More feature films, television movies, and television series would be filmed at Old Tucson Studios than any other man-made location outside Hollywood.

The studio began its next life in 1960 under the auspices of entrepreneur Robert Shelton, who transformed the ghost town into a family fun park as well as a movie studio. Today at Old Tucson Studios are western town sets along Front Street and Kansas Street, the Mexican Plaza courtyard, the High Chaparral Ranch, a ghost town and a railroad.

ARKANSAS

Biloxi Blues

(1988). Matthew Broderick, Christopher Walken. Young recruits experience boot camp in Mississippi during World War II.

Hollywood returned to Fort Chaffee to evoke army life in the

ARKANSAS

1940s to film this adaptation of a Neil Simon play. The recruits were brought to camp on the Arkansas & Missouri Railroad in World War I–vintage Pullman Car #104 and deposited at the Old Frisco Depot (813 Main Street, Van Buren). Tourists can ride the train as far as Springdale today. The town of Van Buren stood in for Biloxi, and at 627 Main Street is where Broderick and his buddies are serviced by good-hearted prostitutes.

Boxcar Bertha

(1972). Barbara Hershey, David Carradine. Union leader and young woman take revenge on the railroad during Great Depression.

The railroad used for director Martin Scorsese's debut film was the Possum Trot Line of the Reader Railroad. The short-line railroad was built in 1880 to haul logs to a sawmill. Today tourists can take a seven-mile trip from Reader to Waterloo, pulled by a wood-burning steam engine. The trip includes wooden trestles and the 1880 Winslow Tunnel. Diner Club Car #52 was used in the movie.

Designing Women

(1986–1993). Delta Burke, Dixie Carter. The work and personal lives of four women running a design business.

The Atlanta house from which the women ran their business in the television series was played by a house on 14th & Scott streets in Little Rock. Tours are conducted by the Quapaw Quarter Association.

A Face in the Crowd

(1957). Andy Griffith, Patricia Neal. Singing hobo is thrust into national prominence as a television star.

Most of the streets around the town of Piggott look about the same as they did when Griffith played this star-making role as Lonesome Rhodes. Gone, however, are the jail and the courthouse. Many original

In *Biloxi Blues*, new Army recruits arrived for military taining at the Old Frisco Depot in Van Buren, Arkansas.

photographs and memorabilia from the movie can be found at the Enchanted Forrest (193 West Main Street).

Frank and Jesse

(1994). Rob Lowe, Bill Paxton. Outlaw James brothers become folk heroes in the aftermath of the Civil War.

Small towns and woodlands in Arkansas played the Midwestern towns where the James brothers rose to fame. King's Opera House (427 Main Street, Van Buren) played the Bank of Northfield in Minnesota, which the James boys and the Youngers targeted as a big score. The town of Winslow became Liberty, Missouri, and Chester played Gallatin, Missouri. The Arkansas & Missouri Scenic Railroad along Highway 71 between Springdale and Eureka Springs was the stage for a daring train heist. The Borden House in Prairie Grove Battlefield State Park (US 62, Prairie Grove), a Civil War battlefield, was where Jim Flowers shoots Rob Lowe, playing Jesse James.

Sling Blade

(1996). Billy Bob Thornton, Dwight Yoakam. Simple man hospitalized since his childhood murder of his mother and lover is released into a small town.

Thornton used his hometown of Benton entirely to film his career-

The Borden House in Prairie Grove, Arkansas, stood at the center of a withering Union assault during the Civil War and was destroyed. Rebuilt after the war, the house was where Jim Flowers, as Bob Ford, shot Rob Lowe, playing Jesse James, in *Frank and Jesse*.

making movie. Thornton first meets his benefactor Lucas Black at the Fun Wash (2205 Military Road). Several scenes were shot along the Saline River, including the old iron bridge and Thornton's baptism site. The State Nervous Hospital where Thornton is released and eventually returns to is the Arkansas Health Center (671 Highway 67).

A Soldier's Story

(1984). Howard Rollins, Jr., Adolph Caesar. Murder investigation on an army base in World War II triggers racial tension.

Fort Chaffee, a 72,000-acre army base open to the public, was used as the setting for this drama. In addition to the base, baseball sequences were shot at Lamar Porter Field (3107 West Capitol, Little Rock), and street scenes were created on Main Street in Clarendon. The murder was staged in the woods around Ruby.

CALIFORNIA

Addams Family Values

(1993). Raul Julia, Angelica Huston. Family fears uncle is in the clutches of a gold-digging woman.

The summer camp to which Christina Ricci and Jimmy Workman are sent is at Sequoia Lake in Fresno County.

Adventures of Robin Hood

(1938). Errol Flynn, Olivia de Havilland. A Saxon lord fights against oppressive British rule.

Sherwood Forest was portrayed in this telling of the Robin Hood legend by Bidwell Park (Fourth and Pine streets, Chico). Robin Hood Glade is located on the north side of Big Chico Creek where Highway 99 crosses the park. The 1017-acre Golden Gate Park in San Francisco was also used to create Flynn's fiefdom.

The Adventures of Rocky and Bullwinkle

(2000). Rene Russo, Jason Alexander. FBI agent calls on two famous cartoon characters to help thwart evil plan for world domination.

The hay truck accident and the climax with the state trooper were filmed southwest of Woodland at the intersection of County Roads 25 and 97. Jefferson Avenue in Clarksburg stood in for Kansas.

American Graffiti

(1973). Ron Howard, Richard Dreyfuss. Four high school graduates ponder their future on the last day of summer.

Petaluma was retrofitted to 1962 to film this quintessential cruising movie in 29 days. The hop was at the Petaluma High School gym (201 Fair Street); Dreyfuss visited

Wolfman Jack's remote radio station on Ravina Lane; Paul LeMat and Mackenzie Phillips smear shaving cream and deflate the tires of the 1960 Cadillac at the intersection of Petaluma Boulevard and Western Avenue; and the final drag race takes place on Frates Road. Mel's Drive-In, where everyone meets and sometimes eats, was recently closed at the time and completely demolished after filming.

Angels in the Outfield

(1994). Danny Glover, Tony Danza. An angel helps a boy realize his baseball dreams.

Although set in Anaheim, the stadium used for baseball sequences in the film was Network Associates Coliseum (66th Avenue, Oakland). Joseph Gordon-Levitt and Milton Davis, Jr. live in a foster home at the corner of Douglas and Hale in Oakland.

The Bachelor

(1999). Chris O'Donnell, Renee Zellweger. Young man has 24 hours to get married to receive a $100 million inheritance.

San Francisco locations include the Palace of Fine Arts (3601 Lyons Street), the Steinhart Aquarium of the California Academy of Sciences in Golden Gate Park (55 Concourse Drive), and Moose's Restaurant (1652 Stockton Street). The horde of brides, including several men in drag, chase O'Donnell down Columbus Avenue and corner him on 2nd Street.

Basic Instinct

(1992). Michael Douglas, Sharon Stone. Prime suspect in a series of sex murders is a predatory woman.

The production was filmed across the Bay area, including Oakland, where George Dzunza is murdered at the former John Breuner Company building (2201 Broadway); Petaluma, where a car chase takes place on Petaluma Boulevard from B Street to East Washington; and Carmel, where Douglas and Stone flirt on Garrapatta State Beach. In San Francisco, Douglas drinks with his fellow cops at Tosca Cafe (242 Columbus Avenue) and dances with Stone at the Rawhide 2 Country and Western Bar (280 Seventh Street).

Bedazzled

(2000). Brendan Fraser, Elizabeth Hurley. Man is granted seven wishes by the Devil in exchange for his soul.

The 30-car pile-up was staged at Columbus and Vallerjo in San Francisco. The police station was depicted by the Agriculture Building at Market Street for the exterior and the War Memorial Building for the interiors. Another San Francisco location used was the Vaillancourt Fountain in Justin Herman Plaza.

Beverly Hills Cop 3

(1994). Eddie Murphy, Jon Tenney. Detective's trail of car theft ring leads to amusement park.

Paramount's Great America amusement park (Great America

Parkway, between US 101 and SR 237, Santa Clara) played Wonder World, where Murphy saves children trapped on the Triple Wheel. Another ride used in the movie was the Alien Attack at Universal Studios Theme Park in Universal City.

The Birds

(1963). Tippi Hedren, Rod Taylor. Flocks of birds begin gathering in a seaside town and become increasingly more menacing.

The Potter Schoolhouse, which was the particular object of the birds' attention, has been repaired and rebuilt, and stands today as the School House Inn (17110 Bodega Lane, Bodega Bay). The Tides Restaurant (800 SR 1), where Hedren first reports the aggressive behavior of the birds, is still there but was used only for exterior shots in the movie. The interior scenes were filmed at Universal Studios. The featured drive is taken along Bay Hill Road above Bodega Bay.

Breakdown

(1997). J.T. Walsh, Kurt Russell. Man searches for his missing wife after his car breaks down in the middle of the desert.

Walsh and Russell confront the tractor trailer on the American River Parkway, a 23-mile strip of protected habitat from Folsom Lake to old Sacramento. In Nevada, scenes were shot at Nelson's Landing on Lake Mohave near Hoover Dam.

Bullitt

(1968). Steve McQueen, Robert Vaughn. Policeman battles politicians and hit men as he tries to keep an informant alive and solve his friend's murder.

Locations from this quintessential San Francisco movie include the Filbert Steps on Greenwich Street, hospital scenes shot at San Francisco General (1001 Patterson) and the Kennedy Hotel (end of Howard Street at Embarcadero). The car chase, considered the greatest in film history, took three weeks to film and consumed nine minutes and 42 seconds of screen time. It began with a U-turn on Cesar Chavez, just east of Bryant, at the base of Bernal Heights. From there, it roughly followed eastbound on Filbert, downhill on Taylor, cuts to the Marina District on Marina Boulevard and into McLaren Park's Mansell Street.

The Candidate

(1972) Robert Redford, Peter Boyle. United States senatorial candidate abandons winning for shaking up the established power structure.

The Paramount Theater (2205 Broadway, Oakland) served as Redford's campaign headquarters. Other Bay area locations included the Marin Art and Garden Center (30 Sir Francis Drake Boulevard, Ross) and the Schlumberger Gallery (709 Davis Street, Santa Rosa).

Cannery Row

(1982). Nick Nolte, Debra Winger. Romance of biologist and wandering floozy is played out against wharf district.

Exteriors were shot on the waterfront in Monterey and the sand dunes north of the marina, but most of the scenes were filmed on a sound stage in Culver City.

Class Action

(1991). Gene Hackman, Mary Elizabeth Mastrantonio. The truth is more powerful than law when father and daughter lawyers square off.

The Tech Mart Building (corner of Great America Parkway) houses fictional Argo Motors, the manufacturer implicated in the class-action suit. The Bix Restaurant (56 Gold Street, San Francisco) also plays a role in the film.

The Conversation

(1974) Gene Hackman, Frederic Forrest. Surveillance expert suspects he is spying on a couple that may be murdered.

The opening aerial shot was taken from the roof of Nieman-Marcus at Union Square, where Hackman secretly tapes the conversations of Cindy Williams and Forrest as they stroll through the square. The grisly murder took place in Room 773 of the Cathedral Hill Hotel at Van Ness at Geary, playing the Jack Tar Hotel.

Cujo

(1983). Daniel Hugh Kelly, Danny Pinteuro. Once friendly St. Bernard contracts rabies and begins terrorizing small town.

Cujo, played by five real dogs, a mechanical dog and an actor in a dog suit, lived in Glen Ellen on Sonoma Mountain Road. Interiors were shot in a private home off Chanate Road in Santa Rosa.

Dark Passage

(1947). Humphrey Bogart, Lauren Bacall. Escaped convict hides out in woman's apartment while plastic surgery heals.

Bacall shields San Quentin escapee Bogart in an art deco apartment at 1360 Montgomery Street on San Francisco's Telegraph Hill. The climactic fight scene is staged in the Golden Gate Recreational Area at Fort Point.

Dirty Harry

(1971). Clint Eastwood, Harry Guardino. Cop throws away rules to hunt down serial killer.

Sniper Andy Robinson shoots from the roof of the Bank America Building (555 California Street) across Washington Square at victim in swimming pool atop the Holiday Inn (750 Kearney Street) two blocks away. In another scene he aims his rifle from the Dante Building (1606 Stockton) across Washington Square at targets in front of Saints Peter and Paul Church (666 Filbert Street). Scenes were shot in the actual mayor's office, but most of the action set on San Francisco streets was shot on a Hollywood lot.

The Doors

(1991) Val Kilmer, Kathleen Quinlan. The life of a mercurial 1960s rock icon.

Scenes of the Fox Warfield Theater (Market Street and Taylor, San Francisco) appear in the film. The Pulgas Water Temple (Canada Road, San Mateo) stands in for the Hollywood Bowl.

Ed TV

(1999). Matthew McConaughey, Jenna Elfman. Video store clerk agrees to have his everyday life filmed for national television.

McConaughey rides the Zamboni machine during a hockey game at the San Jose Arena (525 W. Santa Clara Street, San Jose). The scene was filmed during an actual National Hockey League game in front of a sold-out crowd. McConaughey worked the day shift at North Beach Video at the corner of Grant Avenue and Green Street in San Francisco.

Erin Brockovich

(2000). Julia Roberts, Albert Finney. Unemployed single mother hired as go-fer at law firm uncovers events leading to major class-action suit.

Scenes for the film, including the barbecue and town meeting, were shot in the town of Hinkley, whose residents were being poisoned by ground water emitted by a nearby Pacific Gas & Electric Company Compressor Station. The real-life Barstow Courthouse (235 East Mountain View Avenue) was also used to recreate the trial of the class action suit.

Escape from Alcatraz

(1979). Clint Eastwood, Patrick McGoohan. Dramatization of the closest successful attempt to escape "The Rock."

The cells of the real-life inmates involved in the escapade—138, 140, 144—were located on a bottom row of B Block known as Michigan Avenue. The cells used in the film were shot in C Block of the maximum security federal prison, in the middle of a bottom row known as Broadway. Tours of Alcatraz Island leave from Pier 41 at Fisherman's Wharf.

Fearless

(1993). Jeff Bridges, Isabella Rossellini. Man walks away from a horrific plane crash with a sense of immortality.

The field where the plane crash was staged was in Arvin on Bear Mountain Boulevard near the intersection with South Union Avenue. Exterior mall scenes were shot at the Bayfair Mall (East 14th Street, San Leandro), and interiors were filmed above the food court in Southland Mall (Winton Avenue, Hayward).

Flubber

(1997). Robin Williams, Marcia Gay Harden. Wifty professor discovers a substance with amazingly elastic properties.

Several scenes were shot on University Avenue in San Jose near the Rose Garden, including the exteriors of Williams' house, the flubber bouncing around the neighborhood, and the car flying over the town. The exterior shots of the basketball stadium were filmed on the campus of Stanford University.

Forever Young

(1992). Mel Gibson, Jamie Lee Curtis. A man frozen in a cryogenic experiment for one year in 1939 is not awakened until 1992.

The lighthouse where Gibson and Isabel Glasser played as children and are reunited in the film's finale is the Point Arena Lighthouse at the end of Lighthouse Road off Highway 1 in Point Arena. The Berkeley shingle cottage and gazebo were built specifically for the movie and destroyed in a training session for the local fire department. The 115-foot-tall concrete lighthouse opened in 1908 to replace an 1870 structure destroyed in the 1906 earthquake. Tours are available.

Foul Play

(1978). Goldie Hawn, Chevy Chase. Shy librarian and bumbling cop fall in love and solve a crime.

Filmed in various locations around San Francisco, Hawn's apartment was at 430 Vallejo. She worked in the Pasadena Public Library (285 East Walnut Street).

Full House

(1987–1995). Bob Saget, John Stamos. Young widower raises three young girls.

The television series, set in San Francisco, was shot in Los Angeles. The opening credits show Saget's house on Steiner Street and the Golden Gate Bridge.

The Game

(1997) Michael Douglas, Sean Penn. Wealthy financier gets a live-action game for this birthday that consumes his life.

Douglas' home is the Filoli Mansion (Canada Road, Woodside). The fountain out front is a Hollywood creation, and the graffiti on the walls was written on foamboard adhered to the real walls, but the interior shots were made in the actual time-worn kitchen seen on tours. The taxi races down Harrison Street in San Francisco before crashing into the bay at the Embarcadero. The denouement takes place in Maxfield's at Sheraton Palace (2 New Montgomery, San Francisco).

Gattaca

(1997). Ethan Hawke, Jude Law. In futuristic society the world is divided into the artificially perfected beings and the flawed natural-borns.

The interiors and exteriors of the Gattaca Corporation Headquarters were filmed at the Marin County Civic Center (3501 Civic Center Drive, San Rafael). The Civic Center was the largest design by Frank Lloyd Wright ever built, completed after his death in 1959. The central dome seen in the roof-cleaning scene contains the Marin County library. Tours of the building are available.

George of the Jungle

(1997). Brendan Fraser, Leslie Mann. Baby raised by an ape after a plane crash is discovered and brought to America.

The canoeing scenes were staged in the rapids of the American River near Auburn. Fraser discovers the world he has been missing in Nieman-Marcus at Union Square. The film's finale takes place on the Bay Bridge between San Francisco and Oakland.

Getting Even with Dad

(1993). Ted Danson, Macauley Culkin. Boy steals his robber-father's stolen coins and hides them.

Filmed across San Francisco, the blackmailed Danson takes Culkin to the Steinhart Aquarium (55 Concourse Drive), 3 Com Park (Giants Drive and Gilman Avenue), the Scandia Mini-Golf in Rohnert Park and the Paramount's Great America amusement park (Great America Parkway, Santa Clara). Danson pulls off the heist at the San Francisco Department of Public Health (101 Grove Street).

The Graduate

(1967) Dustin Hoffman, Katherine Ross. Young man just out of college doesn't know what to do with his life.

Some of the scenes were shot in Berkeley along Telegraph Avenue and on the University of California campus at Sproul Plaza but most of the college scenes were staged at the University of Southern California in Los Angeles.

Harold and Maude

(1971). Ruth Gordon, Bud Cort. Relationship develops between death-obsessed young man and lively 79-year-old woman.

Cort's home was played by the Rose Court Mansion (Stacey Court, Hillsborough), with most of the interior scenes taking place in the music room and library. The Sunnyvale High School marching band played outside the St. Thomas Aquinas Church (745 Waverly, Palo Alto). Gordon falls through the cement in the Sutro Bath ruins in Sutro Park, San Francisco, and rescues a street tree at the Redwood City Hall of Justice (Marshall Street between Hamilton and Winslow, Redwood City). She tosses Cort's gift into the water at the Santa Cruz Boardwalk (400 Beach Street, Santa Cruz), where Cort uses a machine to stamp out the coin that reads "Harold Loves Maude." The final setting, where Cort drives to the ocean, can be found up a dirt road behind the Moose Lodge on Route 1 in Pacifica.

Heart and Souls

(1993). Robert Downey, Jr., Elisabeth Shue. Four people killed in a bus accident try to use a baby boy born at the exact moment to wrap up their mortal loose ends.

The fatal bus mishap is staged in San Francisco's Chinatown at the Stockton Street Tunnel. Also featured is the War Memorial Opera House (Van Ness at McAllister Street) and Downey's house at 3365 25th Street at Lilac, which ages dramatically through the story. Downey commits to Shue in the ending at the Conservatory of Flowers on John F. Kennedy Drive in Golden Gate Park.

Heaven Can Wait

(1978). Warren Beatty, Julie Christie. Pro quarterback is accidentally taken to heaven by an overanxious angel but returns to earth in millionaire's body to buy his former team.

Beatty's palatial home was the eclectic-styled, 43-room mansion Filoli (Canada Road, Woodside), built by the owner of the hard-rock Empire Gold Mine in 1917. The 654-acre estate at the southern end of Crystal Springs Lake is open for tours.

High Anxiety

(1977). Mel Brooks, Madelaine Kahn. A psychiatrist framed for murder must confront his fear of heights to prove his innocence.

Brooks is framed for murder by a gunman in a Mel Brooks mask at the Hyatt Regency (5 Embarcadero Center, San Francisco). In an homage to Alfred Hitchcock's *Vertigo*, Brooks filmed scenes at the same spot Kim Novak was saved — at Fort Point near the Golden Gate Bridge.

High Noon

(1952). Gary Cooper, Grace Kelly. Retiring lawman has one more battle to fight and he's not getting any support from the townsfolk.

Fictional Hadleyville was put together across northern California. The house was in Columbia State Park (Highway 49), a preserved gold rush town; Cooper and Kelly were married at St. Joseph's Catholic Church in Tuolumne City; and Kelly rode on the Sierra Railroad in passenger car number 3, whose brakes were failing at the time. The passenger car is in the roadhouse at Railtown in Jamestown (Highway 49).

Homegrown

(1998). John Lithgow, Billy Bob Thornton. Three bungling small-time marijuana growers try to go big-time.

The Henry Cowell Redwoods State Park (101 North Big Trees Park Road, Aptos) was used for the marijuana plantation.

Hotel

(1983–1988). James Brolin, Connie Sellica. Elegant San Francisco hotel is setting for drama and romance.

The Fairmont Hotel (California Street on Nob Hill, San Francisco) played the St. Gregory Hotel in the television series.

Indiana Jones and the Temple of Doom

(1984). Harrison Ford, Kate Capshaw. Archaeologist agrees to search for a village's missing magic stone.

The mountains around Mammoth Lakes played the Himalayas where Ford and Capshaw escape from a crashing plane and raft down the American River on the side of Mammoth Mountain. The scene at the airport where Ford boards the plane was shot at Hamilton Air Force Base, east of the Ignacio section of Navato in Marin County.

The Insider

(1999) Al Pacino, Russell Crowe. Tobacco executive exposes nefarious industry practices.

Pacino uses the phone outside the Cheese Board Bakery (1504 Shattuck Avenue, Berkeley). One of the private investigator's offices was filmed on Masonic Avenue in San Francisco.

Invasion of the Body Snatchers

(1978). Donald Sutherland, Brooke Adams. Man realizes bodies are being infiltrated and can't determine who his real friends are as he tries to escape.

Sutherland works as a public health inspector for the Department of Public Health (101 Grove Street, San Francisco). Elsewhere in San Francisco, Adams lives at 720 Steiner Street, across from Alamo Square, and Sutherland lives on Union Street near the corner of Castle. When the house is surrounded by aliens, Sutherland, Adams, Jeff Goldblum and Veronica Cartwright flee down Montgomery Street to the wooden steps on Filbert Street. The classic final scene was filmed outside the City Hall building.

Inventing the Abbotts

(1997). Joaquin Phoenix, Liv Tyler. Two brothers court three rich sisters.

The high school attended by the characters was Santa Rosa High School (717 S. 3rd Street, Santa Rosa). In Healdsburg, the fire department (601 Healdsburg Avenue) was disguised to look like a feed store. In Petaluma the adjacent Mystic Theater and McNear's Restaurant (21–23 Petaluma Boulevard) became the Haley Theater and the Lake Hotel, respectively. Dom Ivana (15 Western Avenue, Petaluma) played the Iron Skillet Restaurant.

It's a Mad Mad Mad Mad World

(1963). Spencer Tracy, Jonathan Winters. Dying words of thief trigger a cross-country race to find hidden treasure.

The sequence involving the plane and control tower was staged at Sonoma County Airport (2200 Airport Road, Santa Rosa). The mountain driving scenes were filmed on Highway 74 in Palm Desert.

Jack

(1996). Robin Williams, Diane Lane. 10-year-old boy has unique aging disorder that makes him look 40.

Williams' school was the Ross School (Laguintas Road and Allen Avenue, Ross), and his house was next door to the school. The exterior of the bar was shot at the Pacific Bell office on Turney Street in Sausalito, painted odd colors and draped in neon lights. The treehouse scene was filmed on Mare Island, a naval base built in 1854 under Admiral David Farragut.

Jack Frost

(1998). Michael Keaton, Kelly Preston. Father who dies in car accident becomes a better father when he comes back as a snowman.

Snow scenes were filmed at Sugar Bowl Ski Resort in Norden. Shooting took place in the commercial district of historic Truckee, and the featured school was Tahoe Lake Elementary School (375 Grove Street, Tahoe City).

The Joy Luck Club

(1993) Kieu Chinh, Tsai Chin. Four American-born Chinese women explore their ties with mothers born in feudal China.

France Nuyen's apartment is at 901 Union Street in San Francisco, and Tamlyn Tomita's home is at 180 Manchester Street in the city's Bernal Heights section. The church hall and auditorium were shot at Horace Mann School (3351 23rd Street, San Francisco).

Junior

(1994). Arnold Schwarzenegger, Danny DeVito. Male scientist tests a new fertility drug by impregnating himself.

The University of California-Berkeley plays the fictional Leland University. Schwarzenegger and Emma Thompson work as scientists in the Valley Life Sciences Building. The fertility clinic was set up in the Bancroft Hotel (2680 Bancroft Way at College Avenue, Berkeley).

Life

(1999). Eddie Murphy, Martin Lawrence. Two small-time crooks are stunned to suddenly get sentenced to jail for life.

The town of Locke doubled as a Mississippi shanty town. Prison scenes were shot at the Presidio in San Francisco's Golden Gate National Recreation Area. The Presidio served as a military post under the flags of Spain (1776–1822), Mexico (1822–48), and the United States (1848–1994).

The Lost Boys

(1987) Jason Patric, Corey Haim. After moving to a new town, brothers meet boys claiming to be vampires.

The teenage vampires hang out at the amusement park at the Santa Cruz Boardwalk (400 Beach Street). The Sting and the Giant Dipper are two of the rides that are featured.

Lucky Numbers

(2000). John Travolta, Lisa Kudrow. Television weatherman scams the state lottery.

The story was set in Harrisburg, Pennsylvania, but filmed mostly in Sacramento along 44th Street between I and M streets. In Pennsylvania, interior scenes were shot at a Denny's restaurant at Beach Boulevard and Malvern Avenue in Buena Park, and exterior shots were from a Denny's in Mechanicsburg (5505 Carlisle Pike).

Made in America

(1993). Whoopi Goldberg, Ted Danson. Young black woman discovers her father was a white sperm donor.

The opening shots of the movie are of the "Campanile" (Sather Tower) and Wheeler Hall on the University of California campus at Berkeley. Goldberg operates the African Queen Bookstore at the H. Tulanian & Sons Rug Company (2998 College Avenue, Berkeley). Later a car dealer rides a four-ton elephant into Lake Merritt during the filming of one of his commercials. Lake Merritt was once a finger of San Francisco Bay before 12th Street was dammed to provide Oakland with a lake. The movie ends with a rousing singing sequence at the graduation of Nia Long filmed at Oakland Technical High School (4351 Broadway, Oakland).

Mrs. Doubtfire

(1993). Robin Williams, Sally Field. Man poses as an English nanny so he can be close to his kids.

Field's home, where Williams poses as a nanny, is at 2640 Steiner Street at Broadway in Pacific Heights. The children's school is at City College of San Francisco's Chinatown campus 9840 Filbert Street at Taylor), and the TV station where Williams works as a shipping clerk is seen as the studios of KTVU in Oakland at Jack London Square.

Mumford

(1999). Loren Dean, Hope Davis. Psychiatrist moves to small town and quickly becomes a trusted counselor, despite his murky past.

The United States Coast Guard Training Center (559 Tomales Road, Petaluma) stood in for the fictional Panda Modem headquarters; the skateboard ramp used by eccentric founder Jason Lee was built out front. Dean and Lee meet at Old Main Street Saloon (153 North Main Street, Sebastopol). The pharmacy shots were filmed at Adobe Drug (303 West Napa Street, Sebastopol). Dean's house was in Petaluma on Liberty Street, and the lookout he used as an escape was at Clover Flat Landfill above Calistoga.

Murder in the First

(1995). Christian Slater, Kevin Bacon. Petty criminal thrown into solitary confinement becomes a madman.

Filmed on location in Alcatraz. The scene with the cable cars was filmed at Hyde and Lombard.

Murder, She Wrote

(1984–1996). Angela Lansbury, Tom Bosley. Mystery writer finds herself called on for help in real criminal cases.

The fictional town of Cabot Cove in the television series was played by Mendocino. The Victorian Blair House Inn (45110 Little Lake Street), a bed and breakfast, served as Lansbury's house in the show.

My Blue Heaven

(1989). Steve Martin, Rick Moranis. FBI agent is assigned to protect Mafia informant who refuses to lie low.

Joan Cusack works in Atascadero City Hall (6550 El Camino Real), an ornate Italian Renaissance brick building crafted from locally fired bricks during World War I.

National Velvet

(1944). Mickey Rooney, Elizabeth Taylor. Young wanderer trains horses for England's greatest race.

In her first starring role, Taylor prepares for the Grand National at the Pebble Beach polo fields.

The Net

(1995) Sandra Bullock, Jeremy Northern. Software engineer too involved in cyberspace encounters the real world on vacation.

The AIDS march takes place in San Francisco on Montgomery Street and Post Street. The car chase races through Oakland at Glascock Avenue and Park Street Bridge.

Nine Months

(1995). Hugh Grant, Julianne Moore. Man confronts girlfriend's pregnancy with gusto.

The exterior of the doctor's office was shot at Marathon Plaza in Oakland (302 2nd Street); interiors were created at 60 Spear Street. Veterans Memorial Building (200 Grand Avenue at Harrison, Oakland) was used to film the ballroom, lounge and gym. Jeff Goldblum lived at Jack Kerouac Alley between Columbus and Grant. Hospital scenes were shot at the closed Los Medanos Hospital in Pittsburg.

Outbreak

(1995). Dustin Hoffman, Rene Russo. Deadly airborne virus is imported into the United States and starts killing people at an alarming rate.

The Ferndale Repertory Theater (447 Main Street, Ferndale), one of the first theaters in northwest California to be built specifically for movies when it opened in 1920, played the State Theater of Cedar Creek, the first point of contact with the lethal virus. The theater still stages eight live productions a year. The story was shot in various locations around the Victorian-style town of Ferndale. A mercenary camp was filmed in Hawaii along the Huleia River with the Ha'upu Range in the background.

Pacific Heights

(1990). Michael Keaton, Matthew Modine. Tenant barricades himself in apartment and refuses to leave.

Although some establishing street scenes were shot in Pacific Heights, the Queen Anne Victorian town house where Keaton torments Modine and Melanie Griffith is in San Francisco's Potrero Hill district at 1243 19th and Texas streets. The townhouse, which was artificially aged, was used for exterior shots only; interiors were filmed on a sound stage.

Pal Joey

(1957). Frank Sinatra, Rita Hay-

CALIFORNIA

Joan Cusack worked at the Atascadero, California, City Hall during *My Blue Heaven*. (Atascandero Chamber of Commerce)

worth. Wise guy tries to build a swanky San Francisco nightclub.

The Spreckles Mansion (2080 Washington Street, San Francisco) played Sinatra's Chez Joey nightclub. Coit Tower was transformed into Hayworth's Telegraph Hill mansion.

The Parent Trap

(1961) Hayley Mills, Maureen O'Hara. Twins separated by divorce meet at summer camp and begin scheming to reunite parents.

Mills implements her plans at the Lodge of Pebble Beach (17-Mile Drive, Pebble Beach), overlooking the famous 18th hole of the Pebble Beach Golf Links. Scenes were also filmed at the baggage counter of the Monterey Peninsula Airport (Highway 68 and Olmsted Road). Brian Keith's house, which set many a young couple to dreaming, was a set built at Disney Studio's Golden Oak Ranch in Placerita Canyon.

The Parent Trap

(1998) Lindsay Lohan, Dennis Quaid. Twins separated by divorce meet at summer camp and begin scheming to reunite parents.

In this remake the summer camp is at Lake Arrowhead in the San Bernadino Mountains. The home setting has been changed to the villas and vineyards of Napa Valley. Filming took place at the Staglin Family Vineyard in Rutherford, which is open periodically during the year for special events.

Patch Adams

(1998). Robin Williams, Daniel London. Man uses unconventional methods for healing against all standards of medical community.

The school scenes were shot at the University of California-Berkeley at Wheeler Hall and LeConte Hall. The naval hospital at Marc Island stood in for Folsom State Asylum.

Peggy Sue Got Married

(1986). Kathleen Turner, Nicholas Cage. After fainting at her high school reunion, a woman finds herself back in her senior year.

Turner's high school reunion takes place at Santa Rosa High School (1235 Mendocino Avenue, Santa Rosa). She is transported back to Petaluma and her childhood Queen Anne home (226 Liberty Street). Cage's home is at 1006 D Street. Petaluma businesses featured in the movie include Bodell's Appliances (120 Petaluma Boulevard North) and Millie's Chili Bar, which was painted green and covered in glitter to play the Donut Hole I (600 Petaluma Boulevard).

Petticoat Junction

(1963–1970). Bea Benaderet, Edgar Buchanan. Woman runs family hotel on railroad line with help from friendly uncle and three daughters.

The original Hooterville *Cannonball* in the credits "rolling down the tracks" was filmed in Sonora. Too costly to keep traveling north from Hollywood for individual episodes, the *Cannonball* was filmed using a plastic shell originally built for the film *Ticket to Tomahawk*, modeled after a real train in Sonora, California. When the television series went to color after two years, the producers went to shoot the real 1891 steam engine. Today the train, powered by Locomotive No. 3, which starred as the Hooterville *Cannonball*, resides at the California State Railroad Museum at Railtown 1897 in Jamestown, California. The water tower featured in the opening credits is in Sonora with a sign reading "Shady Rest Hotel."

Petulia

(1968). George C. Scott, Julie Christie. Divorcing man trying to sort out new life is entangled in the life of an impulsive young socialite.

Christie lived in a San Francisco house at Montgomery and Filbert; other scenes were shot at Fort Point in the Golden Gate National Recreational Area.

Phantasm

(1979). A Michael Baldwin, Bill Thornberry. Young boys face off against mysterious grave robber.

Dunsmuir House and Gardens (2960 Peralta Oaks Court, Oakland) appears as a mausoleum in this film. Sadly, it may be the most appropriate of the many movie roles the Neoclassical Revival mansion has played. Built in 1899 as a wedding gift for his bride Josephine by Alexander Dunsmuir, son of a wealthy Canadian coal baron, he never got a chance to enjoy it, as he died on the honeymoon. Today Dunsmuir House is owned by the city of Oakland and available for tours every Wednesday and the first and third Sunday of each month between April and September.

Phenomenon

(1996). John Travolta, Kyra Sedgwick. Ordinary man looks at a bright light in the sky and becomes super-intelligent.

Most of the film is shot in Auburn, an old mining town dating to 1848 and the Gold Rush days. Forrest Whitaker's house was at 5421 Blank Road. Many of the mid–1800s buildings in the historic old Auburn district have been restored.

Play It Again Sam

(1972). Woody Allen, Diane Keaton. Mild-mannered film critic dumped by his wife seeks dating advice from Humphrey Bogart.

Susan Anspach leaves Allen in San Francisco at the corner of Vallejo and Kearney. Another San Francisco street scene was filmed at 22nd Avenue and Balboa, where the sheet of glass is broken. Allen plays pool with a blind date in Snarley's Tavern in Bolinas and spends a weekend with Keaton and husband Tony Roberts at Stinson Beach State Park.

Play Misty for Me

(1971). Clint Eastwood, Jessica Walker. Radio disc jockey is terrorized by a fan with whom he spent a brief romantic interlude.

Eastwood picks up Walker at the Sardine Factory Restaurant (701 Wave Street, Monterey). There are several scenes in downtown Carmel where Eastwood would become mayor, including the Crossroads Shopping Center (where the KRML radio station was filmed). Eastwood and Walker exchange words at the Windjammer restaurant at number 9 Municipal Wharf number 2 in Monterey, now the Sandbar and Grill.

Poetic Justice

(1993). Janet Jackson, Tupac Shakur. After witnessing the murder of her boyfriend, a young woman sinks into her poetry.

The movie is set in Oakland, filmed around 18th and Market Streets. The Alice Restaurant (17288 Skyline Boulevard, Woodside) appeared as the Lazy Janey I.

Pollyanna

(1960). Hayley Mills, Jane Wyman. Little girl spreads cheer through embattled town.

Santa Rosa stands in for a New England town in this remake of the 1920 Mary Pickford silent treatment of the Eleanor Porter story. The house in the movie was the Mableton Mansion at 1015 McDonald Avenue.

The Principal

(1987) James Belushi, Lou Gossett, Jr. Teacher beats his wife's boyfriend and is transferred, becoming the principal of a gang-riddled high school.

Bat-wielding Belushi tries to instill lessons in self-respect at Northgate High School (425 Castle Rock Road, Walnut Creek) and on the former Merritt College campus (Martin Luther King Jr. Way, Oakland).

Pump Up the Volume

(1990). Christian Slater, Andy Romano. High school kid runs a pirate radio station at night, infuriating the town's adults.

Saugus High School (21900 West Centurion Way, Saugus) played the fictional Hubert Humphrey High School. In one scene a sign identifying the Saugus High School library can be seen above the library door.

The Puppet Masters

(1994) Donald Sutherland, Eric Thal. Earth is invaded by giant slugs that can control human minds.

The Fresno City Hall (2600 Fresno Street) stands in for the Des Moines, Iowa, City Hall, where Thal rescues Julie Warner.

Raiders of the Lost Ark

(1981). Harrison Ford, Karen Allen. Archeologist is hired by the government to find the Ark of the Covenant.

The Conservatory of Music at the University of Pacific in Stockton was used as Ford's archaeology classroom.

Raising Cain

(1992). John Lithgow, Lolita Davidovich. Child psychologist is obsessed with mind control experiments.

Locations were used across the Bay Area, including Menlo Park City Hall (701 Laurel Street, Los Altos) and the Stanford Shopping Center (El Camino Real, Palo Alto) next to Stanford University.

Return of the Jedi

(1983). Mark Hamill, Harrison Ford. As the Empire builds a new Death Star, a warrior is imprisoned by evil creature.

Combining the magic of movies with the splendor of 300-foot-tall trees, battle scenes were shot across several square miles in Jerediah Smith Redwoods State Park (4241 Kings Valley Road, Crescent City). Laser gunfire crackled from combatants on air cycles through the redwood giants.

The Right Stuff

(1983) Sam Shepherd, Scott Glenn. Story of America's original Mercury 7 astronauts.

Most of the action was filmed at Hamilton Air Force Base, the NASA research center near Sunnyvale. Two scenes were shot at Mountain View/Moffett Field; one with journalists hanging by a hangar and another with Ed Harris complaining about waiting.

The Rock

(1996) Sean Connery, Nicolas Cage. Only man to escape Alcatraz helps commando unit storm island held by terrorists.

In addition to the shooting at Alcatraz Island, there were many locations used in San Francisco. Connery meets his estranged daughter at the Palace of Fine Arts (3301 Lyon

Street), the last remaining structure from the 1915 Panama-Pacific Exposition. He accepts the job in a penthouse suite meeting at the Fairmont Hotel (950 Mason Street). Also featured is the Golden Gate National Cemetery in San Bruno.

The Rookie

(1990) Clint Eastwood, Charlie Sheen. Veteran cop is forced to team with a rookie.

The opening chase sequence takes place on Highway 680 in San Jose, and the climax is filmed at San Jose International Airport, three miles northwest of downtown on I-880.

Same Time, Next Year

(1978). Alan Alda, Ellen Burstyn. Man and woman meet at romantic inn and decide to rekindle their love on the same weekend every year.

The inn where Alda and Burstyn rendezvous is the Heritage House (5200 North Highway 1, Mendocino).

Scream

(1996). David Arquette, Neve Campbell. Psychopathic killer stalks teens like in the movies.

Sonoma Community Center (276 East Napa Street, Sonoma) became Woodsboro High School. The Woodsboro town square was played by the Healdsburg Town Square in Santa Rosa. Drew Barrymore's house was on Sonoma Mountain Road in Glen Ellen, next to the *Cujo* house; Rose McGowan's house was on McGowan Avenue in Santa Rosa; and Campbell's house was on Calistaga Road in Santa Rosa.

Shadow of a Doubt

(1943). Teresa Wright, Joseph Cotten. Psychotic killer visits adoring niece who slowly learns of his unsavory past.

Alfred Hitchcock shot what he often referred to as his favorite film in the town of Santa Rosa, using many local residents as extras. Shooting took place around Courthouse Square (Fourth Street and Mendocino Avenue) and at the Santa Rosa Railroad Depot using Northwestern Pacific Engine number 140. The 1904 basalt stone-and-redwood timber station has recently been restored. I comes to visit Wright at 904 McDonald Avenue.

Shoot the Moon

(1982). Albert Finney, Diane Keaton. Man and woman find it difficult to walk away from stormy 15-year marriage.

Finney and Keaton live in Jack London's Wolf House at Jack London State Historic Park on London Ranch Road in Glen Allen. Included on the 800-acre property are the author's ranch house and the burnt ruins of Wolf House, a 26-room mansion London built but never occupied.

Sneakers

(1992). Robert Redford, Dan Aykroyd. Oddball security team attempts to steal secret "black box" with explosive contents.

Redford and his band of computer hackers work out of the art deco Fox Theater (1815 Telegraph Avenue, Oakland). Built in 1928, the 2,500-seat theater was a regular on the Vaudeville Circuit. It closed in the early 1970s and is currently being renovated.

So I Married an Axe Murderer

(1993). Mike Myers, Nancy Travis. Man suspects his new girlfriend kills off her past husbands.

This movie is virtually a travelogue for the city of San Francisco. Aside from the famous city landmarks used, locations included Prudente's Italian Deli (1462 Grant Avenue at Union), where Travis worked; the live-work lofts in the old Sears Building (Valencia and Cesar Chavez), where Travis lived; the site of the double-take scene at Fog Diner (1300 Battery Street at the Embarcardo), and the Swedenborgian Church (2107 Lyon Street at Washington), where the wedding reception was held.

Star Trek IV: The Voyage Home

(1986). William Shatner, Leonard Nimoy. To save the earth from an alien probe, a futuristic space crew must return to present day earth.

The crew of the Enterprise come to earth in San Francisco, dividing into teams at the intersection of Columbus, Kearny and Pacific Avenues. Shatner and Nimoy board a bus for Sausalito and Nimoy asks, "What does it mean, exact change?" as he boards the bus in front of Happy Donuts at 145 Columbus Avenue. Shatner convinces Spock to curb his "colorful metaphors" while walking at Fort Point Historic Site and Torpedo Wharf in the San Francisco Presidio. The Monterey Bay Aquarium (886 Cannery Row, Monterey) is transformed into the Sausalito Cetacean Institute where Shatner and Nimoy find two humpback whales needed to be brought back to the 23rd century.

Sting II

(1983). Jackie Gleason, Mac Davis. Further adventures of con men.

The chase scene through the amusement park was filmed at the Santa Cruz Boardwalk (400 Beach Street, Santa Cruz). Stunt men leap off a moving car of the Giant Dipper, a roller coaster built in 1924.

Stop or My Mom Will Shoot

(1992). Sylvester Stallone, Estelle Getty. Detective's mom comes to visit and immediately inserts herself into his job and love life.

Although filmed mostly in Los Angeles, an elaborate action sequence was shot at the inactive Santa Rosa Air Center (Northpoint Parkway, Santa Rosa).

Storm Center

(1956). Bette Davis, Brian Keith. Small town librarian gets fired when she refuses to remove a Communist book from the shelves.

The library used in the film was the original Carnegie Library on Sonoma Plaza in Santa Rosa. Town scenes included shots at McMullen's Soda Fountain on 4th Street.

Sudden Impact

(1983). Clint Eastwood, Sandra Locke. Trail of serial killer leads from San Francisco to a small coastal town.

At Burger Island (695 Third Street, San Francisco), now a McDonalds, Eastwood grunts his famous promise to a hostage-taker: "Go ahead. Make my day." The climactic scenes take place on the Santa Cruz Boardwalk (400 Beach Street, Santa Cruz), including a shoot-out on the park's carousel, which opened in 1911, seven years after the boardwalk was established.

The Sure Thing

(1985) John Cusack, Daphne Zuniga. Mismatched students share rides across the country.

The University of the Pacific stood in for an eastern college. Dorms were used in Grave Hovell Hall and South, West Hall, and a classroom was filmed in Sears Hall. Exterior shots were staged in Anderson Quad. Cusack's "sure thing" was waiting for him at UCLA, where the Delta Tau Delta fraternity was used to film a party.

Terminator 2: Judgment Day

(1991). Arnold Schwarzenegger, Linda Hamilton. Cyborg killer from the future is sent back to eliminate the future leader of the Resistance.

The Cyberdyn Systems Building (47131 Bayside Park, Fremont) played the headquarters of a nuclear weapons manufacturer and the site for the high-powered shootout featuring the Terminator riding a motorcycle through a second-story office window and dodging helicopter fire. The newly constructed building was not yet occupied, and a real explosion was detonated inside.

Time After Time

(1979) Malcolm McDowell, David Warner. H.G. Wells must pursue Jack the Ripper into the 20th century after the slasher uses the futuristic writer's time machine.

Once Warner, as Jack the Ripper, visits San Francisco, he concludes he would be an amateur in modern times. Scenes were shot at the Hyatt Regency (5 Embarcadero Center) and the Palace of Fine Art (3301 Lyon Street).

Too Close for Comfort

(1980–1985) Ted Knight, Nancy Dussault. Two grown sisters share a duplex with parents.

Knight and his family live in the gaily colored Victorians on Steiner Street, depicted in the opening credits of the television series.

Towering Inferno

(1974) Paul Newman, Steve McQueen. Massive fire threatens to destroy an office tower and all inside.

The Bank of America Building (555 California Street, San Francisco) was used as the base for the skyscraper to which Hollywood added 86 mythical stories for the filming. Bar scenes were filmed in the main lobby in the Hyatt Regency at 5 Embarcadero Center. Richard Chamberlain's house was shot at 2898 Vallejo Street at Baker Street in Pacific Heights.

True Crime

(1999) Clint Eastwood, James Woods. Journalist covering inmate's execution believes him to be innocent and only has hours to prove it.

Oakland was used extensively throughout this action thriller. The exterior of the *Oakland Tribune* at the corner of Franklin was used, but the Contra-Costa Newspapers (2640 Shadeland Road, Walnut Creek) stood in for the *Tribune* press room. Tracking the case, Eastwood meets witness Dale Porterhouse at Cafe Cheneville (499 9th Street, Old Oakland), playing the Bread Company Restaurant, and is filmed with Lucy Liu at Cynthia's Toys and Games (501 14th Street, Oakland). He also visits the Oakland Zoo (9777 Golf Link Road). The final shot is of the sculpture in Oakland City Center with the *Tribune* headquarters in the background.

Tucker: A Man and His Dream

(1988) Jeff Bridges, Joan Allen. Renegade car designer challenges the auto industry with his own revolutionary concept car.

Northern California stood in for the state of Michigan in the late 1940s. The Armstrong estate in Sonoma was used as the Tucker family home in Ypsilanti. Bridges, as Preston Tucker, tested his car at the Petaluma Speedway (East Washington Street, Petaluma). He introduces the car at an auto show recreated at the Paramount Theater (2025 Broadway, Oakland). The final parade of Tucker cars—there were only 51 ever made—was shot on Oakland's Telegraph Avenue.

Turner and Hooch

(1989) Tom Hanks, Mare Winningham. Detective must adopt the dog of a dead man to find his murderer.

Pacific Grove, founded as a Methodist retreat in 1875, played the fictional Cypress Grove. Hanks and his saliva-challenged friend are seen downtown, on Ocean View Boulevard and at the bank turned into City Hall (southwest corner of Lighthouse and First).

Vertigo

(1958) Jimmy Stewart, Kim Novak. Detective battles fear of heights while trailing a woman.

Novak leaps to her death from the Mission San Juan Bautista (2nd and Mariposa Street, San Juan Bautista), founded in 1797 and the largest of the mission churches. The famous bell tower was taken down before filming, and the tower seen in the film was a Hollywood creation. Still an active Catholic church, the mission is open daily. Earlier, Stewart saved Novak by jumping into San Francisco Bay at Marina Drive under the south end of the bridge. Novak lived in the Brocklebank Apartments (1000 Mason Street, San Francisco), and Stewart lived at 900 Lombard Street at Jones. Novak visits the grave of her great-grandmother and assumes her identity in the Mission San Francisco De Asis (3321 16th Street at Dolores Street), established in 1776. For many years the tombstone of the fictional Carlotta Valdes was left in the mission's graveyard. The mission is open daily.

A View to a Kill

(1985). Roger Moore, Tanya Roberts. Only James Bonds stands between a mad industrialist and the destruction of Silicon Valley.

Moore fights off thugs at Dunsmuir House and Gardens (2960 Peralta Oaks Court, Oakland), the house owned by Roberts in the film. Although shot mostly in England, several recognizable locations in San Francisco were used, including the Peace Pagoda designed by Yoshiro Taniguchi in Japan Center of Golden Gate Park (Buchanan and Post) and City Hall (Polk Street between McAllister and Grove), which psychopath Max Zorin sets on fire. Moore leads police on a chase in a commandeered hook-and-ladder down Market Street to the Third Street Bridge, eluding the pursuers as they crack up near a drawbridge.

The Wedding Planner

(2000) Jennifer Lopez, Matthew McConaughey. Wedding planner is too busy to have her own love life.

Filoli Mansion (Canada Road, Woodside) does double duty as the elegant Napa Inn and City Hall. The Moroccan wedding was staged at the Athenaeum on the campus of California Polytechnic Institute (551 South Hill Road, Pasadena). Bridgette Wilson's wedding was created in Golden Gate Park, with globe lanterns strung from the hulking sycamore trees.

What's Up Doc?

(1972) Barbra Streisand, Ryan O'Neal. Strange woman distracts man competing for a research grant.

The San Francisco Hilton (333 O'Farrell Street) stood in for the fictional Hotel Bristol. Streisand and O'Neal race through Alta Plaza Park, where the stairs are still chipped from the filming.

When a Man Loves a Woman

(1994) Andy Garcia, Meg Ryan. Alcoholic woman goes through rehabilitation and returns to her family.

The opening scene with Ryan and Garcia is at the Buena Vista Cafe (2765 Hyde Street, San Francisco). Other San Francisco scenes include the hospital shot at 766 Vallejo and the school played by the International Studies Academy (693 Vermont Street).

The Woman in Red

(1984) Gene Wilder, Kelly LeBrock. Man's life is changed by encounter with exciting woman in a red dress.

Wilder and Judith Ivey live in one of San Francisco's "painted ladies" on Steiner Street at Alamo Square between Hayes and Fulton. Wilder tap dances on a Ninth story window ledge while dodging LeBrock's husband at the Brocklebank Apartments (1000 Mason Street, San Francisco).

Popular California Locations

ALGODONES DUNES

About 15 miles west of Yuma, Arizona, are the Algodones Dunes, the great sand dunes of the lower Colorado River Valley. Stretching for 40 miles and as wide as ten miles, the Algodones Dunes on the California-Mexico border is one of the largest open dune systems in the United States. And they have been appearing on movie screens almost since the beginning of Hollywood. The Rudolph Valentino starrer *The Shiek* filmed across the sandy wastelands, which were once crossed by a wooden road.

Through the years, it has been a good bet that any movie calling for scenes of neverending sand was staged in the Algodones Dunes. Such sand-choked classics as *Beau Geste* (Cary Grant, Gary Cooper) and *Sahara* (Humphrey Bogart, Lloyd Bridges) were shot here. The 1960s television series *Rat Patrol* was filmed in the desert west of Yuma.

Hollywood still travels out I-8 to the Algodunes dunes. Recent productions have included *Return of the Jedi* (Mark Hamill, Harrison Ford), *Stargate* (Kurt Russell, James Spader), *Rambo III* (Sylvester Stallone, Richard Crenna) and *Three Kings* (George Clooney, Mark Wahlberg).

BIG BEAR

In the movie world, Canada is about 95 miles from Los Angeles. In the eastern regions of the San Bernadino National Forest, up among the pine and oak trees, is a 12-mile valley dominated by Big Bear Lake. Moviemaking here predates World War I, and early movie moguls like D.W. Griffith, filming *Birth of a Nation*, and Cecil B. DeMille, working on *Call of the North*, came here. Whenever a script called for a story set in Canada or the northern Rockies (or any high country setting), crews packed their cameras and headed for Big Bear.

In 1936, *Trail of the Lonesome Pine* became the first outdoor movie filmed in Technicolor. Over the next 20 years, more than 100 productions would use Big Bear. Often the titles alone would tell the movie fan that Big Bear was the shooting location: *Yukon Gold* (Frances Charles, Sam Flint), *North of the Great Divide* (Roy Rogers, Penny Edwards), *The Royal Mounted Patrol* (Charles Starrett, Russell Hayden).

The most filmed Big Bear loca-

CALIFORNIA

The distinctive round boulders at Boulder Bay on Cedar Lake in Big Bear, California, were seen in dozens of motion pictures in the 1940s and 1950s. (Big Bear Film Commission)

tion in the 1940s and 1950s was Boulder Bay on Cedar Lake, with its distinctive round boulders along the shoreline. Other recognizable Big Bear landmarks include craggy Butler Peak and the I.S. Ranch outside Big Bear Village on Tulip Lake.

In addition to exploring the area 30 miles northeast of San Bernadino on one's own, there are guided tours of the lake, the valley and the surrounding mountains available.

Lone Pine

Lone Pine rests in the shadow of Mt. Whitney, the highest mountain in the continental United States. Founded in the early 1800s to supply pioneer ranchers and, later, miners, Lone Pine got its name from a single pine tree that grew in the boulder-strewn foothills of the Cascades beside the creek meandering through the area. The majestic backdrops and rugged rock formations began attracting the attention of Hollywood, 212 miles to the west, in the 1920s.

Most of the filming in Lone Pine takes place in the Alabama Hills, named after the Confederate warship responsible for wreaking havoc on northern shipping during the Civil War. News of her victorious naval exploits trickled across America's frontier, and prospectors sympathetic to the Southern cause named their mining claims after the Alabama. The CSA *Alabama* was sunk by Yankee warships off the coast of France in a running gun battle with the *Kearsarge* in the summer of 1864. Union miners wasted no time in naming a whole mining district, mountain pass, peak and town, "Kearsarge."

The Alabama Hills consist of rounded, weathered granite boulders placed across desert flatlands that form a sharp contrast to the sharply sculptured ridges of the Sierra. Movie Flat Road, that runs through the Alabama Hills, is one of the most recognizable movie sets in Hollywood history. Beginning with Tom Mix in the silent era, every major Western star rode down the road on horseback at one time or another.

Roy Rogers appeared here in his first starring role in *Under Western Stars*, and Bill Boyd, known on the screen as Hopalong Cassidy, filmed so many roles in Lone Pine that he moved here. The Alabama Hills hosted one of the largest location shoots in history when 1200 extras staged the climactic battle scene of *Gunga Din*. Other notable Westerns among the more than 100 films shot here include *The Lone Ranger*, *How the West Was Won*, and *The Gunfighter*.

Although the golden age for Lone Pine has gone the way of the Hollywood western, film crews occasionally still appear. *Bad Day at Black Rock* (Spencer Tracy, Ernest Borgnine) used the area to build an entire town along the railroad tracks in 1955, and, more recently, Fred Ward and Kevin Bacon battled giant earthworms in the Alabama Hills in *Tremors*.

Lone Pine is public land managed by the Bureau of Land Management as part of the Alabama Hills Recreation Area.

Pioneertown

In location shooting, a real town becomes a movie set; Pioneertown is a movie set that became a real town. In 1946 a group of Hollywood people formed a consortium and bought 32,000 acres of land in Yucca Valley on the fringe of the Mojave Desert from the government and the Southern Pacific Railroad. They built an old western movie set here, 130 miles east of Hollywood on Highway 62.

The flat desert land in the mountains, at an altitude of nearly one mile high, had an advantage other western sets did not. Tricky downdraughts in the mountains meant airplanes — and their scene-destroying noise — would not be flying overhead. Filmmakers could work at Pioneertown without one of the most irritating and expensive nuisances of location shooting. And one other thing — the town was a movie set built with permanent structures, not false fronts. Major studios used the old wooden buildings and soundstage for a string of Westerns featuring cowboy actors such as Roy Rogers and Gene Autry.

Eventually box office interest in Westerns died out, and visits from Hollywood became less and less frequent. But some of the people stayed around and built homes around the old sets and an odd business here and there. Today, Pioneertown lives on as a small, unincorporated town. Many of the original set buildings are gone, but Main Street, scarcely 500 yards long but still extremely wide and unpaved, and the surrounding area are still occasionally used for commercials and movie filming. Re-enactments and Old West shows are staged during special events in the town that was built as a movie set.

COLORADO

American Flyers

(1985). Kevin Costner, David Marshall Grant. Brothers challenge each other in the world of bicycle racing.

Filmed around Grand Junction, the movie features a climb up the Rim Rock Drive in Colorado National Monument through the Grand Mesa National Forest. The restaurant scene was filmed in McPherson, Kansas, and the parade scene staged in Lindsborg, Kansas.

Butch Cassidy and the Sundance Kid

(1969). Paul Newman, Robert Redford. Western outlaws stay one step ahead of the law before deciding to flee to Bolivia.

The real Butch Cassidy robbed his first bank in Telluride, and the famous jump scene off the cliff was filmed nearby, 13 miles north of Durango near Baker's Bridge (off CR 250). The shot was created in three separates stages. Newman and Redford run towards the cliff edge above the Animas River; then stuntmen are filmed jumping 30 feet into the gorge, while the camera shoots without the water to create the illusion of a much longer drop to the water; and finally Newman and Redford are shot landing in the water back in California. The scene where Newman rides Katharine Ross around on the handlebars of his bicycle was shot in Grafton, a deserted Mormon community six miles west of Springdale on State Road 9, just outside of Zion National Park. Cassidy's actual home was nearby, five miles south of Circleville on US 89.

Cliffhanger

(1993). Sylvester Stallone, John Lithgow. Mountain ranger unwittingly rescues gang of thieves searching for $100,000,000 in the Colorado Rockies.

Although the film is set in Colorado, producers were not allowed to shoot in the state due to concerns by the Environmental Protection Agency. After establishing shots in Denver's Union Station (1701 Wynkoop Street) and airplane hijack scenes taken from the air over the Ute Indian Reservation in Towaoc, the rest of the action was shot in the Italian Alps.

Denver and Rio Grande

(1952). Edmund O'Brien, Sterling Hughes. Fictional story set against the building of the Denver & Rio Grande Railroad.

In Hollywood, train wrecks were

nearly always filmed in miniature until the first actual train crash filmed in Technicolor was staged for this movie on the Durango & Silverton Railroad in Animas County. Two old engines, No. 319 and No. 345, were loaded with black powder and dynamite to create the explosion in a 30-mph head-on collision. The location of the crash was 23 miles north of Durango at Milepost 475. Locomotive No. 319 played itself, while No. 345 played No. 268, which was used for most of the action scenes. No. 268 was retired from freight service in 1955 and is on display in Gunnison.

Die Hard II

(1990). Bruce Willis, Bonnie Bedalia. Mercenaries seize control of an airport and threaten to cause plane crashes.

Although the setting was Washington DC, a warm winter put the filming crew on the road, and the snow scene at the airport was filmed at Stapleton Airport in Denver. William Sadler commandeers the Highland Lake Congregational Church (Weld County Road 5, Mead) and battles Willis 50 miles northwest of Boulder on the edge of Highland Lake. The tiny church was built in 1896 and is used once a year for a service. Another plane crash in the snow was filmed on the tarmac of the airport in Alpena, Michigan.

Dumb and Dumber

(1994). Jim Carrey, Jeff Daniels. Good-hearted bumblers drive cross-country to return a briefcase left in a limousine.

Carrey and Daniels head for Aspen, but neighboring resorts were used to depict the fashionable ski spa. Street scenes were shot in Breckinridge, and the scene of Daniels sticking his tongue to a frozen ski lift pole was filmed at Copper Mountain Resort (Exit 195 off I-70).

Every Which Way but Loose

(1978). Clint Eastwood, Sandra Locke. Drifter and pet orangutan travel the cow towns.

Eastwood stays at the Royal Host Motel (930 East Colfax, Denver), riding the glass elevator to the curb. He drives down East Colfax Street, eventually getting in a fistfight at the Zanzibar, a former country and western bar in Aurora. In New Mexico, Eastwood searches for a mate for his traveling simian friend, Clyde, at the Albuquerque Biological Park (903 Tenth Street SW).

Flashback

(1990). Kiefer Sutherland, Dennis Hopper. Young FBI agent has his hands full while escorting an aging hippie to jail.

Sutherland and Hopper board the train at the stone and brick Glenwood Springs Train Depot (339 First Street, Glenwood Springs), with the dueling spires. The train station in Oakland is played by Denver's Union Station (1701 Wynkoop Street). Hopper meets Sutherland while autographing his autobiography at City Lights (261 Columbus Street, San Francisco), the bohemian bookstore founded by poet Lawrence Ferlinghetti.

How the West Was Won

(1962). John Wayne, Henry Fonda. One pioneer family's history tells the tale of American westward expansion.

Part of this sprawling epic was filmed at Bent's Old Fort National Historic Site (35110 Highway 194 East, La Junta). The adobe trading post today looks much as it did when it opened in 1828 and became the crown jewel of the Santa Fe Trail. The fort, abandoned by owner William Bent in 1848, has been reconstructed, and tours are available.

Ladybugs

(1992). Rodney Dangerfield, Jackee Harry. Groveling employee agrees to coach the soccer team of his boss' daughter.

The soccer scenes were filmed at the soccer field at St. Mary's Academy (4545 South University Boulevard, Englewood). Other shots featured Kent Denver School (4000 East Quincy Avenue, Englewood).

Mork and Mindy

(1978–1982). Pam Dawber, Robin Williams. Alien comes to earth and boards with a young woman.

The television series was set in Boulder, with Dawber and Williams living at 1619 Pine Street, a mansion with four apartments used for exterior shots. The characters frequented stores at the Pearl Street Mall, including the former New York Deli at 1117 Pearl Street.

National Lampoon's Christmas Vacation

(1989). Chevy Chase, Beverly D'Angelo. Family misadventures continue during holiday break.

The tree-cutting and sledding scenes were shot in Breckinridge. Also used for filming was Summit County High School (16202 US Highway 9, Frisco).

Sleeper

(1973). Woody Allen, Diane Keaton. Health store owner is frozen and brought back 200 years in the future during a government coup.

The home of Evil Eye was filmed at the I.M. Pei–designed National Center for Atmospheric Research (I-70 at Genessee Mountain, Denver). Pei drew inspiration for his futuristic creation on top of a 6,200-foot mesa from the cliff dwellings of the Anasazi Indians. The building was constructed of polyurethane foam sprayed over metal forms.

Strangeland

(1998). Dee Snider, Linda Cardenelli. Sadist uses the Internet to lure teens into his traps.

The horror scenes were filmed mostly in Colorado Springs, notably on the street around the City Administration Building (30 S. Nevada Avenue). During a chase sequence

Pam Dawber and Robin Williams lived in this downtown Boulder, Colorado, dwelling as stars of the television series *Mork and Mindy*.

produced in Denver, filming was disrupted when a real escaped prisoner mixed into the crowd scene.

Things to Do in Denver When You're Dead

(1995). Andy Garcia, Christopher Walken. Men face imminent death after contracts are put out on their lives.

The producers almost didn't film in the titled Denver because they didn't believe it looked enough like their image of Denver. Many scenes were shot around town, including Union Station (1701 Wynkoop Street), where hired assassin Steve Buscemi makes his first appearance.

Three Ninjas: High Noon at Mega Mountain

(1998). Hulk Hogan, Loni Anderson. Three young brothers and the girl next door try to save amusement parks from evil woman.

The besieged Mega Mountain is Six Flags Elitch Gardens Amusement Park (Speer Boulevard, Exit 212A off I-25, Denver). The obstacle course was constructed in the basement of the old Denver Post building on 16th Street.

A Ticket to Tomahawk

(1950). Marilyn Monroe, Walter Brennan. Stagecoach line owner tries to prevent a competing train from running on time.

The railroad scenes were filmed in Animas Canyon north of Durango and in the Rockwood Area on the narrow gauge Durango & Silverton Railroad, using No. 20. The spectacular Durango & Silverton, now a tourist railroad, began operating in the San Juan Mountains in 1881 and was in danger of being abandoned until thousands of people became interested in riding the train seen onscreen. Engine No. 20 starred (with Monroe and Brennan) as Tomahawk & Western No. 1; and after the movie, rail officials painted three coach cars "Rio Grande gold," like the coach in the movie, and launched the popular tourist railroad.

True Grit

(1969). John Wayne, Kim Darby. Young woman recruits a grizzled lawman to avenge her father's death.

Wayne won his only Best Actor Academy Award for his performance in the Colorado Rockies. The first image in the film is of the 14,000-foot Wilson peaks in the San Miguel Range, and Darby's ranch was located along Big Bear Creek on the Wilson Mesa. Owl Creek Pass, an 1885 cattle trail (now a gravel road), was used for trail sequences through the open range. The ferry sequence, where Wayne and Glen Campbell try and send Darby home, was constructed at Blue Mesa Reservoir, 38 miles east of Montrose on Route 50. The courtroom scenes and the staircase where Darby and Wayne have their first conversation were shot in the red brick Ouray County Courthouse (541 4th Street, Ouray). The courtroom is located at the top of the front stairway near the main entrance to the courthouse.

Under Siege 2

(1995). Stephen Seagal, Eric Bogosian. Nuclear terrorists hijacking a train are unprepared for an ex–Navy SEAL passenger.

The Grand Continental passenger train bound for Los Angeles pulls out of Union Station (1701 Wynkoop Street, Denver). The confrontation between Seagal and the hijackers then takes place aboard the train, with the Rocky Mountains as the backdrop.

Vanishing Point

(1971). Barry Newman, Cleavon Little. Car delivery man uses the help of a blind disc jockey to win a bet.

Newman begins his epic dash from Denver to San Francisco in a 1970 Dodge Challenger from the Hendrie and Bolthoff pipe warehouse (1743 Wazee Street, Denver), built in the lower downtown in 1907. Little monitors police whereabouts on his radio from the Goldfield Hotel (US Highway 95, Goldfield, Nevada). Goldfield was founded in 1902, and the hotel, built on an abandoned gold mine and considered the finest hostelry between Denver and the Pacific Coast, was completed in 1908. Today Goldfield is a virtual ghost town. Newman crashes the Challenger in Cisco, Utah.

Popular Colorado Locations

BUCKSKIN JOE'S

In the late 1800s mining boom in Colorado, the village of Buckskin Joe's boomed as well. When the mines played out, the buildings in town sat silent and abandoned, like many of the ghost towns of the West. But Buckskin Joe's got a second life 90 miles to the southeast as a tourist attraction. Buckskin Joe Frontier Town became a rustic reconstructed mining-era town, eight miles west of Canon City off US 50.

Today there are log buildings, many of them restored originals moved to the site, and costumed actors and recreated gunfights in the streets. Hollywood has also staged its share of productions at Buckskin Joe's. Among the movies filmed here were *Cat Ballou* (Lee Marvin, Jane Fonda), *Conagher* (Sam Elliott, Katherine Ross), *The Sacketts* (Tom Selleck, Sam Elliott) and *The Cowboys* (John Wayne, Bruce Dern).

CONNECTICUT

Everybody Wins

(1990). Nick Nolte, Debra Winger. Detective finds more than his client wants as he tries to prove a teen killer innocent.

The movie was filmed partly at Norwich City Hall (100 Broadway) and at private homes along Washington Street and Broadway.

Mystic Pizza

(1988). Julia Roberts, Annabeth Gish. Young waitresses dream of better things while working at a pizza joint.

The real-life Mystic Pizza (56 West Main, Mystic) was too small and couldn't shut down for the many weeks involved in shooting the film, so interior scenes were filmed in the nearby Anguilla Gallery (Water Street, Stonington). Shots of downtown Mystic include a sequence at the Mystic Drawbridge, built in 1922.

Other People's Money

(1991). Danny DeVito, Gregory Peck. Corporate raider falls for the daughter of his take-over target.

The exteriors of the plant DeVito attempts to take over were shot at the Gilbert & Bennett Wire Mill in the Georgetown section of Redding. Interiors were created at Seymour Specialty Wire in Seymour. The 1878 wire mill was heavily damaged by an arson fire at the 64-acre site and subsequently purchased by a grocery retail chain.

Scenes from a Mall

(1991). Woody Allen, Bette Midler. Husband and wife admit to affairs during an excursion to the local mall.

The Stamford Town Center, an enormous mall built on the old Boston Post Road (Main Street) in Stamford, doubled as the Beverly Center in Los Angeles. A replica of the mall was also constructed on a Hollywood sound stage.

Sleepers

(1996). Kevin Bacon, Robert DeNiro. Boys released from a brutal detention center after 10 years seek their revenge.

The central reformatory scenes were shot at the closed Fairfield Hills Hospital in Newtown, where the 250 acres of rolling countryside belie the horrors within the mental institution. Most of the Hell's Kitchen section of New York in the 1960s was recreated in Brooklyn's Greenpoint. The church central to the storyline was the Holy Trinity Church (20 Cumming Street, Brooklyn). Bacon is shot and killed by two assailants in the Elysian Cafe (1001 Washington Street, Hoboken, New Jersey).

Stanley and Iris

(1990). Robert DeNiro, Jane Fonda. Illiterate cook tries to romance newly divorced woman in company cafeteria.

Waterbury, "the Brass City," played fictional Laurel, Connecticut. The movie was filmed in the White City area of Waterbury where the Waterbury Brass Company built 73 white houses for workers. Fonda's house was at 40 Sycamore Lane, and DeNiro lived at 46 Pond Street. The abandoned Waterbury Brass building at 835 South Main Street, now offices, was transformed into the Nevins and Davis Bakery where Fonda and DeNiro worked.

Stepford Wives

(1975). Katherine Ross, Paula Prentiss. Suburban women are replaced by robots to please their husbands.

This adaptation of the science fiction novel was filmed in various towns around southern Connecticut. A stone and wood barn converted to a private home in Westport (open occasionally during special town tours) served as the primary setting. The Men's Association Building and other exteriors were shot in Norwalk, and the psychotherapist's office was in Weston.

Valley of the Dolls

(1967). Patty Duke, Sharon Tate. Three young women struggle to make their way in show business.

The Congregational Church (Center Town Green, Redding) appears as a backdrop in one of the scenes.

Woman Wanted

(1999). Michael Moriarty, Holly Hunter. Father and son both fall in love with a woman who comes to work in their house.

The movie was shot mostly in Canada, but the filmmakers received a rare permit to shoot on the Yale campus in New Haven, using a dining hall for one scene. Other scenes establishing where the characters live were shot on St. Ronan Street. The Grove Street Cemetery (Grove Street between Prospect and Ashman streets, New Haven), where 130 Revolutionary patriots (including Noah Webster and Eli Whitney) rest, appears briefly. The cemetery is open daily.

DELAWARE

Beloved

(1998). Oprah Winfrey, Danny Glover. A slave is visited by the spirit of her deceased daughter.

The movie marked the first time filmmakers had returned to New Castle since an 1899 documentary of the public whipping post where the county sheriff demonstrated the exact way to administer lashes to the back of a prisoner with maximum effect. Here, Second Street was covered with dirt to play a time in America 150 years earlier. Seeking out a location to stand in for mid–nineteenth century rural Ohio, Hollywood scouts flew concentric circles outward from Philadelphia, where the movie's city scenes were set. Producers spotted the rolling terrain of the Fair Hill Natural Resources Area near the Delaware-Maryland border, the former estate of William duPont, Jr. They selected Fair Hill for the film's farm scenes. A ramshackle tenant farm was constructed,

Oprah Winfrey's tenant farm set built in Fair Hill Natural Resources Area near the Delaware-Maryland border was left to deteriorate naturally after the filming of *Beloved*.

and much of the movie was filmed here. Producers decided to leave the movie set intact, to deteriorate naturally. When visiting the park, visitors can wander among the fake buildings and even knock on the Styrofoam stones. Fair Hill lies near the Delaware-Maryland border on Route 273, east of the intersection with route 213.

Dead Poets Society

(1989). Robin Williams, Ethan Hawke. English professor uses poetry and a secret society to encourage students to reject conformity.

The leafy campus of Gothic-style buildings was St. Andrew School (Noxontown Pond Road, Middletown). The play at the film's end was staged at the Everett Theater (45 West Main Street, Middletown). The historic performing arts building has housed an opera, a vaudeville hall and a cinema, and is today a theater.

DISTRICT OF COLUMBIA

All the President's Men

(1976). Dustin Hoffman, Robert Redford. Reporters uncover a scandal that brings down the President of the United States.

The *Washington Post* did not allow filming of its most famous story in its newsroom but shipped tons of actual trash, newspapers and even stickers from editor Ben Bradlee's desk to Hollywood to use in the movie. Only the entrance to the *Washington Post* building (1150 15th Street NW), elevators, some production facilities and the parking lot appeared in the movie. The famous bungled burglary was recreated at the Watergate Hotel (2650 Virginia Avenue NW). Redford, playing Bob Woodward, lived in the reporter's actual building at Webster House (1718 P Street NW); but the apartment used was no. 519, while Woodward lived in no. 617.

American President

(1995). Michael Douglas, Annette Bening. Widowed United States president falls for an environmental lobbyist.

Bening worked for the Cato Institute (1000 Massachusetts Avenue NW), and Douglas stops in to buy flowers at Carmen's House of Flowers in the Williard Inter-Continental Hotel (1401 Pennsylvania Avenue NW).

Born Yesterday

(1993). John Goodman, Melanie Griffith. Oafish tycoon hires reporter to give his showgirl girlfriend some smarts, but she already has some.

Washington was used for establishing exteriors. In addition to the usual landmarks, there is a scene shot at the Willard Intercontinental Hotel (1401 Pennsylvania Avenue NW).

Broadcast News

(1987). Albert Brooks, Holly Hunter. Two rival television reporters jockey professionally and for the attentions of a female producer.

William Hurt's apartment was located at 2039 New Hampshire Avenue NW, no. 301; Brooks' place was at 600 East Capitol Street SE, where an 1878 three-story Victorian brick home was completely refitted with contemporary furniture; Hunter's house was on the one-block long Hillyer Place.

Chances Are

(1989). Robert Downey, Jr., Cybil Shepherd. Reincarnated man begins to remember his past life.

Ryan O'Neal, playing a *Washington Post* reporter, shows recent Yale graduate Downey around the newsroom. Shepherd works as curator of the First Ladies Gowns Exhibit in the Smithsonian Institution American History Museum, and a scene was also shot in the Enid A. Haupt Garden of the Smithsonian Castle (1000 Jefferson Drive SW). The Castle was the Smithsonian's first building, designed by James Renwick and completed in 1855. The grounds are landscaped so that "ground level" rises three stories from the front of the building (which opens onto a pedestrian mall) to the back (which is the street side). Hence the 42-acre Victorian rooftop garden is actually at street level.

Dave

(1993). Kevin Kline, Sigourney Weaver. A look-alike is hired to impersonate the President after he suffers a stroke.

Kline runs a temporary help service at 1442 Wisconsin Avenue NW in Georgetown and lives at 1737 Kenyon Street NW in Mount Pleasant. Production designers were not allowed to film or even take measurements of the inner White House, so they took measurements from the Oval Office replica at the Reagan Library in Simi Valley for Kline's office. Washington eateries featured include the Argentine Grill (2433 18th Street NW) and Cafe Lautrec (2431 18th Street NW). The Virginia Capitol, designed by Thomas Jefferson (Capitol Square, Richmond), stood in for the back portico of the white House, and its interior also provided the setting for the United States House of Representatives. Kline throws out a baseball season–opening ball at Camden Yards in Baltimore.

The Day the Earth Stood Still

(1951). Patricia Neal, Michael Rennie. An alien arrives with a message that earthlings must live peacefully or face destruction as a danger to other planets.

The usual landmarks, such as the White House, the Jefferson Memorial, the Smithsonian Institution, and the Supreme Court Building, are utilized. A frustrated spaceman, Michael Rennie goes to the Lincoln Memorial searching for one reasonable man and laments that he can't speak to the man depicted in the statue. The H. Cornell Wilson House (1609 16th

Street NW) was the home of Sam Jaffe.

Deep Impact

(1998). Morgan Freeman, Robert Duvall. A comet is on a collision course with planet Earth.

Washington was a focal point of the race to save Earth from destruction. Locations used around the nation's capital include the reflecting pool of the Lincoln Memorial; the DC Department of Employment Services (500 C Street NW), which stood in for the city morgue; the Francis Scott Key Bridge; the Sequoia restaurant (3000 K Street NW); and rooftop sequences atop the Housing and Urban Development Building (451 Seventh Street NW).

Dick

(1999). Michelle Williams, Kirsten Dunst. High school students experience the Watergate scandal after wandering away from a White House tour.

The movie was shot almost entirely in Canada, but there are scenes of the real Watergate Hotel (2650 Virginia Avenue NW), exteriors of the White House, the Washington Monument and a sequence at the Chesapeake & Ohio Canal Historical Park (1057 Thomas Jefferson Street NW, Georgetown). Begun in 1828, the 184.5-mile canal operated from 1850 until 1924.

Enemy of the State

(1998). Will Smith, Gene Hackman. Lawyer becomes target of National Security Agency after accidentally receiving evidence of a politically motivated crime.

Lambda Bookstore (DuPont Circle) was redecorated to look like Ruby's lingerie shop, from which Jason Lee emerges, chased by two National Security Agency agents. He grabs a courier's bike, pedals through oncoming cars and evades pursuers in an underpass tunnel of Connecticut Avenue and Q Street beneath DuPont Circle — only to pop out at the far end of the tunnel on the losing end of an encounter with a speeding fire engine. Smith drives his car through the ventilator shaft under the Fort Henry Harbor Tunnel in Baltimore.

Eraser

(1996). Arnold Schwarzenegger, James Caan. Elite marshall with the Federal Witness Protection Program works to protect corporate whistle blower.

In Washington, scenes were shot at the 17th Street Rainbow Pool on the National Mall and at the Phoenix Park Hotel (520 North Capitol Street).

The Exorcist

(1973). Ellen Burstyn, Linda Blair. A priest is called in to purge a young girl of a possessive demon.

The setting for the famous horror film is Georgetown University. The long stair next to Linda Blair's house — 97 stone steps — where Jason Miller is thrown to his death out a window, is at 3600 Prospect Street. The steps were padded to film the death scene. Also featured is the Dahlgren

Chapel, constructed in 1893 and the main Catholic church on campus, and the office of the president, which became the Cardinal's office.

The Exorcist III

(1990). George C. Scott, Ed Flanders. A serial killer executed on the night of the original exorcism reappears.

Georgetown locales starred once again, with the Ascension St. Agnes Church (Massachusetts Avenue & 12th Street NW) playing a central role.

A Few Good Men

(1992). Tom Cruise, Jack Nicholson. Novice military lawyer draws a case defending marines who claim they murdered on orders from their commanding officer.

St. Elizabeth's Hospital (2700 Martin Luther King Jr. Avenue) in Congress Heights doubled as the grounds of the United States Naval Academy. Later in the film Cruise and Kevin Pollack can be seen walking Pollack's baby at 20th Street NW and Belmont Place NW in the Adams-Morgan section.

In the Line of Fire

(1993). Clint Eastwood, John Malkovich. Aging Secret Service agent races to stop presidential assassination.

The Secret Service is housed in the Treasury Building (1500 Pennsylvania Avenue NW), where Eastwood flirts with Rene Russo on the steps. Eastwood subsequently takes Russo to the Lincoln Memorial on their first date. Chase scenes were shot through the Adams-Morgan section of Washington around 18th Street, and Eastwood has a drink with supervisor John Mahoney at the Old Ebitt Grill (675 15th Street NW). Malkovich shoots duck hunters at the Isaac Walton League Ponds in Patuxent River Park (Governors Ridge Park, Bowie, Maryland).

Jackal

(1997). Bruce Willis, Richard Gere. A master of disguise is hired for $70 million to assassinate a Washington politician, and only an imprisoned terrorist can help stop him.

In Washington, a stretch along Pennsylvania Avenue near the United States Capitol, and residential streets and private homes in Georgetown were used for filming.

Mercury Rising

(1998). Bruce Willis, Alec Baldwin. An ostracized FBI agent protects a nine-year-old autistic savant.

Featured in the film is the Eastern Market (7th & C Streets), built in 1873 from a design by Adolph Closs, where a man fearing for his life buys an antique typewriter at a flea market. Another location used in Washington was Rock Creek Park in the northwest section of the capital, established in 1890 and one of the oldest parks in the National Park Service.

Mr. Smith Goes to Washington

(1939). Jimmy Stewart, Jean Arthur. Idealistic average man is appointed to Senate where he is forced to deal with political corruption)

All of the major landmarks are featured in the classic Washington film, but only as background. All the scenes, including the speeches in a meticulously reproduced United States Senate chamber, were filmed in Hollywood.

Murder at 1600

(1997). Diane Lane, Wesley Snipes. Secret Service agents investigate a murder at the White House.

Since no filming is allowed inside the White House, set designers go to extreme lengths to create realistic interior scenes, including consulting books, interviewing former staffers and even taking the public tour. For this movie set designers constructed a 30,000-square foot White House set that featured a laser-cut reproduction of the carpet in William Clinton's Oval Office.

My Fellow Americans

(1996). James Garner, Jack Lemmon. Ex-Presidents on opposite ends of the political spectrum join forces to battle spurious charges.

Extensive sets were constructed in Hollywood for the White House scenes. The finale on the White House lawn was recreated on the lawn at the Biltmore Estate in Asheville, North Carolina. Scenes shot in Washington include shots at the Lincoln and Jefferson memorials, and at the Headquarters of the Daughters of the American Revolution (1776 D Street NW), where the rooftop doubled as the White House rooftop.

No Way Out

(1987). Kevin Costner, Gene Hackman. A cover-up begins when a politician accidentally kills his mistress.

Some scenes were shot in corridors in the Pentagon (Washington Boulevard, Arlington, Virginia), but most of the interior filming was accomplished on an MGM sound stage in Hollywood. Tours of the Pentagon, built in 1943 and one of the world's largest office buildings, are available Monday through Friday. Costner becomes infatuated with Sean Young during a party at the Omni Shoreham Hotel (2500 Calvert Street NW). Another featured hotel in this thriller is the Hay-Adams Hotel (16th and H Streets NW). Chases around the city include a driving sequence on the Whitehurst Freeway in Georgetown and a foot race near the Chesapeake & Ohio Canal.

Pelican Brief

(1993). Julia Roberts, Denzel Washington. Law student stumbles onto plot to assassinate Supreme Court justices.

Roberts and Washington investigate their case at the Georgetown University Law Center (600 New Jersey Avenue NW). Roberts goes to the Riggs National Bank (1503 Pennsylvania

Avenue) to pick up an incriminating videotape; she is almost killed in the parking garage, but that garage scene was filmed in Bethesda, Maryland. Also featured is the main atrium of the Warner Theater overlooking Freedom Plaza and Pennsylvania Avenue. Roberts was a student at Tulane University in New Orleans, Louisiana (6823 St. Charles Avenue). She dines with Sam Shepherd at Antoine's (713–717 Rue St. Louis, New Orleans) before he is killed in a car explosion.

FLORIDA

Absence of Malice

(1981). Paul Newman, Sally Field. The son of a mob boss is hounded by newspaper stories.

Newman contests the charges of a reporter in the offices of the *Miami Herald* (One Herald Plaza, Miami). Field confronts Melinda Dillon at the Vizcaya Museum and Gardens (3251 South Miami Avenue, Miami), an Italian Renaissance villa built in 1916. The 34 rooms of the 10-acre villa are open for tours.

Ace Ventura: Pet Detective

(1994). Jim Carrey, Courteney Cox. A detective specializes in finding missing animals.

In his search for Snowflake, the missing Miami Dolphins' mascot, Carrey attends parties at the Vizcaya Museum and Gardens (3251 South Miami Avenue, Miami) and the Biltmore Hotel (1200 Anastasia Avenue, Coral Gables). Carrey rescues Snowflake and Dan Marino at a basin in Fort Lauderdale at 2001 SW 20th Street. Stadium sequences were filmed in Joe Robbie Stadium (2269 NW 199th Street, Miami).

Armageddon

(1998). Bruce Willis, Billy Bob Thornton. The world's best deep-core drilling team is sent to blow up an asteroid headed for earth.

The crew take off for its rendezvous with the earthbound asteroid from Kennedy Space Center (State Road 405, Kennedy Space Center). Actual shuttle launch footage from lift-offs at Cape Canaveral Air Station is used for the blast-off. Similar missile launches can be viewed from Cocoa Beach or along the Indian River in Titusville. Current shuttle blast-off schedules are available from NASA's shuttle hotline at 800-572-4636. The asteroid sequences were filmed at the Badlands National Park in South Dakota.

Bad Boys

(1995). Will Smith, Martin Lawrence. Two policemen have to pretend to be each other to retrieve stolen contraband.

A hanger at the Opa-Lacka Airport in Miami that was scheduled for demolition was blown up for the movie.

The Bellboy

(1960). Jerry Lewis, Milton Berle. Bellboy at posh hotel resembles show business star.

Lewis shot the movie during four weeks in which he was performing at the Fontainebleu Hilton Resort and Spa (4441 Collins Avenue, Miami).

Black Sunday

(1977). Robert Shaw, Bruce Dern. Demented war veteran plots to kill thousands at the Super Bowl.

The filming of the hijacked blimp terrorizing fans at the Orange Bowl (1501 NW Third Street, Miami) took place the day before the actual Super Bowl X. Game footage was obtained the next day with cameras disguised as CBS television cameras.

Body Heat

(1981). William Hurt, Kathleen Turner. A woman convinces a lawyer to help eliminate her husband.

Many of the town scenes were staged in Lake Worth. Hurt first spots and tries to pick up Turner at the Amphitheater at the end of Lucerne; his office is on Lakeview Street. Turner's home is a private mansion in Hypoluxo at the corner of Federal Highway and Hypoluxo Road. Turner suns herself at the end of the film not in Florida but in Hawaii, at Ke'e Beach on the island of Kauai.

Caddyshack

(1980). Chevy Chase, Rodney Dangerfield. An exclusive golf club gets an abrasive new member.

The Rolling Hills Golf & Tennis Club (3501 W. Rolling Hill Circle, Davie) played the Bushwood Country Club in both the original and the sequel.

Cape Fear

(1991). Robert DeNiro, Nick Nolte. Psychopathic rapist released from jail seeks revenge on his lawyer.

Florida does duty as the Carolinas in this stylish remake. Nolte first realizes he is being followed by ex-convict DeNiro at the Rainbo Cafe (1909 Hollywood Boulevard, Hollywood), which has been transformed into an ice cream shop. Nolte later tries to bribe DeNiro into leaving him alone on the Hollywood Boardwalk. The theater where DeNiro entices Juliette Lewis is a lecture hall at Broward Community College in Davie. The climactic scene on the houseboat was filmed in a 90-foot water tank.

Cocoon

(1985). Don Ameche, Wilford Brimley. Senior citizens get revitalized after swimming in pools containing alien cocoons.

Filmed around St. Petersburg, the movie shows the newly-spry oldsters dancing at the Coliseum Ballroom (535 Fourth Avenue North). When the ballroom opened in 1924 the wooden dance floor was the largest in the southeastern states.

Cocoon: The Return

(1988). Don Ameche, Wilford Brimley. Pensioners come back to earth to visit relatives.

Jack Gifford and Elaine Stitch have their first date at the Desiree Supper Club (9674 SW 24th Street, Miami). The high-powered basketball game occurred at Morningside Park (850 NE 55th Terrace, Miami).

Cop and a Half

(1993). Burt Reynolds, Norman D. Golden II. An eight-year-old witness to a murder withholds information until Tampa police agree to make him a cop.

The movie used locations throughout Tampa and the old cigar-rolling historic section of Ybor City. The Ybor City Chamber of Commerce and Ybor City State Museum offer a guided walking tour of historic Ybor City (1818 E. Ninth Avenue).

Creature from the Black Lagoon

(1954). Richard Carlson, Julie Adams. A scientific expedition to the Amazon uncovers a humanoid amphibian.

The South American jungle was recreated at Wakulla Springs State Park (1 Spring Drive, Wakulla Springs), site of one of the largest and deepest freshwater springs in the world. Objects 185 feet down on the bottom can still be seen clearly. Wakulla Springs was believed to be the pool tabbed as the "Fountain of Youth" by Ponce de Leon in 1513. In addition to all three *Creature* movies, several early Tarzan films were shot here as well.

Crisscross

(1992). Goldie Hawn, David Arnott. A boy tries to sell cocaine to get his mother out of a career as a stripper.

Single mother Hawn and Arnott live in rooms 203 and 204 of the Eden House Hotel (1015 Fleming Street, Key West). The 1920s guest house was distressed to play Hawn's Esquire Lounge in 1969.

D.A.R.Y.L.

(1985). Mary Beth Hurt, Michael McKean. A family takes in amnesic boy with special powers.

Barret Oliver's Barketon School was played by Kaley Elementary School (1600 E. Kaley Avenue, Orlando). School children earned money as extras during filming over Christmas break. The movie's big chase sequence was filmed on the East/West Expressway.

Devil's Advocate

(1997). Al Pacino, Keanu Reeves. Hotshot lawyer discovers his new boss is Lucifer himself.

Reeves makes his reputation at the Duval County Courthouse (330 E. Bay Street, Jacksonville), designed in 1902 by Rutledge Holmes.

Doc Hollywood

(1991). Michael J. Fox, Julie Warner. A young doctor is sentenced to work a few shifts in a small-town hospital after a traffic accident.

On his way to his dream job in

California, Fox swerves to avoid a cow on Baden Powell Road in Melrose. The large house used as a prop in Camp Shands, south of Melrose and east of SR 21, is still standing. The town of Micanopy, Florida's oldest inland town, plays the fictional Grady, South Carolina, the squash capital of the South. The parade of marching squashes was staged through the center of town. The House of Hirsch antique store (209 NE Cholokka Boulevard, Micanopy) became the hospital where Fox serves his sentence.

Edward Scissorhands

(1990). Johnny Depp, Winona Ryder. An Avon lady adopts manmade boy whose creator died before he was able to complete his hands.

In a small subdivision called Carpenter's Run in Wesley Chapel, 44 of the 50 homeowners agreed to have their houses painted in a mad palette of pastel colors for this fable. Depp's new home was on a cul-de-sac called Tinsmith Circle. Scientist Vincent Price's 80-foot-high Gothic mansion was created on Platt Road overlooking Dade City. The topiary structures that Depp fashioned were created in a warehouse on Route 41 and placed on the lawns in Carpenter's Run. Depp goes to a beauty shop to sharpen his hands at South Gate Plaza (2500 South Florida Avenue, Lakeland).

Ernest Saves Christmas

(1988). Jim Varney, Douglas Seale. Obnoxious cab driver looks for a replacement for retiring Kris Kringle.

Varney first picks up Santa Claus at the Orlando International Airport. Later, the Orlando Science Center (777 East Princeton Street, Orlando) stands in for a children's museum. Varney's house is on the backstage tour of Universal Studios.

Fair Game

(1995). William Baldwin, Cindy Crawford. A policeman tries to protect woman from renegade KGB agents.

Filming took place all over south Florida; the closing sequence featured the sinking of the 180-foot freighter Tortuga off Key Biscayne specifically for the movie. The wreck is now a popular spot for recreational divers and has been renamed Fair Game.

The First of May

(2000). Mickey Rooney, Julie Harris. Unwanted boy and forgotten old lady find home with circus.

Although it appears that the circus is traveling, the circus scenes were all filmed in the winter home of the Clyde Beatty Cole Brothers Circus (1038 Main Street, DeLand). There is also footage of the community of Lake Helen, which is listed on the National Register of Historic Places.

Folks

(1992). Don Ameche, Tom Selleck. A man's life falls apart when his parents come to live with him.

While wife Anne Jackson is in the hospital, a senile Ameche burns down the family home at Briny Breezes

The Orlando (Florida) Science Center played a children's museum in *Ernest Saves Christmas*. (Orlando Science Center)

Mobil Home Community (5000 N. Ocean Boulevard, Briny Breezes). Jackson is hospitalized at the Boca Raton Resort Hotel and Club (501 East Camino Real, Boca Raton), which played an upscale medical center.

Forever Mine

(1999). Joseph Fiennes, Ray Liotta. Wife's affair triggers a 16-year vendetta between two men.

The hotel scenes in Miami were created at the Don Ce Sar Beach Resort (3860 Gulf Boulevard, St. Petersburg Beach).

Frogs

(1972). Ray Milland, Sam Elliott. A wealthy despoiler of nature meets his doom via a savage herd of murderous frogs.

The film was shot at Eden State Gardens and Museum (County Road 395, Point Washington), overlooking Choctawhatchee Bay. The 10-acre estate was built for William Wesley, whose 1898 Greek Revival mansion was also used in the movie. Many of the 500 frogs and 100 giant South American toads escaped onto the grounds, which are open to tours, after the filming.

GI Jane

(1997). Demi Moore, Anne Bancroft. Naval intelligence officer is recruited to become the first female SEAL.

The United States Capitol, which does not permit interior filming, was played by the temporarily vacant Interstate Commerce Commission Build-

Ray Milland was besieged by amphibians at Eden State Gardens in *Frogs*.

ing (Constitution Street and 12th Street). Moore is put through her paces at Camp Blanding (Route 1, Starke), which is still an active training center for the Florida National Guard. Tours are available of the camp, which was a major training center during World War II; a refurbished barracks features a small museum. Producers hauled 50 tons of white sand to the wooded location to simulate a Navy shore base. Shooting moved to South Carolina at Hunting Island State Park near Beaufort to shoot war games and POW camp scenes.

Goldfinger

(1964). Sean Connery, Gert Frobe. British spy tries to save American gold supply from being contaminated.

Despite the American setting for most of the movie, Connery never set foot in America. His scenes were filmed in England and integrated with footage shot on location in the United States. The hotel scene where Connery catches Frobe cheating at cards was set in the Fontainebleau Hilton Resort and Spa (4441 Collins Avenue, Miami). The conclusion at the United States Bullion Depository in Fort Knox, Kentucky, was also recreated in England, but there were establishing shots of Highway 31-A leading to Fort Knox. Visitors can tour the base and see the outside of the vault.

Great Expectations

(1998). Ethan Hawke, Gwynneth Paltrow. Painter pursues unrequited childhood love in New York City.

The principal set in the movie is

Anne Bancroft's crumbling mansion, played by Cá d'Zan, circus impresario John Ringling's Venetian Gothic mansion on Sarasota Bay. Filmmakers gave the 1920-built Venetian palace a distressed look by adding vines and gray-green paint. The grounds were covered with dead palm fronds. Special effects left the 30-room terracotta mansion roofless at film's end. Cá d'Zan is part of the Ringling Circus Museum (5401 Bay Shore Road, Sarasota), and is recently restored and open to the public. Hawke's growing-up scenes were shot in the fishing village of Cortez Island.

The Greatest Show on Earth

(1952). Charlton Heston, Jimmy Stewart. The professional and personal lives of performers in the circus business.

John Ringling brought the Ringling Brothers and Barnum & Bailey Circus to Sarasota in 1927. The circus wintered here through 1959, and the headquarters were used in making the film. The site remains as part of the Ringling Center for the Cultural Arts (5401 Bay Shore Road, Sarasota).

Instinct

(1999). Anthony Hopkins, Cuba Gooding. Anthropologist living with gorillas kills poachers and is sent to a Florida mental institution.

The Student Services Building at Valencia Community College East Campus (701 N. Econlockhatchee Trail, Orlando) served as a Miami medical university.

Just Cause

(1995). Sean Connery, Laurence Fishburne. Law professor tries to convince police to consider new evidence in favor of convicted killer.

The University Auditorium at the University of Florida played Harvard, where Connery taught. Blair Underwood kidnaps Kate Capshaw at the Eden Roc Resort and Spa (4525 Collins Avenue, Miami Beach), and Connery chases the kidnapper along the MacArthur Causeway between Miami and Miami Beach. At the 90,000 acre Crescent B Ranch southeast of Punta Gorda, the first Florida cattle ranch to convert into a tourist attraction, the Cracker Shack was built for the movie. It now serves as a small museum.

Let It Ride

(1989). Richard Dreyfuss, Teri Garr. After a gambler promises never to bet again he gets on the hottest streak of his life.

Dreyfuss feeds his gambling compulsion at Hialeah Park (2200 East Fourth Avenue, Hialeah), with its trademark flamingos in the background.

Lethal Weapon III

(1992). Mel Gibson, Danny Glover. supercops team with equally tough policewoman in pursuit of crooked cop.

The implosion in the opening scene was the demolition of the old Orlando City Hall on south Orange Street.

License to Kill

(1989). Timothy Dalton, Robert Davi. Spy leaves Her Majesty's Secret Service to avenge attack on best friend.

Dalton and David Hedison parachute into Hedison's wedding in the opening scene at St. Mary's Catholic Church (1010 Windsor Lane, Key West). The power lines had to be removed around the area for the scene. Dalton's license to kill is revoked at the Ernest Hemingway Home and Museum (907 Whitehead Street, Key West). The scene was staged on the second floor balcony of the 1851 Spanish Colonial-style mansion where Dalton dodged gunfire from a nearby lighthouse. Stripped of his license, Dalton tips a literary hat to the setting by observing, "I guess it's a farewell to arms." The descendants of Hemingway's cat still roam the grounds, which are open for tours. The *Sea Eagle* used in the ocean scenes is a 60-foot dive boat available for dive trips out of Key West at the Ocean Key House, Zero Duval Street.

Married to the Mob

(1988). Michelle Pfeiffer, Matthew Modine. Dead mobster's wife attracts amorous attention from a mob king and an FBI agent.

The climactic scene where Pfeiffer accompanies Dean Stockwell to the hotel was shot at the Eden Roc Resort and Spa (4525 Collins Avenue). In Massapequa Park, New York, Pfeiffer tries to avoid Mercedes Ruehl in the Foodtown on 4938 Merrick Road.

Matinee

(1993). John Goodman, Cathy Moriarty. Showman takes over a small town's movie theater.

Goodman has big plans for his Strand Theater, played by the Cocoa Village Playhouse (300 Brevard Avenue, Cocoa). The ornate brick building, opened as an early "talkie" house known as the Alladin Theater in 1924, was used for exterior shots; interiors were completed at Universal Studios.

Mean Season

(1985). Kurt Russell, Mariel Hemingway. Reporter becomes spokesman for a killer, who then targets his girlfriend.

The newsroom scenes were filmed in the real *Miami Herald* newsroom (One Herald Plaza, Miami).

My Girl

(1991). Macauley Culkin, Dan Aykroyd. Young girl feels abandoned when her widowed father falls in love.

Aykroyd and Anna Chlumsky live in the Stanford Inn (555 East Stanford Street, Bartow), a 1906 Victorian mansion designed by Leo Elliot and now a bed and breakfast. Chlumsky and Culkin ride their bikes through downtown Bartow along Main Street. Chlumsky and Aykroyd are eating at Cafe Jake's (112 East First Street, Sanford) when they see Glenda Chism.

Palmetto

(1998). Woody Harrelson, Elisabeth Shue. Former reporter released from prison after a trumped up charge is hired to fake a kidnapping.

The two-story brick building where Harrelson sips beer in the middle of his caper is The Gator Club (1490 Main Street, Sarasota). The building is on the National Register of Historic Places.

Parenthood

(1989). Steve Martin, Mary Steenburgen. Childrearing examined from different points of view in the same large family.

The ballgame in the opening scene, filmed in 20 takes because the batter couldn't hit the ball to centerfield, was shot at Tinker Field (287 South Tampa Avenue, Orlando). The sequence at the Chuck E Cheese was shot in Altamonte Springs on Highway 436. Century Tower at the University of Florida is where Martin dreams his son turns into a sniper shooting into Turlington Plaza.

Passenger 57

(1992). Wesley Snipes, Tom Sizemore. Airline security expert is trapped on passenger jet seized by terrorists.

The hijacking scene was filmed at Orlando Sanford Airport (2735 Mellonville Avenue, Sanford). Orlando International Airport was also used for filming.

Police Academy 5: Assignment in Miami Beach

(1988). Bubba Smith, David Graf. Former chief of police academy goes to Florida to accept an award.

The contrivance to move the characters in this film series to Florida is the 50th Annual National Police Chiefs Convention held in the Fontainebleu Hilton Resort and Spa (4441 Collins Avenue, Miami).

Problem Child

(1991). John Ritter, Amy Yasbeck. Monster child teams up with his new stepsister to create even more mischief.

Ritter and Yasbeck unite their new families in marriage at the Harry P. Leu Botanical Gardens (1920 North Forest Avenue, Orlando). The 56 acres of camellia forests and avenues of giant camphor are open daily for tours. The site of the movie's food fight is Pete's Bubble Room restaurant (1351 South Orlando Avenue, Maitland). They adopt Michael Oliver in Fort Worth, Texas, at the orphanage at the Gladney Center (2300 Hemphill Street), playing the St. Brutus orphanage.

PT 109

(1963). Cliff Robertson, Ty Hardin. Dramatization of John Kennedy's war-time experience in the South Pacific.

The South Pacific was shot on Little Palm Island, a resort 28 miles east of Key West. The island, which became a resort in 1988, had no running water or electricity before Joseph Kennedy requested it for the film. President Kennedy, who favored Warren Beatty for the role, came to the island to watch some of the shooting.

Ruby in Paradise

(1993). Ashley Judd, Todd Field. Young woman arrives in Florida resort town to make a new start.

Judd's destination is Panama City Beach, where she takes in a Better Buns Contest at Spinnaker on Thomas Drive, dances at Thunderbirds (4300 West Highway 98) and parties at Sharky's Beach Bar on Front Beach Road. In her down time she climbs the dunes of St. Andrew's State Recreation Area (three miles east of Panama City Beach via SR 392).

Rude Awakening

(1989). Eric Roberts, Cheech Marin. Former hippies find a changed world after 20 years in a South American commune.

Roberts and Marin lived in the commune created in Wekiwa Springs State Park (four miles northwest of I-4, off US 441 near Apopka). The namesake spring forms a crystal clear pool that is seldom more than five feet deep.

Running Scared

(1986). Billy Crystal, Gregory Hines. Chicago cops lose their edge after vacationing in Key West.

Crystal and Hines dream of buying a bar while sitting in Mallory Square in Key West. The fishing boat Corsina, which they used, can be rented at 3367 Donald Avenue. The climactic shootout takes place in the

Sharky's Beach Club was one of Ashley Judd's destinations when she came to Panama City Beach, Florida, to start a new life in *Ruby in Paradise*.

cavernous central atrium of the James R. Thompson Center (100 West Randolph Street, Chicago).

Semi-Tough

(1978). Burt Reynolds, Kris Kristofferson. Two football players share a condo with the owner's daughter.

Football sequences were staged at the Orange Bowl Stadium (1501 NW Third Street, Miami). The stadium is home to the University of Miami Hurricanes.

Something About Mary

(1998). Ben Stiller, Cameron Diaz. Man gets the chance to meet his dream girl from high school.

After a brief start in Rhode Island, Stiller follows Diaz to south Florida. The high school was shot at Plantation City Hall (400 NW 73rd Avenue, Plantation).

Something Wild

(1986). Jeff Daniels, Melanie Griffith. Humdrum life of businessman changes when he meets a sexy stranger.

Griffith swims at the former Tallahassee Motor Lodge across Lake Ella on land now occupied by restaurants.

The Specialist

(1994). Sylvester Stallone, Sharon Stone. Ex-CIA bomb expert helps woman seek revenge against underworld.

Florida hotels take a beating in this thriller: Stallone blows Room 1205 of the Fontainebleu Hilton Resort and Spa (4441 Collins Avenue, Miami Beach) into the Atlantic Ocean, and a cabana explodes at the Biltmore Hotel (1200 Anastasia Avenue).

Stick

(1985). Burt Reynolds, Candice Bergen. Ex-con tries to straighten out his life but must avenge the death of an old friend.

The stunt featuring a fall from a 20-story condominium complex was shot at the Grove Towers (7950 NW 58th Street, Coconut Grove).

Traces of Red

(1992). James Belushi, Lorraine Bracco. Detective becomes entangled in string of murders that can all be traced to him.

Belushi investigates his case in the Palm Beach-Fort Lauderdale area. He and Tony Goldwyn turn up leads in Squeeze (2 South New River Drive, Fort Lauderdale) nightclub. Belushi testifies at the South County Courthouse (200 West Atlantic Avenue, Delray Beach), and the sheriff's headquarters was fashioned at the imposing Twin Lakes High School, now the Dreyfoos School of the Arts (501 South Sapodilla Avenue, West Palm Beach). Suspect Bracco sponsors a political fundraiser at the exclusive Breakers Hotel (One South County Road, Palm Beach). The grand Italian villa–style hotel was built in 1896 by pioneer Florida developer Henry Flagler.

True Lies

(1994). Arnold Schwarzenegger, Jamie Lee Curtis. Computer salesman/secret agent tries to save the world and his marriage.

Schwarzenegger rides a horse through the lobby of the Renaissance Mayflower Hotel (1127 Connecticut Avenue NW) in Washington DC. He chases nuclear terrorist Art Malik through shops at the Georgetown Park Mall (M Street and Wisconsin Avenue, Washington DC) after riddling the mens room with bullets in a scene that was filmed on a Hollywood set. For the scene where he rescues his daughter in a harrier jet — rented for $20,000 an hour — from the penthouse hide-away, producers built an additional two stories atop the Terremark Building (1220 Brickell Avenue, Miami) so that the windows could be blown out. The harrowing rescue of Curtis from the limousine before it careened off the bridge took place on the old Seven-Mile Bridge between Miami and the Florida Keys, which was no longer in use.

Truman Show

(1998). Jim Carrey, Ed Harris. Man discovers his entire life has been a television show.

Producers searched for a planned community to play the part of a town as television set and decided on Seaside, a Victorian-style community built in 1990, near Panama City. Seaside became the fictional Seahaven, where every street name referred to a movie.

Ulee's Gold

(1997). Peter Fonda, Patricia Richardson. Reclusive beekeeper fights to hold his dysfunctional family together.

All the swamplands and bee yards in the movie belong to L.L. Lanier & Sons Tupelo Honey, east of Panama City on Highway 22. The old truck where the money was hidden is still there along the Apalochicola River.

Up Close and Personal

(1996). Robert Redford, Michelle Pfeiffer. ambitious television journalist falls in love with her boss.

Scenes were shot at Bahia Honda State Park (36850 Overseas Highway, Bel Glade on Bahia Honda Key). The prison riot scene was staged in Philadelphia's Holmesburg Prison.

Waterboy

(1998). Adam Sandler, Kathy Bates. football team waterboy discovers he has a unique ability to tackle.

Stetson University in DeLand, named for hat magnate John Stetson, became the fictional South Central Louisiana State University. Vines were placed on the entrance gates and an aged plaque covered the Stetson seal. Other locations on campus included the Holler Fountain and the Cummings Gym. Practices and regular season Mud Dog game footage was staged at Spec-Martin Stadium (260 East Euclid, DeLand), and the climactic game at the "Bourbon Bowl" was filmed with 8000 extras at the Florida Citrus Bowl (1 Citrus Bowl Place, Orlando). Bates and Sandler lived in a clapboard house built on the main boat launch at Highbanks Marina (488 West Highbanks Road, DeBary). The banks of the St. Johns River here stood in for the Louisiana bayou.

Where the Boys Are

(1960). George Hamilton, Dolores Hart. College students head for Fort Lauderdale on spring break in search of fun.

The movie put this beach town on the radar screen for fun-seekers everywhere, and it took three decades for the town to erase its image as "Fort Liquordale." Now the college crowd gravitates toward Daytona Beach. The Elbow Room popularized in the movie is still on Las Olas Boulevard, open 24 hours.

Wild Things

(1998). Kevin Bacon, Matt Dillon. High school counselor is accused of raping one of his students.

Dillon's remote hut was built in Bill Baggs State Park (1200 South Crandon Boulevard at the end of Key Biscayne). Other scenes were shot in Oleta River State Recreational Park (3400 NE 164th Street, North Miami).

Wilder Napalm

(1993). Debra Winger, Dennis Quaid. brothers are pyrotechnics who can start fires with their minds.

The county fair was assembled in the parking lot of Sanford Plaza (30th Street, Sanford). Additional scenes were filmed at Orlando Sanford Airport (2735 Mellonville Avenue, Sanford), which handles commercial and personal aircraft.

Wrestling Ernest Hemingway

(1993). Robert Duvall, Richard Harris. Two lonely old men meet in a park and forge a friendship.

Harris lives in the Lone Palm, played by the vintage 1938 Ocean Hacienda Inn (1924 North Atlantic Boulevard, Fort Lauderdale).

GEORGIA

The Bingo Long Traveling All Stars and Motor Kings

(1978). Billy Dee Williams, James Earl Jones. Tired of dictatorial Negro League owner in the 1930s, star pitcher starts his own team.

The baseball scenes were filmed in two historic Georgia ballyards: Grayson Stadium (Victory Drive in Daffin Park, Savannah) and Luther Williams Field (Central City Park, Macon). Grayson was built in 1926 and remodeled in 1941, and features a brick facade with large covered grandstand. Luther Williams was constructed in 1929 with a traditional brick archway and all 4000 seats covered by the grandstand roof.

Boxing Helena

(1993). Sherilyn Fenn, Julian Sands. A horrible accident leaves a woman at the mercy of her demented ex-boyfriend surgeon.

The mansion at the corner of West Paces Ferry and Castlegate in the Buckhead section of Atlanta was the home of Sands' mad doctor.

Consenting Adults

(1992). Kevin Kline, Kevin Spacey. New neighbors turn couples' lives upside down.

Producers searched for a generic subdivision that could be anywhere and settled on the Atlanta suburb of Sweetbottom Plantation, a community of homes based on 19th century historically reproduced mansions. The couples lived on Pleasant Hill Road. Also appearing is the Gwinnett County Detention Center (2900 University parkway, Lawrenceville). The first vacation spot chosen by the wife-swapping couples was the Rice Hope Plantation (206 Rice Hope Drive, Moncks Corner, South Carolina), a rice plantation started in 1696. The 1840s plantation house is open to guests.

Deliverance

(1972). Jon Voight, Burt Reynolds. Four friends run into problems on a weekend canoeing trip.

Despite the gruesome nature of the plot, the beauty of the northeast Georgia scenery from the movie sparked a boom in whitewater rafting.

Wife swappers Kevin Spacey and Kevin Kline chose Rice Hope Plantation, established in 1696 and an inn since 1987, as a vacation spot in *Consenting Adults*. (Rice Hope Plantation)

Doing his own stunts, Jon Voight climbed up this cliff and out of Tallulah Gorge in Georgia to escape a disastrous canoeing trip in *Deliverance*.

Doing his own stunts, Voight climbed out of the Tallulah Gorge in Tallulah Falls State Park (US 441). The inn featured is the York House (US 441, Mountain City), built in 1851 in the wilderness of what would become the Chattahoochee National Forest.

Driving Miss Daisy

(1989). Morgan Freeman, Jessica Tandy. Elderly woman is forced to rely on hired chauffeur to get around.

The home where Tandy lived was at 822 Lulwater Road in the turn-of-the-century Druid Hills section of Atlanta. Abandoned after shooting, the house is now completely restored. The home of the real Miss Daisy, upon whom the character is based, is at 1284 Fairview Road. Walking tours of the filming locations are offered by the Atlanta Preservation Center.

Dutch

(1991). Ed O'Neill, Ethan Embry. Construction worker agrees to drive his girlfriend's snobbish son home from boarding school.

The private school where O'Neill picks up Embry is Berry College on US 27 in Rome, site of the plantation home of Martha Berry, who began teaching local children in a one-room log cabin in 1902. Her single classroom would evolve into Berry College and earn the cotton broker's daughter eight honorary degrees. A museum on campus is dedicated to her work.

Forces of Nature

(1999). Sandra Bullock, Ben Affleck. Soon-to-be-wed man's plans are sidetracked by an exciting stranger.

There are scenes of Savannah, including the famous globe built by Savannah Gas in 1957 to store natural gas. Located south of DeRenne Avenue at 73rd Street, the globe has been called the largest in the world. Also featured are businesses on Broughton Street, and the bus and train depots. The airport where the action is triggered is Dulles in Washington, playing La Guardia in New York. A scene on the road takes place at South of the Border (I-95, Dillon, South Carolina). Much of the action in South Carolina takes place at The Castle (411 Craven Street, Beaufort), an 1850s private residence where the wedding was staged.

Forrest Gump

(1994). Tom Hanks, Gary Sinese. Simple man has knack for appearing on the scene of famous events.

Although set in Alabama, Hanks sits on a bus bench and tells his life story to a succession of strangers in Savannah's Chippewa Square on Bull Street. The bench was removed after the filming, but it was put back to appease tourists before being removed again. There are replicas of the bench in places around the country, but the real bench is on a lot at Paramount Pictures in Hollywood. Michael Humphreys, playing Hanks as a boy, grows up along Main Street in Varnville, South Carolina, playing a fictional Alabama town. Also in South Carolina, Hanks ties up his shrimp boat at Lucy Creek on Lady's Island, south of Beaufort. The Beaufort Performing Arts Center (801 Cataret Street) plays the Bayou le Batre hospital that is named for Forrest Gump. Hanks saves Vietnam soldiers in sequences shot in South Carolina's Hunting Island Park in what is now the Ocean Point Golf Club. The scene with the Black Panthers took place at Independence and Third streets in Washington DC. This movie marked the first time permission had been granted to shoot in the reflecting pool of the Lincoln Memorial, where Hanks and childhood friend Robin Wright run into each other. Hanks gives Wright his Congressional Medal of Honor at the Palace of Fine Arts in San Francisco, California (3601 Lyons Street). Hanks ends a leg of his three-year cross-country run at the Marshall Point Lighthouse in Port Clyde, Maine.

Freejack

(1992). Emilio Estevez, Mick Jagger. An auto racer is snatched by time travel an instant before a fatal explosion.

The Fulton Cotton and Bag Mill, built in 1881 by Atlanta's largest employer and left decaying until a conversion into lofts, was the backdrop for 21st century Atlanta. The extended car chase takes place on the streets of Atlanta until Estevez plows through a roadblock.

Fried Green Tomatoes

(1991). Kathy Bates, Jessica Tandy. Unhappy housewife is inspired by an old woman in a nursing home.

GEORGIA

The tapered brick pillars of the Whistle Stop Cafe in Juliette, Georgia, are familiar to fans of *Fried Green Tomatoes*.

Juliette, 90 miles south of Atlanta, was essentially an abandoned town until the popular movie came out. The train depot was a dilapidated building found in the woods. Today there are more than a dozen businesses serving the tourist trade stopping to see the Whistle Stop Cafe with the brick pillars on McCrackin Road. So many people came, the eatery had to change its name to that of the fictional cafe in the movie. Fried green tomatoes can be ordered separately or come free with the meal.

The General's Daughter

(1999). John Travolta, Madeleine Stowe. Army officer with the power to arrest any military person of any rank investigates high-ranking suspects in murder of famous general's daughter.

Myrtle Grove Plantation in Richmond Hill, an 1850s-era plantation now known as Folly Farms, stood in for James Cromwell's house. To create fictional Fort McCallum, the tree-lined entrance to the 1736 plantation of Noble Jones at Wormsloe (Skidaway Road, Isle of Hope) was filmed, and then the grounds of Savannah State University and the Oatland Island Educational Center (711 Sandtown Road, Savannah) were used to represent Fort MacCallum. Other locations included the Laurel Grove Cemetery (Anderson Street, Savannah) and the Crab Shack (Chimney Creek on Tybee Island).

Glory

(1989). Matthew Broderick, Denzel Washington. A Boston gentleman leads the first company of black soldiers into battle in the Civil War.

Savannah stood in for Civil War–era Boston, and an elaborate set was constructed behind the Cotton Exchange on River Street. Broderick lived in the private Hugh W. Mercer home on Bull Street. The storming of Fort Wagner in the film's finale was staged on the beach at Jekyll Island, the southernmost of the Golden Isles.

In the Heat of the Night

(1988–1994). Carroll O'Connor, Howard E. Rollins, Jr. Small town sheriff in American South does his job amidst political and racial tension.

All but the first six episodes of the television series were filmed in Covington, mostly in the square around the 1884 Newton County Courthouse. The former Porter Memorial Library, now a telecommunications company, at 1174 Monticello Street served as the Sparta police station.

Invasion USA

(1985). Chuck Norris, Richard Lynch. Russians landing in Miami Beach meet a recluse living in the Everglades.

The invaders head for Atlanta, where scenes were filmed on Auburn Avenue, a gritty thoroughfare once known as Old Wheat Street.

Kalifornia

(1993). Juliette Lewis, Brad Pitt. Journalists go on a tour of serial

The former Porter Memorial Library, now a private business, in Covington, Georgia, is better known to viewers of the long-running television series *In the Heat of the Night* as the Sparta police station.

The distinctive Newton County Courthouse commands the town square in Covington, Georgia where *In the Heat of the Night* filmed for seven seasons.

killer's murder sites with a man who turns out to be the killer himself.

The opening scenes were filmed in the west part of the Murray's Mill complex (1200 Foster Street, Atlanta), an old avatar that became do-it-yourself loft space. The water tower of the early 1880s machine shop shows up several times. Filming also took place in Loft 409 at White Provision Company (Howell Mill & 14th Street), an old brick slaughterhouse on the Southern Railway Line built in 1910.

The Legend of Bagger Vance

(2000). Will Smith, Matt Damon. Struggling golfer turns to mystical caddy for advice after returning from war.

The golf scenes were filmed at Kiawah Island, South Carolina, on the Ocean Course. A new 18th hole was built on the sand dunes near the practice range to replicate the mythical links at Krewe Island. Off-the-course action used locations in downtown Savannah, including the Massie School (207 East Gordon Street), founded in 1856 and the oldest school in Georgia, and the Lucas Theater for the Arts (37 Abercom Street). The ornate theater built in 1921 was restored over 12 years at the cost of $11 million. Additional scenes were shot at the Jekyll Island Club, an 1888 retreat for America's wealthy.

The Longest Yard

(1974). Burt Reynolds, Eddie Albert. Ex–football player convict organizes a game against the warden's team.

Reynolds organizes the game against the guards at Georgia State Prison (GA Highway 147, Reidsville). The car chase at the start of the film is on the Sidney Lanier Bridge in Brunswick.

Love Potion Number 9

(1989). Ted Donovan, Sandra Bullock. Biochemist changes her luck with women after visit to a gypsy.

The conclusion, with hundreds of extras chasing Donovan down the street, was filmed on Auburn Avenue in Atlanta.

Midnight in the Garden of Good and Evil

(1997). Kevin Spacey, John Cusack. Insular Savannah society is rocked by murder involving one of their own.

In a story where Savannah is a bigger character than the actors, there are many identifiable locations on-screen. The gates of the Bonaventure Cemetery (330 Bonaventure Road) were used as props to show the graveyard's avenue of oaks. The voodoo expert Minerva makes her first appearance at Forsyth Park, laid out in 1851 on Gaston Street between Whitaker and Drayton streets. Other landmarks include Christ Episcopal Church (28 Bull Street) and the Owens-Thomas House, a Regency-style mansion designed by English architect William Jay on Oglethorpe Square at 124 Abercorn Street. The elegant English villa is open for tours.

My Cousin Vinny

(1992). Joe Pesci, Marisa Tomei. Vacationer mistaken for murderer calls on his novice lawyer cousin for help.

The prison scenes were shot at Lee Arrendale Correctional Institution in Alto. The courthouse where Pesci tries the case is the Jasper County Courthouse (On the Square, Monticello), a Neo-Classical marble and brick structure built in 1907.

The Real McCoy

(1993). Val Kilmer, Kim Basinger. Reformed cat burglar is pressured into one more job when her son is kidnapped.

The interior of the Nations Bank (55 Marietta Street, Atlanta) was transformed into Basinger's target — the supposedly impregnable Citizens and Southern National Bank. Also featured is the Silver Skillet (200 14th Street, Atlanta).

Remember the Titans

(2000). Denzel Washington, Will Patton. Black high school football coach deals with first season of integrated team.

Based on a true story in Norfolk, Virginia, the movie was filmed at several schools in Georgia. The press conference and scenes in the gym were shot at Henry W. Grady High School (929 Charles Allen Drive); the football and training scenes were filmed at Etowah High School (6565 Putnam Ford Road, Covington); and the stadium and locker room for the championship game in Roanoke were staged at Sprayberry High School (2525 Sandy Plains Road, Marietta). There is an eating scene at the Silver Skillet (200 14th Street, Atlanta), a 1950s-style diner with a distinctive rooftop sign.

Scream 2

(1997). David Arquette, Neve Campbell. A movie is made about the original murders, and the killings begin again.

Decatur's Agnes Scott University plays the fictional Windsor College. The first building constructed on campus was Agnes Scott Hall, which was built in 1891 and originally housed the entire College. The building's bell tower, where seniors accepted to graduate school or hired for their first jobs are invited to ring the bell each Friday, is featured in the opening scenes of the movie.

HAWAII

Black Widow

(1986). Debra Winger, Theresa Russell. Federal investigator tracks a woman whose heavily-insured husbands keep dying.

Winger befriends her quarry Russell at the Mauna Lani Hotel and Bungalows on the Kohala Coast of the island of Hawaii. Russell saves Winger when she loses her oxygen supply scuba diving in Lava Tree State Monument (off Pahoa-Pohoiku Road/ Highway 132, Pahoa, Hawaii). The wedding scene was held at the Cathedral of Our Lady of Peace (1184 Bishop Street, Honolulu, Oahu). Built of coral blocks in 1843, the church is one of the oldest Catholic cathedrals in the United States. Winger works as an investigator in Seattle, Washington, for the Department of Justice in the Group Health Administration Building (521 Wall Street).

Blue Hawaii

(1961). Elvis Presley, Angela Lansbury. A man just out of the Army eases his way back into civilian life.

The definitive island movie was shot in part at the Polynesian Cultural Center (55-370 Kamehamecha Highway, Laie, Oahu), where Presley performs. The center preserves and displays the heritage of the South Sea islands in a 42-acre park.

Donovan's Reef

(1965). John Wayne, Lee Marvin. The appearance of a man's daughter threatens the good time carousing of a group of friends.

Although more than 200 films have been shot in Hawaii since Thomas Edison first brought a camera here in 1898, this was one of the first features made in the new state. Wayne and Marvin brawl in locations all over the island of Kauai.

Fantasy Island

(1978–1984). Ricardo Montalban, Herve Villechaize. Visitors pay $50,000 for a chance to visit unique resort and fulfill their dreams.

The waters tumbling 80 feet in the opening credits are the Wailua Falls on Kauai. The falls are visible from Highway 583 (Maalo Road), four miles northwest of Kapaia. In ancient times Hawaiian chiefs would dive over the cliff into the pool to demonstrate courage.

From Here to Eternity

(1953). Burt Lancaster, Deborah Kerr. The lives and loves on a military base on the eve of the attack on Pearl Harbor.

The famous beach scene with Lancaster and Kerr was shot at Halona Cove, eight miles south of Waikiki on Oahu.

Hawaii Five-O

(1968–1980). Jack Lord, James McArthur. Adventures of elite branch of Hawaii state police answerable only to the governor.

Most of this long-running police series was filmed on location in Hawaii. Lord's police headquarters were at the Iolani Palace (South King and Richards Street, Honolulu, Oahu). Completed in 1882 by King Kalakaua, the palace is the last official royal residence in the United States. Guided tours are available Tuesday through Saturday.

Jurassic Park

(1993). Sam Neill, Laura Dern. Scientists clone dinosaurs to create a modern theme park, with disastrous results.

The lush island of Kauai provided the setting for dinosaur-filled Jurassic Park, although most of the locations can be seen only by helicopter tour. The waterfall at the beginning of the movie where the helipad was erected is Manawaiopuna Falls in Hanapepe Valley. Scenes were also filmed at the National Tropical Botanical Garden (3530 Papalina Road, Kalaheo, Kauai).

South Pacific

(1958). Rosanno Brazzi, Mitzi Gaynor. Navy nurse tries to convince an island planter to scout nearby Japanese islands.

Gaynor sings "I'm Gonna Wash That Man Right Outta My Hair" while lathering on Lumahai Beach, a small beach two miles west of Hanalai on Highway 56 on Kauai, the northernmost of the Hawaiian Islands. Haena, a small village near the north end of Highway 56, provided the setting for the story.

IDAHO

Dante's Peak

(1997). Pierce Brosnan, Linda Hamilton. Volcanologist tries to convince town at the foot of a volcano that an eruption is imminent.

Most of the exteriors were shot in Wallace, with the fictional Dante's Peak added digitally to the background. Sixty miles north, at Mirror Lake Resort near Sandpoint, designers built Elizabeth Hoffman's log cabin in a small dirt parking lot next to the lake.

Pale Rider

(1985). Clint Eastwood, Michael Moriarty. Small mining town looks to gun-toting preacher for protection against local gangster.

Much of the filming took place in Sun Valley, and there is a slide show about the making of the movie at Sawtooth National Recreation Area headquarters north of Ketchum (Route 75). Included in its 756,000 acres of forest are three mountain ranges featuring peaks exceeding 10,000 feet.

ILLINOIS

About Last Night

(1986). Rob Lowe, Demi Moore. Man and woman carry on a romance after a one night stand.

The characters hang out at Mother's (26 West Division Street, Chicago). Moore and Lowe bump into each other at Kelly's (949 Webster Avenue at North Sheffield Avenue). After they break up Lowe watches Moore at the Biograph Theater (2433 North Lincoln Avenue at West Fullerton, Chicago), where John Dillinger was gunned down after seeing the movie *Manhattan Melodarma*. Lowe and James Belushi play softball in Grant Park, south of Buckingham Memorial Fountain. The scene was shot in the fall, and leaves had to be taped to trees around the field.

Above the Law

(1988). Steven Seagal, Pam Grier. Cop investigates the dealings of his former organization — the CIA.

Seagal tries to prevent a drug deal from going down at the Fulton Street Market in Chicago. Also used on location was the St. Mary of the Angels Church at 1850 N. Hermitage in the West Loop.

Adventures in Babysitting

(1987). Elisabeth Shue, Maria Brewton. Girl takes young charges with her to pick up stranded friend in downtown Chicago.

Many suburban and downtown Chicago locations were used to craft this tale, including the Dan Ryan Expressway, where Shue blows a tire and is picked up by a crazed tow truck driver; Fitzgerald's (6615 Roosevelt Road), where Shue sings the blues; and scaling down the Y Building at film's end. The unique design was created for Yaskawa Electric America headquarters on a 15-acre site at the northwest corner of Norman Drive South and Waukegan Road in the Norman Woods Business Park of Waukegan.

The Babe

(1992). John Goodman, Kelly McGillis. Tale of Babe Ruth's life plays up the legends surrounding baseball's biggest hero.

Wrigley Field (1060 West Addison Street) in Chicago did triple duty in the film, appearing as the Polo Grounds and Yankee Stadium in New York, and as itself for Ruth's famous "called shot" in the 1932 World Series. Danville Stadium (9th and Highland streets, Danville), built in 1946, stood in for Forbes Field in Pittsburgh and Fenway Park in Boston. St. Vincent DePaul Church (1010 West Webster Street, Chicago) was turned into Goodman's boyhood home, Baltimore's St. Mary's Home for Boys.

Baby's Day Out

(1994). Joe Mantegna, Lara Flynn Boyle. Kidnappers keep losing a stolen baby, who seems to be outsmarting them.

The baby's day out in Chicago includes stops at Marshall Fields (111 North State Street), the Daley Center (50 West Washington at Dearborn), and Grant Park. Boyle's home was portrayed by Cantigny mansion (One South 151 Winfield Road, Wheaton) on the 500-acre estate built by Colonel Robert R. McCormick, editor and publisher of the *Chicago Tribune*. The restored Georgia residence is open for tours.

Backdraft

(1991). Kurt Russell, Robert De-Niro. The search for an arsonist forces two firefighting brothers to work together.

Firehouses used for establishing shots in Chicago include DeNiro's Chinatown firehouse offices at 22nd and Rinston, and a firehouse at Archer and Sacramento streets. The parade honoring a fallen firefighter is held near City Hall.

Betrayed

(1988). Debra Winger, Tom Berenger. Rookie FBI agent is assigned to infiltrate white supremacist organization.

A bank robbery is staged at Midcity Bank (Halsted and Madison, Chicago). Winger eventually kills Berenger at the construction site where the RR Donnelly Building stands today (77 West Wacker Drive, Chicago).

Blink

(1994). Madeleine Stowe, Aidan Quinn. An eye operation restores a blind woman's eyesight, but she's not sure if what she sees is reality or hallucination.

Quinn lived on Sheffield Avenue with a view of Wrigley Field; Stowe's apartment was depicted by the Flat Iron Building (Milwaukee North and Damen avenues in Wacker Park, Chicago). Stowe is cured of her blindness at Illinois Masonic Hospital (836 West Wellington, Chicago). The St. Patricks Day parade scenes were shot from the staging area at Dearborn and Wacker streets in Chicago.

The Blues Brothers

(1980). Dan Aykroyd, John Belushi. Brothers attempt to save the Catholic home where they were raised.

Thirteen cars were used to star as the Bluesmobile, which Aykroyd and Belushi drive around Chicago. They drive the Bluesmobile through the mall at the former Dixie Square Shopping Center (15201 S. Dixie Highway, Harvey). The abandoned shopping center now has trees growing through the cement in the parking lot. The Bluesmobile also jumps over the 95th Street and Calumet River Bridge. Aykroyd and Belushi drive the Bluesmobile into the lobby of the Richard J. Daley Center (50 West Washington at Dearborn), through a plate glass window and out another window before slamming to a stop in front of the Cook County Building to pay the overdue tax bill on their childhood home. Other locations used in this classic Chicago movie include Nate's Deli (807 W. Maxwell), playing the Soul Food Cafe; the Plymouth Baptist Church (3235 E. 91st), starring as the Triple Rock Church; and the South Shore Country Club (south end of 71st Street), standing in as the Palace Ballroom and Viaduct. Belushi is released from the Joliet Correctional Institution (Route 171, Joliet), where the Blues Brothers wind up performing. The scene featuring the car flying off the highway was filmed at an unfinished ramp of the Milwaukee (Wisconsin) Freeway connecting I-794 to the Hoon Bridge. Although the storyline is still set in Chicago, the Milwaukee skyline can be seen in the background.

Breakfast Club

(1985). Emilio Estevez, Judd Nelson. Five very different kids trapped together for detention open up to one another.

Maine North High School, the setting for the Sharmer High School, is closed and is today an Illinois State Police station (9511 Harrison Street, Des Plaines). At the time of shooting the library where detention was scheduled wasn't big enough, so the library set was built in the gym. The final shot of Nelson crossing the football field was shot at the Glenbrook North High School football field (2300 Shermer Road, Northbrook).

Chain Reaction

(1996). Keanu Reeves, Morgan Freeman. Chief scientist on team discovering alternative fuel sources is murdered, and fellow researchers are framed for the crime.

A fake laboratory used for the research scenes was built in the United States Department of Energy's

Argonne National Laboratory (9700 Case Avenue, Argonne). The main action sequence was filmed on the two-level Michigan Avenue Bridge, and the chase sequence melds the Field Museum (1400 South Lake Shore Drive) and the Museum of Science and Industry (57th and Lake Shore Drive) into a Washington DC museum. The rotunda and Supreme Court Chamber of the Wisconsin State Capitol in Madison stood in for the United States Capitol.

Class

(1983). Jacqueline Bisset, Rob Lowe. Country boy arrives at sophisticated prep school and begins affair with roommate's mother.

The dorms at Northwestern University in Evanston doubled as the prep school where Lowe and Andrew McCarthy get an education. Bisset seduces McCarthy in the glass elevator of Water Tower Place (835 North Michigan Avenue, Chicago).

The Color of Money

(1986). Tom Cruise, Paul Newman. Pool hustler takes on a talented but undisciplined protégé.

Chicago played Atlantic City in this continuation of the classic 1960s *The Hustler*. Cruise is beaten up at St. Paul's Billiards (1415 West Fullerton), and Cruise and Newman tangle at the North Center Bowling Alleys (4017 North Lincoln). The Blackstone Hotel (636 South Michigan Avenue) played the hotel where Cruise stayed in Atlantic City, and the climactic pool tourney was staged in the auditorium of the Navy Pier (600 East Grand Avenue) on the lakefront. The pier opened as an amusement park in 1916.

Curly Sue

(1991). James Belushi, Kelly Lynch. Vagabond con man working with little girl decides to find her a real home.

The school featured is the Haven Middle School (2417 Prairie Avenue, Evanston). Lynch's law practice is in the Leo Burnett Building (35 West Wacker, Chicago).

ER

(1994–). Anthony Edwards, Eriq LaSalle. Workers in a Chicago hospital emergency room.

The exterior for the hospital entrance in the television series is that of the University of Illinois-Chicago Hospital at 1740 West Taylor.

Ferris Bueller's Day Off

(1986). Matthew Broderick, Alan Ruck. High school wise guy takes a day off from school.

The high school were Broderick picks up Mia Sara is Glenbrook North High School (2300 Shermer Road, Northbrook). His adventures in Chicago take him to the Sears Tower (233 S. Wacker) to look at the city; to the Chicago Board of Trade (La Salle Street at Jackson Boulevard); the Art Institute of Chicago (111 South Michigan Avenue); Wrigley Field (1060

West Addison Street), where he catches a foul ball; the Daley Center (Randolph and Washington), where he walks past pigeons; and City Hall (121 N. La Salle Street), where he joins in the German American Day parade. Ruck's house, where the Ferrari was garaged, was at 370 Beech Street in Highland Park. The blue water tower that proclaimed "Save Ferris "was off of Cedar Road next to the Northbrook Public Library in Northbrook.

Flatliners

(1990). Keifer Sutherland, Julia Roberts. Medical students explore the world of near death experiences with experiments on themselves.

The Jesuit residence at Loyola University (96525 North Sheridan Road, Chicago) served as the university hospital, and the combustible scene on the hospital steps was staged at the Museum of Science and Industry (5700 South Lake Shore Drive, Chicago). The museum is a reproduction of the Palace of Fine Arts from the 1893 Columbian Exposition.

The Fugitive

(1993). Harrison Ford, Tommy Lee Jones. Man must find real killer to clear himself of the murder of his wife.

Ford escapes from Jones by merging into the St. Patrick's Day Parade at Chicago's City Hall. The climax of the chase occurs throughout the Chicago Hilton and Towers (720 South Michigan Avenue), ending with the apprehension in the laundry department. Two of the more memorable stunts from the movie were filmed in North Carolina. The spectacular train crash that enabled Ford to flee from Jones was filmed at the Great Smoky Mountains Railway (Everett Street, Dillsboro) on a specially built track next to the main track. The two mangled engines were left there and can be seen on the tourist train between Dillsboro and Bryson City. The dam Ford leaps off to escape Jones was the Cheoah Dam, which can be reached by hiking on the Rock Trail from the River Bridge on US 129. Six dummies of Ford were tossed over the 225-foot dam into the turbulent waters to film the sequence; the subterranean tunnels he raced through to reach the spot were constructed in a Chicago warehouse.

Groundhog Day

(1993). Bill Murray, Andie MacDowell. Flippant weatherman finds himself trapped in February 2.

Almost all interior and exterior shots were filmed in Woodstock, with many scenes in the town square playing Punxsutawney, Pennsylvania. Murray throws himself from the bell tower in the Woodstock Opera House (121 Van Buren Street). Every February 2 there is a Groundhog Day Festival in Woodstock with a free showing of the film and a tour of all the sites used in the movie.

Hero

(1992). Andy Garcia, Dustin Hoffman. Thief rescues passengers from airline crash and watches someone else claim the credit.

Hoffman convinces Garcia not to commit suicide on a ledge outside Suite 1030 of the Drake (140 East Walton Place, Chicago). The ledge was specifically built for the scene in the movie. The Drake has been the hostelry of choice for the rich and famous in Chicago since the 1920s. Geena Davis worked as a reporter in NBC Tower (454 North Columbus Drive); tours of the studio are available.

High Fidelity

(2000). John Cusack, Jack Black. Music-obsessed record store owner recounts his top five break-ups with girlfriends.

Cusack's struggling Championship Vinyl record store was built in an unoccupied storefront on the corner of Honore and Milwaukee in Chicago. Additional scenes were shot in Well's Street Bridge, Lincoln Park and Roscoe Village. The proposal scene took place in the Rainbo Club (1150 N. Damen, Chicago).

Hill Street Blues

(1981–1987). Daniel J. Travanti, Barbara Babcock. The work and personal lives at inner city police precinct.

The exterior of the police station in the opening credits is the Maxwell Precinct Station in Chicago at the corner of 14th and Morgan.

Home Alone

(1990). Macauley Culkin, Joe Pesci. Young boy accidentally left behind when family leaves for vacation defends home against burglars.

The house where Culkin is left alone is at 671 Lincoln Avenue in Winnetka. Other locations in Winnetka include the railroad track bridge behind the Hubbard Woods Metro station; the St. Louis Bread Company (Green Bay Road and Gage Street), which played a pharmacy; and the gazebo across the street on Green Bay Road. The Christmas Choir was staged at Haven Middle School (2417 Prairie Avenue, Evanston).

Home Alone II: Lost in New York

(1992). Macauley Culkin, Joe Pesci. Boy's family flies to Florida while he winds up in New York.

Blocks of Chicago's LaSalle Street became Manhattan streets; the Rookery Building (La Salle and Adams streets) housed the fictional Eddie Bracken's toy store that Culkin discovers is about to be robbed on New Year's Eve. In New York City, Culkin lives is Room 411 of the Plaza Hotel (Fifth Avenue and Central Park South), and meets Pesci and Daniel Stern out front. He escapes their clutches at the intersection of Central Park South and Fifth Avenue by pinching a woman who turns around and clobbers the goons.

The Hudsucker Proxy

(1994). Tim Robbins, Paul Newman. Mail room employee is appointed head of a major conglomerate in scheme to drive down stock price so insiders can buy at distressed prices.

The Merchandise Mart (between Wells and Orleans Street), a two-block commercial building in Chicago, was used for exterior shots of the fictional Hudsucker Industries. The Crystal Ballroom of the Blackstone Hotel (636 South Michigan Avenue) was used for several scenes.

The Hunter

(1980). Steve McQueen, Eli Wallach. Professional bounty hunter struggles with bail jumpers and existential questions.

McQueen chases criminal up spiral parking lot of Marina City, and on the 15th floor the car goes out of control and goes off the building into the Chicago River.

In the Heat of the Night

(1967). Sidney Poitier, Rod Steiger. Black Philadelphia detective investigates a murder in racist Southern town.

Sparta, Illinois, played the fictional Sparta, Mississippi, in the film, with most of the shooting done in Sparta and Freeburg. The railroad sequences were shot in the former Missouri and Illinois railroad yard in Sparta. The railroad depot that features prominently is located at 611 W. 2nd Street in Sparta and has been renovated and converted into the Roscoe Misselhorn Art Gallery.

Kissing a Fool

(1998). David Schwimmer, Mili Avital. Man tests fiancée by convincing his best friend to try and seduce her.

The bridge of the lagoon in Chicago's Lincoln Park is the site of the blind date between Schwimmer and Avital. Schwimmer works as a sportscaster at WGW Studios on State and Wacker streets. The characters visit The Green Mill (4802 North Broadway) for an evening of jazz. The club was a favorite haunt of Al Capone in the 1920s.

Love Jones

(1997). Larenz Tate, Nia Long. Poet and photographer try to weather vagaries of a relationship.

Tate and Long live in Wicker Park and can be seen strolling around the illuminated Buckingham Fountain in Grant Park.

Lucas

(1986). Corey Haim, Kerri Green. Nerdy boy seeks popularity by trying out for the football team and attaching himself to the star player.

The outside school scenes were shot at Glenbard High School (670 Crescent Boulevard, Glen Ellyn), which was built in 1917.

Mad Dog and Glory

(1993). Robert DeNiro, Bill Murray. Nerdy police photographer saves the life of a crime boss who wants to then be his benefactor.

DeNiro lives in a greystone apartment in Chicago's Lincoln Park in the 500 block of West Belden. Many bars and restaurants were used for filming in the Wicker Park and Bucktown sections.

Married ... with Children

(1987–1997). Ed O'Neill, Katey Segal. Shoe salesman battles the daily grind of life.

The fountain in the opening credits is the Clarence Buckingham Memorial Fountain (Congress Street in Grant Park, Chicago), dedicated in 1927 as the world's largest decorative fountain and built to resemble Versailles' Latona Basin Fountain.

My Best Friend's Wedding

(1997). Julia Roberts, Dermot Mulroney. When a woman's long-time friend announces his engagement, she decides to marry him herself.

The film was shot entirely in Chicago. Locations included a romantic dinner at Charlie Trotter's Restaurant (816 West Armitage); the Gold Coast Room of the Drake Hotel (140 East Walton); and Comiskey Park (333 W. 35th Street), where Cameron Diaz' father owns the White Sox. Philip Bosco's pink stucco home was at Cuneo Estate and Gardens (1350 N. Milwaukee Avenue, Vernon Hills), built in 1914 by Samuel Insull, Thomas Edison's partner and first president of Commonwealth-Edison. Tours are available of the opulent Venetian-style mansion. The wedding was staged at Fourth Presbyterian Church on Michigan Avenue.

My Bodyguard

(1980). Chris Makepeace, Adam Baldwin. New kid in school hires a bodyguard to deal with school bullies.

Makepeace lives in luxury at the Omni Ambassador Hotel (1301 North State Parkway, Chicago).

The Negotiator

(1998). Samuel Jackson, Kevin Spacey. Police negotiator accused of murder takes hostages in a government office.

The modern glass RR Donnelly Building (77 West Wacker Drive, Chicago) stood in for the Chicago Police Department where Jackson takes hostages.

Never Been Kissed

(1999). Drew Barrymore, Michael Vartan. Young newspaper copy editor goes undercover at her old school to get story on today's high schools.

Most of the movie was shot in southern California, but since Barrymore worked for the *Chicago Sun Times*, there are shots inside the Sun Times Building (401 North Wabash).

New Port South

(2000). Raymond Barry, Kevin Christy. Road trip from Chicago to California turns dangerous for group of teens.

Scenes of the high school where plans are launched for the road trip was shot in the Brainerd Building of Libertyville High School (416 W. Park Avenue, Libertyville).

Next of Kin

(1989). Patrick Swayze, Liam Neeson. Cop seeks revenge for the murder of his brother.

The mob family's meal is held at The Green Mill (4802 North Broadway, Chicago), a popular jazz club opened in 1907 as Pop Morris's Garden.

Nothing in Common

(1986). Jackie Gleason, Tom Hanks. Man's business success is tempered by problems in his parents' marriage.

Gleason drinks at Mother's (26 West Division Street, Chicago); Hanks works as an advertising executive in the Wrigley Building (400 North Michigan Avenue, Chicago); and Bess Armstrong teaches at Northwestern University in Annie May Swift Hall in Evanston.

Only the Lonely

(1991). John Candy, Ally Sheedy. Man can't devote his life to mother and new girlfriend both.

Candy lived with mother Maureen O'Hara at 930 West Roscoe in Chicago. He introduces Sheedy to his controlling mother at the Pump Room in the landmark Omni Ambassador East Hotel (1301 North State and Goethe Street). The walls leading into the dining area are lined with photos of immortal Hollywood stars who have dined here. Another Chicago eatery featured was the Bento Restaurant (3369 North Clark), which starred as O'Neil's, the Irish hangout where a corpse is brought for one final celebration. Candy and Sheedy dine alone in the infield of Comiskey Park watching fireworks (this was the last movie to shoot in the stadium before its demolition). Candy boards a train for New York to commit to Sheedy at the station in Niles, Michigan (598 Dey Street).

Ordinary People

(1980). Donald Sutherland, Mary Tyler Moore. Family tries to come to terms with the death of youngest son.

Filming took place at Lake Forest Academy, a private prep school in the Chicago suburbs that opened in 1857 with an enrollment of four boys.

The Package

(1989). Gene Hackman, Tommy Lee Jones. Army sergeant on simple mission to deliver a prisoner is thrown into the maelstrom of Russian-American espionage.

Hackman's Washington government offices are portrayed by the Field Museum of Natural History (1400 South Lake Shore Drive), and the Chicago Hilton and Towers (720 South Michigan Avenue) hosted a presidential banquet in its Grand Ballroom. The Cermak Road Bridge at Canal Street was disguised as the Berlin, Germany, exchange point where Jones is handed over to Hackman. Willow Springs in Pulaski Woods became Germany's Black Forest.

Planes, Trains and Automobiles

(1987). John Candy, Steve Martin. Obnoxious salesman latches onto man traveling home for Thanksgiving.

Two motel scenes were filmed in Illinois—the first at the Sun Motel (originally the Braidwood Motel) on Route 55 in Braidwood, and the other, where Candy and Martin wind up in the same bed, in Gurnee at the El Rancho Motel on Highway 41. In New York, the train breaks down at the South Dayton train station and everyone disembarks into a field, and Candy falls asleep while driving on the not-yet-opened 219 Expressway near Springville.

Prelude to a Kiss

(1992). Alec Baldwin, Meg Ryan. While on his honeymoon a man begins to suspect his new wife is not what he imagined.

Baldwin's Chicago office is located at One South Wacker Building at Madison. The honeymoon is filmed in Jamaica, West Indies.

Primal Fear

(1996). Richard Gere, Edward Norton. Lawyer defends altar boy accused of murdering a powerful priest.

The film was shot in Chicago along the 1800 block of South Prairie Street. The William W. Kimball Residence, built in 1892 by Solon S. Beman, served as the murdered archbishop's home.

Red Heat

(1988). Arnold Schwarzenegger, James Belushi. Russian policeman teams with Chicago policeman on drug case.

Among the many locations used in Chicago was the Wacker and Wabash intersection, where Schwarzenegger and Belushi drive a borrowed bus through a fountain and into a building.

The Relic

(1997). Penelope Ann Miller, Tom Sizemore. Mystery surrounds museum researcher's crates that arrive from South America.

The Field Museum of Natural History (1400 South Lake Shore Drive) in Chicago's Grant Park substitutes for a Washington DC museum. Most scenes were shot on a Hollywood sound stage, however.

Return to Me

(2000). Minnie Driver, David Duchovny. Man falls in love with the woman who receives his dead wife's heart.

The opening scene with Duchovny on top of a building under construction was shot in Chicago just west of Northwestern Station on Washington. Other Chicago shooting locations include the Great Ape House at Lincoln Park Zoo, where Joely Richardson works; the Twin Anchors Restaurant (1655 N. Sedgwick Street); and the Michael Reese Hospital and Medical Center (2955 South Vernon Street), where director Bonnie Hunt's brother works as a physician.

Risky Business

(1983). Tom Cruise, Rebecca DeMornay. Teenager goes into business with a prostitute to pay for father's wrecked Porsche.

Cruise's father's Porsche slips into Lake Michigan at the marina in Belmont Harbor (end of Belmont Street, Chicago). The exteriors of his house were shot on Linden Street in Highland Park, with the interiors created in the gym of Kokie's former East Niles High School. Scenes were also shot in The Drake (140 East Walton, Chicago) in Palm Court, and at the Gold Coast Room.

Rookie of the Year

(1993). Thomas Ian Nicholas, Gary Busey. 10-year-old boy joins major leagues after a broken arm heals in such a way as to give him a super fastball.

The doctor's office where the arm is examined is at Oak Park Avenue and Lake Street in Chicago. The baseball scenes were shot at Wrigley Field (1060 West Addison Street) in the fall after baseball season, so a green tarp had to be placed over the outfield walls to hide the dying ivy vines.

She's Having a Baby

(1988). Kevin Bacon, Elizabeth McGovern. Newlyweds try to live up to everyone's expectations for a family.

Bacon and McGovern get married at the Winnetka Congregational Church (725 Pine Street, Winnetka). Bacon's advertising office was filmed at the Leo Burnett Building (35 West Wacker Drive).

Silver Streak

(1976). Richard Pryor, Gene Wilder. Passenger thinks he sees man thrown from the train but no one believes him.

The Silver Streak crashes into Union Station (210 Canal Street, Chicago) at the end of its journey. After establishing shots, the scene where the train plows through several restaurants and shops and comes to rest in the Great Hall, was filmed in an airplane hangar at Los Angeles (with a toolbox placed on the accelerator).

Sixteen Candles

(1984). Molly Ringwald, Justin Henry. Young girl's chaotic life is epitomized when her family forgets her 16th birthday.

Interiors and exteriors were filmed at Niles East High School (7700 Lincoln Avenue, Skokie), which was torn down in 1992 and replaced with the Oakton Community College. The church used for the movie was Glencoe Union Church (Park Street, Glencoe). Anthony Michael Hall drives the Rolls Royce down Central Street in Evanston.

The Sting

(1973). Paul Newman, Robert Redford. Young con man teams up with legendary scam artist to seek revenge for partner's murder.

Producers went looking for an El station in Chicago to portray a train station in the 1930s and selected the

ILLINOIS

oldest station in Chicago—at 43rd and Calumet.

Stir of Echoes

(1999). Kevin Bacon, Kathryn Erbe. Hypnotized man sees ghost of young woman and jeopardizes his family to find out her story.

Exteriors of Wicker Park, Polish Village and Brighton Park were woven into a single Chicago neighborhood for the supernatural story. Interior shots were staged on sets built in the abandoned Lakeside Press building in downtown Chicago. An additional location was the Rialto Theater (9102 N. Chicago Street, Joliet), opened in 1926 and digitally altered in the film.

Straight Talk

(1992). Dolly Parton, James Woods. Small town woman accidentally finds herself on the radio in Chicago dispensing down-to-earth advice.

Parton's radio station was in an empty office on north Lincoln in Chicago. Woods and Parton have their first date at The Pump Room in the Omni Ambassador Hotel (1301 North State Parkway). The two stage a happy reunion on the Irv Kupcinet Bridge in Wabash at the end of the movie.

Uncle Buck

(1989). John Candy, Jean Louisa Kelly. Loutish uncle babysits for brother's kids.

The elementary school scene was shot in New Trier Township High School (385 Winnetka Avenue, Winnetka), and the high school was at the New Trier West High School (now a community center at 7 Happ Road, Northfield). Candy takes his young charges bowling at the Windy City Bowling Alley in Cicero.

The Untouchables

(1987). Kevin Costner, Sean Connery. Federal agent assembles an elite squad to battle Prohibition-era bootleggers.

In Chicago, Costner lived at 22nd Place and Hoye; Connery's apartment was located at 1634 South Racine; and Robert DeNiro, as Al Capone, was headquartered at the Lexington Hotel, which was played in the movie by Roosevelt University (430 South Michigan Avenue) and the lavishly decorated Chicago Theater (175 N. State Street). Burnham & Root's Rookery (LaSalle and Adams, Chicago) was used for the exterior of police headquarters. The climactic shootout scene with the teetering baby carriage in the crossfire was staged at Union Station (210 South Canal Street, Chicago). Forty miles south of Great Falls, Montana, on a bridge across Hardy Creek (exit off I-15 across the Missouri River), Costner and Connery try to intercept a shipment of Canadian whiskey.

U.S. Marshals

(1998). Tommy Lee Jones, Wesley Snipes. marshal hunts down criminal after plane transporting prisoners crash-lands.

Chicago stood in for New York; the plane crash was filmed at O'Hare Airport. The plane used in the movie was hauled to a flooded rock quarry near Marmet, Illinois, and is now part of a dive park. Jones' headquarters was shot at 444 N. Michigan Avenue, and Snipes is arrested at St. Ann's Hospital on the west side. The climactic chase scene was staged at the Bohemian National Cemetery (5255 North Pulaski). The graveyard, established in 1877, was standing in for a Queens, New York, cemetery.

Vice Versa

(1988). Judge Reinhold, Fred Savage. Mysterious oriental skull transforms a father into his son and vice versa.

Percy Julian Junior High School (416 South Ridgeland, Oak Park) played the fictional Ernest Hemingway Junior High where Savage attends school. Reinhold worked at Marshall Fields (111 North State Street).

Wayne's World

(1992). Mike Myers, Dana Carvey. Two slackers hype their local cable public access television show from a basement.

The shot of eight cars impaled on a 40-foot-tall spike, known as "The Spindle" (a public sculpture by artist Dustin Shuler), was taken in the Cermak Plaza Shopping Center at Cermak Road and Harley Avenue in Berwyn. Myers and Carvey cruise past a large saluting Indian atop a building promoting the Eye Care Center at 6254 S. Pulaski Road in Chicago. Myers and Carvey meet their idol Alice Cooper in the US Cellular Arena (500 W. Kilbourn Avenue, Milwaukee, Wisconsin).

Weird Science

(1985). Anthony Michael Hall, Kelly LeBrock. Two boys attempt to create the perfect woman.

The high school the young scientists attend is the former Niles East High School (Lincoln Avenue, Skokie). The Northbrook Court Shopping Center (Lake-Cook Road/Northbrook), since remodeled, was used for mall scenes. The sports car chase in the movie's finale was filmed through downtown Highland Park.

While You Were Sleeping

(1995). Sandra Bullock, Bill Pullman. Woman seeking a family pretends to be engaged to unconscious man.

Bullock works at the Randolph Street El Station in Chicago (this marked the first time the Chicago Transit Authority had ever shut down service at a station). The hospital scenes where Peter Gallagher lay unconscious were filmed mostly on Hollywood sets, but the exterior of the hospital was filmed at Northwestern Memorial Hospital (251 East Huron Street, Chicago); his condominium was at Lake Point Towers (505 N. Lake Shore Drive). The mass and wedding were shot at Mount Carmel Catholic Church (709 W. Belmont). Later, Pullman and Bullock stroll past the water cannon on the main branch of the Chicago River.

Wildcats

(1986). Goldie Hawn, Swoosie Kurtz. Woman takes job coaching high school football team.

Lane Technical High School (2501 West Addison, Chicago) does double duty as Prescott High, the suburban school Hawn leaves, and the football field of Central High, the inner-city school where she goes to coach.

INDIANA

Blue Chips

(1994). Nick Nolte, Mary McDonnell. Basketball coach thinks he can't stay competitive without breaking rules to get the best players.

Nolte's fictional Western University Dolphins play their games at Frankfort Senior High School (One Marsh Road, Frankfort).

Breaking Away

(1979). Dennis Christopher, Dennis Quaid. Bike race becomes focal point for clash between college kids and local town boys.

Filmed in and around the Indiana University campus in Bloomington, the film builds to a climax with the school's legendary bike race, The Little 500, a spring tradition since 1951.

Brian's Song

(1971). James Caan, Billy Dee Williams. Professional football players fight for the same position and forge close friendship.

Training camp scenes were filmed at St. Joseph's College in Rensselaer.

Eight Men Out

(1988). Jace Alexander, John Cusack. Dramatization of 1919 Black Sox Scandal when Chicago played to lose the World Series.

Bush Stadium, named after Owen "Donnie" Bush (now called 16th Street Speedway), in Indianapolis doubled for both the Chicago and Cincinnati ballparks in 1919. The train scenes were staged at the Railway Museum of Greater Cincinnati (315 W. Southern Avenue, Covington, Kentucky). Main Street in Over-the-Rhine between 12th and Liberty streets (Cincinnati, Ohio) was used to portray Chicago street scenes, and fans burn Shoeless Joe Jackson in effigy in Piatt Park, Cincinnati's first park, located at Eighth Street between Vine and Elm.

Hard Rain

(1998). Christian Slater, Minnie Driver. Dam failure floods a small town while an armored car robbery is going down.

Filming began by shooting in five-foot flood water engulfing a replica of the town of Huntingburg in the tank of an aircraft carrier. The Main Street was flooded for real with shallow water to simulate the early stages of the flood as sandbags were piled up in front of the storefronts.

Hoosiers

(1986). Gene Hackman, Barbara Hershey. Small town Indiana basketball team seeks the state championship.

Fictional Hickory High School's home court was in the 1921 gymnasium of Knightstown Academy (355 N. Washington, Knightstown). The old basketball court, which doesn't meet current standards for length and width, can be seen by appointment. The site of the final state playoff game was in the Hinckle Fieldhouse on the campus of Butler University (4600 Sunset Avenue). The hospital scene was staged at Wishard Memorial Hospital (1001 W. 10th Street, Lebanon).

A League of Their Own

(1992). Tom Hanks, Geena Davis. Story of America's first female professional league seen through the lives of two sisters.

Two Indiana ballparks were used in the filming: Bosse Field (Garvin Park between North Main and Heidlebach streets, Evansville), where the final game was played, and Huntingburg Stadium (First and Cherry streets, Huntingburg), which played the home field of the Rockford Peaches. (Garry Marshall's estate was the Cantigny Mansion (One South 151 Winfield Road, Wheaton, Illinois), the former home of *Chicago Tribune* publisher Robert McCormick. A private home at the corner of 5th and Main streets in Henderson, Kentucky, served as a boarding house where the players stay. At the end of the movie Davis and her peers are recognized at the National Baseball Hall of Fame (Main Street, Cooperstown).

Prancer

(1989). Sam Elliott, Cloris Leachman. Little girl finds injured reindeer and assumes it belongs to Santa Claus.

Rebecca Harrell nurses a wounded reindeer on director John Hancock's childhood home at Hancock Fruit Farm (7355 North Fail Road, LaPorte). Town scenes were shot in nearby Three Oaks, Michigan.

Rudy

(1993). Sean Astin, Ned Beatty. Undersized, underskilled student is determined to play football for Notre Dame University.

Filming took place on the campus of Notre Dame University in South Bend, including football scenes at Knute Rocke Stadium. When Sean Astin finally gets to play in his final game, the crowd scenes were shot during an actual Notre Dame-Boston College football game. Scenes were also shot at St. Rita High School (7740 S. Western Avenue, Chicago, Illinois) and Holy Cross College in Notre Dame.

Winning

(1969). Paul Newman, Joanne Woodward. Race driver must balance tenuous marriage and his dream of winning the world's greatest race.

Newman plays a race driver eying Victory Lane at the Indianapolis 500 with scenes shot at Indianapolis Motor Speedway (10267 East US Highway 136). Newman cuts his teeth on the road races through the streets of the village of Elkhart Lake in Wisconsin. These celebrated road races began in the 1950s.

IOWA

The Bridges of Madison County

(1995). Meryl Streep, Clint Eastwood. Wandering photographer falls into love affair with farm woman.

Streep's farmhouse was created from a 35 years–abandoned building eight miles southwest of Des Moines and two miles west of I-35 on a gravel road. The house is now open to the public daily, May through October. Courthouse Square in Winterset was used for several shots, and bridges used in Madison County included the Roseman Bridge and Holliwell Bridge.

Featured in *The Bridges of Madison County*, the Cutler-Donahue Covered Bridge, built in 1871, is at the entrance of Winterset City Park. Just south of this bridge is an arched stone bridge where Clint Eastwood and Meryl Streep go for their "getaway" picnic. (Madison County Chamber of Commerce)

More than a decade after it was built in a Dyersville, Iowa, cornfield, people are still coming to see the "Field of Dreams." (Field of Dreams Movie Site)

Six of Madison County's original 19 covered bridges remain intact.

Field of Dreams

(1989). Kevin Costner, Amy Madigan. An Iowa corn farmer hears voices telling him to build a baseball field.

After scouring Iowa for a farm with just the right features, producers settled on Don Lansing's 100-acre farm (28963 Lansing Road, Dyersville). A wraparound portion of the porch was constructed on the turn-of-the-century farmhouse, and three days were used to transform 2½ acres of cornstalks into a pristine baseball diamond. After movie fans from across the world began arriving to see the magical field, it was decided not to plow it over. Today the "Field of Dreams" is open for play daily from April to October. Costner sees the message on the scoreboard that inspires him to build his diamond in Iowa farmland in Fenway Park (Kenmore Square, Boston, Massachusetts). James Earl Jones' apartment was on Central Avenue in Dubuque.

Penitentiary

(1938). Walter Connolly, John Howard. Prison drama of men behind bars.

The first movie filmed in Iowa was set in the Iowa Men's Reformatory, now the Anamosa State Penitentiary (406 N. High Street, Anamosa). The Gothic fortress, known as the "White Palace of the West," was built of dolomite stone, beginning in 1873.

Straight Story

(1999). Richard Farnsworth, Sissy Spacek. 73-year-old man drives a vintage 1966 riding mower from Iowa to Wisconsin to make amends with estranged brother.

Filming followed the approximate path the real-life Alvin Straight followed and closely matched the length of time he required to make the journey (to allow for the proper scenic backgrounds). The path included the towns of Laurens, New Hampton, West Bend, Cleremont, Prairie du Chien and Mt. Zion.

KANSAS

The Day After

(1983). Jason Robards, Jo Beth Williams. The aftermath of a nuclear attack on Lawrence, Kansas, is dramatized.

While bombed-out downtown Lawrence is scarcely recognizable, survivors are cared for at Lawrence Memorial Hospital (325 Main Street) and in the Allen Field House on the campus of the University of Kansas. The scene of mass graves and people huddling in tents was shot along the Kansas River.

In Cold Blood

(1967). Robert Blake, Scott Wilson. True story of two young killers who slaughter a family in an isolated farmhouse.

For authenticity, the film was shot in all the actual locations, including the Clutter house where the family was killed (Holcomb). The family horse Babe was featured. Also used were scenes shot in Olathe, the killers' hometown; in Garden City, the largest town near the murder site; and Leavenworth prison.

Kansas

(1988). Matt Dillon, Andrew McCarthy. Drifter implicates stranded traveler in bank robbery.

McCarthy saves the daughter of the governor of Kansas in Valley Falls. Other Kansas towns used in the shooting include Lawrence, Edgerton, Gardner and Linwood.

Mars Attacks!

(1996). Jack Nicholson, Glenn Close. Martians invade Earth with powerful weapons and a sly sense of humor.

Looking for a desolate town, producers settled on Burns, which played the rural enclave of Perkinsville. The DoNut World, with a 26-foot chocolate donut on top, was built here so it could be obliterated by invading forces. The opening scene showing a farm family watching a flaming herd of cattle stampede by was shot in Lawrence. The aliens first land in Pahrump, Nevada, and footage of the implosion of the Landmark Hotel and Casino in Las Vegas was used.

Paper Moon

(1973). Ryan O'Neal, Tatum O'Neal. Con man/bible salesman hooks up with an orphan girl during the Depression.

Several of the heartland's historic hotels made appearances, including the Midland Hotel in Wilson, built of native limestone. Boasting the only modern amenities for miles, occupancy often hovered about 120 percent with many guests sleeping on floors. No longer in use, the Midland Hotel is still standing. The McCracken Hotel in McCracken was once the finest hotel between Kansas City and Denver after it was built in 1909. It did not last much longer than its starring turn in this movie. The old St. Charles Hotel (St. Josephs, Missouri) is empty but still standing as well, the last historic downtown hotel still extant in St. Josephs.

KENTUCKY

Fire Down Below

(1997). Stephen Seagal, Kris Kristofferson. EPA agent fights businessmen dumping toxic waste in the Kentucky hills.

The mine scene was filmed at Great Saltpetre Cave in Mt. Vernon, a 3500-foot cave discovered in 1798. The cave's Echo Auditorium doubled as one of the story's abandoned mines. The cave is presently closed to public tours. The house and church were constructed in Hazard County above Carr Fork Lake. The movie's chase sequence was staged in an operational strip mine.

Flim Flam Man

(1967). George C. Scott, Sue Lyon. Young man travels with legendary con man.

Scenes were filmed along North Main Street in Winchester, named after the former Virginia home of its founder, John Baker. Other towns visited by the con men include Lawrenceburg and Georgetown. The Vaughn Tobacco Warehouses in Lexington were converted into sound stages.

In Country

(1989). Bruce Willis, Joan Allen. Teenage girl becomes obsessed with discovering the story of her father's death in Vietnam.

Most of the movie was filmed in Mayfield at a private home. The Graves County Courthouse, a two-story brick building on Courthouse Square in Mayfield, also appears. Chuck's Restaurant, with a plastic chicken on the roof, was specially built for the movie and is based on Emma's in Mayfield. The sequence in the Maplewood Cemetery features the Woolridge Monument, (the grave of a Civil War soldier surrounded by statues of his family, childhood sweetheart and hunting dog). Colonel Henry, the only one buried here, is atop his horse "Fop." Emily Lloyd comes to look for her father's name at the Vietnam Memorial.

The Mighty

(1998). Sharon Stone, Gena Rowlands. Two outcast boys travel to lands of knights and heroes in their storybooks.

The outdoor scenes were filmed in Devou Park in Covington; scenes of the Cincinnati skyline were shot from here. Also appearing is the Roebling Suspension Bridge across the Ohio River.

Rain Man

(1988). Dustin Hoffman, Tom Cruise. Man discovers father left bulk of estate to autistic brother he didn't know he had.

Cruise learns the identity of the beneficiary of his father's will at the Cincinnati Trust, a fictional bank played by the Dixie Terminal (120 East Fourth Street, Cincinnati, Ohio). St. Anne's Convent (Highway 8, Melbourne) was transformed into Wallbrooks, the facility for the developmentally disabled where Cruise discovers he has an autistic brother. Hoffman begins to reveal his ability with numbers when he counts at a glance 246 toothpicks that tumble to the floor at Pompilios Restaurant (600 Washington, Newport). The brothers attend their father's funeral at Evergreen Cemetery (24 Alexandria Pike, Southgate). When Cruise and Hoffman reach Las Vegas, they head for Caesars Palace (3750 Las Vegas Boulevard South), where Hoffman counts cards in a former pit area near Cafe Roma and receives a makeover in Cleopatra's Salon. In Oklahoma, Cruise begins to run a hot bath in the Big 8 Motel (1705 East 66th Highway, El Reno) and realizes Hoffman was institutionalized after scalding him as a child. The sequence was shot in Room 117. Hoffman is confused by a DON'T WALK sign in the middle of an intersection in Guthrie, Oklahoma.

Raintree County

(1957). Montgomery Clift, Elizabeth Taylor. Civil War romance between teacher and Southern belle.

Filmed partly in Paducah and Danville, the movie featured an opening scene shot at an old church that used to stand at the edge of the property that now houses the Raintree Inn Bed and Breakfast (3314 Old Highway 10, Somerset). The cemetery appears in the background. The scenes involving Abraham Lincoln's funeral train were shot near Danville, featuring the old Baltimore & Ohio *William Mason* locomotive and several coaches draped in black.

Simpatico

(1999). Nick Nolte, Jeff Bridges. Successful horse racing couple are threatened by a racing con they pulled 20 years earlier.

The horse racing scenes were filmed at Churchill Downs (700 Central Avenue, Louisville), and a private horse farm in Lexington was used for the farm scenes.

Some Came Running

(1958). Frank Sinatra, Shirley MacLaine. World War II vet returns to Indiana hometown and grapples with his future.

Much of the filming took place in Hanover, Indiana. The final scene, with the burial of MacLaine, was shot in Moffett Cemetery (Moffett Cemetery Road, Milton) on the Ohio River.

Stripes

(1981). Bill Murray, Harold Ramis. Two friends decide to quit their jobs and join the Army for kicks.

The film was shot partly at the United States Armor Center at Fort Knox (4554 Fayette Avenue), although the barracks used in the movie are no longer active. The fort has been home to the United States Army Armor School and Center since the inception of the Armored Forces in 1940.

LOUISIANA

Angel Heart

(1987). Mickey Rourke, Robert DeNiro. Routine missing persons case for small-time private eye takes a more sinister turn.

Brownie McGhee performs at and Rourke gets beat up in, the Maple Leaf Bar (8316 Oak Street, New Orleans), which was started as a chess and music club. Also used as a New Orleans filming location was St. Louis Cathedral on Jackson Square, a modified Spanish-style church completed in 1794. St. Anthony's Garden in the back of the church was once a notorious dueling ground.

The Beguiled

(1971). Clint Eastwood, Geraldine Page. Wounded Yankee soldier during Civil War is brought to Southern girls school to recuperate, sparking jealousy and deceit on campus.

The film was shot entirely at Ashland-Belle Helene Plantation (State Highway 75, Darrow), which served as the school. The mansion house is one of the largest ever built in Louisiana and is one of the best surviving examples of the Classical Revival style. Eight massive pillars stretch across each facade.

The Big Easy

(1987). Dennis Quaid, Ellen Barkin. New Orleans police detective tries to solve a string of murders while under investigation for accepting bribes.

The exterior of Quaid's apartment was shot at the Pontalba Buildings (St. Ann Street/Jackson Square, New Orleans), thought to be the oldest apartment buildings in the country. The dignified red brick apartment houses were built by the Baroness Micaela Almonester de Pontalba. The Lower Pontalba, at 523 St. Ann Street, is open for guided tours. Interiors were shot at the Germaine Wells Mansion at the corner of Chartres and Esplanade streets. Barkin hears of Quaid's arrest on bribery charges while eating at Antoine's (713–717 Rue St. Louis, New Orleans), founded by Antoine Alciatore in 1840.

Blaze

(1989). Paul Newman, Lolita Davidovich. Governor Earl Long of Louisiana moves in with a stripper, to the glee of his opponents.

Some of the filming took place at Long's Pea Patch Farm in Winnifield. Davidovitch's apartment was on the 1200 block of Royal Street in New Orleans. Newman was committed at Jackson State Hospital, which stood in for Mandeville Hospital. A former Woolco on Florida Boulevard became a Bourbon Street nightclub. A 1956 pep rally, with 1500 students carrying torches, was recreated at the 34-story State Capitol (State Capitol Drive, Baton Rouge). The building was constructed from 26 varieties of marble from every marble-producing country in the world.

Cat People

(1982). Nastassja Kinski, Malcolm McDowell. Feline-like humans must mate with like creatures, and seemingly only a brother and sister remain.

The story begins with black panthers at the Audubon Zoo (6500 Magazine Street, New Orleans). The panthers are part of the African Savanna exhibit in the 58-acre park. Kinski's house was at the corner of Chartres and Esplanade streets.

Dead Man Walking

(1995). Sean Penn, Susan Sarandon. A nun balances her compassion for a murder victim's family with her work as a prison spiritual advisor.

The interiors and exteriors were shot in the Louisiana State Penitentiary at Angola. A small museum is on the grounds. Sarandon was supposed to have lived in the St. Thomas housing project in the lower garden district between Race Street and Jackson Avenue.

Double Jeopardy

(1999). Tommy Lee Jones, Ashley Judd. Woman framed for murder is released from jail and sets out to find her son and solve the mystery of the crime.

The charity gala at the film's climax was filmed in the courtyard of the historic Hermann-Grima House adjacent to Bourbon Street in the French Quarter. The courtyard garden features the only horse stable and functional outdoor kitchen in the French Quarter. The house is open to the public. Judd walks into the lobby of the Hotel Monteleone (214 Royal Street, New Orleans) to buy a dress, and is trapped in a casket at Lafayette Cemetery No. 1 in the Garden District between Washington Avenue and Prytania, Sixth and Coliseum streets.

The Drowning Pool

(1975). Paul Newman, Joanne Woodward. Big city cop is brought to Louisiana bayou on a blackmail case and finds out it involves an old girlfriend.

Scenes were shot at the Lafayette Police Station (900 E. University Avenue, Lafayette) and at Oaklawn Manor (five miles northeast of Franklin on Irish Bend Road). With 20-inch-thick walls built upon a massive foundation, this 1837 Greek Revival manor was the centerpiece of one of the region's first sugar cane plantations. The plantation's aviary was built as a set for the movie. Tours are available daily.

Easy Rider

(1969). Peter Fonda, Dennis Hopper. Long-haired bikers hit the road en route to New Orleans for Mardi Gras.

Fonda and Hopper take many stumbles at St. Louis Cemetery No. 1 (425 Basin Street, New Orleans), established in 1789 as the first of New Orleans' Cities of the Dead (where all the dead are buried in tombs above ground). Jack Nicholson meets his grisly end in Morganza; the diner where he angered the locals is gone, but the foundation remains. In New Mexico, Hopper and Fonda show up at a commune and frolic in the hot springs at Taos Pueblo in Arroyo Hondo. The tallest pueblo in the Southwest, some parts have been continuously occupied for 1000 years. The jail scene was also filmed in Taos, at the Hedgecock Building, an 1882 Italianate store at 157 Bridge Street.

Evangeline

(1929). Dolores Del Rio, Roland Drew. Young Canadian woman follows the man she loves after he is imprisoned in exile by the British.

Evangeline follows her love to the bayous of Louisiana in this silent-era film which was shot at St. Martinsville, Avery Island and Catahoula Lake. A statue of Del Rio as Evangeline stands in the shadow of the St. Martin de Tours Church in St. Martinsville (133 Main Street). Established in 1765, the present church building was built in 1844.

Everybody's All-American

(1988). Dennis Quaid, Jessica Lange. A college football hero and his homecoming queen sweetheart have to live a real life.

The pep rally that opens the movie was staged on the steps of the State Capitol (State Capitol Drive, Baton Rouge). College football scenes were shot at Mumford Stadium at Southern University and Tiger Stadium at Louisiana State University. At Tiger Stadium the scenes were shot during an LSU-Alabama game, with real fans cheering on the actors after the game; but since LSU lost, the only fans remaining were from the visiting

Crimson Tide. Another football scene was filmed at Mile High Stadium (1900 Eliot Street, Denver, Colorado).

Hurry Sundown

(1967). Jane Fonda, Michael Caine. Ruthless land owner tries to buy cousin's land.

The state prison farm was located near St. Gabriel. Other locations include a roadside diner in St. Francisville and the Goodwood House in Baton Rouge.

Hush Hush Sweet Charlotte

(1964). Bette Davis, Olivia DeHavilland. Woman lives for 40 years under suspicion in her small town after her fiancé is murdered.

The story is staged at Houmas House Plantation (40136 River Road/Highway 942, Burnside), the state's largest sugar plantation in the 19th century. Tours of the 20,000 acre plantation, including the first Spanish and French–style house built in the late 1700s, are available. Scenes were also shot at Afton Villa Gardens (9247 US Highway 61, St. Francisville). The villa was destroyed by fire in 1963 but the 20 acres of garden are open to the public.

Interview with a Vampire

(1994). Tom Cruise, Brad Pitt. A vampire reveals the loves and longings of his life.

The opening scenes depict San Francisco standards. The interview took place at the four-way corner of Market Street, Golden Gate Avenue, Tryor Street and 6th Street, directly across from the Golden Gate Theater and the Fox Warfield Theater. Cruise sucks the life from Christian Slater as he pulls away from the toll booth and drives across the Golden Gate Bridge in the closing scene. In Louisiana, Pitt's home was played by Oak Alley Plantation (3645 Los Angeles Highway 18, Vacherie), a massive Greek Revival mansion supported by 28 columns and approached on a drive under dual rows of 250-year-old oak trees. Oak Alley Plantation is open to the public. The fight scene where Pitt kills an old woman and her poodles was filmed at Destrehan Plantation (13034 River Road, Destrehan).

The Life and Assassination of the Kingfish

(1977). Ed Asner, Nicholas Pryor. Dramatization of the flamboyant life of controversial Louisiana governor Huey Long.

The movie was shot in and around the State Capitol (State Capitol Drive, Baton Rouge). Huey Pierce Long was shot at the State Capitol Building on September 8, 1935, and died two days later at Our Lady of the Lake Hospital, Baton Rouge, which was used in the movie but has since been destroyed. Governor Long is interred in the sunken garden at the State Capitol Grounds.

Live and Let Die

(1973). Roger Moore, Yaphet Kotto. British secret agent tries to cripple heroin smuggling operation.

The chase scene was staged near

Brad Pitt lived at Oak Alley Plantation in Vacherie, Louisiana, named for the majestic rows of centuries-old oaks, in *Inteview with a Vampire*. (Oak Alley Plantation)

Slidell in the Irish Bayou. The power boat jump over the causeway during filming set a world record of 110 feet. Many companies offer swamp tours through the area.

The Long Hot Summer

(1958). Paul Newman, Joanne Woodward. Nomadic handyman decides to marry the daughter of an autocratic Southern plantation owner.

The production was filmed in and around the town of Clinton, including scenes at the ornate white East Feliciana Parish courthouse. The two-story Greek Revival building with a circular dome and a surrounding Doric columnade looks much as it did when dedicated in 1840. Orson Welles' home was on False River Road outside the town of New Roads.

Miller's Crossing

(1990). Gabriel Byrne, Albert Finney. Peacemaker between two warring mobs has hands full.

Caspar's Great Room, where Byrne confronts gangster Jon Polito, was staged in Gallier Hall (1118–32 Royal Street, New Orleans). The house has been restored to its 1860s appearance and is open for tours. The exterior of Caspar's house was shot at Louise McGehee School (2343 Pryania Street, New Orleans). The killing scene was staged on Highway 190, four miles west of Hammond across from the Hidden Oaks Camp.

Out of Sight

(1998). George Clooney, Jennifer Lopez. Career bank robber accidentally kidnaps FBI agent during jail break.

The jail break scene was filmed at the Louisiana State Penitentiary at Angola, playing the Glades Correctional Institute in Florida. The car crash takes place on the US 190 bridge in Krotz Springs. Lopez and Clooney get better acquainted at the 73-story

Marriott Renaissance Center in Detroit, Michigan (Jefferson Avenue). Other Detroit locations include the State Theater (2115 Woodward Street), Dot and Etta's Shrimp Hut (10300 McNichols Road) and the Kronk Gym (8925 Binwood Street), home to 27 world champion boxers. The boxing sequences were staged in a rebuilt gym upstairs to accommodate the lights needed for filming.

The Pistol: Birth of a Legend

(1991). Adam Guier, Nick Benedict. Film treatment of the greatest scorer in the history of college basketball.

Southeastern Louisiana University stood in for Pete Maravich's Louisiana State University. Some filming took place in downtown Hammond at the Columbia Theater.

Pretty Baby

(1978). Brooke Shields, Keith Carradine. 12-year-old prostitute teams with a photographer in New Orleans during World War I.

Shields hangs out at a bar in Column's Hotel (3811 St. Charles Avenue, New Orleans) and is auctioned off to a big-hearted bidder. The hotel was built in 1883 as a home for Simon Hernsheim, a wealthy tobacco manufacturer.

Savage Bees

(1976). Ben Johnson, Michael Parks. Killer bees from South America invade the United States.

The deadly bees swarm towards New Orleans and are led into the Louisiana Superdome (1550 Poydras Street, New Orleans) by a Volkswagen, where they are immobilized by the air conditioning. Tours of America's largest indoor arena, as tall as a 27-story building, are available.

Sex, Lies and Videotape

(1989). James Spader, Andie MacDowell. Man's habit of interviewing women on videotape changes a couple's life.

Filmed in Baton Rouge, the movie opens as Spader arrives at Ray's Bait Shop on Airline Highway. His house is on Bedford Avenue, one block north of Government Street. MacDowell's house was in a subdivision off Highland Road, and Laura San Giacomo's house was on Eugene Avenue. Other scenes in Baton Rouge include a dining sequence at Zeezee Gardens on Perkins Road (which now contains memorabilia from the movie) and a scene at The Bayou on Chimes Street.

Steel Magnolias

(1989). Sally Field, Dolly Parton. Six friends rendezvous at the local beauty parlor to discuss their lives.

Natchitoches, founded in 1714 as the oldest settlement in the Louisiana Purchase, stood in for the fictional southern town of Chinquapin. The Natchitoches Parish Tourist Commission provides a detailed tour of 17 locations used in the filming, with most clustered between Lafayette and Keyser on the west bank of the Red River.

Tarzan

(1918). Elmo Lincoln, Enid Markey. English nobleman is raised by apes in the jungle after his parents die.

The first film treatment of Lord Greystone, starring Lincoln as Tarzan, was filmed in the swamps outside Morgan City. Young men from the New Orleans Athletic Club played ape parts.

Tightrope

(1984). Clint Eastwood, Genevieve Bujold. Serial killer chooses victims with a connection to the cop on his trail.

Shootouts were filmed in New Orleans at Dixie Brewery (2401 Tulane Avenue) and Jackson Brewery on Decatur Street, a complex of shops and eateries overlooking the Mississippi River.

The Undefeated

(1969). John Wayne, Rock Hudson. Ex–Union colonel and ex–Confederate colonel find themselves on the same side in a battle with Mexicans.

Hudson's home was filmed at the Shades plantation near Wilson; to keep the Yankees from invading his estate, he torches the plantation set built inside the Richards Ford building on Florida Boulevard in Port Hudson.

Undercover Blues

(1993). Dennis Quaid, Kathleen Turner. Husband-and-wife-team of spies try to leave the espionage business behind on maternity leave but can't.

Quaid and Turner evade hit men at the Napoleon House (500 Chartres Street, New Orleans).

MAINE

The Man Without a Face

(1993). Mel Gibson, Margaret Whitton. Boy befriends the town recluse, who gave up teaching after a disfiguring accident.

The fictional Holyfield Academy was actually on the campus of Bowdoin College in Brunswick, including Whittier Field, a pine-encircled field used for athletics since 1896. Town scenes were shot in Rockport, where Gibson goes after hours to avoid any people.

Message in a Bottle

(1999). Kevin Costner, Robin Wright. Reporter finds sad love letter in a bottle on the beach and tracks down the author.

Wright's Chicago home was portrayed by a 130-year-old house at 97 Danforth Street in Portland. Beach scenes were shot at Popham Beach, south of Bath, playing the seashore of North Carolina. The diner was constructed near Shaw's Wharf in New Harbor, and Costner built his sailboat at the Boat Shop and Maine Maritime Museum (243 Washington Street, Bath), a 10-acre site located on a 19th century shipyard where large sailing ships once were birthed. Airport shots were filmed at an American Airlines terminal at O'Hare International Airport in Chicago.

Myth of Fingerprints

(1997). Julianne Moore, Blythe Danner. Family's troubles come to a head during Thanksgiving reunion.

The family home where most of the action takes place is the isolated Chandler Estate in Andover.

Peyton Place

(1957). Lana Turner, Lee Philips. Woman looks back on small town she grew up in whose secrets lie beneath a placid surface.

Many locations in Camden were used to create fictional Peyton Place, including a house on Chestnut Street (where Turner lived) and the Main Street business section (where she owned a shop). The Knox Mill Museum at Washington and Mechanic streets was Harrington Mill, now a bank headquarters. One room inside the building is a museum devoted to the history of the old woolen mill.

MARYLAND

Absolute Power

(1997). Clint Eastwood, Gene Hackman. Aging thief accidentally gets involved in illicit affairs of the President.

The Walters Art Gallery (600 N. Charles Street, Baltimore) stood in for the National Portrait Gallery where Eastwood sketches. The municipally-owned gallery houses more than 25,000 works of art. Other area shooting sites included the Towson courthouse, Patapso Park, and Maryvale Prep–Brooklandville.

And Justice for All

(1979). Al Pacino, Jack Warden. Corrupt judge charged with rape hires a lawyer with whom he has clashed in the past.

The Baltimore courthouse is the Clarence Mitchell Courthouse on 100 North Calvert Street. Other locales include the Chesapeake Bay Bridge and Baltimore City Hall (100 N. Holliday Street), featuring some of the finest examples of architectural ironwork in America. Guided tours of the 1867–75 restored building are available.

Avalon

(1990). Leo Fuchs, Eva Gordon. Immigrant family comes to America in search of a better life.

Primary shooting locations were Fells Point and Mount Vernon Place in Baltimore. Armin Mueller-Stahl grows up on Cliffmont Avenue, and the family camps out on Lake Drive in Druid Hill Park to escape the heat.

The street car crash was staged at the Senator Theater (5904 York Road).

The Bedroom Window

(1987). Steve Guttenberg, Elizabeth McGovern. Secret lovers witness an assault which threatens to blow their affair into the open.

Guttenberg's apartment, where his lover and boss' wife Isabelle Huppert looks down on Mount Vernon Square and witnesses the assault, was at 12 Mount Vernon Place in Baltimore. The Baltimore Museum of Art at North Charles and 31st Street became the opera house where Huppert is stabbed. In North Carolina, scenes were shot at the Performing Arts Center of the North Carolina School of Arts (1929 Stevens Center, Winston-Salem) and the North Carolina Aquarium at Fort Fisher.

The Blair Witch Project

(1999). Heather Donahue, Joshua Leonard. Footage from three missing student filmmakers is found in the woods a year after their disappearance.

The fictional account of the Blair Witch, shot documentary style, was so convincing it sent fans scurrying across the western Maryland countryside in search of the nefarious sorceress. Backdrops for the movie include locations in Burkittsville in Frederick County and in Seneca Creek State Park in Montgomery County. The Blair Witch House, where the characters are actually killed, is the Griggs House in Patapsco State Park (Route 40, Ellicott City), Maryland's first state park. The badly dilapidated 200-year-old Federal-style house was slated to be torn down until the success of the movie, and still stands in the park.

Clara's Heart

(1988). Whoopi Goldberg, Neil Patrick Harris. Housekeeper bonds with child of quarreling parents.

Kathleen Quinlan spies her philandering husband Michael Ontkean at a luncheon at Belvedere Condominiums (Charles Street at East Chase, Baltimore). Other Baltimore locations include St. Anne's Church (528 East 22nd Street) and the final scene at Children's Hospital (3825 Greenspring Avenue).

Diner

(1982). Steve Guttenberg, Mickey Rourke. Young friends prepare to get on with their lives.

The original Hollywood Diner was trucked in from New Jersey and placed on an empty lot at Boston and Montford streets for shooting. It was subsequently moved to its present location at the corner of Holliday Street and Saratoga Street. Other Baltimore area filming locations include the waterfront opposite the American Can Company, the pier at the foot of Broadway and the Roland Park Shopping Center.

For Richer or Poorer

(1997). Tim Allen, Kirstie Alley. Rich New Yorkers find a fulfilling life hiding out from the IRS on an Amish farm.

A rural farm in Westminster was the main setting for filming. Main Street in Westminster stood in for Intercourse, Pennsylvania. Additional footage was shot in Muddy Creek Forks, Pennsylvania, at the A.M. Grove General Store (New Park Road), built in 1900 by A.M. Grove and also housing the town's railroad station.

Guarding Tess

(1994). Nicholas Cage, Shirley MacLaine. Former first lady hand picks a man who hates her as her Secret Service protector.

Ex-Presidential wife MacLaine's house was located on South Road in Baltimore's Mount Washington neighborhood, standing in for Columbus, Ohio.

He Said, She Said

(1991). Kevin Bacon, Elizabeth Perkins. The lives of two journalists are seen from a male and a female perspective.

Bacon and Perkins worked for the *Baltimore Sun* on Calvert Street before embarking on their television careers. They are shown in Baltimore's Bolton Hill section and at the top of the Clarion Hotel (612 Cathedral Street).

Her Alibi

(1989). Tom Selleck, Paulina Porizkova. Writer of detective stories pretends to be alibi for beautiful woman arrested for murder.

Selleck spies on Porizkova at the Kelmscott Bookstore (32 West 25th Street, Baltimore) and tells his publisher about her at Budlows (1501 Budlow Street). A cocktail reception is staged for author Selleck at the Baltimore Museum of Art (Art Museum Drive and North Charles and 31st Street), designed by John Russell Pope.

Home for the Holidays

(1995). Holly Hunter, Robert Downey, Jr.. A woman, having just lost her job, goes to her dysfunctional family home for Thanksgiving.

Hunter flies from Chicago to land in the Baltimore-Washington International Airport. While in Baltimore, she spends time at the Baltimore Museum of Art (Art Museum Drive and North Charles and 31st Street).

Homicide: Life on the Street

(1993–1999). Yaphet Kotto, Kyle Secor. Homicide squad works to close cases in the city of Baltimore.

The Broadway Recreation Pier in Fells Point (Thames Street at Broadway, Baltimore) was used for the exterior shots of the police station.

Liberty Heights

(1999). Adrien Brody, Bebe Neuwirth. Families deal with a changing America in 1950s Baltimore.

Many scenes were shot on Baltimore's Redwood Street, including an eating scene at Werner's (231 E. Redwood). Another featured location is the Hippodrome Performing Arts

Center on North Eutaw Street, built as the Vaudeville House in 1914 and one of the last of the remaining Thomas Lamb theaters.

Men Don't Leave

(1990). Jessica Lange, Arliss Howard. Woman struggles to keep life together after the untimely death of her husband.

Lange meets musician Howard while delivering lunch to George Peabody Library (17 East Mount Vernon Place, Baltimore), with its five ornate iron balconies enveloping a marble atrium. A tense family lunch is staged at the B & O Railroad Museum (901 West Pratt Street, Baltimore), once known as "Railroad University" and home of one of the world's most spectacular collection of locomotives.

Patriot Games

(1992). Harrison Ford, Anne Archer. CIA agent on vacation saves member of England's Royal family and is targeted by the IRA for assassination.

Though the movie was shot mostly in England, Ford does have to defend himself from an IRA assassin outside Gate 3 of the United States Naval Academy in Annapolis. Additional scenes were filmed in Calvert Cliffs State Park in southern Maryland's Calvert County.

The Replacements

(2000). Keanu Reeves, Gene Hackman. Football coach and quarterback get a second chance at success.

Football scenes were filmed in PSI Net Stadium (1101 Russell Street, Baltimore).

Runaway Bride

(1999). Julia Roberts, Richard Gere. Reporter is assigned to do story on woman who has left a string of grooms at the altar.

The 1790s town of Berlin was the centerpiece for locations on this film, shot entirely in Maryland. Many of the shops in the red brick buildings along Main Street appear in the movie and set memorabilia is on display in the windows of Berlin Hardware. Other nearby locales outside Berlin include the Saint Paul Methodist Church in New Windsor and the Snow Hill High School in Snow Hill. Berlin is in Worcester County, seven miles east of Ocean City on Route 346.

St. Elmo's Fire

(1985). Judd Nelson, Rob Lowe. Recent college graduates cope with realities of real life.

Although the movie is set in Georgetown, no university buildings appear in the film. The graduation scene was filmed at the University of Maryland in College Park, and the football scene took place in front of the Sigma Kappa sorority house on Fraternity Row.

Serial Mom

(1994). Kathleen Turner, Sam Waterston. Protective mother kills off anyone who threatens her family values.

Turner eludes police in a chase sequence at the Church of the Good Shepherd (1401 Carrolltown Avenue, Baltimore) and is finally arrested at Hammerjacks (now the Inner Harbor Concert Hall), to the cheers of the band and dancers at 1101 South Howard Street. Turner's trial is staged at the Baltimore County Courthouse (400 Washington Avenue, Towson). Also featured in Towson is Towson High School (69 Cedar Avenue).

Silent Fall

(1994). Richard Dreyfuss, John Lithgow. Unconventional therapist tries to find couple's murderer through their autistic son.

The story was filmed at the Ashby Bed and Breakfast (27448 Ashby Drive, St. Michaels). A dining scene was shot at the Crab Claw (156 Mill Street, St. Michaels).

Tin Men

(1987). Richard Dreyfuss, Danny DeVito. The lives of two aluminum siding salesmen collide — quite literally, in an auto accident.

DeVito's house is at 3107 Cliffmount Street; he drinks and quarrels with Dreyfuss at the Belvedere Condominiums (Charles Street at East Chase), which played the Belvedere Hotel. The two rivals also ate at the Hollywood Diner (corner of Holiday and Saratoga streets).

Violets Are Blue

(1986). Kevin Kline, Sissy Spacek. High school sweethearts reunite and try again, despite a marriage and a busy career.

Filming was accomplished on location in Ocean City; Baltimore played Dublin, Ireland.

Washington Square

(1997). Albert Finney, Jennifer Jason Leigh. Rich man and daughter clash over her choice of suitor.

The stately brick homes of Baltimore's Union Square stood in for 19th century New York; Mount Vernon Place played Paris.

MASSACHUSETTS

Alice's Restaurant

(1969). Arlo Guthrie, Patricia Quinn. A strange odyssey begins when a man can't dump trash because City Dump is closed for Thanksgiving.

Theresa's Restaurant is at the original location of Alice's Restaurant (40 Main Street, Stockbridge). Alice lived in the Old Trinity Church (4 Van Deusenville Road, Housatonic). Guthrie purchased the church, and today it is the Guthrie Center, a headquarters for community volunteers.

Ally McBeal

(1997). Calista Flockhart, Robert Downey, Jr. Young woman deals with life, love and work.

The exterior shot of Flockhart's law firm (with the Palladian windows) is of the redbrick 19th Century Congregational House (14 Beacon Street, Boston).

Blown Away

(1994). Tommy Lee Jones, Jeff Bridges. Bomb squad expert tries to retire, but his successor is killed in an explosion.

Bombs go off all over Boston in this thriller. Jones blows a police car off the ground in Copley Square, and an ocean liner is exploded in East Boston Harbor. The ship was exploded with a little too much gusto, and 8000 windows were shattered in the surrounding neighborhoods, adding an additional $20,000 to the filming budget.

Boston Public

(2000). Jessalyn Gilsis, Chi McBride. Lives of ten faculty members in city public school.

East Boston High School (Marion Street, Boston) was used for school exteriors; Doyle's Cafe (3484 Washington Street) in Jamaica Plains was shot as the outside of a popular teachers' hangout.

The Bostonians

(1984). Christopher Reeve, Vanessa Redgrave. Boston women agitate for voting rights in the late 1800s.

Locations were used on Martha's Vineyards, Oak Bluffs, Ocean Park and in and around Beacon Hill to depict Boston a century ago. In Newport, Rhode Island, scenes were shot in the harem-style upstairs sitting room of the Chateau-sur-Mer (Bellevue Avenue). The 1852 stone mansion of High Victorian architecture is open for tours.

Captains Courageous

(1937). Spencer Tracy, Lionel Barrymore. Big-hearted fisherman befriends sodden old salt.

The schooner race to Gloucester was filmed off the coast of Mexico, but the fishing port (including a wharf by the sea and a home on Lookout Street) made it to the screen in several scenes. Also featured is Our Lady of Good Voyage Church (142 Prospect Street). The most famous site in Gloucester, The Fishermen's Memorial looking out on the sea from Stacy Boulevard, makes an appearance in the movie as well. The 1923 Leonard Craske sculpture, dedicated to the memory of all Gloucester fishermen, is inscribed with a line from Psalms: "They that go down to the sea in ships."

Charly

(1968). Cliff Robertson, Claire Bloom. Scientific experiment turns retarded adult into a genius.

The movie was filmed around South Boston, including John Hancock Observatory (St. James Avenue and Trinity Place) — at 740 feet, said to be the highest vantage point in New England; Faneuil Hall (Faneuil Square on Merchant Row), and also the town of Nahant.

Cheers

(1982–1993). Ted Danson, Shelly Long. Ex-ballplayer and reformed alcoholic buys a bar.

The Bull and Finch Pub (84 Beacon Street, across from the Boston Common, Boston), located beneath the Hampshire House, was used in the opening credits. Although the television series was never filmed on location, and the fictional set differs from the inside of the Bull and finch, it is now the biggest tourist attraction in Massachusetts, drawing more than one million fans each year.

A Civil Action

(1998). John Travolta, Robert Duvall. Injury lawyer enters a whole new league when he assumes a toxic waste dumping case.

The film is based on a true case in Woburn. Locations were used all around Massachusetts, including the Boston Public Garden, dating to 1859 and adjacent to the Boston Common; the Atheneaum (Ten½ Beacon Street); Jamaica Plain, the better part of a string of connected parks designed in the nineteenth century by Frederick Law Olmsted to ring Boston; and the Metropolitan State Hospital (475 Trapelo Road, Waltham).

Good Will Hunting

(1997). Robin Williams, Matt Damon. Working class genius tries to live in two worlds.

Damon hangs out and says farewell to his friends at Woody's L Street Tavern (658 E. Eighth Street, South Boston). Damon and Ben Affleck can also be seen walking into the Bow & Arrow Pub on Harvard Square in Cambridge.

Hocus Pocus

(1993). Bette Midler, Sarah Jessica Parker. Town is visited by witches and a boy turned into a cat 300 years before.

Downtown Salem and Salem 1630 Pioneer Village in Salem's Forest River Park (at the junction of SR114/1A and West Street) provided the setting for this story taking place across three centuries. The living history museum recreates the first English settlement in Salem, with thatched cottages and wigwams.

Housesitter

(1992). Steve Martin, Goldie Hawn. Con artist moves into man's empty house and poses as his new wife.

The towns of Cohasset and Concord blended into the fictional Dobbs Mills; Martin's movie house was torn down after shooting. Martin meets Hawn at Cafe Budapest (90 Exeter Street, Boston).

Jaws

(1975). Roy Scheider, Robert Shaw. Shark threatens bathers in resort community.

Opposite: Some of the explosions staged for *Blown Away* on the streets of Boston were a little too real — producers paid for the repair of more than 8000 windows. (Massachusetts Film Office)

MASSACHUSETTS

Robin Williams sought solace in the Boston Public Garden during *Good Will Hunting*. (Massachusetts Film Office)

The filming of the big fish tale and all its sequels was completed mostly on Martha's Vineyard. Shaw's home port was on North Street in the Menemsha Fishing Village; his boathouse was built specially for the movie and destroyed on Joseph Sylva State Beach. Also featured is the red brick Gay Head Lighthouse, built in Aquinnah in 1844. All the shark scenes in Massachusetts utilized a mechanical shark named after director Steven Spielberg's lawyer; live shark footage was filmed at Seal Rocks in Australia.

Love Story

(1970). Ryan O'Neal, Ali McGraw. Harvard law student is disinherited when he marries a poor girl.

Scenes were shot of O'Neal and McGraw at Harvard University in the school's Tercentuary Theater, and of them walking through the historic "yard" surrounded by buildings virtually describing the history of architecture in America. Additional footage was used from the United States Equestrian Team headquarters in Hamilton and 119 Oxford Street in Cambridge. O'Neal's family home was at Old Westbury Gardens (71 Old Westbury Road, Old Westbury, New York).

Malice

(1993). Alec Baldwin, Nicole Kidman. Wife's operation has dire effects on couple's lives.

Smith College in Northampton stood in for fictional Westerly College. Other locations included Lord Jeffrey Inn (30 Boltwood Avenue, Amherst) and The Abbey (448 W. Second Street, South Boston).

Mermaids

(1990). Cher, Winona Ryder. Mother navigates relationships with lovers and daughters in 1960s.

Two blocks of Main Street in Rockport were transformed to look like the fictional Eastport in 1963, including Cher's office and Bob Hoskins' shoe store. The family home was specially built on Coolidge Point near Manchester. Hospital scenes were staged at Needham-Glover Hospital in Gloucester. The swim scenes were filmed at William E. Tolman High School (150 Exchange Street, Pawtucket).

Never Too Late

(1965). Maureen O'Sullivan, Paul Ford. Middle-aged woman shocks family when she becomes unexpectedly pregnant.

The town of Concord on Main Street and Concord Center became Calvertown for the movie; traffic was directed at Main and Walden streets. A house on Nashawtuc Road was used for interiors.

The Next Karate Kid

(1994). Pat Morita, Hilary Swank. Karate master takes on troubled teenaged girl as pupil.

Swank attends Brookline High School (115 Greenough Street, Brookline), and her prom is staged at Tufts University in Somerville. The climactic fight scene was staged on the docks in East Boston. Also featured was the 1927 Stuart-style Crane Estate, known as Castle Hill, in Ipswich (Argilla Road). Concerts and lectures are scheduled in the mansion during the summer.

Next Stop Wonderland

(1998). Hope Davis, Philip Seymour Hoffman. Mother places personal ads for daughter.

Locations were used around the Boston area, including Union Park in South Boston, the New England Aquarium at Central Wharf off Atlantic Avenue, the Copley Plaza Hotel on Copley Plaza and the neighborhood commercial center of Davis Square in Somerville.

One Crazy Summer

(1986). John Cusack, Linda Warren. Teen adventures during a summer on Nantucket.

The ferry dock at Woods Hole looks much as it did when it was used as a filming location, although it runs to Martha's Vineyard, not Nantucket as it does in the movie.

The Out of Towners

(1997). Steve Martin, Goldie Hawn. Couple's trip to New York City is fraught with complications.

In the original version the unlucky travelers wind up in Boston via train at South Station; in this version Martin and Hawn begin their trip by flying in to Logan International Airport. After that there are aerial views of their car going through Boston to get back to New York.

The Paper Chase

(1973). Timothy Bottoms, John Houseman. First year law student studies under his idol.

Although no university is ever mentioned in the television series spawned by the movie, the law school in the original film was Harvard University Law School, the oldest continuously operating law school in the United States. The law school's main building, in which Bottoms drinks in

Houseman's every word, dates to the 1920s.

The Perfect Storm

(2000). George Clooney, Mark Wahlberg. Unusually intense storm catches commercial fishermen at sea.

The Crow's Nest, the gritty hotel/bar where commercial fishermen congregate, is located on Main Street in Gloucester, across the street from the dock where the ill-fated *Andrea Gail* set sail. The set for the Crow's Nest was built on Harbor Loop. Actual footage was shot on the edge of Hurricane Floyd for the early portions of the storm.

The Practice

(1997–). Dylan McDermott, Camryn Manheim. Lives and loves of defense attorneys.

The old Suffolk County Courthouse in Pemberton Square is used for establishing exterior shots; the interior is replicated on a Los Angeles set.

The River Wild

(1994). Meryl Streep, Kevin Bacon. Two armed robbers force their way into a family's whitewater rafting trip.

Streep trains as a rower at the Weld Boat House on the Chrales River at Harvard University in Cambridge.

School Ties

(1992). Brendan Fraser, Matt Damon. Jewish boy in 1950 tries to hide his religion at an elite prep school.

Fraser starred as quarterback in footage shot at Middlesex School (1400 Lowell Road, Concord). Additional gym and campus scenes were obtained at Worcester Academy (81 Providence Street, Worcester). The movie opens with Fraser driving past the Roxy Theater (2004 Main Street) in Northampton, Pennsylvania, a 1000-seat art deco theater opened in 1921.

A Small Circle of Friends

(1980). Brad Davis, Karen Allen. Three college students buck the system in the 1960s.

Set at Harvard University, Memorial Hall played the school administration building in Cambridge. Bridgewater State College doubled as Harvard during a riot scene.

The Spanish Prisoner

(1997). Steve Martin, Campbell Scott. Web of intrigue surrounds a secret formula.

The closing scene was staged on a water taxi in Boston Harbor. There are also scenes at Logan International Airport and Rowes Wharf. In New York, Scott brings a book to be repaired to Weitz, Weitz and Coleman Booksellers (1377 Lexington Avenue, Manhattan) and waits for an FBI contact at the Carousel in Central Park on Park Drive.

Spenser: For Hire

(1985–1988). Robert Urich, Avery Brooks. Private investigator never wants for murder cases.

Urich's private eye works out of an empty 1947 firehouse at the corner

The Crow's Nest hotel bar in Gloucester, Massachusetts, was the nerve center for those on shore in *The Perfect Storm*. (Massachusetts Film Office)

of Mount Vernon and River streets in Boston.

State and Main

(2000). Alec Baldwin, William Macy. Hollywood film crew overruns a small town while shooting on location.

Manchester-by-the-Sea did double duty for the film, first standing in as fictional modern-day Waterford, Vermont, and then being dressed up as an 1880s frontier town for Macy's movie, "The Old Mill." The town star was Seaside No. 1, an old firehouse with a newly restored cupola which played itself in the movie — an old firehouse. One of its vintage fire engines also appeared in the movie. Elsewhere, Hooper's Market on School Street became Hooper's Coffee Corner, and an apartment building on the corner of School and Central became the Grain and Feed store.

Tell Me That You Love Me, Junie Moon

(1970). Liza Minnelli, Robert Moore. Three outcast misfits move in together to better deal with the world.

Much of the location shooting was done in Manchester-by-the-Sea on the granite outcropping of Cape Ann. The nude scene in the cemetery was filmed in Blue Hill Cemetery (700 West Street, Braintree).

To Gillian on Her 37th Birthday

(1996). Peter Gallagher, Michelle Pfeiffer. Man finds it difficult getting on with his life after his wife dies.

Partly filmed on Nantucket, locations included Brant Point Lighthouse and the Hy-Line Ferry Terminal. The sandcastle competition was staged at Wrightsville Beach, North Carolina.

The Verdict

(1982). Paul Newman, James Mason. Washed-up lawyer gets a chance at redemption.

Newman does his sleuthing from an office in the Massachusetts State House (Beacon Street, Boston). The original brick front of Charles Bullfinch's design remains virtually unchanged from its completion in 1798. The trial sequences were staged in New York City at the Tweed Courthouse (52 Chambers Street).

Who's Afraid of Virginia Woolf?

(1966). Elizabeth Taylor, Richard Burton. Young college instructor and wife are invited to home of older professor and his vituperous wife.

The Tyler Annex at Smith College served as Taylor and Burton's claustrophobic home in this drama where all four members of the cast earned an Academy Award nomination.

Wings

(1990–1997). Tim Daly, Steven Weber. Brothers operate a small commuter airline.

The opening credits feature Tom Nevers Field (Airport Road, Nantucket Island) as the home of Sandpiper Air.

The Witches of Eastwick

(1987). Jack Nicholson, Cher. When three lonely women with witch-like powers conjure up the perfect man he turns out to be the devil.

Primary shooting took place in the cramped business district of Cohasset, including the Cohasset Common. In Boston the Grand Lobby of the Wang Center for the Performing Arts (270 Tremont Street) makes an appearance. Nicholson lived in the Great House at Castle Hill (290 Argilla Road, Ipswich) which is open for tours.

With Honors

(1994). Brendan Fraser, Joe Pesci. Squatter finds law student's thesis and blackmails him one page at a time.

Fraser loses the only copy of his thesis under a sidewalk grate outside the Widener Library inside Harvard Yard on the campus of Harvard University; interiors were filmed at the Boston Athenaeum (Ten½ Beacon Street, Boston).

MICHIGAN

Anatomy of a Murder

(1959). Jimmy Stewart, Lee Remick. Lawyer agrees to defend Army Lieutenant who claims temporary insanity after killing a man who had been with his wife.

The film was shot entirely on location on the Upper Peninsula. Ben Gazzara, as the accused soldier, was stationed at Big Bay Point Lighthouse (3 Lighthouse Road, Big Bay), and the murder scene was filmed at the Lumber Jack Tavern in Big Bay, where the real-life shooting of the bar owner occurred on July 31, 1952. Among the many sites used in Big Bay was the Thunder Bay Inn (County Road 550), a guest house once owned by Henry Ford.

Blue Collar

(1978). Richard Pryor, Harvey Keitel. Auto workers rob the local union for kicks and find more than money in the vaults.

Filmed in Kalamazoo, the car factory scenes were shot at the now closed Checker Motor Company (2016 N. Pitcher Street). Morris Malkin, an immigrant Russian tailor, purchased the Dort body plant in Kalamazoo in 1922 and formed the Checker Cab Manufacturing Company. The last of the famous cabs was manufactured in 1982, but body parts for General Motors are still fabricated there.

Grosse Pointe Blank

(1997). John Cusack, Minnie Driver. Hit man returns home to complete a contract job and attend a high-school reunion.

Producers were set to shoot in Grosse Pointe, but the school board denied access after reading the script, and the John Marshall High School in Los Angeles stood in for Grosse Point. Although there are scenes of the Detroit skyline and establishing exteriors in Grosse Point, most of the streets and houses were shot in southern California.

Hoffa

(1992). Jack Nicholson, Danny DeVito. Account of powerful union leader as seen through the eyes of a friend.

The 1957 Teamsters convention where Nicholson, as Jimmy Hoffa, was elected president was staged at the Cobo Arena (Civic Center Drive, Detroit). A clash between union and non-union workers was recreated at the Detroit Produce Terminal (7201 West Fort Street). The Detroit Public Library, an Italian Renaissance building crafted of Vermont marble (5201 Woodward Avenue) played the role of the Senate Office Building in Washington. In Pittsburgh, Pennsylvania the Carnegie Mellon Institute on Fifth Avenue doubled for a Washington DC courtroom.

Midnight Run

(1988). Robert DeNiro, Charles Grodin. Accountant is pursued by bounty hunters, the FBI and gangsters.

Yaphet Kotto boards a train searching for DeNiro and Grodin in Niles (598 Dey Street). The town was once at the intersection of so many major railroads that the original depot was known as the "Gateway of Commerce and Settlement" for the west. In Arizona, the scene in the Flagstaff train station featured the depot built in 1926 in a distinctive Tudor Revival/Chalet style. In Las Vegas,

Nevada, the casino shots were in the Aladdin (3667 Las Vegas Boulevard South), and the finale occurs at McCarran Airport (4270 South Valley View Boulevard).

Polish Wedding

(1998). Claire Danes, Lena Olin. Pregnancy triggers events in large matriarchal family.

In street scenes the Martha Washington Bakery (10335 Joseph Campau, Hamtramck) is featured.

Presumed Innocent

(1990). Harrison Ford, Brian Dennehy. Prosecutor is under suspicion for his former girlfriend's murder.

The opening scene is on a ferry in the Detroit River, playing New York City. Later, Ford's trial is held at the Frank Murphy Hall of Justice (600 Randolph Street, Detroit).

Renaissance Man

(1994). Danny DeVito, Gregory Hines. Fired advertising man finds meaning in teaching unskilled army recruits.

DeVito's advertising office was located in the Renaissance Center (East Jefferson Street, Detroit), and his unemployment office was portrayed by the Olde Brokerage (Griswold and Lafayette, Detroit). DeVito turns English teacher at Fort Jackson in Columbia, South Carolina, which portrays Fort McClane. In an attempt to prove to his students that anything is possible, a rotund DeVito conquers the 40-foot-high Victory Tower on the base. America's largest army basic training center was established in 1917 and offers tours and a base museum.

Roger and Me

(1989). Michael Moore, Pat Boone. Film director pursues head of General Motors to discuss damage to community from loss of jobs.

The General Motors headquarters where Moore fruitlessy dogs his quarry is on 3044 West Grand Boulevard and Woodward. Designed by Albert Kahn, this was the largest office building in the world when it opened in 1920. Today it is mostly empty.

The Rosary Murders

(1982). Donald Sutherland, Charles Durning. Priest is conflicted when serial killer of priests and nuns confesses to him.

The movie was filmed entirely in Detroit and set principally in the Holy Redeemer High School at Vernor and Junction, the producer's alma mater. Also featured prominently is Duly's Coney Island, directly across the street. Duly's, opened in 1921, features 24-hours-a-day counter seating in a building that is only 12 feet wide.

Somewhere in Time

(1980). Jane Seymour, Christopher Reeve. Playwright uses self-hypnosis to travel back in time to meet a young stage actress.

Reeve lived in Chicago on North Halsted near the Steppenwolf Theater and did his research in Blackstone Library at 4904 S. Lake Shore Drive.

Christopher Reeve travels back in time to the Grand Hotel on Mackinac Island in search of Jane Seymour in *Somewhere in Time*. (Grand Hotel)

When he travels back in time the scenes are filmed at the Grand Hotel on Mackinac Island. The historic resort opened in 1887. Also featured on the island is Round Island Lighthouse.

True Romance

(1993). Christian Slater, Patricia Arquette. defending his new bride puts a man on the wrong side of police and gangsters.

MINNESOTA

Beautiful Girls

(1996). Timothy Hutton, Uma Thurman. Piano player at crossroads of his life returns home.

Stillwater, settled in 1843 at the spot where the St. Croix River widens into Lake St. Croix, stands in for Knight's Ridge, New York. The reunion location was filmed in Hopkins, and town scenes were shot in Marine on St. Croix.

Drop Dead Gorgeous

(1999). Kirsten Dunst, Ellen Barkin. Mock documentary of fictional beauty pageant in Mount Rose.

Barkin and Dunst live in the Ardmore Village trailer park in Lakeville. The auditorium for the centerpiece pageant is at Wayzata West Junior High School (North Barry Avenue, Wayzata), and the swan float goes down Main Street in Waconia during the pageant parade.

Fargo

(1996). Frances McDormand, Steve Buscemi. Man's plan to kidnap his wife goes awry when he hires bungling hit men.

The scene of the crime was shot at Moose Lake State Park (4252 County Road 137, Moose Lake). William Macy meets with Buscemi at the King of Clubs Bar (Central Avenue NE, near 3rd Ave NE, Minneapolis). The massive statue of Paul Bunyan welcoming travelers to Brainerd that is featured in the movie does not exist, although there is a large 26-foot animated storytelling woodsman at The Paul Bunyan Amusement Center in Brainerd (junction of SRs 210 and 371). The Paul Bunyan statue for the movie was created on the side of a North Dakota highway. Another scene in North Dakota was of a man shoveling his walk, with a grain elevator in the background, shot in Hallock.

Foolin' Around

(1980). Gary Busey, Annette O'Toole. Poor boy tries to win rich girl's love.

O'Toole's family lives in a mansion on Lake Minnetonka in Excelsior, a natural lake with 110 miles of shoreline. Other Twin Cities locations include St. Anthony Falls, an historic flour milling district; and St. John's Basilica, where the hang-gliding Busey crashes in a bid to stop O'Toole's wedding.

Grumpier Old Men

(1995). Walter Matthau, Jack Lemmon. New bait shop owner stirs up feuding neighbors again.

Bass Lake, where Matthau and Lemmon fish (and Sophia Loren turns the bait shop into an Italian restaurant) was shot just west of Stillwater. Slippery's Bar and Grill was portrayed by the Halt Time Rec. Bar (1013 Front Avenue, Saint Paul). The wedding scenes were filmed in the old lumber town of Marine on St. Croix.

Grumpy Old Men

(1993). Walter Matthau, Jack Lemmon. Neighbors continually fuel a 50-year quarrel.

Although the movie is set in Wabasha, the houses where Matthau, Lemmon and Ann-Margret live are in East Saint Paul on the 1100 block of Hyacinth Street. The train station in the opening scenes is actually the Depot Bar and Grill (311 Heritage Place, Faribault). Ice fishing scenes were shot on Rebecca lake near Delano. Lemmon marries Ann-Margret at the end of the movie in Memorial Lutheran Church (12112 Earl Street, Faribault).

Here on Earth

(2000). Chris Klein, Leelee Sobieski. Rich college kid is taught a lesson after joy ride destroys a restaurant.

The town of Welch stood in for the Massachusetts Berkshire Mountains. The baseball sequences were staged at Jack Ruhr Field (14475 240th Street East) in Miesville.

Iron Will

(1994). Mackenzie Astin, Kevin Spacey. Boy enters cross-country dog-sled race to win money for mother.

Two Harbor Depot in Duluth served as the finish line for the 1917 marathon race between Winnipeg, Canada, and Saint Paul, Minnesota. The Winnipeg City Hall was portrayed by the Central Administration building (215 N. Second Ave. E., Duluth). Footage of the frozen wilderness for the race was obtained on the north shore of Lake Superior in Gooseberry Falls State Park, 1662 acres of forest highlands 13 miles north of Two Harbors on Route 61.

Jingle All the Way

(1996). Arnold Schwarzenegger, Sinbad. Father tries to get the year's hot toy the day before Christmas.

Schwarzenegger's upscale home was located in Edina Park outside of Minneapolis; his children attend Falcon Heights Elementary School (1393 Garden Avenue West, Falcon Heights). He tries to find his Christmas present in the Mall of America in Bloomington. A haggard Schwarzenegger eats in a booth at Mickey's Diner (36 West 7th Street, Saint Paul). Built in 1937 in New Jersey, the distinctive red-and-cream dining car was transplanted to Saint Paul, where it has remained open 24 hours a day for over 60 years. It is one of only two diners in America on the National Register of Historic Places.

Little Big League

(1994). Luke Edwards, Jason Robards. Young boy inherits the Minnesota Twins from his grandfather.

Edwards attended Groveland Park Elementary School (St. Claire Avenue, Saint Paul) and fished in the Minnehana Creek from the bridge in Minnehaha Park until he became a baseball owner. Then he began showing up in Comiskey Park, Fenway Park, Yankee Stadium and the Hubert H. Humphrey Metrodome at 34 Kirby Puckett Avenue.

Mallrats

(1995). Ben Affleck, Shannen Doherty. Two best friends left by their girlfriends seek solace in local mall.

Shooting took place at the Eden Prairie Center in Eden Prairie; the mall was chosen for its generic look and relative lack of distractions as an overlooked shopping destination in the shadow of the Mall of America.

Mary Tyler Moore

(1970–1977). Mary Tyler Moore, Ed Asner. Single woman finds her way at Minneapolis television station.

Moore flings her beret into the air at the end of the opening credits in front of IDS Crystal Court (corner of 7th Street and Nicollet Avenue, Minneapolis). Exteriors of the Victorian mansion where Moore and Valerie Harper live is at the southwest corner of Keenwood Parkway and West 22nd Street, near the Lake of Isles in Minneapolis.

The Mighty Ducks

(1992). Emilio Estevez, Josh Ackland. Lawyer is sentenced to coach a peewee hockey team.

Estevez gathers his young charges at the Peavey Park ice rink at Chicago and Franklin avenues in south Minneapolis. Other Twin Cities locations include courtroom scenes in St. Cloud; Rice Park (140 Washington Street, St. Paul); IDS Crystal Court (Seventh Street and Nicollet Avenue); and the inner city neighborhood of Elliot Park.

The Mighty Ducks II

(1994). Emilio Estevez, Kathryn Erbe. Former ragtag hockey mites go up against the world's best team from Iceland.

Action was filmed in four rinks: Parade Ice Arena (600 Kenwood Parkway, Minneapolis); New Hope Ice Arena (4949 Louisiana Avenue North, New Hope); Blake School Ice Rink in Hopkins; and Pickwick Ice in Burbank, California.

Overnight Delivery

(1998). Reese Witherspoon, Paul Rudd. Suspicious boyfriend sends girlfriend inflammatory letter and must stop delivery.

A Federal Express office was recreated behind Williamson Hall on the University of Minnesota campus. Additional scenes were shot at the OK Corral Livery stable (20201 Johnson Memorial Drive, Jordan).

The English-style country estate of Glensheen in Duluth, Minnesota, was the setting for the story in *You'll Like My Mother.* (Glensheen)

Purple Rain

(1984). Prince, Apollonia Kotero. Young Musician struggles for acceptance of his music.

Prince used more than 30 locations around his hometown of Minneapolis to complete his first feature film; the bar featured at the end of the movie is First Avenue (701 First Avenue N.).

A Simple Plan

(1998). Bill Paxton, Billy Bob Thornton. Two brothers find millions of dollars in a crashed plane.

The crashed plane was filmed in the woods near Delano, although the scene with Paxton getting pecked by crows was shot on a sound stage at Energy Park Studios in Saint Paul. An abandoned house was used to stage the shotgun duel. When production had to move to Wisconsin in search of snow, the changing of the tire and the murder of the snowmobiler was shot in Ashland. The barber shop scene with the sheriff featured the actual town barber in his shop.

Sugar and Spice

(2001). Marla Sokoloff, Marley Shelton. High school cheerleader turns to crime after she becomes pregnant.

The football scene was filmed at Eastview High School (6200 140th Street, West Apple Valley). Some of the locations used in Saint Paul include Arlington High School (1495 Rice Street); the Hamm building on Payne Avenue; the corner of Concord and Robert streets; and the Macalester/Groveland area.

Untamed Heart

(1993). Christian Slater, Marisa Tomei. Busboy rescues waitress from rapist and begins a relationship.

The rescue takes place along Main Street in Minneapolis Riverplace; Tomei and Slater work at Jim's Coffee Shop and Bakery (328 Central Avenue West).

You'll Like My Mother

(1972). Patty Duke, Richard Thomas. Pregnant widow makes a troubling visit to her late husband's mother.

The movie was filmed almost entirely at the Glensheen Historic Estate (3300 London Road, 5 miles north of Duluth on SR 61), which served as Rosemary Murphy's home. The 22-acre English country estate on the shore of Lake Superior was built in 1908 by mining baron Chester A. Congdon and opened to the public in 1979 after a notorious double-murder took place in the home in 1977. In addition to regularly scheduled tours of the Jacobean mansion and formal gardens, there is a separate tour of the third floor and attic which explains the house's steel beam construction.

MISSISSIPPI

Adventures of Huck Finn

(1993). Elijah Wood, Courtney B. Vance. Boy fakes his death and travels down Mississippi River with escaped slave.

On the run, Wood heads for a small town portrayed by Jefferson College (US 61 near US 84E, Washington). Incorporated in 1802, the school is being restored as a historic landmark, and several buildings are open to the public. The stately homes of Natchez are used for several scenes, including the Rosalie Mansion (Canal Street at Broadway Street), where Wood impersonates the mansion's owners. Daily tours are available of the 1820s brick mansion built on the site of Fort Rosalie. Footage was also shot near the Mississippi River at Natchez-under-the-Hill, on Silver Street, once a haven for gamblers, thieves and riverboat roughnecks. Caves dug into the bluffs sheltered stolen contraband.

The Chamber

(1996). Chris O'Donnell, Gene Hackman. Young lawyer tries to win reprieve for grandfather on death row.

The execution "chamber" of the title was filmed in Parchman Penitentiary (Highway 49 West, Indianola). The Edison Walthall Hotel (225 East Capitol Street, Jackson) was used for room scenes.

Cookie's Fortune

(1999). Glenn Close, Julianne Moore. Suicide of matriarch in small town leads family to try and hide the truth.

Due to budget constraints, the entire town of Holly Springs was used as the movie set. To save money, the story was altered to fit the town, and even the town signs were not changed. The Holly Springs Square, which endured 62 raids during the Civil War, featured nearly 100 nineteenth century buildings.

Ghosts of Mississippi

(1991). Alec Baldwin, James Woods. Retelling of assassination of civil rights leader Medgar Evans and the 30-year struggle to bring his killer to justice.

Mississippi locations included Yazoo City, Port Gibson and Natchez. The film was also shot at the actual Evers home at 2332 Guyner Street in northwest Jackson and at the Hinds County Courthouse.

The Gun in Betty Lou's Handbag

(1992). Penelope Ann Miller, William Forsythe. Meek librarian seeking attention claims to be murderer of a gangster.

The movie was filmed on location in Oxford at the town square and on the University of Mississippi campus.

Miss Firecracker

(1989). Holly Hunter, Mary Steenburgen. Woman sees beauty pageant as ticket out of small-town life.

Filmed in Yazoo City, the movie utilized the house at Grand Avenue and Canal Street as its primary setting. The Miss Firecracker Contest took place at a carnival set up on the south end of Main Street.

Mississippi Burning

(1988). Gene Hackman, Willem Dafoe. FBI agents investigate disappearance of civil rights activists in 1964 in the Deep South.

Although the movie was filmed in dozens of locations around Mississippi, the courthouse selected for the trial was the Chambers County Courthouse in Lafayette, Alabama (Courthouse Town Square), an 1899 two-story brick building with Palladium windows. The site of the slain men's funeral eulogy and procession was the Cedar Hill Cemetery (3201 Clay Street, Vicksburg).

My Dog Skip

(2000). Diane Lane, Kevin Bacon. Young boy comes of age during World War II with the help of a stray dog.

The town of Canton was transformed to play 1930s Mississippi. Many storefronts were changed, an old gas station became the bus depot, and a baseball park became a football field. Downtown scenes were shot around Courthouse Square.

O Brother Where Art Thou

(2000). George Clooney, Jon Tuturro. 1930s rural prison escapees record a hit song while on the lam.

The rollicking finale takes place inside the Trolio Hotel on Canton Square in Canton and spills out into the courthouse square. The chain gang sequences were filmed along the backroads of Madison County.

Ode to Billie Joe

(1976). Robby Benson, Glynnis O'Connor. Infatuated teen is forbidden to see the girl he loves.

Filmed on location in Mississippi, the production utilized locations in the Greenwood and Itta Bena areas. Benson commits suicide by jumping into the Tallahatchie River from a bridge near Vaiden in Rising Sun (County Road 559).

A Time to Kill

(1996). Sandra Bullock, Matthew McConaughey. Young lawyer takes racially charged case when black father murders two white men who raped his daughter.

The movie was filmed entirely on location in and around Canton, standing in for fictional Clanton. Many exteriors were of buildings around the town square, including the 1855 Madison County Courthouse and the abandoned Malony Building (where McConaughey's law office was created). The interior courtroom was built on a sound stage outside of town.

MISSOURI

Article 99

(1991). Ray Liotta, Kiefer Sutherland. Doctors break rules to serve patients in understaffed and undersupplied hospital.

St. Marys Hospital in Blue Springs is used as Veteran's Hospital. The Liberty Memorial (100 W. 26th Street, Kansas City), the only public museum in the United States dedicated to World War I, gets a feature role. The 217-foot memorial tower was dedicated in 1926.

The Big Brass Ring

(1999). William Hurt, Nigel Hawthorne. Presidential hopeful is confronted by a secret in his past during a campaign stop in St. Louis.

Most of the principle St. Louis landmarks make an appearance, including the Gateway Arch, the cobblestones of Laclede's Landing (the site of the city's original settlement), and St. Louis City Hall (1200 Market Street).

Escape from New York

(1981). Lee Van Cleef, Kurt Russell. President must be rescued from futuristic Manhattan, which is a maximum security prison.

All of the Manhattan scenes were filmed in St. Louis. The Chain of Rocks Bridge became the 59th Street Bridge, where Russell and Donald Pleasence are rescued; the wreckage of the plane crash was staged at Broadway and St. Charles Street; Russell meets Ernest Borgnine at the Rox Theater at Grand Avenue and Washington Street; and the Grand Hall of Union Station was used for a fight scene.

Kansas City

(1996). Jennifer Jason Leigh, Miranda Richardson. Crime drama played out against the jazz backdrop of Kansas City in the 1930s.

The movie was shot on location throughout director Robert Altman's hometown of Kansas City, although the Hey Hey Club, central to the action, was recreated.

King of the Hill

(1993). Jesse Bradford, Lisa Eichhorn. Boy must fend for himself during the Depression when his mother is forced into a sanitarium.

Most of the film was shot on a set built in the vacant Kiel Auditorium at 14th and Market streets in St. Louis, which has since been torn down and replaced by the Kiel Center. Locations outside the sound stage include the Lister Building (North Taylor Avenue and Olive Street), which portrayed the distressed Empire Hotel. Bradford graduates in a scene staged at the Sheldon Concert Hall (3648 Washington); his school was played by the New City School (Lake and Waterman in the Central West End).

Larger Than Life

(1993). Bill Murray, Janeane Garofolo. Motivational speaker inherits an elephant from his circus clown father and must transport her across the country to sell the pachyderm.

St. Louis stood in for Baltimore, where Murray comes into possession of his elephant. Many of the locations in the industrial area around 1st Street were used. Murray tricks a trucker into giving him a ride at Johnson's Corner truck stop (2842 SE Frontage Road, Loveland) off I-25, Exit 254. The famous rest area opened in 1951, three years before the interstate highway came through.

Mr. and Mrs. Bridge

(1990). Paul Newman, Joanne Woodward. Grown children clash with conservative parents.

Shooting took place at the Jackson County Courthouse (415 East 12th Street, Kansas City). The Art Deco limestone building was built during the Depression in 1934.

Ride with the Devil

(1999). Skeet Ulrich, Tobey Maguire. Fictional accounts of battle in pre–Civil War "bloody Kansas".

During flood season the Mississippi River town of Pattonsburg was deserted, as residents moved to higher ground; filmmakers came in and removed 118 telephone poles, and 500 truckloads of dirt later the ghost town was Lawrence, Kansas, in the 1850s. Additional footage was obtained north of Hays, Kansas, along the Saline River Valley.

Sometimes They Come Back

(1991). Tim Matheson, Brooke Adams. Schoolteacher returns to his home town where he is haunted by the ghosts of thugs killed in a train crash with his brother.

The high school where Matheson teaches is played by Liberty Junior High School (Liberty Square, Liberty).

White Palace

(1990). Susan Sarandon, James Spader. Older working class waitress gets involved with younger widowed yuppie.

Sarandon works at the White Knight Cafe (1801 Olive Street, St. Louis), the eatery that inspired the story. The St. Louis waterfront is featured in scenes at the Memorial Arch and the upscale, converted buildings in Laclede's Landing. The bachelor party was staged at Lemp Mansion (3322 DeMenil Place, St. Louis), and Sarandon and Spader reunite in the final scenes at Duff's restaurant (392 North Euclid Avenue, St. Louis), which portrayed a Greenwich Village restaurant in New York.

MONTANA

Always

(1989). Richard Dreyfuss, Holly Hunter. Daredevil aerial forest fighter can't give up his job for the woman he loves.

A scene at the beginning of the movie where a plane flies so low two fishermen jump from a boat was shot at Bull Lake on Highway 2. The firefighters' home base was built at the Libby Airport in Libby; part of the airport control set is still in place. Actual fires were burning in Yellowstone National Park below Dreyfuss and John Goodman during filming. The Ephrata Airfield at the Port of Ephrata (1990 Division Avenue East), a former World War II Army Air Corps training base and now a popular recreational airport in Washington, was also used in the filming.

Diggstown

(1992). James Woods, Lou Gossett, Jr. Man makes a bet he can find a boxer to knock out 10 men in 24 hours.

The fight-mad fictional town of Diggstown was created in the old Montana Territorial Prison in Deer Lodge, the first built in the American West. The four-tiered brick cell block with the Gothic facade has been unused since 1979. Today it is a museum open to the public, with self-guiding tours.

Heaven's Gate

(1980). Kris Kristofferson, Christopher Walken. Montana sheriff struggles to protect immigrant farmers from cattle ranchers.

The fictional town of Sweetwater in the film that bankrupt United Artist Studios was built in a parking lot on the edge of Two Medicine Lake in Poleridge, outside of Glacier National Park.

The Horse Whisperer

(1998). Robert Redford, Kristin Scott Thomas. Young girl and horse injured in accident are taken to Montana to horse healer of mystical talents.

In Montana, outdoor scenes were filmed at the base of the Absaroka and Beartooth mountain ranges south of Big Timber in McLeod. The accident scene at the beginning of the movie was staged in Saratoga Springs, and Scott Thomas is brought to a hospital set up in Saratoga Spa State Park (19 Roosevelt Drive).

Rancho Deluxe

(1975). Jeff Bridges, Sam Waterston. Two drifters become cattle rustlers in modern-day Montana.

Bridges and Waterston sit in steaming water and plan the biggest rustle of their lives in the Chico Hot Springs Resort (Chico Road, Pray).

A River Runs Through It

(1992). Brad Pitt, Craig Sheffer. Two very different friends bond through fly fishing while growing up in Montana.

The town of Livingston at the head of Paradise Valley portrayed Missoula, with many false fronts built along commercial buildings on Front Street, across the Union Pacific railroad tracks. Fishing scenes were filmed on the Yellowstone River south of Livingston, along the Gallatin River south of Bozeman and on the Boulder River south of Big Timber.

NEBRASKA

Boys Town

(1938). Spencer Tracy, Mickey Rooney. Priest creates school for juvenile delinquents.

The movie was filmed in an actual village for abused children, now the Boys and Girls Town (2.5 miles west of I-680 in Omaha on Dodge Street). Tracy won an Academy Award for his portrayal of founder Father Flanagan, and his Oscar statuette is on display in the Hall of History. Guided and self-guided tours are available on the 900-acre site.

Election

(1999). Matthew Broderick, Reese Witherspoon. Teacher decides to sabotage the class presidential campaign of an overachieving student.

The movie was shot on location in Omaha, mostly in the Papillon/La Vista High School, which played the fictional George Washington Carver High School. Broderick has an uncomfortable meeting with parents at Grandmother's Restaurant and Lounge (8989 West Dodge Road).

Terms of Endearment

(1983). Shirley MacLaine, Debra Winger. Story of love and conflict between mother and daughter.

Winger confronts philandering husband Jeff Daniels outside Architectural Hall (14th and R streets, Lincoln) on the campus of the University of Nebraska-Downtown; a room inside was transformed into a doctor's office, where Winger learns she has cancer. She is later hospitalized at Lincoln General Hospital (2300 South 16th Street, Lincoln), which was used for interiors and exterior shots. Winger has dinner with John Lithgow at Kay's Restaurant in the Piedmont Shops (1265 South Cotner Boulevard, Lincoln). Earlier, he had bailed her out when she was short of cash at Leon's Food Mart, which was in the same shopping center but is now out of business. The swimming pool scenes were filmed at the Inn of Lincoln (5250 Cornhusker Highway, Lincoln). In Texas, Jack Nicholson and MacLaine live in Locke Lane in the Avalon section of Houston. Their first date is at Brennan's Restaurant (3300 Smith Street, Houston), and Nicholson drives her into the Gulf of Mexico at East Beach in Galveston.

To Wong Foo, Thanks for Everything, Julie Newmar

(1995). Patrick Swayze, Wesley Snipes. Three drag queens in an old

Cadillac traveling across country break down in a small town.

Location scouts sought a small town that looked as if it was placed in the midst of a vast landscape. To play the fictional town of Snydersville, they settled on Loma, a town of 23 people, 35 miles northwest of Lincoln. The tiny settlement is not even on most maps. In Jersey City, New Jersey, the Drag Queen Beauty Pageant was held in the exotic gold and red interior of the Canton Tea Garden (920 Bergen Avenue).

NEVADA

Another Stakeout

(1993). Richard Dreyfuss, Emilio Estevez. Police detectives stake out the home of a Mafia trial witness.

There are interior scenes at the Crowne Plaza Las Vegas (4255 South Paradise Road), but when the quarry steps outside, he leaves the Binions Horseshoe (128 E. Fremont Street, Las Vegas).

Austin Powers: International Man of Mystery

(1997). Mike Myers, Elizabeth Hurley. British secret agent frozen in the 1960s is thawed in the 1990s.

Although mostly shot in Los Angeles, there are interior scenes of the Riviera Hotel and Casino (2901 Las Vegas Boulevard South) and the Stardust Casino (3000 Las Vegas Boulevard). Myers also cruises down Las Vegas Boulevard in an English double-decker bus.

Baby Geniuses

(1999). Kathleen Turner, Christopher Lloyd. Babies are super-intelligent and actually lose brain power as they grow up and abandon baby-talk.

Part of the movie was filmed in Adventuredome at Circus Circus (2880 Las Vegas Boulevard South, Las Vegas).

Blind Fury

(1989). Rutger Hauer, Terry O'Quinn. Blinded Vietnam vet calls on a Samurai fighter to protect son of a dead comrade.

The casino scenes were staged in the Riverside Casino (17 South Virginia Street, Reno).

Bob and Carol and Ted and Alice

(1969). Natalie Wood, Robert Culp. Hip couple shares liberated sexual theories with another couple.

The final sequences in the movie, where both couples wind up in bed, was shot at the Riviera Hotel and Casino (2901 Las Vegas Boulevard South, Las Vegas).

The Bodyguard

(1992). Kevin Costner, Whitney Houston. Former Secret Service agent takes job guarding pop singer.

Costner takes Houston to a private lakeside cabin by Fallen Leaf Lake on the south shore of Lake Tahoe (Highway 89, Camp Richardson). The hotel where he guarded Houston was the Fontainebleu Hilton Resort and Spa (4441 Collins Avenue, Miami, Florida).

Bonanza

(1959–1973). Lorne Greene, Michael Landon. Widower and three sons run a ranching empire.

The Ponderosa Ranch owned by Greene did not exist on Lake Tahoe's north shore when the television series began in 1959. But so many people were showing up at Bill and Joyce Anderson's property at the approximate location indicated on the map during the show's opening credits that Anderson approached NBC with a plan to build a real Ponderosa. It was completed in 1967, and the Western-style theme park now contains the original Cartwright ranch house on 600 acres in Incline Village (100 Ponderosa Ranch Road).

Casino

(1995). Robert DeNiro, Sharon Stone. Bookie rises through the ranks of Midwestern mobs to reach Las Vegas.

The interior of the Riviera Hotel and Casino (2901 Las Vegas Boulevard South, Las Vegas) and the exterior of the demolished Landmark Hotel combined to create the fictional Tangiers Casino. The Peppermill Inn (Las Vegas Boulevard South) was used to help evoke the Las Vegas of the 1970s.

Cherry 200

(1987). David Andrews, Jennifer Balgobin. When a futuristic man breaks his robot/wife he travels across apocalyptic wasteland seeking a replacement.

Las Vegas, in the movie's pessimistic vision, is abandoned and covered with sand in the year 2017. Scenes were shot in Valley of Fire State Park (State Road 169) and many Nevada ghost towns, such as Rhyolite and Tonopah.

Chicken Every Sunday

(1948). Dan Dailey, Celeste Holm. Wife is forced to take in boarders to pay for husband's wild investment schemes.

The family home was in Carson City at 406 North Montana Street, built in 1873 by Marshall Robinson, founder of the *Carson Daily Appeal*. Footage was also used of the Virginia & Truckee Railway, the original tracks of which ran through the Carson River Canyon, 17 miles from Virginia City to Carson City. Today the train runs 2½ miles from Virginia City to Gold Hill.

Con Air

(1997). Nicholas Cage, John Cusack. Prisoners seize control of convict transport plane.

At the controls, Cage clips the guitar of the Hard Rock Hotel & Casino (4455 Paradise Road, Las

Vegas) and incongruously crashes the plane into the former Sands Hotel on Las Vegas Boulevard prior to its demolition.

Cool World

(1992). Brad Pitt, Gabriel Byrne. Comic strip seductress tries to convince creator to let her cross into the real world.

The climax involves a spike at the top of the Crowne Plaza Las Vegas (4255 South Paradise Road), which allows cartoon characters to enter Las Vegas and terrorize gamblers.

Desert Hearts

(1985). Helen Shaver, Patricia Charbonneau. 1950s woman going to Reno for quickie divorce finds herself attracted to a vivacious young lesbian.

Several locations in Reno were used, including the train station at East Commercial Row and Lake Street; the Park Wedding Chapel (136 South Virginia Street, near the courthouse), which was founded in 1957 as "Reno's Original Wedding Chapel"; the Riverside Casino (17 South Virginia Street); and Parkers Western Wear (151 North Virginia Street), where Shaver goes to replace her Eastern clothes.

Electric Horseman

(1979). Robert Redford, Jane Fonda. Rodeo star-turned-pitchman steals a Las Vegas showhorse and rides towards the open range.

Redford rides the prized steed out of Caesars Palace (3750 Las Vegas Boulevard South, Las Vegas) and up the Strip on his way to Utah's Snow Canyon on Highway 8. The denouement takes place at Dick's Cafe (114 E. George Boulevard) in downtown St. George, Utah.

Five Against the House

(1955). Guy Madison, Kim Novak. College students plan and execute a Reno casino robbery after overhearing a cop say it cannot be done.

The casino heist takes place at Harold's Club, which stood at 236 N. Virginia Street in Reno from 1935 to 1996.

Fools Rush in

(1997). Matthew Perry, Salma Hayek. Man decides to spend his entire life with a woman after one night.

There are scenes at Hoover Dam, McCarran Airport (4270 South Valley View Boulevard, Las Vegas) and Caesars Palace (3750 Las Vegas Boulevard South, Las Vegas). In New York City, Perry's favorite eating place is Gray's Papaya at 72nd Street and Amsterdam Avenue. He confronts the strange man urging him to follow his heart at the 72nd Street subway entrance.

Funny Bones

(1995). Oliver Platt, Jerry Lewis. Stand-up comedian fails in Las Vegas debut and returns to his childhood home.

Platt tries to make his mark in comedy at the Las Vegas Hilton (3000 Paradise Road, Las Vegas) but bombs. He then flies back to England, where the rest of the movie is set.

The Godfather Part II

(1974). Al Pacino, Robert Duvall. Mafia don's assuming power of organization in the 1950s contrasts with his father's early days as an immigrant.

Pacino's mansion was played by the private Fleur de Lac on the west side of Lake Tahoe. The grounds of the former Henry Kaiser estate, built in 1939, are easily seen from one of the many boat tours that use the lake. The movie estate was torn down and replaced by condominiums shortly after filming, and the only structures left from the movie are the complex of old native stone boathouses with wrought iron gates. It is from here that John Cazale is rowed into the mist for his last boat ride.

The Greatest Story Ever Told

(1965). Max Von Sydow, Michael Anderson. The life of Christ.

An expansive replica of Jesus' city of Capernaum was built on Pyramid Lake, doubling as the Sea of Galilee. Nevada's largest natural lake stretches 30 miles and is seven to nine miles across, surrounded by rugged sandstone mountains. Complete with a Tufa Pyramid lurking in the background, the location was on State Road 445 in Sutcliffe, 35 miles northeast of Reno. Von Sydow delivered his "Sermon on the Mount" speech from the Green River Overlook in the Island in the Sky section of Canyonlands National Park. A rock next to a fence marks the exact spot.

Honey, I Blew Up the Kid

(1992). Rick Moranis, Marcia Strassman. Inventor's new machine accidentally inflates his son to 50 times his normal size.

The huge baby walks down Fremont Street in Las Vegas in front of the Pioneer Club (25 East Fremont).

Honeymoon in Vegas

(1992). James Caan, Nicholas Cage. Wealthy gambler offers to erase man's debt in exchange for weekend with loser's fiancée.

Cage, as part of the Flying Elvis jump team, parachutes into the parking lot at Bally's Casino resort (3645 Las Vegas Boulevard South, Las Vegas). He tangles with Caan in Kauai, Hawaii, at the Inn on the Cliffs (3610 Rice Street) when he tries to get Sarah Jessica Parker back.

Honky Tonk Man

(1982). Clint Eastwood, Kyle Eastwood. Broken down country-and-western singer and nephew head for the Grand Ole Opry for a once-in-a-lifetime audition.

Eastwood hits the stage and sings at the Wild Horse Saloon and Gold Canyon Steakhouse, portraying the Victorian-style Europa Bar. The tavern was started in 1887 and is at 160 Main Street in Dayton.

Indecent Proposal

(1993). Robert Redford, Demi Moore. Married woman accepts one million dollars to sleep with another man.

Max Von Sydow delivered "The Sermon on the Mount" from this rock at the edge of a cliff overlooking the Green River in Canyonlands National Park for *The Greatest Story Ever Told*.

Redford meets and makes his offer to Moore while she and Woody Harrelson are staying at the Las Vegas Hilton (3000 Paradise Road).

An Innocent Man

(1989). Tom Selleck, F. Murray Abraham. Crooked cops break into the wrong house and frame homeowner for drug dealing.

The Nevada State Penitentiary (3301 East Fifth Street, Carson City) was used for the exterior shots of the prison where Selleck is wrongly incarcerated. Filmmakers gave the building a more sinister appearance by adding barbed wire, cyclone fencing, perimeters and two guard towers. Prison officials liked the enhancements to their sandstone-walled encampment so much that they retained them after filming was completed. Other prison scenes were staged in The Ohio State Reformatory (100 Reformatory Road, Mansfield, Ohio).

Leaving Las Vegas

(1995). Nicholas Cage, Elisabeth Shue. Writer goes to Las Vegas determined to drink himself to death.

There are scattered street scenes in Las Vegas, including the first time Shue and Cage see each other outside the Stardust Hotel and Casino (3000 Las Vegas Boulevard); he propositions her outside the Flamingo Hilton (3555 Las Vegas Boulevard South); and she asks him to live with her outside

Circus Circus (2880 Las Vegas Boulevard South). Interiors were staged at the River Palms (2700 S. Casino Drive) in Laughlin.

Lethal Weapon 4

(1998). Mel Gibson, Danny Glover. Cops get put on hit list of Asian underworld.

The stunt with the tractor-trailer and the mobile home, where Gibson slides down the highway on a coffee table, was filmed on Highway 215 between Henderson and Las Vegas before it opened.

Lost in America

(1985). Albert Brooks, Julie Hagerty. Yuppies quit their jobs and hit the road as carefree travelers in a motor van.

Brooks loses all their money at the Desert Inn (3145 Las Vegas Boulevard South, Las Vegas) before heading to the Hoover Dam. At the end of their odyssey, Brooks and Hagerty park their van in front of the skyscraper at 9 West 57th Street in New York City.

Melvin and Howard

(1980). Jason Robards, Paul LeMat. Man helps old man with broken motorcycle in desert who claims to be Howard Hughes.

Some of the scenes were shot in Gabbs, the smallest incorporated city in Nevada, 140 miles southeast of Reno. In Las Vegas the courtroom scenes were staged in the Clark County Courthouse (200 South Third Street).

The real Melvin Dummar, the down-on-his-luck factory worker who claimed a part of Howard Hughes' estate, appears in a scene with Mary Steenburgen at the bus station in Reno (Second and Grant Street).

Misery

(1990). Kathy Bates, James Caan. Novelist crashes car and is rescued by deranged fan who imprisons him.

The story is set in the Colorado Rockies but was shot near Lake Tahoe. Caan crashes his car on the old Donner Pass, 30 miles west of Reno in California. The road is accessed off I-80 to Donner, up past Donner Lake and into the town of Soda Springs. The cabin where much of the action takes place is a Forest Service lodge off limits to the public. The store in the movie is the Genoa Country Store (2299 Main Street, Genoa).

The Misfits

(1961). Clark Gable, Marilyn Monroe. Divorcee hooks up with cowboys with an unsavory scheme for wild horses.

The movie, the last for both Gable and Monroe, was shot principally on Main Street in Dayton, ten miles east of Carson City on Highway 50. The rodeo was staged here, and Mia's Restaurant in Odean Hall, which the characters frequent, was built in 1863. In Reno, scenes were filmed in the Mapes Casino (featuring one of three skyrooms in the United States), which operated from 1947 until 1982 and is being restored, and the Washoe County Courthouse (117 South Virginia Street). The original brick building dates to 1873, with a leaded glass dome in the second floor ceiling that was put in by Frederick De Longchamps in 1910.

Ocean's Eleven

(1960). Frank Sinatra, Dean Martin. Eleven friends from World War II plan to rob five of the biggest casinos in Las Vegas in one night.

The five hotel casinos that Sinatra and his cronies plan to hit just after midnight on New Year's Day are the Sahara Hotel & Casino (2535 Las Vegas Boulevard South), the Riviera Hotel and Casino (2901 Las Vegas Boulevard South), the Desert Inn (3145 Las Vegas Boulevard South), the Flamingo Hilton (3555 Las Vegas Boulevard South) and the defunct Sands Hotel and Casino.

Oh, God! You Devil

(1984). George Burns, John Doolittle. God and Satan mix it up over the soul of a young rock star.

Burns, as God, plays Burns, as the Devil, in poker at the Galleria Bar in Caesars Palace (3750 Las Vegas Boulevard South, Las Vegas).

Over the Top

(1987). Sylvester Stallone, Robert Loggia. Man competes with rich father-in-law for the affection of his son.

The climax takes place with Stallone participating in the International Arm Wrestling Championships at the Las Vegas Hilton (300 Paradise Road, Las Vegas).

Oxford Blues

(1984). Rob Lowe, Ally Sheedy. Young American must enroll at Oxford in England to pursue the girl of his dreams.

Before going to England, Lowe lived in Las Vegas, parking cars at the Dunes. It was imploded in 1993.

Pay It Forward

(2000). Kevin Spacey, Helen Hunt. Teacher inspires student to make the world a better place.

Among the many Las Vegas locations used was the All-American Sports Park at 121 East Sunset Road. A homeless camp was built at the southern end of the Strip near Mandalay Bay Road. Spacey teaches at the Centennial School (10200 Centennial Parkway) near Red Rock, 30 miles northwest of Las Vegas.

Pink Cadillac

(1989). Clint Eastwood, Bernadette Peters. Bounty hunter agrees to help his quarry's wife get her baby back.

The Cadillac showroom was Good Deals on Wheels (901 South Virginia Street, Reno), and Eastwood hangs onto the hood of the car as it smashes through the glass doors of the Eldorado Hotel and Casino (345 North Virginia Street, Reno). Other casinos used for interiors were Harrah's (219 North Center, Reno) and John Aseuaga's Nugget (1100 Nugget

Avenue, Sparks). Fuji Park in Carson City (Clear Creek Road off Highway 395) was transformed into the rodeo where Eastwood played a clown.

Play It to the Bone

(1999). Woody Harrelson, Antonio Banderas. Friends agree to box as last-minute fill-ins on a Mike Tyson undercard.

Sequences were shot at Mandalay Bay (3950 Las Vegas Boulevard, Las Vegas) and at the Mad Greek Cafe (Freeway 15 and Baker Boulevard, Baker, California), a popular stop-off for travelers between Las Vegas and Los Angeles.

The Professionals

(1966). Burt Lancaster, Lee Marvin. Four hard-edged adventurers are hired to rescue a kidnapped woman.

Location shooting took place in the Valley of Fire State Park, dedicated in 1935 as Nevada's first state park. The stone ruins of the set can be seen on the White Dome Trail, 1/4 mile from the picnic area. It is the only movie set in the park, as filmmakers are no longer allowed to abandon their sets.

Promised Land

(1988). Jason Gedrick, Tracy Pollan. High school basketball star and cheerleader girlfriend sink from the heights after graduation.

Kiefer Sutherland and Meg Ryan get married at the yellow and white trimmed Silver Bells Wedding Chaple (628 North Virginia Street, Reno).

Roadside Prophets

(1992). John Doe, Adam Horovitz. Two bikers on independent quests team up on the road.

The quirky journey of Doe and Horowitz takes them through Valley of Fire State Park (State Road 169) and on to Lake Mead. Interiors were staged at the Four Jacks Casino (Highway 93, Jackpot).

The Shootist

(1976). John Wayne, Lauren Bacall. Dying gunfighter tries to live out his final days with dignity.

Bacall's boarding house was the Krebs-Peterson House (500 N. Mountain Street, Carson City), built in 1914 and open during the annual Victorian Christmas tour. Wayne, in his last film role, takes Bacall for a buggy ride in Washoe Lake State Park on Highway 395.

Showgirls

(1995). Elizabeth Berkley, Kyle MacLachlan. Young dancer heads to Las Vegas where she is forced to work as a stripper.

Las Vegas Strip locations included the Luxor and Forum Shops (3900 Las Vegas Boulevard), and the exterior of the Stardust (3000 Las Vegas Boulevard).

Sister Act

(1992). Whoopi Goldberg, Maggie Smith. Street-wise lounge singer witnesses mob crime and hides in a convent.

Goldberg witnesses her boyfriend being killed at Fitzgerald's Club (255 North Virginia Street, Reno). Elsewhere in Reno, St. Thomas Aquinas Church (310 West Second Street) plays the Catholic school Goldberg attended as a child, and the Reno Post Office (50 South Virginia Street) doubled as the police station. St. Paul's Catholic Church (221 Valley Street, San Francisco) was transformed into St. Katherine's Convent, where Goldberg hides while waiting to testify.

Star Trek: Generations

(1994). William Shatner, Patrick Stewart. Dead starship captain must help future captain save star system.

The climax occurs as Shatner dies on a mountaintop near the parking lot at the end of Fire Canyon in Valley of Fire State Park (SR 169, Overton). The jagged red sandstone formations of the park appear to be on fire when reflecting the sun's rays.

Swingers

(1996). Jon Faureau, Vince Vaughn. Young men try to get into the dating scene by immersing themselves in lounge culture.

After a long night of gambling, Faureau and Vaughn eat at the buffet in the Fremont Hotel and Casino (200 East Fremont Street) in downtown Las Vegas, although they are shown walking into the Stardust Casino Hotel (3000 Las Vegas Boulevard).

Things Change

(1988). Don Ameche, Joe Mantagna. Shoe-shiner is paid to take murder charge for mafia don.

The Cal-Neva Lodge Resort (Number 2 Stateline Road, Crystal Bay) portrays the fictional Galaxy Hotel where Mantegna takes Ameche for one last fling after coaching him on his phony confession. The original Cal-Neva Lodge was put in business in 1926; after it burned to the ground in 1937, it was rebuilt in just over a month, with 500 men working around the clock.

This Is My Life

(1992). Julie Kavner, Dan Aykroyd. Divorced mother neglects her daughters to pursue a career in comedy.

Kavner uses McCarran Airport (4270 South Valley View Boulevard, Las Vegas) and tests her stand-up act at the Tropicana Hotel (3801 Las Vegas Boulevard South).

Vega$

(1978–1981). Robert Urich, Phyllis Davis. Private detective works cases in Las Vegas.

Urich operated out of the Desert Inn (3145 Las Vegas Boulevard South), and location shots of Las Vegas appeared in nearly every episode.

Vegas Vacation

(1997). Chevy Chase, Beverly D'Angelo. Things go wrong for family on vacation in Nevada.

Most of the casino sequences were shot at the Mirage (3400 Las Vegas Boulevard South, Las Vegas). Also featured is the Chapel of the Bells (2233 Las Vegas Boulevard, Las Vegas). This was the last movie to shoot at the YESCO neon sign graveyard, which no longer exists; the most famous of the signs became the foundation for the Las Vegas Neon Museum (731 S. 4th Street).

Viva Las Vegas

(1964). Elvis Presley, Ann-Margret. Race driver heads for Las Vegas to earn money for a new engine.

The race track scenes were filmed in Henderson, but there is footage of Las Vegas from the 1960s. One sequence features cars zipping across the Hoover Dam, flying around Mt. Charleston and through downtown Las Vegas on Fremont Street.

The Winner

(1996). Rebecca DeMornay, Vincent D'Onofrio. Player wins at roulette each and every Sunday, and low-lifes fight to take advantage of him.

The fictional "Pair-A-Dice" Casino was created at the Liberace Museum (1775 East Tropicana Avenue, Las Vegas), set up by the flamboyant entertainer in 1979 to display his collection of jewelry, antique cars, rare pianos and elaborate costumes from his million-dollar wardrobe.

NEW HAMPSHIRE

The Good Son

(1993). Wendy Crewson, Macauley Culkin. Mother must choose between evil son and visiting nephew.

Culkin throws the dummy he calls "Mr. Highway" from an overpass into traffic on Route 16 in Newington. Culkin lets his sister Quinn Culkin fall through the ice on Mirror Lake (Route 16) in Jackson. In Massachusetts, the exterior of the Pyle House is on Harbor Street in Manchester-by-the-Sea; Culkin and Elijah Wood throw rocks through the window of the Cape Ann Anchor & Forge Company on Whittemoore Street; and the interior scenes with the psychiatrist were shot in the Pegleg Inn (2 King Street, Rockport). The climax was filmed on the cliffs of Palisade Head at the southern end of Tettegouche State Park (Highway 61, Silver Bay, Minnesota).

Jumanji

(1995). Robin Williams, Bonnie Hunt. Kids playing a magic board game find a man trapped inside.

Main Street in Keene, once known for its glass and white pottery, became desolate and graffiti-stained; wild animals stampeded through Central Square.

On Golden Pond

(1981). Henry Fonda, Katharine Hepburn. Woman tries to communicate with distant father through her new step-son.

Now twenty years old, the movie remains the only Hollywood film shot entirely in New Hampshire. The private home in the movie is visited on Squam Lake in Holderness by two boat tour companies.

Return of the Secaucus Seven

(1980). Bruce MacDonald, Maggie Renzi. Seven college friends arrested on the way to protest a march reunite ten years later.

The setting for the reunion was the century-old Ski-Wheelers Lodge, also known as Winwood Lodge (Kearsage Road, North Conway), in the Mt. Washington Valley.

NEW JERSEY

The Amityville Horror

(1979). James Brolin, Margot Kidder. Family moves into new house only to find demonic inhabitants already living there.

Filming took place in Toms River at 18 Boroks Road. The boathouse built for the movie is still there, but the actual house has been renovated, repainted and moved one lot over.

Annie

(1982). Albert Finney, Carol Burnett. Spunky orphan wins over cold-hearted industrial baron.

Woodrow Wilson Hall at Monmouth College in West Long Branch played Finney's Fifth Avenue townhouse mansion in New York City; the lawn of the school library stood in for the White House lawn. The bridge scene in the finale is in East Newark.

Baby It's You

(1983). Rosanna Arquette, Vincent Spano. In 1966 a high-school girl is relentlessly pursued by Frank Sinatra-loving classmate.

Featured in the movie is the Roadside Diner (Collingswood Circle at Routes 33 and 34, Wall), with its bright red roof and equally bright yellow awnings. Interior dormitory shots were filmed at Upsala College in East Orange.

Big

(1988). Tom Hanks, Elizabeth Perkins. Boy wishes to be big at a carnival magic wish machine, and the next day he awakes fully grown.

Filmmakers rented a traveling carnival and staged the beginning and ending scenes on the banks of the Hudson River in Palisades Interstate Park (Alpine Approach Road, Alpine). Hanks and Robert Loggia play "Heart and Soul" and "Chopsticks" with their feet on the giant piano keyboard at FAO Schwarz (767 Fifth Avenue). The scene took two days to shoot in the toy store.

Boys on the Side

(1995). Whoopi Goldberg, Drew Barrymore. Three women travel across the country and become entwined in one anothers' lives.

Mary Louise Parker, suffering from AIDS, gets sick at the Bendix Diner (Route 17 and Williams Avenue, Hasbrouck Heights).

Chasing Amy

(1997). Ben Affleck, Joey Lauren Adams. Man's crush on lesbian friend threatens their relationship.

The movie was filmed in large part in downtown Red Bank; locations include Jacks Music (3 Broad Street), where Affleck and Jason Lee hang out. Affleck learns that Adams is involved with a woman when he hears her sing at the Meow Mix (East Houston and Suffolk streets, Manhattan, New York). Affleck confronts Adams about her past outside the Ocean Ice Palace (197 Chambersridge Road, Brick), and the lead characters fall in love on the swings in Victory Park (River Road, Rumson).

Clerks

(1994). Brian O'Halloran, Jeff Anderson. Disinterested clerk at convenience store tries to get life together.

The central location was the Quick Stop and RST Video (58 Leonard Avenue, Leonardo), the actual store filmmaker Kevin Smith worked at while making the movie when the business was closed. The funeral home was at 59 E. Lincoln Avenue in Atlantic Highlands.

Cop Land

(1997). Sylvester Stallone, Harvey Keitel. Small-town sheriff looks the other way as crooked New York cops settle in.

The fictional New Jersey town of Garrsion was created from scenes shot in Edgewater and Fort Lee. Fort Lee was Hollywood before Hollywood — between 1907 and the end of the silent film era, seven movie studios and 21 movie companies operated here. The cops go to New York City for a bachelor party at Scores (333 East 60th Street).

Coyote Ugly

(2000). Piper Perabo, Tyra Banks. Woman pursues songwriting career and gains notoriety as barmaid in hip Manhattan club.

The Coyote Ugly country bar (153 First Avenue and 9th Street, New York) gained a national reputation as a rowdy dive after it opened in 1993; it subsequently became so overrun by tourists that a sign over the bar snarls, "this ain't the movie." The New Jersey Turnpike toll booth scenes were filmed at the toll booths on Atlantic Beach Bridge on Long Island. Scenes set where the characters live were filmed in Asbury Park, Keansburg and Sea Bright.

Donnie Brasco

(1997). Al Pacino, Johnny Depp. FBI agent goes undercover in the Mob and gets too close.

A featured player in the film is the Tic Toc diner on the north side of Route 3, east on Exit 153 off the Garden State Parkway in Clifton.

Ed

(2000–). Thomas Cavanaugh, Julie Bowen. Lawyer returns to home town and buys bowling alley, where he sets up law practice.

The closed-down Country Club Bowling in Northvale serves at the Stuckeybowl, which Cavanaugh buys. Producers retained 16 of the lanes for bowling scenes and gutted the rest of the building for sound stages. Montclair High School portrays Stuckeyville High School, where Bowen teaches.

Eddie and the Cruisers

(1983). Michael Pare, Tom Berenger. Dead rock and roller is remembered by old band members when an early record is re-released.

The car in which Pare apparently was killed was pulled from the Raritan River near the bridge in Port Republic. Tony Mart's, where the band played in Somers Point, no longer exists. The junkyard scene where Pare hid his lost tapes was filmed at the Auto Recyclers (Route 561, Atco), marked by the distinctive airplane out front.

Family Man

(2000). Nicholas Cage, Tea Leoni. Investment banker gets a chance to see how his life would have turned out had he been married.

Much of the filming took place in Teaneck in the orthodox Jewish neighborhood around Cherry Lane, Morrison and Prince streets and Grange Road. As the movie is about a Christmas story, residents had to get special permission from their rabbis to hang decorations, and they erected a small sign assuring passersby that the Christian icons would be removed immediately after shooting.

Friday the 13th

(1980). Betsy Palmer, Adrienne King. 11 years after boy drowns at a lakeside camp, counselors at newly reopened camp are being murdered.

The camp at Cape Crystal Lake was played by Camp No-Be-Bo-Sco (North Bergen Boy Scouts) at 11 Sand Pond Road in Blairstown.

In and Out

(1997). Kevin Kline, Joan Cusack. High school teacher about to get married is identified as gay by a former student making a speech accepting an Academy Award.

Kline's Greenleaf High was portrayed inside and out by the red brick Pompton Lakes High School (44 Lakeside Avenue, Pompton Lakes). The bar scene with Cusack and Tom Selleck was filmed in the empty Slater's Mill in Riverdale. Lincoln Center in New York City doubled as the exterior for the Oscar ceremony.

IQ

(1994). Tim Robbins, Meg Ryan. Albert Einstein intervenes on behalf of grease monkey suitor of his niece.

Some scenes were filmed in Albert Einstein's actual backyard at 112 Mercer Street in Princeton; the larger home next door was used for interior shots. Andy's Tire and Service Center (130 West Broad Street, Hopewell) became the gas station where Robbins pumps gas and meets Ryan.

It Could Happen to You

(1994). Nicholas Cage, Bridget Fonda. Man promises to share lottery ticket with waitress in lieu of a tip and wins the grand prize.

Cage chases Fonda through the ornate hallways and rotunda of the William F. Brennan Courthouse (575 Newark Avenue, Jersey City). The 1910 building was on its way to being torn down when a single man confronted wrecking crews on the roof, leading to a reprieve and triggering a restoration effort. Yvonne's Diner, where Fonda works and the action for the story is triggered, was specially built for the movie and later disassembled.

Lean on Me

(1989). Morgan Freeman, Beverly Todd. Tyrannical principal takes over decaying inner city school with plans to instill discipline.

The actual Eastside High School in Patterson (150 Park Avenue), where bat-wielding principal Crazy Joe Clark (played by Freeman) worked, was used for filming.

Mortal Thoughts

(1991). Demi Moore, Glenne Headly. Detectives question woman about incidents involving the death of her best friend's abusive husband.

A drunken Bruce Willis is killed in the parking lot of Bowcraft Amusement Park (Route 22, Scotch Plains).

North

(1994). Jason Alexander, Julia Louis Dreyfuss. 11-year-old boy decides to divorce his too-busy parents.

John Ritter and Kate Capshaw take Elijah Wood on an outing to the Bowcraft Amusement Park (Route 22, Scotch Plains). Wood meets Bruce Willis (as the Easter Bunny) in Bridgewater Commons Mall (400 Commons Way, Bridgewater); his secret place to go is a furniture store in the mall.

On the Waterfront

(1954). Marlon Brando, Karl Malden. Priest tries to convince errand boy to testify against racketeers.

The movie was filmed entirely in Hoboken; the docks and the warehouses that provided the gritty backdrop are gone but the Cafe Elysian (1001 Washington Street) and Our Lady of Grace Church (Park Avenue between 4th and 5th streets), where Brando and Eva Marie Saint rendezvous, remain. Filming also took place in Elysian Park (Hudson Street between 10th and 11th streets), site of the first official baseball game in 1846, with a great view of the Manhattan skyline.

One True Thing

(1998). Meryl Streep, Renee Zellweger. Career woman reassesses her life when she quits her job to care for cancer-stricken mother.

The Halloween scene with Zellweger and William Hurt was staged at the Maple Leaf Coffee Shop (165 Maplewood Avenue, Maplewood Village). Some of Hurt's scenes as the head of the English Department at Princeton University were filmed on campus.

Rounders

(1998). Matt Damon, Edward Norton. Reformed gambler returns to poker table to help friend pay off loan sharks.

Rutgers Law School portrayed the fictional City Law School in New York City. Damon helps Norton try an win money at the Trump Taj Mahal (1000 Boardwalk at Virginia Avenue, Atlantic City).

Snake Eyes

(1998). Nicholas Cage, Gary Sinese. Murder takes place in the audience of an important boxing match.

A replica of the Atlantic City boardwalk was built in the parking lot of the Egg Harbor Township High School (24 High School Drive, Egg Harbor Township); special effects were used for the boardwalk scene where the globe rolls down and through a news van. Cage and Sinese make an actual appearance on the Boardwalk in Brighton Park beside the automated sidewalk leading to the Sands (Indiana Avenue and Park Place).

The Sopranos

(1999–). James Gandolfini, Lorraine Bracco. Everyday life of mid-level Mafia family.

The TV series is filmed on location all over north Jersey; one of the most recognizable stars is Satin Dolls (Route 17, Lodi), which plays the Bada Bing Club. The Green Grove retirement community is Green Hill in West Orange (103 Pleasant Valley Way). The family home is in North Caldwell. Interior scenes are shot at the Silvercup Studios in Queens, New York.

Stardust Memories

(1980). Woody Allen, Charlotte Rampling. Successful film director attends festival in honor of his works.

The 6400-seat Great Auditorium in Ocean Grove, the largest auditorium in the world devoted to evangelical Christianity, portrayed the fictional "Hotel Stardust." While making the movie, the impressive white cross above the entrance was replaced. Free organ concerts are held in the Great Auditorium on the world famous 1908 Hope-Jones pipe organ every Wednesday and Saturday.

Stealing Home

(1988). Jodie Foster, Mark Harmon. Man handles ashes of childhood sweetheart who committed suicide.

The beach scenes which Foster and Harmon drive to were shot at Island Beach State Park. In Philadelphia, Harmon and Harold Ramis relive their high school baseball moments at Veterans Stadium (Broad and Pattison streets), and Harmon reveals the truth about his high school romance at Bob's Diner (Lyceum and Ridge avenues).

Wise Guys

(1986). Danny DeVito, Joe Piscopo. Errand boys lose $250,000 and are set up by the Mob to kill each other.

Mafia boss Dan Hedaya runs his operation out of the Castrelo Restaurant (61 Ferry Street, Newark), and threatens DeVito and Piscopo at St. Lucy's Church (corner of Grove and 15th Street, Jersey City). The boys bet on the wrong horse at the Meadowlands Race Track (50 Route 120 East Rutherford).

The World According to Garp

(1982). Robin Williams, Glenn Close. Story of quirky man and mother who writes a feminist book that makes her a magnet for all sorts of troubled women.

Gubernational candidate Close is assassinated in front of the Hartley Dodge Memorial Building (Kings Road and Green Avenue, Madison). The plane crash was staged at Lincoln Park Airport in Lincoln Park, where a house was built on the airstrip. Williams character is forged in his early years at the Steering School, played by Millbrook School (School Road, Millbrook, New York).

NEW MEXICO

And God Created Woman

(1988). Victor Spano, Rebecca DeMornay. Woman marries man to secure her release from prison and then ignores him.

Museum worker Spano is caught in bed with wife DeMornay at the Randall Davey Audubon Center (1800 Upper Canyon Road, Santa Fe) as a tour group comes through.

Contact

(1997). Jodie Foster, Matthew McConnaughy. Astronomer realizes a dream when she detects intelligent radio signals from outer space.

The opening sequences were filmed at the Very Large Array at the National Radio Astronomy Observatory, one hour west of Socorro near the intersection of US highway 60 and New Mexico route 36. Twenty-seven large white antennas are placed across the landscape in the shape of a Y — not to make "contact" but as radio telescopes to accumulate data for computers. A visitor center and self-guiding tours are available to explain radio astronomy. The final scene, as Foster gazes pensively into a canyon sunset, was created on the south rim of Canyon de Chelly National Monument (US 191, Chinle).

The exact spot was near a turnout above the White House Ruins at mile marker 6.4 on the South Rim auto tour. In Washington DC, the balcony scene with Foster and McConaughey was filmed at the Hotel Washington (15th & Pennsylvania Avenue NW).

The Cowboy Way

(1994). Woody Harrelson, Kiefer Sutherland. Two rodeo riders travel to New York to find missing friend.

Before the protagonists leave for the big city, rodeo scenes were shot at the Rio Arriba Fairgrounds in Espanola. Upon arriving in New York City, Sutherland and Harrelson are denied a room at the Waldorf Astoria (301 Park Avenue, New York City) and leave without paying for dinner. They say farewell to cowboy-wannabe Ernie Hudson at Central Park West and Seventh Avenue before heading back to New Mexico.

Gas Food Lodging

(1992). Ione Skye, Brooke Adams. Teen sisters dream of leaving their dreary desert town.

The desert town scenes were filmed on location in Deming; additional sequences were shot among the agate, jasper, fire opal, quartz and amethyst-filled geodes in Rockhound State Park, fourteen miles southeast of town on SR 11.

Hi-Lo Country

(1998). Woody Harrelson, Billy Crudup. Hard-living cowboys fall for the same married woman.

The annual fictional Hi-Lo Rodeo was shot in the town of Galisteo; the house and cemetery were built on the high prairie above Las Vegas; and snow scenes were created on a sound stage built at the College of Santa Fe. In Pritchett, Colorado, three downtown blocks were dressed up to recreate street scenes in the 1940s.

Indiana Jones and the Last Crusade

(1989). Harrison Ford, Sean Connery. Archaeologist and father look for the Holy Grail and battle Nazis.

The opening sequence, with River Phoenix being chased atop a circus train, was staged on the Cumbres and Toltec Scenic Railroad between the Antonito, Colorado, and Chama, New Mexico, stations. Railroad trips aboard the old narrow-gauge coal-burning trains climb through the rugged San Juan and Sangre de Cristo mountain ranges. The final scene, with Ford and Connery riding off into the sunset, was created at the Cowboy Morning Figure 3 Ranch (Route 1 off I-27, Claude). The guest ranch is open to the public.

King Solomon's Mines

(1950). Stewart Granger, Deborah Kerr. African guide falls in love with woman as they search for her husband.

Carlsbad Caverns National Park stood in for the Sahara Desert for Granger, Kerr and their collection of porters. The desolate terrain around the enormous limestone cave lies in the foothills of the Guadalupe Mountains.

The Man Who Fell to Earth

(1976). David Bowie, Rip Torn. Humanoid is sent to earth to get water for his dying planet.

The primary location for the alien landing was Fenton Lake State Park (455 Fenton Lake Road), a 35-acre lake set in a forest of ponderosa pines.

The Milagro Beanfield War

(1988). Ruben Blades, Richard Bradford. Dispute over water between farmers and real estate developer in small desert town.

The movie was filmed entirely in the small town of Truchas near Taos on the Old High Road to Taos. The subsistence agricultural community was established by a Spanish land grant in 1754.

Natural Born Killers

(1994). Woody Harrelson, Juliette Lewis. Psychopathic lovers and serial killers become media darlings.

The prison riot scene was shot at the Stateville Correctional Facility (Highway 53, Crest Hill) where 342 maximum security prisoners were cleared to act in the melee. The exterior of the courthouse was shot at the Chicago Cultural Center (78 East Washington Street, Chicago). Harrelson and Lewis are "married" on the Taos Gorge Bridge, and are captured in the old Phar-Mor Grocery off Coors Road in Rio Rancho.

Red Dawn

(1984). Patrick Swayze, C. Thomas Howell. Eight Midwestern teens defend their homeland against the Russians at the start of WWIII.

The invasion begins with Russian paratroopers jumping into the football field at Memorial Middle School (Old National Road and Legion Drive). The Russians then set up headquarters in the La Castaneda Hotel (524 Railroad Avenue, Las Vegas). The secret hideout for the tiny band of underaged defenders was filmed in an abandoned grocery store. The Center Block (corner of Grand and East Lincoln streets), an 1899 pharmacy with distinctive Richardsonian arches was set on fire for the movie, which was tabbed by the Guinness Book of World records for most acts of violence. Although the century-old building has been since renovated, some of the fire damage can still be seen on the outside.

Silkwood

(1983). Meryl Streep, Kurt Russell. Death of nuclear plant worker may have been linked to wrongdoing at the plant.

Scenes were filmed in Albuquerque at the Albuquerque Airport and at the Los Alamos National Laboratories.

Speechless

(1994). Michael Keaton, Geena Davis. Two political speechwriters fall in love and discover they are working for opposing candidates.

Keaton and Davis meet in the La

Castaneda Hotel (524 Railroad Avenue, Las Vegas), a mission Revival-style hotel that was the crown jewel in Fred Harvey's chain of Harvey Houses serving the passenger train trade. Other scenes were filmed in Albuquerque, Santa Fe and Los Alamos.

Twins

(1988). Arnold Schwarzenegger, Danny DeVito. Mismatched brothers of a failed genetic experiment discover each other after 35 years.

Twins Schwarzenegger and DeVito come to terms with their family ties eating lunch outside the Palace of Governors (105 W. Palace Avenue, Santa Fe), built in 1610 and one of the oldest public buildings in the United States. Guided tours are available. Later they buy identical clothes at The Plaza. The Randall Davey Audubon Center (1800 Upper Canyon Road, Santa Fe) played the artist colony called Whispering Pines, where the twins search for their mother. After driving across the Rio Grande Gorge Bridge they continue the hunt at the Mabel Dodge Luhan House (240 Morada Road, Taos).

White Sands

(1992). Willem Dafoe, Mickey Rourke. Sheriff finds body in the desert with $500,000 in a suitcase and sets out to impersonate the man.

Sheriff Dafoe meets suspect Rourke at the La Fonda Hotel (100 East San Francisco Street, Santa Fe). Mary Elizabeth Mastantonio's home is the Mabel Dodge Luhan House (240 Morado Road, Taos), two blocks east of Taos Plaza. The titular white sands were filmed at the White Sands National Monument in south central New Mexico.

Popular New Mexico Locations

NEW MEXICO MOVIE RANCHES

In 1985 a pasture in northeastern New Mexico outside Santa Fe was swiftly transformed into a Western town with three streets and 38 building fronts for the filming of the movie *Silverado* (Kevin Kline, Scott Glenn). The Cook Ranch quickly became a favorite for Hollywood directors needing clear skies and big spaces. Warner Brothers purchased Cook Ranch in anticipation of the shooting of *Wild Wild West* (Will Smith, Kevin Kline); during special effects explosions a wind-whipped fire burned down many of the wooden buildings, which the studio planned to rebuild.

Other New Mexico movie ranches have also enjoyed heavy Hollywood traffic. The Eaves Movie Ranch, 14 miles from Santa Fe on the way to Cerillos, hosted movies such as *Chisum* (John Wayne, Forrest Tucker) and *Wyatt Earp* (Kurt Russell, Val Kilmer); Bonanza Creek Ranch was the setting for *Man from Laramie* (Jimmy Stewart, Arthur Kennedy) and *The Legend of the Lone Ranger* (Klinton Spilsbury, Michael Horse); and the Ghost Ranch was where *City Slickers* (Billy Crystal, Jack Palance) and *The Groove Tube* (Chevy Chase, Richard Belzer) among many other movies, was shot.

NEW YORK

Addicted to Love

(1997). Matthew Broderick, Meg Ryan. Man and woman seek to break up happy couple who used to be their lovers.

Jilted lovers Broderick and Ryan plot their revenge at the Performance Pit in Washington Square Park in Manhattan. As part of his scheme, Broderick takes a job as a dishwasher in Raoul's Restaurant Francais (180 Prince Street) to get back at owner Tcheky Karyo. Also featured is the Sproul Observatory on the campus of Swarthmore College (Route 320, Swarthmore, Pennsylvania).

An Affair to Remember

(1957). Cary Grant, Deborah Kerr. Shipboard lovers agree to reunite six months later.

Grant waits in vain for Kerr, who has suffered an accident en route to the prearranged meeting place on the observation deck of the Empire State Building (350 Fifth Avenue, Manhattan).

After Hours

(1985). Griffin Dunne, Rosanna Arquette. The later it gets the stranger it gets in one night of a man's life in New York City.

Dunne spends most of his time learning about life in the wee hours at the Club Berlin, once the historic Half Note jazz club and now the Thomas Nordanstad Gallery at 289 Hudson Street in Manhattan. He meets Arquette at the River Diner (452 11th Avenue and 37th Street) and finds Teri Garr waitressing at the Emerald Pub at 308 Spring Street. His late night odyssey began after a normal work day in the Metropolitan Life Insurance Company building (11 Madison Avenue).

The Age of Innocence

(1993). Daniel Day-Lewis, Michelle Pfeiffer. Well-bred Victorian-age man is set to marry similarly well-bred young woman, but he is more attracted to a somewhat scandalous beauty.

The 19th century New York opera house in the opening scene where Day-Lewis first sees Pfeiffer is played by the Academy of Music (Broad and Locust streets) in Philadelphia. In New York, Old Bethpage Village was brought back to the 1870s for the movie. The Rensselaer Polytechnic Institute's Pi Kappa Phi fraternity house (Second Street, Troy) played the New York City home of Miriam Margolyes. Day-Lewis' law office on Wall Street was portrayed by the Rice Building (First and River streets). Washington Park in Troy, one of only two private parks in the nation, stood in for the other — Manhattan's Gramercy Park. The garden can be viewed from beyond a fence, but only residents may enter.

Alice

(1990). Mia Farrow, Joe Mantegna. Ailing woman consults herbalist who prescribes magic potion.

Rendered invisible by magic, Farrow enters the Ralph Lauren Store (867 Madison Avenue, Manhattan). Farrow and Mantegna carry on their affair with a meal at Barbetta (321 West 46th Street, Manhattan) where she offers up the magic potion that turns them both invisible.

Analyze This

(1999). Robert DeNiro, Billy Crystal. Psychiatrist's main patient is an insecure mobster.

In a flashback to the 1950s, the cop sits on his motorcycle in front of The Muscoot, a bar at the corner of Route 35 and 100 in Somers. DeNiro suffers a panic attack at Elmhurst General Hospital (79–01 Broadway, Elmhurst, Queens), which he believes to be a heart attack. He meets with fellow mobsters in the Old Lion Social Club (Todt Hill, Staten Island).

Annie Hall

(1977). Woody Allen, Diane Keaton. Neurotic singer hooks up with equally neurotic girlfriend.

Keaton and Allen people-watch at Bethesda Fountain in Central Park. Allen's favorite film, *The Sorrow and the Pity*, played at the now-closed Thalia (250 West 95th Street, Manhattan). The break-up lunch was filmed in an outdoor cafe at 8301 Sunset Boulevard in West Hollywood, California.

The Apartment

(1960). Jack Lemmon, Shirley MacLaine. Man tries to climb the corporate ladder by loaning his apartment to executives for secret trysts.

Lemmon waits for MacLaine to show up in front of the Majestic Theatre (245 West 44th Street, Manhattan), unaware that she is at his apartment with his boss, Fred McMurray.

Arthur

(1981). Dudley Moore, Liza Minnelli. Unambitious drunk set to inherit a fortune by marrying falls in love with a poor girl.

Locations for Moore's home on Long Island were filmed at Old Westbury Gardens (71 Old Westbury Road, Old Westbury) and at the entrance gate to Planting Fields Arboretum, a 400-acre recreation park designed by the Olmstead brothers on Planting Fields Road in Oyster Bay. In New York City, Moore brings a hooker to the Oak Room in the Plaza Hotel (Fifth Avenue and Central Park South) and walks out on his marriage to Jill Eikenberry in the final scene at St. Bartholomew's Church (Park Avenue between 50th and 51st streets). The exterior for Geraldine Fitzgerald's home in Manhattan was shot at the National Design Museum (2 East 91st Street), built as Andrew Carnegie's 64-room mansion in 1898.

Bang the Drum Slowly

(1973). Robert DeNiro, Michael Moriarty. Baseball player opens season knowing he has terminal disease.

The scenes featuring Moriarty

pitching and DeNiro catching and delivering clutch hits for the fictional New York Mammoths were filmed at Shea Stadium in Flushing.

Barefoot in the Park

(1967). Robert Redford, Jane Fonda. Newlyweds make their way in a fifth-floor walk-up apartment.

Although the interiors were shot in Hollywood, the exteriors for the building where Fonda and Redford lived were shot at 111 Waverly Place in Manhattan. They honeymoon at the Plaza Hotel (Fifth Avenue and Central Park South). The park in which Redford dances barefoot near the end of the movie is Washington Square.

The Bonfire of the Vanities.

(1990). Tom Hanks, Bruce Willis. Car accident causes world to fall apart for successful commodities trader.

Willis begins to tell Hank's story at a party staged at the World Financial Center (200 Liberty Street, Manhattan). Hanks and Kim Cattrall lived in a multi-level apartment at 800 Park Avenue, and his mistress (Melanie Griffith) lived in an apartment at 346 East 55th Street. Willis and Clifton James discuss the hit-and-run incident in the Bronx while walking through the Atlas Building (630 Fifth Avenue) and past the statue of Atlas.

Breakfast at Tiffanys

(1961). Audrey Hepburn, George Peppard. Young woman kept by rich older man meets young man kept by rich older woman.

Hepburn admires the window displays in the windows of Tiffany & Company (727 Fifth Avenue at 57th Street, Manhattan) early in the morning after being up all night on a date. Later, she gets to go inside with suitor Peppard, and they ask for something in the $10 range. Tiffany's, which dates to 1837, stationed 40 security guards around the store during a Sunday shoot. The exteriors of Hepburn's brownstone were filmed at 171 East 71st Street; the interiors were shot on a Hollywood sound stage.

Bright Lights, Big City

(1988). Michael J. Fox, Keifer Sutherland. Young man from Kansas has trouble adjusting to faster lifestyle in New York City.

Fox worked as a fact-checker for the fictional Graham magazine at the Art Deco Fred French Building (551 Fifth Avenue). One of the places he went was Chumley's in Greenwich Village, a signless tavern that was once a speakeasy during Prohibition, at 86 Bedford Street. The term "to 86 something" (as in getting rid of it) originated here in reference to the removal of a drink off the table in a hurry.

Broadway Danny Rose

(1984). Woody Allen, Mia Farrow. Talent agent is more father than agent while handling fringe acts.

Old comedians tell the story of Allen's hard-luck talent agent at the Carnegie Deli (854 Seventh Avenue, Manhattan). Also featured is the Waldorf Astoria (301 Park Avenue).

Brothers McMullen

(1995). Edward Burns, Mike McGlone. Three brothers use strong family bonds to navigate through relationships with women.

Shooting locations in and around New York City included writer and director Burns' family home. Others included the running track beside the Central Park Reservoir, where McGlone confronts Shari Albert about their relationship, and the Grange Hall, where Burns dines with Peter Johansen (50 Commerce Street).

Buffalo 66

(1998). Christina Ricci, Vincent Gallo. Newly released convict kidnaps a teenage girl and convinces her to pose as his wife to impress his parents.

Recckio's Lanes (2426 S. Park Avenue, Buffalo) was used for the bowling sequences. The lockers were imported, but the phone booth featured is there; the bowling took place on Lane number 13.

Bullets Over Broadway

(1994). John Cusack, Jack Warden. Young playwright in the 1920s turns to a gangster to get his play produced.

Cusack is finally able to stage his play "God of Our Fathers" at the Belasco Theater (111 West 44th Street, between 6th and 7th avenues, Manhattan). The theater, started by David Belasco in 1906, is housed in a Colonial Revival building designed by George Keister.

Cocktail

(1988). Tom Cruise, Elisabeth Shue. Hip bartenders play fast with the drinks and the ladies.

Cruise and Bryan Brown "reigned as they poured" as bartenders at the Northeast Corner (First Avenue and 63rd Street, Manhattan). Cruise and Lisa Banes break up in volatile fashion on Broadway between 67th and 68th streets. The island bar scenes were shot on location in Jamaica.

Coming to America

(1988). Eddie Murphy, Arsenio Hall. African prince arrives in New York to find a bride.

James Earl Jones stays at the Waldorf Astoria (301 Park Avenue, Manhattan) when he comes to retrieve the free spending Murphy. Murphy and Hall naturally assume that Queens is where they can find suitable brides and head for that borough, where they visit a McDowell's fast food joint — which was played by a Wendy's on Queen Boulevard in Elmhurst.

Cosby

(1984–1992). Bill Cosby, Phylicia Rashad. Doctor and lawyer raise large family in New York City.

The exteriors of the Cosby family home in the television series were shot at 10 St. Luke's Place, a block of 15 elegant Italianate townhouses between Seventh Avenue South and Hudson Street.

The Cotton Club

(1984). Richard Gere, Gregory Hines. Stories about patrons who frequent a famous jazz club in Harlem in the 1920s.

James Remar keeps his moll Diane Lane in bohemian style at the Apthorp Apartments (2017–2109 Broadway, Manhattan). In the film's finale, Gere and Lane board the Twentieth Century Limited for California in the 1913 Beaux Arts Grand Central Terminal (42nd Street between Lexington and Vanderbilt avenues).

Crimes and Misdemeanors

(1989). Woody Allen, Martin Landau. The paths of one man trying to end an affair and another trying to initiate one entwine.

Allen and Landau discuss the emotional ramifications that come with getting away with murder at a wedding held in the Waldorf Astoria (301 Park Avenue, Manhattan). Later, a reception is held for Landau at the Tavern on the Green (Central Park at West 67th Street); his mistress, Anjelica Huston, lives at 359 East 68th Street.

Crocodile Dundee

(1986). Paul Hogan, Linda Kozlowski. Australian adventurer escorts American reporter through bush country and then accompanies her to even more dangerous New York City.

When he came to New York, Hogan stayed at the Plaza Hotel (Fifth Avenue and Central Park South). He thumps a pimp, thinking he is protecting two hookers, outside a corner bar at Avenue B and 7th Street. The scene where a potential mugger pulls a knife on him and Hogan responds, "That's a knife? *This* is a knife," was shot in the abandoned lower level of the BMT Ninth Avenue subway station in Brooklyn.

Crocodile Dundee II

(1988). Paul Hogan, Linda Kozlowski. Australian outback expert must now protect New York girlfriend in his native bush country.

Exteriors for the mobsters' house were filmed at the Vanderbilt Museum (Little Neck Road, 1.5 miles north of SR 25A, Centerport). The Spanish Revival–style mansion overlooking Northport Harbor is open for tours and features a planetarium.

Crossing Delancey

(1988). Amy Irving, Peter Riegert. Modern woman resists the efforts of her Old-World grandmother to get her married.

Riegert works as a pickle man at Guss's Pickle Stand (35 Essex Street, Manhattan). Jeroen Krabbé takes Irving to the Restaurant Provence (38 MacDougal Street, Manhattan) on their first date.

Desperately Seeking Susan

(1985). Rosanna Arquette, Madonna. Bored woman assumes the identity of a woman she learns about in the personal ads.

Arquette first reads the personal ad for Desperately Seeking Susan in the Nubest and Company Salon (1482 Northern boulevard, Manhasset). Madonna trades her pyramid jacket—which Arquette eventually purchases—for some rhinestone boots at the Love Saves The Day boutique (119 2nd Avenue, Manhattan). While tracking Madonna, Arquette follows her from Battery Park to St. Marks Place, where she spills a vendor's cart in front of the Dojo Restaurant (14 W. 4th Street in Greenwich Village). Aidan Quinn works as a projectionist in the Bleecker Street Cinema, which operated in the Federal-style building of the Mori Restaurant (144 Bleecker Street). The two-screen art house is no longer in business.

Dog Day Afternoon

(1975). Al Pacino, Penelope Allen. Man's desperate bank robbery turns into a hostage situation and then a media circus.

The story is based on a true robbery of a Chase Manhattan branch in Brooklyn. The bank that Pacino robs to pay for his male lover's sex change operation was created from a transformed garage on 10th Street in Brooklyn's Flatbush section.

The Dream Team

(1989). Michael Keaton, Christopher Lloyd. Four mental patients become separated from their doctor on a field trip to New York.

When their trip to Yankee Stadium ends in shambles, Keaton, Lloyd, Peter Boyle and Stephen Furst make their way across the 44th Street Median between Broadway and Seventh Avenue with an empty refrigerator carton over their heads to protect them from the rain. The four show up at the Kenilworth (151 Central Park West at 75th Street), where Keaton's girlfriend lives.

Everyone Says I Love You

(1996). Edward Norton, Drew Barrymore. Love story among rich Manhattanites spills over to Europe and gets complicated.

Norton sings to Barrymore near the fountains in front of the Metropolitan Museum of Art (1000 Fifth Avenue and 82nd Street) and buys her an engagement ring during a shopping spree at Harry Winston Jewelers (718 Fifth Avenue). Julia Roberts buys her airline ticket to Paris at the Air France office on 120 West 56th Street.

Eyewitness

(1981). William Hurt, Sigourney Weaver. Janitor with a fixation on local newscaster gets a chance to meet her when he finds a corpse in the building where he works.

Hurt happens upon a dead man while doing his job as a janitor at the high-rise at 330 Park Avenue South in Manhattan and pretends to know something more to keep Weaver interested in him. Weaver lives in the Apthorp Apartments (171 West 71st Street). Hurt and Christopher Plummer grapple among horses at the

Claremont Riding Academy (175 West 89th Street) in the finale.

Fame

(1980). Irene Cara, Lee Curreri. Four aspiring performers get accepted at New York's High School for the Performing Arts.

The actual High School for the Performing Arts did not permit shooting, so filming took place at the abandoned Haaren High School building on 899 Tenth Avenue and 59th Street. The exotic seven-story Flemish-style building began life in 1906 as DeWitt Clinton high School.

Fatal Attraction

(1987). Michael Douglas, Glenn Close. Woman from one-night stand begins to stalk man and his family.

Douglas meets Close for the first time at a Saturday meeting in the HarperCollins Building (10 East 53rd Street, Manhattan). After Close kidnaps Ellen Hamilton Latzen, she takes her to Playland Amusement Park (Playland Parkway off Exit 19 of I-95, Rye) and rides the Dragon Coaster. The 1923 fun park still features many original Art Deco buildings and was one of the earliest totally planned amusement parks in America.

The First Wives Club

(1996). Goldie Hawn, Diane Keaton. Three divorced women seek revenge on husbands who left them for younger women.

Old friends Keaton, Hawn and Bette Midler reunite after the funeral of a friend and hatch their plans at Cafe des Artistes (1 West 67th Street, Manhattan). Elsewhere in New York, Keaton auctions off all the belongings of Victor Garber and Hawn at Christie's, now Hotel Dominico (502 Park Avenue); Hawn tries to drink away her troubles at the King Cole Bar in the St. Regis Hotel (2 East 55th Street); Hawn appears as a mother in the play "Of a Certain Age" at the Plymouth Theatre (236 West 45th Street); and the E.S. Vandam gallery (100 Vandam Street) makes an appearance.

The Fisher King

(1991). Jeff Bridges, Robin Williams. Suicidal radio disc jockey finds redemption through unusual homeless man who was the victim of his horrible mistake.

Before his life disintegrated after making irresponsible comments about a shooting spree on the radio, Bridges lived at 146 West 57th Street in New York City. Bridges searches for the Holy Grail at the castle-like Armory at Hunter College (Madison Avenue between 94th and 95th streets). The rush hour throng begins to waltz as Williams chases his beloved Amanda Plummer through the Main Room of Grand Central Station.

For Love or Money

(1993). Michael J. Fox, Gabrielle Anwar. Hotel concierge falls for mistress of powerful tenant.

Fox works every angle for money while running the concierge at the fictional Bradbury in Manhattan, played by the Pierre Hotel (Fifth Avenue between 60th and 61st streets). Fox spies on Anwar through the window of the San Domenico eatery at 240 Central Park South, and buys a large stuffed giraffe at FAO Schwarz (767 Fifth Avenue, Manhattan).

The Freshman

(1990). Marlon Brando, Matthew Broderick. Young student falls in with Mafia family after losing all his belongings.

Much of the movie was filmed in Canada, but scenes were shot at New York University (Fourth Street, Manhattan) where Broderick attends classes. Upon his arrival in New York City, Broderick falls down the staircase at Grand Central Station at the West Balcony and Vanderbilt Avenue with all his luggage and meets con man Bruno Kirby.

Ghost

(1990). Patrick Swayze, Demi Moore. After being killed in a mugging, a man's deep love enables him to remain on earth in spirit.

Swayze and Moore share a loft in New York City at 112 Mercer Street; his death is staged on Crosby Street between Prince and Spring streets. Whoopi Goldberg meets Moore for the first time at Mezzogiorno restaurant (195 Spring Street). Goldberg gives blood money that Swayze helps her liberate from Tony Goldwyn's bank account to two nuns who have set up a station at the base of the statue of George Washington on the site of his first inaugural at Federal Hall (28 Wall Street). The current Greek Revival building was opened in 1842.

Ghostbusters

(1984). Dan Aykroyd, Bill Murray. Three unemployed parapsychology professors start a ghost removal service.

The firehouse for Hook and Ladder Company No. 8 (14 North Moore Street) was used for exterior shots of the Ghostbusters headquarters; interiors were filmed in a decommissioned firehouse in Los Angeles. Sigourney Weaver lived in the building at 55 Central Park West. Since the building was only 19 stories tall, the scenes of the haunted temple on the roof were filmed with models and matte paintings. Murray finally wins a date with Weaver at the Fountain Plaza in Lincoln Center. Rick Moranis is chased through Central Park by a red-eyed terror dog and stops to bang on the window of the Crystal Room of the Tavern on the Green (Central Park at West 67th Street) to get the attention of diners, and the Stay-Puft Marshmallow Man materializes out of the building at Two Columbus Circle.

Ghostbusters II

(1989). Dan Aykroyd, Bill Murray. Too much negative energy from New Yorkers triggers massive slime attack.

The Statue of Liberty on Liberty Island comes to life and brings Murray, Aykroyd and Harold Ramis back into business. Sigourney Weaver works at the fictional Manhattan Museum of Art, portrayed by the National Museum of the American Indian (1 Bowling Green), where a Carpathian painting she is working on springs to life. The triumphant final scene takes place on the steps of this Cass Gilbert–designed Beaux Arts building in lower Manhattan.

The Godfather

(1972). Marlon Brando, Al Pacino. Son of Mafia boss uninvolved in the family business must take over when war breaks out.

Two Tudor-styled homes—at 110 and 120 Longfellow Road in Staten Island—were combined to portray the Corleone estate; the wedding scene was staged in the garden at 120 Longfellow. Richard Conte is gunned down on the courthouse steps of the New York County Supreme Court (60 Centre Street, Manhattan). The scene with the horse head in the bed was shot at Falaise, a 1923 Normandy-style manor house in the Sands Point Preserve (Middleneck Road, Port Washington), which is open for tours. Also on Long Island, James Caan was machine-gunned to death at the toll booth while listening to the 1951 New York Giants–Brooklyn Dodgers play-off game on an abandoned runway in Mitchell Field. The featured burial ground was the Calvary Cemetery (49–02 Laurel Hill Boulevard, Woodside, Queens), opened in 1948. With more than 2,500,000 interments in Queens, there are more people buried there than are living there.

Godzilla

(1998). Matthew Broderick, Jean Reno. Giant radiation-fueled lizard comes to Manhattan to build a nesting site.

Godzilla comes ashore in New York City as mayor Michael Lerner is giving a speech in front of the Federal Building (28 Wall Street); the giant lizard's first step from the east River is onto South Street at the seaport. Broderick tries to lure Godzilla into a trap by dumping truckloads of fish in the intersection between the Flatiron Building and 200 Fifth Avenue.

The Goodbye Girl

(1977). Marsha Mason, Richard Dreyfuss. Man sublets apartment, unaware that owner's girlfriend is still living there.

The apartment which Mason and Dreyfuss agree to share was on Manhattan's Upper West Side at 170 78th Street and Amsterdam.

Goodfellas

(1990). Robert DeNiro, Ray Liotta. Local boy works his way up through the Mob.

Liotta testifies against fellow mobsters DeNiro and Paul Sorvino at the New York County Supreme Court (60 Centre Road, Manhattan).

Green Card

(1990). Andie MacDowell, Gerard Depardieu. Man marries to stay in the United States, but the relationship takes an unexpected turn.

MacDowell and Depardieu get to know each other while strolling about the Bethesda Fountain in New York's Central Park and defend their marriage with a test at 26 Federal Plaza. MacDowell lives in an airy apartment at 60 West 76th Street.

Hannah and Her Sisters

(1986). Woody Allen, Mia Farrow. Lives criss-cross over a holiday weekend.

Allen spies his former "awful blind date" Dianne Wiest at Tower Records (1961 Broadway, Manhattan). Michael Caine arranges to bump into Barbara Hershey at the Pageant Book and Print Shop (114 West Houston Street), and they have the first meeting of their affair at The St. Regis Hotel (2 East 55th Street).

Heartburn

(1986). Jack Nicholson, Meryl Streep. Marriage unravels when husband has affair while wife is pregnant.

Streep's first meeting with Nicholson takes place at the Tavern on the Green (Central Park at West 67th Street) in Manhattan, and she later escapes her marital woes by taking refuge in her father's apartment in the Apthorp Apartments (2207 Broadway). The 12-story limestone Renaissance Revival building was erected in 1908.

Hide in Plain Sight

(1980). James Caan, Jill Eikenberry. Divorced man seeks children after they are placed in the witness protection program with their mother.

Filmed mostly in Buffalo, where this true story occurred in 1967, locations include the steps of City Hall on Niagara Square and Delaware Park on Parkside Avenue.

The House on 92nd Street

(1945). William Eythe, Lloyd Nolan. FBI infiltrates NAZI agents operating in New York City during World War II.

In this groundbreaking film shot almost entirely on location, the house that was a front for German spies was actually Elsa's Gowns on 53 East 93rd Street. Now torn down, its identical twin is now the Alamo Apartments at 55 East 93rd Street.

How to Marry a Millionaire

(1953). Lauren Bacall, Marilyn Monroe. Tired of men with no money going nowhere, three models set out to trap rich husbands.

The centerpiece of Bacall, Monroe and Betty Grable's plan to trap rich guys is the $1000-a-month apartment they set up at 36 Sutton Place on the Upper East side of Manhattan. Only the exterior of the building was used in the movie. Fred Clark, trying to sneak back into New York City after a dud of a weekend with Grable, is stopped at the George Washington

Bridge and given a ride across the Hudson River with great fanfare as the 50 millionth vehicle to cross.

Ironweed

(1987). Jack Nicholson, Meryl Streep. Street people struggle to survive during the Depression in Albany, New York.

Nicholson and Streep enjoy a meal at the Miss Albany Diner (893 Broadway, Albany), distinguished by its rich ceramic tile floor in a brick-colored geometric pattern. In Troy, Washington Park was used. Locations in Hudson included Gold's Scrapyard on Columbia Street and a grave digger scene shot with Nicholson and Tom Waits.

It Should Happen to You

(1954). Judy Holliday, Peter Lawford. Documentary filmmaker falls in love with model who is only interested in advancing her career.

Filmmaker Jack Lemmon discovers Holliday while filming a documentary at the Bethesda Fountain in Central Park; they live at 115 West 69th Street in Manhattan.

Just the Ticket

(1999). Andy Garcia, Andie MacDowell. Man who lords over New York City's illegal ticket trade tries for one big score when the Pope visits.

The Pope's Easter Mass is staged at Yankee Stadium. Other locations include the Metropolitan Museum of Art, Madison Square Garden, Shubert Alley, and Herald Square.

King Kong

(1976). Jeff Bridges, Charles Grodin. An expedition to a strange island captures a giant ape and brings him to civilization.

The classic original 1933 story was filmed completely in Hollywood; and, to the great consternation of its owners, the Empire State Building was passed over for the World Trade Center (1 and 2 World Trade Center, Manhattan, destroyed by terrorists on September 11, 2001) when this remake went shooting on location. The final sequences were filmed amidst great fanfare and thousands of New York City extras. Bridges and Jessica Lange set up a reconnaissance camp on Honopu Beach on the island of Kauai in Hawaii.

King of New York

(1990). Christopher Walken, Laurence Fishburne. Former drug lord returns from prison determined to wipe out all the competition and distribute the profits to New York's poor.

Latter-day Robin Hood Walken uses the Plaza Hotel (Fifth Avenue and Central Park South, Manhattan) as his base of operations. The bloody gang shootout between Walken and Joey Chin takes place at the intersection of Doyers Street and Pell Street in Chinatown.

Kojak

(1973–1978). Telly Savalas, Kevin Dobson. Flamboyant police detective works the streets of New York.

Savalas operated out of the 9th Precinct Police Station (321 East Fifth Street, Manhattan).

Kramer Vs. Kramer

(1979). Dustin Hoffman, Meryl Streep. Newly divorced man learns to take care of his son and then must fight for custody of him.

Hoffman takes Justin Henry on a tour of New York City landmarks, saving his most lavish praise for the Chrysler Building (405 Lexington Avenue). Interiors and exteriors of Federal Hall (28 Wall Street) were used to portray the courthouse for the custody battle scenes; also used was the Tweed Courthouse (52 Chambers Street).

Law and Order

(1990–). Jerry Orbach, Sam Waterston. New York County police work to apprehend criminals, and the district attorney's office works to convict them.

Many scenes of the television series are filmed in the hallways and on the front steps of the New York County Supreme Court building (60 Centre Road, Manhattan).

Legal Eagles

(1986). Robert Redford, Debra Winger. District attorney is drawn into case with attractive defense lawyer and flaky client.

Redford delivers a speech to the Manhattan Legal Society at the Meridien Hotel (118 West 57th Street, Manhattan). He and Winger interrupt Terrence Stamp during an auction at Sotheby's (York Avenue and 72nd Street) and defend Darryl Hannah at the New York County Supreme Court (60 Centre Road).

Life with Mikey

(1993). Michael J. Fox, Christina Vidal. Former child star grows up to be manager of potential child stars.

Fox discovers his next protégé when Vidal tries to pick his pocket outside the American Museum of Natural History (Central Park West at West 79th Street, Manhattan). He worked out of an office in the Seagram Building (375 Park Avenue at 52nd Street, Manhattan).

The Long Kiss Goodnight

(1996). Geena Davis, Samuel Jackson. Amnesic homemaker bumps her head and begins to remember a previous life as a secret agent.

Though the movie was filmed mostly in Canada, the final sequence is shot on the Rainbow Bridge at Niagara Falls.

Love Affair

(1994). Warren Beatty, Annette Bening. Shipboard lovers agree to reunite three months later to see if attraction was real.

Beatty checks into the Essex House (160 Central Park South, Manhattan) upon arriving in New York City to keep the rendezvous with Bening.

Mad About You

(1992–1999). Helen Hunt, Paul Reiser. Young marrieds balance professional and personal lives in New York City.

After meeting at a newsstand while looking for the *New York Times*, Hunt and Reiser make their home in this television series on the southeast corner of 12th Street and Fifth Avenue in Manhattan.

Malcolm X

(1992). Denzel Washington, Angela Bassett. Story of radical American Muslim leader.

Washington and Bassett have their first date at the American Museum of Natural History (Central Park West at West 79th Street); later, Washington checks in to the Hilton Hotel (6th Avenue and 54th Street) against the wishes of his advisors. Ridgewood in Queens stood in for Boston.

Man on the Moon

(1999). Jim Carrey, Danny DeVito. Story of tormented comic Andy Kaufman.

The filmmakers were not able to use Kaufman's real childhood home in Great Neck, but they were able to shoot two houses in the same neighborhood on Bayview Avenue for interiors and exteriors. Most of the movie was filmed in Los Angeles.

Manhattan

(1979). Woody Allen, Diane Keaton. Man's wife leaves him for a woman and starts to write a book revealing private details of his marriage.

In the opening scene, Allen, Mariel Hemingway, Michael Murphy, and Anne Byrne dine at Elaine's (1703 second Avenue between 88th and 89th streets) while engaging in a philosophical discussion. Other Manhattan scenes include Allen and Keaton sitting on a bench at the foot of the 59th Street Bridge; Allen running into Keaton and Murphy at the perfume counter of Bloomingdale's (100 Third Avenue); and an under-dressed Allen taking his son to lunch at the Russian Tea Room (150 West 57th Street). Hemingway attends The Dalton School (108 East 89th Street), where Allen meets her after classes.

Manhattan Murder Mystery

(1993). Woody Allen, Diane Keaton. Wife looks deeper into neighbor's death, over the objections of her husband.

Zach Braff's birthday is celebrated at The 21 Club (21 West 52nd Street, Manhattan), and the HarperCollins Building (10 East 53rd Street) portrays Allen's office. Allen and Keaton find a dead body at the Hotel 17 (225 East Seventeenth Street).

The Manhattan Project

(1986). John Lithgow, Christopher Collet. Teenager breaks into top secret plant and steals some plutonium.

Suffern High School (Viola Road, Suffern) plays Ithaca High

School, where Collet builds an atomic bomb as his school science project. The town of Haverstraw stood in for Ithaca.

Mickey Blue Eyes

(1999). Hugh Grant, James Caan. Art house auctioneer unwittingly gets involved with mob activity when he learns his teacher girlfriend is the daughter of a gangster.

The characters frequent the Knickerbocker Bar & Grill (33 University Place at 9th Street, Manhattan).

Midnight Cowboy

(1969). Dustin Hoffman, Jon Voight. Naive country boy comes to New York with plans to become a gigolo and befriends a sickly street hustler.

Working the streets of New York City, Voight is thrown out of the Peninsula Hotel (700 Fifth Avenue), which played The Barclay, while trying to service women. Sylvia Miles, whose performance was the shortest ever to win an Academy Award, slips Voight past the doorman of her apartment at 114 East 72nd Street.

Mighty Aphrodite

(1995). Woody Allen, Mira Sorvino. Adopted boy's surpassing intelligence inspires parents to search for his biological mother.

Allen walks his new baby along Fifth Avenue and 64th Street, and later runs into Sorvino in FAO Schwarz (767 Fifth Avenue, Manhattan). Sorvino and Michael Rapaport meet for a blind date at the Central Park Bandshell, south of the 72nd Street Transverse.

Miracle on 34th Street

(1947). Maureen O'Hara, John Payne. Lawyer defends old man who is institutionalized for claiming to be Santa Claus.

The original 1947 version was filmed in Macy's (151 West 34th Street, Herald Square, Manhattan), but the 1994 remake was not permitted to shoot in the world's largest department store. The Macy's Thanksgiving Parade in the film begins at the Museum of Natural History's 77th Street Entrance. The trial of Edmund Gwenn's Santa Claus was staged at the New York County Supreme Court (60 Centre Street).

Moonstruck

(1987). Cher, Nicolas Cage. Woman falls in love with her fiancé's brother.

The story is set amid the brownstones and gardens of the Carroll Gardens section of Brooklyn which was developed between 1869 and 1884. Cage worked in the Cammareri Brothers Bakery at 502 Henry Street. Al Capone was married in the neighborhood in 1918.

The Naked City

(1948). Barry Fitzgerald, Howard Duff. Method of detectives working a murder case is followed step by step.

Interiors and exteriors of the Tenth Precinct (230 West 20th Street, Manhattan) were used as the detectives try to solve one of "eight million stories in the naked city." Duff's murdered girlfriend was killed in her apartment at 52 West 83rd Street.

The Natural

(1984). Robert Redford, Robert Duvall. Overage baseball player emerges from nowhere to become the biggest star in the game.

The movie opens with Redford striking out Joe Don Baker in a farmhouse field in South Dayton, after which he boards the train in the refurbished South Dayton train depot. Redford and Glenn Close meet in the Parkside Candy Shoppe (Main and Oakwood, Buffalo). Playing baseball stadiums in the 1930s were All-High Stadium behind Bennett High School (2885 Main Street, Buffalo), which played Wrigley Field, and old War Memorial Stadium, which was the home park for the fictional New York Knights and site of Redford's career-ending home run. The stadium, which stood at Jefferson and Best streets, has been torn down.

Network

(1976). William Holden, Faye Dunaway. Last-place television network airs rantings of deranged anchorman for ratings.

The headquarters of the fictional United Broadcasting System was portrayed by the exterior of the MGM Building at 1350 Avenue of the Americas in Manhattan; studio sequences were filmed in Canada. Holden and Dunaway shared a passion pit in the Anthorp Apartments (2207–2209 Broadway).

New York Stories

(1989). Woody Allen, Mia Farrow. Three separate vignettes about life in New York City.

Heather McComb lived in the Sherry Netherland Hotel (781 Fifth Avenue, Manhattan) in the "Life Without Zoe" segment. In "Oedipus Wrecks," Allen lunches with his overbearing mother Mae Questel at Tavern on the Green (Central Park at West 67th Street) and waits for Farrow outside the MONY Building (1740 Broadway). In his fantasy, a dead Questel barks instructions from her casket at Riverside Memorial Chapel (180 West 76th Street).

Nighthawks

(1981). Sylvester Stallone, Billy Dee Williams. Two cops are reassigned to new anti-terrorist unit just in time to deal with a German terrorist in New York City.

Rutger Hauer takes hostages aboard the Roosevelt Island Tram that links Roosevelt Island with Manhattan; Stallone is lowered from a helicopter to the dangling tram car to receive an infant as proof the terrorists are reasonable folk. The IND Hoyt-Schermerhorn station in Brooklyn was used for both the 57th St. and 42nd St. subway station scenes. The train, consisting of retired equipment, operated on one of the unused outer tracks. The 63rd St. tunnel, then under construction, was used in the underground chase sequence.

Nobody's Fool

(1994). Paul Newman, Bruce Willis. Small town ne'er-do-well reconnects with the family he abandoned years before.

The Hudson Valley town of North Bath was patched together from Beacon (including the 1930s-era Tiffany Diner and the Queen Anne Victorian–style Botsford Briar), Fishkill, Poughkeepsie, Newburgh, and Hudson.

NYPD Blue

(1993–). Dennis Franz, Rick Schroeder. The gritty lives of the cops in a New York police department.

The television series uses the building of the 9th Precinct (321 East Fifth Street, Manhattan) to portray the fictional 15th Precinct.

The Out of Towners

(1970). Jack Lemmon, Sandy Dennis. Couple's trip to New York to take a new job is fraught with misadventure.

The seemingly-hard-to-get-to destination when Dennis and Lemmon depart from MacArthur Airport in Islip, Long Island, is the Waldorf Astoria (301 Park Avenue, Manhattan). The original terminal is now a parking lot, but as the plane takes off the movie provides a clear shot of Holbrook. They eventually spend the night in Central Park and are ultimately forced to scale down the side of the three-story frame house at 17 Grove Street. Built in 1822, the house is one of the few wood-framed structures remaining in Manhattan.

The Paper

(1994). Michael Keaton, Robert Duvall. Frenzied 24 hours in the life of people working on a big-city newspaper.

The office building that played the office of the fictional *New York Sun* was located on Manhattan's John Street. Keaton and Tomei live in the Devonshire House (28 East 10th Street) and Keaton skips out of a dinner with his wife and in-laws at Gus's Place (149 Waverly Place).

A Perfect Murder

(1998). Michael Douglas, Gwyneth Paltrow. Woman's death might prove a boon to both her controlling husband and her lover.

Paltrow and Douglas live in a lavish Manhattan apartment at 7 East 91st Street; she works as an interpreter at the Secretariat of the United Nations (43rd Street and First Avenue). Tours are offered daily. Douglas withdraws $400,000 from a bank at 48 Wall Street to finance his deadly scheme.

The Patty Duke Show

(1963–1966). Patty Duke, William Schallert. Teen's identical cousin comes to stay with family.

The Brooklyn Heights Promenade, built in 1951 to shield Brooklyn Heights residents from the Brooklyn-Queens Expressway rushing beneath it, is featured in the opening credits of the television series.

The Pick-Up Artist

(1987). Robert Downey, Jr., Molly Ringwald. Carefree womanizer gets entangled with the daughter of a degenerate gambler in hock to the Mob.

Ringwald works as a tour guide at the American Museum of Natural History (Central Park West at West 79th Street, Manhattan). Downey and Ringwald enjoy an early morning moment together in a car parked in front of the fountain off the 72nd Street Transverse.

Plaza Suite

(1971). Walter Matthau, Maureen Stapleton. The lives of three couples who stay in the same room at the Plaza Hotel.

The story is set entirely in Room 719 of the Plaza Hotel (Fifth Avenue and Central Park South) in Manhattan.

Prizzi's Honor

(1985). Jack Nicholson, Kathleen Turner. Professional hit man and professional hit woman fall in love and discover their next assignments are each other.

Nicholson lived at 57 Montague Street in Brooklyn with a view of Brooklyn Bridge and don William Hickey lived at 3 Pierrepot Place in Brooklyn Heights. The brick showplace was built in 1857 for Abiel Abbot Law, whose son would go on to become mayor of a consolidated, five-borough New York City.

The Producers

(1968). Zero Mostel, Gene Wilder. Outrageous Broadway producer convinces conservative accountant to invest in his schemes.

Mostel and Wilder agree to produce the play *Springtime for Hitler*, and the waters of The Fountain Plaza at Lincoln Center, the largest cultural complex in the world, dance in celebration. The *Springtime for Hitler* sequences were filmed at Broadway's Playhouse Theater (torn down in 1969); when the theater blows up, the marquee of the Cort Theater, across 48th Street from the Playhouse, is clearly visible. Mostel and Wilder enjoy the Carousel on Park Drive of Central Park during a lunchbreak.

Quick Change

(1990). Bill Murray, Geena Davis. Man executes a clever bank robbery but can't seem to make his way out of New York City.

The bank that Murray, dressed as a clown, robs was a closed branch of Chemical Bank at 120 Park Avenue at 41st Street in Manhattan. Many street scenes of New York City follow.

Radio Days

(1987). Mia Farrow, Julie Kavner. Stories of personalities during the Golden Age of radio in the 1940s.

Farrow works as a cigarette girl in the King Cole Room of the St. Regis Hotel (2 East 55th Street, Manhattan). The radio broadcasting network building was located in the Metropolitan Life Building (11 Madison Square). Also featured in the movie was the last Horn & Hardart's Automat in operation, at 200 East 42nd Street in Manhattan. It closed forever a few years after the filming.

Raging Bull

(1980). Robert DeNiro, Cathy Moriarty. Story of volatile middleweight boxing champion Jake LaMotta.

The Lido Beach Hotel (Maple Boulevard and Broadway, Long Beach), now a condominium complex, played the nursing home where DeNiro tells his story. Moriarty and DeNiro meet for the first time at the public swimming pool on St. Luke's Place.

Ragtime

(1981). James Cagney, Elizabeth McGovern. Man tries to seek justice for the vandalization of his car in the early 1900s.

Although the movie was filmed mostly in London, there were significant locations in New York, including the Victorian mansion at 81 Main Street in Mt. Kisko and the Morgan Library (29 East 36th Street, Manhattan), where Howard E. Rollins, Jr. wages a stand-off until his car is returned in perfect condition.

Ransom

(1996). Mel Gibson, Rene Russo. Father of kidnapped son turns ransom into bounty on the head of the kidnapper.

The Science Fair was held at Bethesda Fountain in the middle of Central Park. The quarry scene at the end was filmed in a quarry in North Haledon.

Regarding Henry

(1991). Harrison Ford, Annette Bening. A lawyer is forced to learn how to walk and talk again after being shot.

Ford and Bening live at 1009 Fifth Avenue at 82nd Street in Manhattan, and he tries a case at the New York County Supreme Court (60 Centre Road) before he suffers a brain injury. After the shooting, the first word Ford utters while trying to recall his former life is "Ritz," in reference to the former name of The Weston (112 Central Park South). He then goes to the hotel, sits in a room and tries to remember his past. Mikki Allen attends school in Dutchess County at the Millbrook School (School Road, Millbrook).

Rich and Famous

(1981). Jacqueline Bisset, Candice Bergen. Two women maintain friendship over twenty years of rivalry in love and career.

This was filmed largely on location in the Algonquin Hotel (59 West 44th Street), where Bisset offers a tour of the hotel and an informal history lesson on the Round Table to a young paramour. Elsewhere, Bergen rents an entire floor of the Waldorf Astoria (301 Park Avenue).

Rosemary's Baby

(1968). Mia Farrow, Ruth Gordon. Young wife is unaware of her husband's involvement with the occult.

Farrow and John Cassavetes, who has made a pact with the devil, move to New York's Upper West Side into the Dakota (One West 72nd Street), which plays the Branford.

Saturday Night Fever

(1977). John Travolta, Karen Lynn Gorney. Brooklyn youth uses disco dancing to escape to better world.

Travolta and his friends scare Donna Pescow by pretending to jump off the Verrazano-Narrows Bridge at the beginning of the movie, and he leaves Brooklyn for good at the end of the movie to grow up in Manhattan by crossing the Brooklyn Bridge. In between he primps for his disco appearances at his family home at 221 79th Street in Brooklyn.

Scent of a Woman

(1992). Al Pacino, Chris O'Donnell. Student agrees to look after a blind man on trip to city.

Pacino's destination for his last big city fling is the Waldorf-Astoria (301 Park Avenue) in New York City. While in town, he and O'Donnell dine at the Plaza Hotel's Oak Room (Fifth Avenue and Park Avenue South), and Pacino tangos with Gabrielle Anwar in the Cotillion room of The Pierre (61st Street and Fifth Avenue). Hempstead House (95 Middleneck Road, Port Washington) portrayed one of the buildings in O'Donnell's prep school. The design of the 1912 house, open for tours from Friday through Sunday, features the traits of an English Tudor castle. Pacino defends O'Connell during a disciplinary hearing at the Emma Willard School (285 Pawlings Avenue, Troy).

Scrooged

(1988). Bill Murray, Karen Allen. Tyrannical network television boss encounters Christmas spirits.

Murray heads the IBC Network in the Seagram Building (375 Park Avenue at 52nd Street, Manhattan), where he wants to air a live version of the "Christmas Carol" on Christmas Eve.

Sea of Love

(1989). Al Pacino, Ellen Barkin. Detective uses personal ads to track a serial killer.

Working his sting, Pacino meets women who answer his personal ads at O'Neill's, now the Iridium Jazz Club, on 48 West 63rd Street in New York City. Barkin worked on 57th Street at Maud Frizon Shoe Store, which no longer exists.

Searching for Bobby Fischer

(1993). Max Pomeranc, Joe Mantegna. Father tries to exploit his son's genius for chess.

Pomeranc develops an affinity for chess while watching Laurence Fishburne and others play games on the permanent tables in Washington Square Park.

Seinfeld

(1990–1998). Jerry Seinfeld, Jason Alexander. Four friends look out for one another in New York City.

The exterior for the restaurant where the characters eat is Tom's Restaurant (2880 Broadway at 112th Street, Manhattan), near the campus of Columbia University. The interior of Tom's looks nothing like the set used for the television series.

Serpico

(1973). Al Pacino, John Randolph. Cop blows the whistle on corruption in department, and his comrades turn against him.

Pacino moves from Brooklyn to Greenwich Village via the Williamsburg Bridge in a Dodge clunker. Once in Manhattan, he takes up residence on the block-long Minetta Street at number 5–7. Also making a brief appearance are the sidewalk tables and awnings of Cafe Reggio (119 MacDougal Street).

Shaft

(1971). Richard Roundtree, Moses Dunn. Black private-eye is hired to find kidnapped daughter of Harlem ganglord.

Shot on location in New York City, from Greenwich Village and Times Square to Harlem and Welfare Island (now the upscale Roosevelt Island), the movie was a guided tour through urban Manhattan in the early 1970s. Roundtree spent a good deal of time at the No Name Bar (621 Hudson Street, now the Piccolo Angolo). His apartment was across the street.

Shaft Returns

(2000). Samuel Jackson, Vanessa Williams. Police detective nephew of famous private detective tracks son of wealthy real estate tycoon in racially motivated murder.

This was filmed around 18th and Broadway at the Metronome. Shooting also took place at the River Diner (452 11th Avenue and 37th Street).

She-Devil

(1989). Meryl Streep, Roseanne Barr. Woman vows revenge on departed husband and his lover.

Barr and Ed Begley, Jr. first meet Streep at the Frank Lloyd Wright–designed Solomon R. Guggenheim Museum (Fifth Avenue at 89th Street, Manhattan).

Single White Female

(1992). Bridget Fonda, Jennifer Jason Leigh. Woman advertises for a roommate after her boyfriend leaves and winds up with a lodger with a secret past.

Fonda's apartment is in the wildly ornate 17-story Beaux Arts Ansonia Apartments residential complex at 2107–2109 Broadway in Manhattan.

Six Degrees of Separation

(1993). Donald Sutherland, Stockard Channing. Mysterious man passes himself off to wealthy New York couple as famous actor's son.

Will Smith enters the lives of Sutherland and Channing at their apartment at 860 Fifth Avenue, between 67th and 68th streets in Manhattan. The interiors were filmed in a 16th floor apartment at 1049 Fifth Avenue. Everyone goes to the Strand Bookstore (828 Broadway) to search its "eight miles of books" for a biography of Sidney Poitier to try and verify Smith's tale. Smith sits in Central Park and ponders his life at the bronze statue of Balto the Wonder Dog (East 67th Street near the East Drive). The real Balto, a heroic sled dog who led the team delivering diphtheria serum to Nome, Alaska, in 1925, is stuffed and on display at the Cleveland (Ohio) Museum of Natural History. The museum displays a film shot in 1925 of Balto and the original team. Smith is eventually apprehended by police at the Waverly Theater (323 Avenue of the Americas).

Soapdish

(1991). Sally Field, Kevin Kline. Ambitious young actress schemes to bring down the long-running star of a popular soap opera.

Kline takes Elisabeth Shue to dinner at the Stage Deli on 834 Seventh Avenue in Manhattan. The Daytime Emmy Awards show was staged at the Plaza Hotel (Fifth Avenue and Central Park South).

Someone to Watch Over Me

(1987). Tom Berenger, Mimi Rogers. Happily married New York City cop becomes infatuated with glamorous woman he is assigned to protect.

Berenger's first assignment as a detective is to protect murder witness Rogers at 8 East 62nd Street. Later, Berenger confronts Andreas Katsulas at a soiree at the Guggenheim Museum (1071 Fifth Avenue, Manhattan).

Sophie's Choice

(1982). Meryl Streep, Kevin Kline. Polish survivor of Nazi concentration camps struggles to adjust to life in America.

Peter MacNicol joins Streep and Kline in a Queen Anne Victorian house at 101 Rugby Road in the Flatbush section of Brooklyn. The house was painted pink for its appearance as a 1940s boarding house. The three drink champagne atop the Brooklyn Bridge.

Splash

(1984). Tom Hanks, Darryl Hannah. Man is reunited with a mermaid who saved him from drowning as a little boy.

Hannah first swims ashore looking for Hanks at the Statue of Liberty on Liberty Island. Once she locates him, they live for a time at Tudor Tower (25 Tudor City Place), a self-contained enclave in the heart of Manhattan. After Hannah is exposed as a mermaid, she is brought to the

American Museum of Natural History (Central Park West at 79th Street) to be examined. In the final sequence Hanks makes the decision to live with Hannah forever by diving into the chilly East River off Pier 17.

Splendor in the Grass

(1961). Natalie Wood, Warren Beatty. Farm girl struggles with morals and desires in Depression-era Midwest.

In a rare reversal of the usual Hollywood location casting, the New York area stood in for rural Kansas, since director Elia Kazan wanted to stay in the East to be near his ailing father during shooting. The search for a suitably agrarian location for Wood's homestead took film crews to the furthest edge of Staten Island, to 4144 Victory Boulevard. Horace Mann High School (231 W. 246 Street, Riverdale) was used for school exteriors, the filming of a basketball game and dance sequences.

Stella

(1990). Bette Midler, Trini Alvarado. Woman refuses to marry the father of her child and sacrifices everything for her.

Midler stands in the rain and watches daughter Alvarado get married in the Terrace Room of the Tavern on the Green (Central Park at West 67th Street) in mid-town Manhattan.

Stepmom

(1998). Julia Roberts, Susan Sarandon. Stricken by cancer, a woman tries to convince her kids' workaholic stepmom to be a better mother.

Liam Aiken disappears under Roberts' care at the boathouse in Central Park; later, Sarandon and Roberts watch Aiken and Jena Malone skate at the park's Wollman Rink. Roberts dines with Malone at the Cowgirl Hall of Fame, a Tex-Mex Restaurant on West 10th Street in Greenwich Village.

Superman

(1978). Christopher Reeve, Margot Kidder. Young boy arrives from distant planet with special powers.

The Daily News Building (220 East 42nd Street, Manhattan) was transformed into the Daily Planet building; Kidder lived in a penthouse apartment at 240 Central Park South on her reporter's salary. Reeve takes Kidder on a private tour of New York city, flying past the Brooklyn Bridge and arriving at the Statue of Liberty. Scenes were also filmed in Red Rock State Park in New Mexico near Church Rock, in an area later renamed Superman Canyon.

The Sweet Smell of Success

(1957). Burt Lancaster, Tony Curtis. Powerful New York newspaper columnist does anything to stay on top.

Lancaster's apartment was located at the Brill Building (1619 Broadway, Manhattan), built by a family of haberdashers and now a show business tower in the heart of New York's musical district of Tin Pan Alley.

Taxi

(1978–1983). Judd Hirsch, Danny DeVito. Taxi drivers make a living while pursuing their dreams.

The fictional Sunshine Cab Company operated out of the Dover Garage at 534 Hudson Street in Greenwich Village, which appears briefly in the opening credits.

Taxi Driver

(1976). Robert DeNiro, Jodie Foster. Mentally unstable cab driver turns his inner rage against the decadent streets of New York City.

DeNiro picks his way ominously through a political rally at the Central Park Entrance at Columbus Circle. He calls Cybill Shepherd from a payphone to apologize for having taken her to a porno movie from the lobby of The Ed Sullivan Theater (1697 Broadway), and he picks her up in front of the St. Regis Hotel (2 East 55th Street, Manhattan) after his shooting spree.

Three Days of the Condor

(1975). Robert Redford, Faye Dunaway. Researcher for the CIA discovers more than he should know and finds himself the target of his own organization.

Top CIA man Cliff Robertson works out of the World Trade Center (1 and 2 World Trade Plaza in lower Manhattan). Redford narrowly escapes being gunned downed in the alley next to the Ansonia Apartments (2107–2109 Broadway) and eventually confronts Robertson on the Brooklyn Promenade.

Three Men and a Baby

(1987). Tom Selleck, Steve Guttenberg. Three bachelors take charge of a baby left by one of their girlfriends.

The sumptuous bachelor pad where Selleck, Guttenberg and Ted Danson live was located in the Prasada (50 Central Park West), although all the interiors were shot on a sound stage. The boys use the baby to their advantage (by flouting their sensitivity to collect women's phone numbers) on the path by Belvedere Castle in Manhattan's Central Park, next to Shakespeare's Garden.

Tootsie

(1982). Dustin Hoffman, Jessica Lange. Unemployed actor dresses in drag to land a role in a popular soap opera.

Hoffman reveals to his agent Sydney Pollack that he is Dorothy Michaels playing his part in drag at the Russian Tea Room in Manhattan at 150 West 57th Street. After being exposed as a man, Hoffman commiserates with Charles Durning at the bar in the yellow, gabled Hurley Mountain Inn (Old Route 209, Hurley) in the Catskill Mountains.

Unfaithfully Yours

(1984). Dudley Moore, Nastassja Kinski. Conductor plans to murder his wife whom he suspects of cheating on him.

Moore conducts the orchestra at Carnegie Hall (57th Street and Seventh Avenue), with its perfect acoustics, and dines at the Russian Tea Room (150 West 57th Street).

Wall Street

(1987). Michael Douglas, Charlie Sheen. Young stockbroker will do anything to jump start his career.

Sheen comes to work for Douglas at 222 Broadway, a vacant highrise used for filming. Douglas gives Sheen a million dollars to invest at a power lunch at The 21 Club (21 West 52nd Street, Manhattan). After Sheen decides to turn Douglas in for insider trading, he carries a tape-recording to federal prosecutors in the restroom of the Tavern on the Green (Central Park at West 67th Street). In the final scene, Sheen accepts responsibility for his misdealings and walks up the steps of the New York County Supreme Court building (60 Centre Street).

The Way We Were

(1973). Barbara Streisand, Robert Redford. Political beliefs drive a wedge in wonderful romance.

Streisand and Redford meet at the Plaza Hotel (Fifth Avenue and Central Park South, Manhattan). Upstate, downtown Ballston Spa was used for street scenes, and Union College in Schenectady portrayed the fictional Wentworth College. Locations included Nott Memorial, the Chester Arthur statue and the Memorial Field House, where the prom scene was staged.

Welcome Back Kotter

(1975–1979). Gabe Kaplan, Marcia Strassman. Man returns to teach in his old high school classroom.

New Utretcht High School (16th Avenue and 79th Street, Brooklyn) played the fictional James Buchanan High School where Kaplan returned to teach.

When Harry Met Sally

(1989). Billy Crystal, Meg Ryan. Friends debate the potential effects of sex on their relationship.

Crystal meets Ryan in the main quadrangle of the University of Chicago's Hyde Park campus off University Avenue at 58th Avenue in Illinois. He drops her off in New York City for law school at the Fifth Avenue Entrance of Washington Park, and it will be five years before they meet again. Also in New York, Carrie Fisher and Ryan enjoy an outdoor lunch at Loeb Boathouse Cafe (Park Drive East at 74th Street), and Crystal bumps into the two women at the Shakespeare and Company bookstore at 2259 Broadway. He realizes he likes Ryan as more than a friend at the Metropolitan Museum of Art (1000 Fifth Avenue at 82nd Street) and commits to her at a New Year's Eve party at the Puck Building (295 Lafayette Street).

The Wiz

(1978). Diana Ross, Michael Jackson. Modern urban version of the Wizard of Oz.

Ross and Jackson encounter the image of the Chrysler Building (405 Lexington Avenue) as they enter the Emerald City (as played by New York City). Other locales included the World Trade Center (1 and 2 World Trade Plaza, Manhattan), where a musical production takes place in the four-acre plaza; Astroland Park on Coney Island in Brooklyn, and Shea Stadium in Queens. Ross and Jackson and a cast of hundreds cross the Brooklyn Bridge.

Wolf

(1994). Jack Nicholson, Michelle Pfeiffer. Man suffers wolf bite and notices his behavior starts to change.

After catching Kate Nelligan cheating on him, Nicholson moves to the Mayflower Hotel on the Park (15 Central Park West, Manhattan). As he evolves into a werewolf, Nicholson stalks the caged animals in the Central Park Zoo (64th Street), sending them into a frenzy. Rival publisher Christopher Plummer's estate is portrayed by the Old Westbury Gardens (71 Old Westbury Road, Old Westbury).

Working Girl

(1988). Melanie Griffith, Harrison Ford. Secretary poses as her boss to carry through her stolen idea.

Griffith took the Staten Island Ferry to work in Manhattan each morning from the Staten Island Ferry Terminal, which features a museum in its large lobby. Ford and Griffith go to a wedding at the National Design Museum (2 East 91st Street), and to the headquarters of the Trask Company at the National Museum of the American Indian (1 Bowling Green).

You've Got Mail

(1988). Tom Hanks, Meg Ryan. Business rivals unwittingly fall in love over the Internet.

Hanks and Ryan are supposed to meet for the first time at the Cafe Lalo (201 W. 83rd Street) on New York's Upper West Side, and Ryan and Hanks try to decipher the screen name "NY 152" at the Ocean Grill (384 Columbus Avenue). Maya Schaper Cheese and Antiques (106 West 69th Street) was used for both the interiors and exteriors of Ryan's bookstore, which is being forced out of business by a big chain.

Zelig

(1983). Woody Allen, Mia Farrow. Human chameleon becomes famous in the 1920s for his ability to blend into famous scenes.

Although this was mostly a tour de force in the editing room, one real scene in the movie took place on the part of the boardwalk in Long Beach known as the Old Promenade.

NORTH CAROLINA

Betsy's Wedding

(1990). Alan Alda, Molly Ringwald. Father prepares emotionally and practically for daughter's wedding.

The North Carolina Queen Anne Cottage-style governor's mansion, one of the few governor's residences in the nation constructed in the nineteenth century still in use, was the site of Ringwald's wedding reception. The executive mansion is located in Raleigh at 200 North Blount Street, two blocks northeast of the State Capitol.

Billy Bathgate

(1991). Dustin Hoffman, Nicole Kidman. Young man rises from gofer through the ranks of the Mob.

The town of Hamlet was made over to play New York in the 1930s. The centerpiece of the set was the two-story Victorian Queen Anne train station built in 1900 (2 Main Street), and several storefronts were converted on Main Street. The Kenan House on the University of North Carolina–Wilmington Campus (1705 Market Street) portrayed the Saratoga Hotel. In New York, Hoffman conducts some business at the Saratoga Equine Sports Center harness track on Nelson Avenue in Saratoga.

Blue Velvet

(1986). Dennis Hopper, Isabella Rossellini. Man discovers severed human ear in a field and races it to a woman involved in a bizarre relationship.

Rossellini lives in the Carolina Apartment (Fifth Avenue and Market Street, Wilmington). Also used in Wilmington was the New Hanover High School (1307 Market Street), which played the Wilmington Police Station.

Bull Durham

(1988). Kevin Costner, Susan Sarandon. Fan picks one minor league baseball player each season with whom to have an affair.

The home of the Durham Bulls (where the movie was filmed), Durham Athletic Park at 428 Morris Street, is no longer used by the team but still stands. Other baseball footage was shot at Burlington Athletic Stadium (1450 Graham Street, Burlington), World War Memorial Stadium (510 Yanceyville Street, Greensboro) and Fleming Stadium (300 Stadium Street, Wilson). The batting cage scene was shot at Par Golf (5715 Fayetteville Road, Garner), but the cages have been removed due to lack of business.

The Butcher's Wife

(1991). Demi Moore, Jeff Daniels. Clairvoyant marries butcher she thinks she saw in a vision.

Three cottages on Bald Head Island, built in 1903 by lighthouse keeper Captain Charlie Swan and lived in with his family until he retired in 1933, were used in the first part of the movie before the action shifts to the butcher shop in Greenwich Village, New York. These three cottages, known collectively as Captain Charlie's Station, are listed in the National Register of Historic Places and available for rent. No cars are permitted on the island.

The Color Purple

(1985). Danny Glover, Whoopi Goldberg. Lifespan of black girl in American South.

Mid–nineteenth century town scenes were filmed in downtown Marshville in Union County. Also featured was the Anson County Courthouse (North Green Street, Wadesboro).

Crimes of the Heart

(1986). Diane Keaton, Jessica Lange. Three grown sisters who have followed very different paths in life reunite over a family tragedy.

Adulterous Sissy Spacek shoots husband Beeson Carroll at Orton Plantation (9149 Orton Road, Winnabow). Built in 1725 on the Cape Fear River, the old rice plantation is private but can be viewed from the garden paths, which are open to the public. The family home to which the sisters return is a private home at 211 Caswell Street in Southport. The original Victorian mansion was built in 1904 and has been renovated slightly since the filming of the movie.

The Crow

(1994). Brandon Lee, Ernie Hudson. Murdered man returns as undead avenger.

Wilmington played Detroit in the movie best remembered for Lee's accidental death on a sound stage. Featured in a dining scene is the Hieronymous Seafood Restaurant (5035 Market Street, Wilmington).

Dawson's Creek

(1998–). James Van Der Beek, Katie Holmes. Teenagers growing up in a small town.

Southport plays the Boston-area seaside town of Capeside. Locations around town include the Groove Jet (112 Princess Street), the Martin Luther King Center (South 8th Street), Mollye's Market (118 Princess Street) and the Ice House (115 S. Water Street).

Dream a Little Dream

(1989). Corey Feldman, Corey Haim. Accident leaves teenager with the mind of a wise old man.

The opening and closing sequences were filmed at Thalian Hall (310 Chestnut Street, Wilmington).

Eddie

(1996). Whoopi Goldberg, Frank Langella. Limousine driver and fanatical basketball fan gets a chance to coach the New York Knicks.

The Charlotte Coliseum (100 Paul Buck Boulevard, Charlotte) was used for the Knicks' practice sessions and home games under the scrutinizing eye of new coach Goldberg.

Hellraiser III: Hell on Earth

(1992). Doug Bradley, Terry Farrell. Killer appears to be working with ambitious television reporter to provide grisly crimes.

The killer claims a victim at the Nations Bank Corporate Center (100 N. Tyron Street, Charlotte). Additional scenes were shot on the campus of Wake Forest University, off Silas Creek Parkway in Winston-Salem.

I Know What You Did Last Summer

(1997). Sarah Michelle Gellar, Jennifer Love Hewitt. A year after accidentally running down a pedestrian and dumping the body in the ocean, murders begin.

Much of the filming took place in Southport, including: the American Fish Company (W. Bay Street); Dosher Memorial Hospital (924 Howe Street); and Port Charlie's Restaurant (317 W. Bay Street). The scenes at the old-fashioned soda fountain were shot at Dee's Drug Store, founded in 1916 in Burgaw.

Kiss the Girls

(1997). Morgan Freeman, Ashley Judd. Police hunt serial killer who has just allowed a first victim to escape.

Morgan pursues his prey through the 2,635-acre Eno River State Park (6101 Cole Mill Road, three miles west of Durham).

The Last of the Mohicans

(1992). Daniel Day-Lewis, Madeleine Stowe. Orphan settler raised by Mohawk Indians nettles both sides of the French and Indian War.

The wilderness of 18th century upstate New York was portrayed by Chimney Rock Park (US 74 and US 64, Chimney Rock). A love scene between Lewis and Stowe was filmed at Inspiration Point, and the climactic fight scene was staged at Hickory Nut Falls. Three different trails lead to the falls, where the 404-foot sheer drop is twice the height of Niagara Falls.

Matlock

(1986–1995). Andy Griffith, Linda Purl. Folksy down-home lawyer charges big fees.

The area around Wilmington, near Griffith's real home, was the base for the shooting of this series set in Atlanta.

Mr. Destiny

(1990). James Belushi, Linda Hamilton. Average man goes back in time to replay a high school baseball game and changes his entire future life.

In his new life Belushi lives at the Biltmore Estate (US 25, Asheville), the largest private home ever built in America. In Winston-Salem an abandoned R.J. Reynolds tobacco plant on RJR Boulevard was transformed into the offices and factory of Belushi's Liberty Republic. Also featured in Winston-Salem were the Grecian Corner (101 Eden Terrace), where Belushi dines with Hamilton; Cafe Piaf (405 West Fourth Street);

and Ernie Shore Field (401 West 30th Street), where Belushi changes his future fortunes with a single at-bat.

Nell

(1994). Jodie Foster, Liam Neeson. Country doctor battles to keep child raised in woods from being turned into a lab experiment.

Psychologist Neeson takes wild child Foster to the Days Inn Uptown (601 North Tyron Street, Charlotte). Foster's backwoods cabin was constructed on Montana Lake in Nantahala National Forest (between Waynesville and Murphy).

Rambling Rose

(1991). Laura Dern, Robert Duvall. Family take in troubled woman who can't avoid getting involved with men.

The Bellamy Mansion (Fifth Avenue and Market Street, Wilmington) was used as the exterior for the Hillier Hotel, operated by Duvall and Diane Lane; the restored antebellum residence is open for tours. The interior of the hotel was filmed in the nearby Graystone Inn (South 3rd and Dock) which features a hand-carved oak, Renaissance–style grand staircase. The movie's wedding was staged at the Black River Presbyterian Church in Ivanhoe (State Road No. 1102).

Raw Deal

(1986). Arnold Schwarzenegger, Kathryn Harrold. Exiled FBI agent is given a chance for reinstatement by going undercover in the Mob.

Schwarzenegger toils as a small-town sheriff, with the small town portrayed by Wilmington, before heading for Chicago to take on gangsters. Locations used in Wilmington were the Dixie Grill (116 Market Street), the Independence Shopping Mall (Oleander Drive) and the Old Wilmington Light Infantry Armory (40 Market Street) which now houses city offices.

Richie Rich

(1994). Edward Herrmann, Macauley Culkin. Rich kid must take over family business while searching for lost parents.

Culkin's house, as the world's richest kid, was the 225-room Biltmore (US 25, Asheville), the largest private residence ever built in the United States. The French Chateau, created for William Vanderbilt between 1889 and 1895, sprawls across 8,000 mountain acres and is open for tours.

The Road to Wellville

(1994). Anthony Hopkins, Bridget Fonda. Man goes to famous health farm to have system cleansed of impurities.

The Wise House (1713 Market Street, Wilmington) served as the interior of Hopkins' house. Also featured in North Carolina were the Airlie Gardens, 67 acres of post-Victorian, European–style gardens with 12 acres of freshwater lakes designed in the early 1900s. Privately owned until 1999, the gardens in

Wrightsville Beach on Airlie Road are now open to the public. In New York, the lakeside Mohonk Mountain House (Mountain Rest Road, New Paltz) portrayed Dr. John Kellogg's Health Sanitarium in Battle Creek, Michigan.

Silver Bullet

(1985). Gary Busey, Corey Haim. Werewolf terrorizes small town.

Wilmington portrayed the fictional Tracker's Mill; one of the location stars was the Dixie Grill at 116 Market Street.

Sleeping with the Enemy

(1991). Julia Roberts, Patrick Bergen. Woman stages her own death to flee from abusive husband.

The college theater was played by Thalian Hall (310 Chestnut Street, Wilmington). Roberts and Bergen live in a high-priced home built on Wrighstville Beach and destroyed after filming. Additional footage was shot on Figure Eight Island. The town of Abbeville, South Carolina, stood in for Cedar Falls, Iowa, where Roberts goes after changing her name and appearance. Abbeville began and ended the history of secession in the United States: both the first secession in the Southern states and the final cabinet meeting of a crumbling Confederacy took place here.

Spies

(1990). Cloris Leachman, David Dukes. Boy sees German submarines in front of his Long Island home.

Southport stood in for New York, and the movie was filmed in houses along Bay Street and on the waterfront. Ship scenes were staged aboard the *USS North Carolina*, docked in Wilmington on the Cape Fear River at the junction of US 17/US 74/US 76 and US 421N. Self-guided tours of the battleship's nine decks are available.

Weeds

(1987). Nick Nolte, Ernie Hudson. Prison inmate writes a play that leads to his parole.

The ex-cons put on their play professionally at the Thalian Hall (310 Chestnut Street, Wilmington), which played the fictional Broadway Theater. Named after Thalia, one of the Muses who presided over comedy and pastoral poetry, the playhouse was designed by John Montague Trimble, a famous theater architect, and built in 1855–56. It remains the only Trimble theater still in existence. Also featured was the Raw Bar's Palm Room in Wrightsville Beach (13 East Salisbury Street).

Weekend at Bernie's

(1989). Andrew McCarthy, Jonathan Silverman. Young corporate climbers try to make murdered company president seem alive.

The beach house used for the weekend was built near the Wrightsville Marina but disassembled after the movie. Recreational scenes with the presidential cadaver were shot on the beach at Bald Head Island, with water skiing filmed at Carolina Beach State Park (10 miles south of Wilmington off NC Hwy 421).

Popular North Carolina Location

WILMINGTON

It all began with a magazine cover in 1983.

In the pre-production process for his upcoming movie *Firestarter* (Drew Barrymore, David Keith), producer Frank Capra, Jr. was searching for a mansion to serve as the setting for the story of a couple who volunteered for scientific experiments while in college and bore a child with the ability to start fires merely by thinking about them. He saw a picture of an antebellum mansion depicted on the cover of *Southern Accents* magazine and sent his location scouts across Texas to search for a similar mansion.

After scouring the Lone Star State, Capra still did not have the house he was looking for. The producers decided to visit the real thing, the plantation house featured on the magazine cover. That mansion was the private Orton Plantation, built on the Cape Fear River in Winnabow, North Carolina, in 1725. After discussions with the owners, the producers worked out an agreement to film *Firestarter* on the old rice plantation.

After working in the Wilmington area for a short while, director Dino DeLaurentis began to recognize the coastal region as the ideal location to realize his long-festering dream of establishing a major East Coast film studio. He bought land on North 23rd Street and began building his dream studio around an old brick warehouse. He christened his new film paradise DEG Studios (DeLaurentis Entertainment Group).

What DeLaurentis discovered in the Wilmington region was a variety of diverse locations able to portray a wide variety of settings, a temperate climate that enabled year-round shooting and, even though no feature films had been previously shot in the area, a skilled, film-savvy technical populace. Most important, North Carolina was a "right-to-work" state, which was conducive to keeping production costs low.

After DeLaurentis blazed the trail, filmmaking in the Cape Fear Region around Wilmington exploded. Virtually nonexistent as a filmmaking location when North Carolina Governor Jim Hunt established a state film program in 1980, within ten years the state ranked second only to California in revenues derived from the film industry. Fully 10 percent of the Wilmington-area economic base was grounded in the nascent movie business. DeLaurentis, however, was no longer sharing in the bonanza. His studio was felled by financial difficulties, and he lost it to Carolco in 1988.

For the better part of a decade, activity in the groundbreaking studio was limited to commercial production. In 1996, the facility was purchased by a subsidiary of Columbia Pictures and was revitalized as the EUE Screen Gems Studio. Frank Capra, Jr. returned as president, and the production lot once again became one of the largest feature film studios east of Hollywood.

Today the studio at 1223 North

23rd Street features a three-block, four-story urban back lot that has portrayed cities across the globe in the movies. The lot covers 15 acres and has a main street, four cross-streets and four complete buildings with shootable interiors. There are nine sound stages, ranging from 7,200 to 35,500 square feet, with more than 100,000 square feet of filming space available. Screen Gems Studio also offers a surface tank of over 600 square feet for aquatic scenes. The studio also offers an ample supply of set lighting, grip, and expendables, production offices, construction mills, plaster and paint shops, props, a screening room, editing suites and a commissary with on-set catering. Weekend tours of the studio lot are available.

With Screen Gems leading the way, the state of North Carolina now boasts seven facilities statewide, 29 stages and more than a million square feet of controlled space for production. Many locations in the Wilmington area are popular with Hollywood scouts as well. Wrightsville Beach was featured in *Sleeping with the Enemy* (starring Julia Roberts), *To Gillian on Her 37th Birthday* (with Michelle Pfeiffer), and *Weekend at Bernie's*. Southport provided the setting for *Spies*, about German submarines spotted off Long Island, and *Crimes of the Heart* (with Sissy Spacek, Diane Keaton and Jessica Lange). Southport is also the filming location for the television series *Dawson's Creek*, standing in for the coastal New England town of Capeside, Massachusetts. The popular teenage soap opera has caused a decided spike in tourism in the town from fans hoping to connect with the show.

All told, the Wilmington area has played host to over 300 feature films, mini-series and television movies, and six television series since Frank Capra, Jr. happened to pick up a copy of *Southern Accents* less than 20 years ago. It is little wonder that Wilmington, North Carolina, has earned the reputation as "Hollywood East."

If you want to see the picturesque mansion that started it all, the Orton Plantation Gardens are 18 miles south of Wilmington on SR 133. Although the mansion is closed to the public, it can be seen from the public gardens, which are open from March through October.

NORTH DAKOTA

Wooly Boys

(2001). Peter Fonda, Kris Kristofferson. Old-fashioned sheep rancher's visit to the big city triggers a series of misadventures.

Much of the film was shot on location in Medora, the town made famous by Theodore Roosevelt. Cosmetic alterations were made to some of the downtown buildings, and a special set, since disassembled, was built. Fonda arrives in Minneapolis to visit his daughter at the Minneapolis Convention Center, which doubled as the bus station.

OHIO

Air Force One

(1997). Harrison Ford, Gary Oldman. Terrorists hijack Air Force One and take President and his family hostage.

Severance Hall (11001 Euclid Avenue at Case Western Reserve University), home of the Cleveland orchestra, doubled as the Kazakhstan Presidential Mansion attacked by United States Special Forces in the opening sequence. Scenes shot at the Ohio State Reformatory (100 Reformatory Road, Mansfield) show guards watching monitors in the central guard room and a general walking through the third tier of the West Cell Block. Rickenbacker International Airport in Columbus stood in for Ramstein Air Base in Germany.

A Christmas Story

(1983). Darren McGavin, Peter Billingsley. Young boy in the 1940s tries to convince parents that a BB gun is the perfect Christmas gift.

The movie was set in Indiana and filmed mostly in Toronto, the downtown scenes were shot in Cleveland. It was a snowless winter when the Christmas parade was staged in Cleveland Public Square, so fake snow had to be added. The department store where Billingsley first sees the Red Ryder gun in the window was Halles Department Store.

City of Hope

(1991). Vincent Spano, Chris Cooper. Old apartment block becomes focal point for struggle between developers and residents.

The interior of Baldwin Hall on the University of Cincinnati's West Campus became City Hall. Playing featured roles in Cincinnati were Arnold's Bar and Grill (210 E. Eighth Street), the city's oldest continuously operated eatery, and Stenger's Cafe (1720 Vine Street).

The Deer Hunter

(1978). Robert DeNiro, John Cazale. The lives of three Pennsylvania factory workers before, during and after the Vietnam War.

The Russian Orthodox wedding sequence was shot at the St. Theodosius Russian Orthodox Cathedral (733 Starkweather Avenue, Cleveland), with its elegant onion domes. The reception was held at the nearby Lemko Hall, an eclectic 1919 social hall (2335 W. 11th Street). The cemetery scene and funeral procession were filmed in Duquesne Heights. The deer hunting sequences were filmed in the state of Washington, on Mount Baker, an isolated volcano in Cascades National Park (Glacier Creek Road, Highway 542).

Fresh Horses

(1988). Molly Ringwald, Andrew McCarthy. College student falls for backwoods teenager who is already married.

The characters hang out at the Serpentine Wall on the Ohio riverfront at the University of Cincinnati; the old Chemistry Building is used as a classroom. The epilogue takes place at Paramount's King's Island (King's Island Drive, off Exit 25A of I-71, King's Mill) during the Winterfest celebration, which is no longer held. The rural scenes were filmed in Kentucky in Boone County, Warsaw County and Gallatin County.

Green Fields of Wyoming

(1948). Lloyd Nolan, Burl Ives. Kids of rival horse-breeding families compete.

Part of the shooting took place at the Lancaster Fairgrounds (Fair Avenue at High Street, Lancaster), with open range shots added to the final film. Square 13, bounded on one side by High Street, features period houses from the early 19th century.

Harper Valley PTA

(1977). Barbara Eden, Ronny Cox. Mother takes on the town.

Eden leads her protest from the steps of the sprawling Berry Middle School in Lebanon (25 Oakwood Drive), built in 1929. The Village Ice Cream Parlor (22 South Broadway, Lebanon) and the Golden Lamb Inn across the street (27 South Broadway) are featured. The Inn was built in 1803. In addition to viewing the historic collections, food is available.

Harry and Walter Go to New York

(1976). James Caan, Elliott Gould. Small-time con men attempt the largest bank heist of the century.

The middle 20 minutes of the movie feature the Ohio State Reformatory (100 Reformatory Road, Mansfield), where Caan and Gould befriend a notorious bank robber and steal his plans to knock over a bank. Later they escape from the Gothic penitentiary.

Light of Day

(1987). Michael J. Fox, Joan Jett. Rock band siblings differ on approach to life and career.

Fox and Jett launch their performing careers at the Euclid Tavern (11629 Euclid Avenue, Cleveland); Fox toils at his day job in the Marshallan Company, a metal stamping plant in the Flats district at West 85th Street.

Little Man Tate

(1991). Jodie Foster, Adam Hann-Byrd. Single mother sacrifices so her genius son can realize his gift and be a little boy.

Foster lives at 12th & Vine in Cincinnati and devotes her life to getting Hann-Byrd a proper education. Along the way she visits the Washington Park Elementary School (13th and Race streets, Cincinnati); 127 McMicken Hall at the University of Cincinnati, which serves as a quantum physics classroom; the Hebrew Union College (3101 Clifton Avenue,

Cincinnati), which doubled as the Grierson Institute; the Wexner Center for the Performing Arts at Ohio State University in Columbus; and Miami University in Oxford, where Hann-Byrd attends classes. Dianne Wiest's home and office are at the Tau Kappa Epsilon fraternity house at Miami University. The Florida hotel where Foster and Debi Mazar stay was portrayed by the Clairmount Motor Inn (650 South High Street, Columbus), now a Best Western.

Lost in Yonkers

(1993). Richard Dreyfuss, Mercedes Ruehl. Widower leaving for World War II leaves children with domineering mother and feeble sister.

Ruehl escapes everyday life with her mother by going to the Murphy Theater (Main and Mulberry streets, Wilmington), an historic art deco theater opened in 1918, given to the town by Chicago Cubs owner Webb Murphy.

Milk Money

(1994). Melanie Griffith, Ed Harris. Hooker tries to make a respectable life.

Griffith hustles customers on Main Street in Lebanon, where the Village Ice Cream Parlor (22 South Broadway, Lebanon) is featured; the sock hop in the finale was filmed in the Kilgour Elementary School (1339 Herschel Avenue, Cincinnati).

Mischief

(1985). Doug McKeon, Catherine Mary Stewart. Shy teen begins to get girls when he becomes friendly with rebellious senior.

Liberty-Union High School (500 Washington Street, Baltimore) was used for exteriors; Hamilton High School in Columbus played Nelsonville High. Scenes were filmed at the Nelsonville town square as well.

My Summer Story

(1994). Charles Grodin, Mary Steenburgen. Summer growing up for an Indiana family in the 1940s.

Like its prequel, A Christmas Story, city scenes were shot in Cleveland, including the Wilbur Wright Elementary School on Parkhurst Avenue. The camping vacation was filmed at Blueberry Hill Campground (735 Pinkney Road, Burgaw, North Carolina).

One Trick Pony

(1980). Paul Simon, Blair Brown. Washed-up pop singer is on the road with marriage and money woes.

Footage was shot at Cleveland Hopkins International Airport, ten miles southwest of town. Simon performed at the old Agora Club near Case Western University on Euclid Avenue in Cleveland. The renowned rock club burned in 1984.

A Rage in Harlem

(1991). Gregory Hines, Forest Whitaker. Woman on the run with gangster's gold is looked after by a naive, bashful man.

Hines and Whitaker go to the Museum Center at Union Terminal, the former art deco Cincinnati train station at 1301 Western Avenue; Whitaker boards a train to follow Robin Givens to New York here. Main Street in Over-the-Rhine, between 12th and Liberty streets, was used for New York street scenes. The Warehouse Nightclub (1313 Vine Street, Cincinnati) was built as a set for the movie and converted into a dance club afterwards.

The Shawshank Redemption

(1994). Tim Robbins, Morgan Freeman. Man accused of slaying his wife and her lover in the 1940s adapts to prison life in unconventional ways.

Freeman and Robbins are incarcerated in the Ohio State Reformatory (100 Reformatory Road, Mansfield), a Gothic masterpiece opened in 1886. The medieval chateaux and castles were intended to provide a transcendent religious experience to the young male prisoners; the East Cell Block is listed in the Guinness Book of World Records for the world's largest free-standing cell block, with six tiers. Cell block scenes were shot on a set built in an old Westinghouse warehouse in downtown Mansfield. Tours are offered on Sunday afternoons in the summer. Scenes were also shot in the town of Mansfield, including Freeman feeding the birds in Central Park; and a sequence at the E & B Market (4th Street), where Robbins and Freeman bag groceries while on parole.

Tango and Cash

(1989). Sylvester Stallone, Kurt Russell. Top cops who don't like each other get framed and jailed together.

Stallone and Russell climb up a water tower pipeline, cross a roof line and slide down a wire into pine trees on the other side of the wall to escape prison at the Ohio State Reformatory (100 Reformatory Road, Mansfield).

Teachers

(1981). Nick Nolte, Jo Beth Williams. Teacher takes on high school full of under-achievers.

Nolte goes to teach at the former Central High School, now the Columbus Center of Science and Industry (333 West Broad Street, Columbus). Four floors and an outdoor science park present more than 1,000 interactive exhibits.

Telling Lies in America

(1997). Kevin Bacon, Brad Reunifier. Immigrant teenager in the 1960s tries to impress classmates by emulating flashy radio disk jockey.

The movie was filmed entirely in Cleveland; a central location is the basement of the West Side Market (Lorain Avenue and West 25th Street), a popular stopping place for hungry European immigrants since 1868. The current brick building dates to 1912.

WKRP in Cincinnati

(1978–1982). Gary Sandy, Gordon Jump. Struggling classical radio station makes a drastic format switch to rock and roll.

To establish Cincinnati in the credits, the television series uses the Tyler Davidson Fountain in Fountain Square. Rising 43 feet high and built of 85 tons of stone and 24 tons of bronze, the fountain was a gift to the city in 1871 by hardware merchant Henry Probasco and named for his brother-in-law.

OKLAHOMA

In the Army Now

(1994). Pauly Shore, Andy Dick. Two youths try to fund crazy schemes by joining the Army reserves, and wind up on the front lines.

Shore and Dick undergo basic training at Fort Sill, north of Lawton on US 62/277/281. Staked out by General Phil Sheridan in 1869, and named for West Point classmate Brigadier General Joshua Sill, the base museum can be visited (437 Quananh Road) and the grounds toured. The old frontier post features the grave of Geronimo.

My Heroes Have Always Been Cowboys

(1991). Scott Glenn, Gary Busey. Rodeo cowboy returns home to care for ill father against the wishes of his sister and her husband.

Ranch scenes were filmed at the C. W. Scheihing Homestead, southwest of Guthrie; the log cabin was built of native oak logs in 1889. Rodeo sequences were shot at the Lazy E Arena, located just minutes north of Oklahoma City on the beautiful 300 acre Lazy E Ranch. Seating capacity in the arena is 6,200.

The Outsiders

(1983). C. Thomas Howell, Matt Dillon. A group of boys grow up on the wrong side of the tracks in hardscrabble times.

Street scenes were staged in the Greenwood-Archer district of Tulsa. The old Bowen Lodge, used as a film set, at 11th Street and Denver has been demolished for a parking lot, but the Tastee-Freeze on 11th Street is still there. Also standing is the Admiral Drive-In.

Rumble Fish

(1983). Nicolas Cage, Matt Dillon. Leader of small gang lives in shadow of popular older brother.

Filmed around Tulsa, the colorful Siamese fighting fish are released into the Arkansas River at the 21st Street Bridge on the western edge of the city.

Tex

(1982). Matt Dillon, Meg Tilly. Two brothers struggle after mother dies and father leaves.

Dillon puts caps in the typewriters at Bixby High School (Riverview and Stadium roads, Bixby).

Other scholastic scenes were shot in the gym at Broken Arrow High School (1901 E. Albany, Broken Arrow). The portion of the park along the Arkansas River in Tulsa where the motorcycles ride through the sand was washed away in a 1986 flood.

Twister

(1996). Bill Pullman, Helen Hunt. Divorcing tornado hunters can't shake each other as they chase storms across the Plains.

The film tornado rips through Wakita; the water tower is real, but most of the 35 buildings destroyed in and around Main Street were fake. Guthrie became the fictional Newkirk, and several buildings—the Rocket hamburger stand, the gas station, the drive-in theater, and the motel—were all built at 5th and Vilas Avenue and obliterated during the filming. Part of the action was around the Blue Tulip restaurant, on Highway 19 west of Marysville, serving the best pies in Oklahoma; but it exists only in the movie.

UHF

(1989). Al Yankovic, Victoria Jackson. Man wins television station in a poker game and turns it over to his unemployed nephew.

The television station was constructed in a not-yet-occupied wing of the newly constructed Kensington Mall, now TV Guide Building (7140 South Lewis, Tulsa). The transmitter was housed in a radio station off the air since the 1970s, on Edison at 57th West Avenue in Tulsa.

OREGON

Animal House

(1978). John Belushi, Tim Matheson. College dean attempts to expel trouble-making fraternity in 1962.

The original setting for the fictional Faber College was to be the University of Missouri, but after reading the script school officials backed out of the project and filming commenced around the University of Oregon in Eugene. Delta House was actually a halfway house for convicts at 751 East 11th Street. The building was torn down in 1986 and the bricks sold off at $5 each. Erb Memorial Union in the center of campus was the site of the food fight; John Belushi perched on a ladder to look into the girls' sorority at the Sigma Nu House; the courtroom scene was staged in 110 Fenton Hall; and the toga party was staged at Kappa Sigma fraternity. The parade scene in the finale was filmed in the coastal town of Cottage Grove.

Breaking In

(1989). Burt Reynolds, Casey Siemaszko. Professional thief takes on an apprentice.

Reynolds hides money after a bank robbery in Oaks Amusement Park (South East Spokane Street,

Portland), one of the oldest continuously operating amusement parks in America. Surrounded by the same stately oak trees for which it was named, the park was built by the Oregon Water Power and Navigation Company in 1905.

Come See the Paradise

(1990). Dennis Quaid, Tamlyn Tomita. Family is torn apart by internment of Japanese-Americans during World War II.

Portland was used to recreate Little Tokyo in Los Angeles in 1936. Footage was obtained from the Portland Meadows quarter-horse track (1001 North Schmeer Road) and Portland International Raceway (at 1940 North Victory Boulevard). The Brooklyn Movie Theater was played by the Moreland Movie Theater (6712 Southeast Milwaukee), which later was destroyed in a fire.

Drugstore Cowboy

(1989). Matt Dillon, Kelly Lynch. Drug addicts sink inexorably into life of crime.

The opening scene features a robbery at the Nob Hill Pharmacy on the corner of Northwest 21st and Glisan in Portland. Dillon and Lynch live in the Irving Apartments (2127 NW Irving, Portland), and the police officer gets shot at the Josephine Apartments, now condominiums, at Northwest 21st and Irving.

Even Cowgirls Get the Blues

(1993). Uma Thurman, Lorraine Bracco. Hitchhiker with oversized thumbs becomes a model and is sent to Western ranch to film a commercial.

Thurman gets sent to the fictional Rubber Hose Ranch, which was set in the Oregon desert around Bend. Filming also took place in the John Day Fossil Beds National Monument. Containing a variety of plant and animal fossils, this region of north-central Oregon was named for a young scout on the Astor overland expedition of 1811.

Fox Fire

(1996). Angelina Jolie, Hedy Burress. Five teenaged girls are empowered after beating up a teacher who has sexually harassed them.

The school used in the movie was Lincoln High School (1600 SW Salmon Street, Portland). Other scenes in Portland were filmed at the Burnside Skate Park under the Burnside Bridge, and the Broadway Bridge over the Willamette River, which Jolie scales.

Free Willy

(1993). Jason James Richter, Lori Petty. Young boy struggles to save a killer whale.

Hammond Mooring Basin (Iredale Street, Hammond) played Dawson's Marina, where the orca is eventually set free. A hot tub in the marina office allowed actors to stay warm during takes and avoid hypothermia. Richter lives with his foster family in Astoria at 3392 Harrison and hunts for scraps to feed Willy on the 14th Street dock at the Columbia River.

Hear No Evil

(1993). Marlee Matlin, D.B. Sweeney. Deaf woman becomes target of corrupt cop.

Although the more famous *The Shining* featured the Timberline Lodge (Timberline Road off of Highway 26, Mount Hood) as the celebrated hotel in its story, none of the interiors were filmed there. This movie, made 13 years later, was the first to use the interior for shooting.

Hysterical

(1983). Bill Hudson, Clint Walker. Burned out writer moves to small town to rekindle his interest in writing.

Hudson rents the Yaquina Head Lighthouse (three miles north of Newport) in which to work, only to find it inhabited by the spirit of a woman who killed herself. Perched on a rocky peninsula thrusting into the Pacific, the Yaquina Head Lighthouse is the tallest on the Oregon Coast — at 93 feet in height. The lighthouse is open for tours on summer mornings.

Men of Honor

(2000). Cuba Gooding, Robert DeNiro. Son of sharecropper becomes first master diver in the United States Navy.

A naval base was built from scratch on the Oregon side of the Columbia River, which stood in for the Bayonne Dive School in 1952. The scene depicting the crippling accident was filmed on the USS *Navajo* in Long Beach, California, which stood in for the USS *Hoist*. The characters go to unwind at the River Rat Tap in Cathlamet.

Mr. Holland's Opus

(1995). Richard Dreyfuss, Glenne Headly. Frustrated composer finds fulfillment as high school music teacher.

Dreyfuss tries to instill a love of music into his students at Grant High School (2245 NE 36th Avenue, Portand). Other scenes were shot at the Christie School in Marylhurst.

My Own Private Idaho

(1991). River Phoenix, Keanu Reeves. Narcoleptic male prostitute hooks up with the son of the Portland mayor.

James Russo, as mayor of Portland, works in City Hall at 1221 SW 4th Avenue.

One Flew Over the Cuckoo's Nest

(1975). Jack Nicholson, Louise Fletcher. Man sent to mental hospital rallies patients against the head nurse.

Nicholson takes over a ward of the Oregon State Mental Hospital

(Center Street between 24th and 25th streets, Salem). He showed up at the hospital two weeks before filming and mingled with the most disturbed patients, eating in their mess halls, observing their speech patterns and body movements, and even watching patients undergoing the same shock treatments his character would be subjected to in the film. Nicholson staged his insurrection in Building J.

Paint Your Wagon

(1968). Clint Eastwood, Lee Marvin. Farmer and prospector team up with big plans for the California gold country.

The film was shot in Baker, where gold was discovered in 1861. In the Baker City Historic District are more than 100 commercial and residential buildings that highlight the ornate architecture of those early gold rush days. There is a layout of the movie set at the Oregon Trail Museum (2840 Grove Street).

Personal Best

(1982). Mariel Hemingway, Scott Glenn. Top athletes try to make it to the Olympics.

Athletic scenes were filmed at Hayward Field (East 15th Avenue and Agate, Eugene) on the campus of the University of Oregon, site of many Olympic Trials.

Shattered

(1991). Tom Berenger, Greta Scacchi. Amnesic man searches for clues to his previous life after car crash.

Berenger and Scacchi's car leaps over a seaside cliff between Cannon Beach and Manzanita along Highway 101 north of Neahkanie Mountain.

The Shining

(1980). Jack Nicholson, Shelley Duvall. Family becomes caretakers of isolated hotel over the winter.

Although the story was set in Colorado, the opening sequence with the car driving up the mountain road was filmed in Glacier State Park in Montana, and the exterior of the Overlook Hotel was shot at Timberline Lodge (Timberline Road off of Highway 26, Mount Hood). All the remaining principle shooting was done at EMI Studios in Borehamwood, England, including the hedge maze in front of the hotel, which was built on the studio lot. The hotel room in the movie was changed from 217 in the Stephen King novel to 237 because Timberline management feared no one would want to stay in Room 217 after watching the movie, and the lodge doesn't have a Room 237.

Sometimes a Great Notion

(1977). Paul Newman, Henry Fonda. Struggles of a logging family in the Northwest.

The first movie ever to air on Home Box Office was filmed along the Siletze River in Lincoln City and Kernville. A featured hangout was the Kernville Tavern, now Kernville Steak and Seafood, at 186 Siletz Highway.

The Temp

(1993). Timothy Hutton, Lara Flynn Boyle. Executive's path to the corporate penthouse is cleared by an efficient temporary worker.

The Princeton Club, now a part of the Governor Hotel, at SW 11th and Alder in Portland, portrayed Mrs. Appleby's Baked Goods Company, where Hutton, Boyle and Faye Dunaway work. Boyle swims and tries to seduce Hutton at Battleground Lake in Washington.

PENNSYLVANIA

All the Right Moves

(1983). Tom Cruise, Craig T. Nelson. High school football player and coach both dream of getting out of their small town.

Location shots took place in Johnstown. Although Greater Johnstown High School has been torn down, the practice football field is still there on 200 Central Avenue. Point Stadium (100 Johns Street) was the home of the Ampipe Bulldogs and site of the climactic muddy football game.

Animal Factory

(2000). Edward Furlong, Steve Buscemi. Young inmate forges bond with seasoned prisoner.

Furlong is sentenced to a stretch in San Quentin, played by Philadelphia's Holmesburg State Prison, for drug trafficking.

Birdy

(1984). Matthew Modine, Nicolas Cage. Man returns from Vietnam with mental problems that make him yearn to be a bird.

Modine and Cage chase pigeons at an empty warehouse in Philadelphia (46th and Market streets). The building was once the Philadelphia Arena and the original home of *American Bandstand*. Traumatized Vietnam vet Modine is hospitalized at Agnews Developmental Center (Montague Expressway and De La Cruz, San Jose, California).

The Blob

(1958). Steve McQueen, Aneta Corsaut. Gelatinous creature from outer space devours countryside as it grows larger and larger.

The opening scene features terror-stricken patrons streaming into the street from the Colonial Theater (227 Bridge Street, Phoenixville). The restored theater shows movies, including special screenings of *The Blob*. The climax of the drive-in horror classic takes place with the Blob devouring a diner in the nearby town of Downingtown. The original diner was replaced in 1965 at the cost of $18,000, and today the Chef's Diner stands on the site at the corner of Lancaster Avenue (Business Route

30) and Downing Avenue. In between the two towns is Historic Yellow Springs, a Revolutionary War hospital, where neighborhood and wooded scenes were filmed.

Blow Out

(1981). John Travolta, Nancy Allen. Soundman accidentally records evidence that a car crash was really murder.

Travolta drives his jeep through the concourse of Philadelphia's City Hall (Broad and Market streets at Penn Square). Designed to be the world's tallest building when it was planned in 1871, it was surpassed by the Washington Monument and the Eiffel Tower by the time it was finished in 1901. Travolta eventually crashes the jeep into the display window across the street at the old John Wanamaker Department Store, now Lord & Taylor's.

Bob Roberts

(1992). Tim Robbins, Alan Rickman. Conservative folksinger runs for the United States Senate by manipulating the people and the press.

Robbins films his live television segment, *The Cutting Edge*, in the studios of WQED-TV (4802 Fifth Avenue, Pittsburgh). Also in Pittsburgh, the council chambers of the City/County Building on Grant Street were converted into a Senate hearing room. On the campus of Penn State University in College Park, Robbins staged a rally in the 2545-seat Eisenhower Auditorium.

The Cemetery Club

(1993). Ellen Burstyn, Olympia Dukakis. Three friends in their 50s all lose their husbands and meet annually at their graves.

The cemetery where Burstyn, Dukakis and Diane Ladd attend funerals is the Allegheny Cemetery (4734 Butler Street, Pittsburgh). Lainie Kazan's many wedding ceremonies and receptions are staged at the Heinz Hall for the Performing Arts (600 Penn Avenue, Pittsburgh). Moskowitz Music is really Spratt Music on Brownsville Road in Brentwood.

Clean and Sober

(1988). Michael Keaton, Kathy Baker. Man checks into drug rehab center to hide from the law and realizes he is an addict.

Keaton and Baker meet for a date at the Colonial Theater (11th and Moyamensing, Philadelphia).

Dawn of the Dead

(1978). David Emje, Ken Foree. Four people try to survive an attack by zombies by sealing themselves inside a shopping mall.

The horror film was shot in the Monroeville Mall (200 Mall Boulevard, Monroeville), shooting from 10 at night until six in the morning while the stores were closed. The weapons store was shot in downtown Pittsburgh and added to the mall in the movie.

The Distinguished Gentleman

(1992). Eddie Murphy, Lane Smith. Con man with the same name as deceased Congressman gets elected to his Washington seat.

The interior of the Pennsylvania State Capitol (Capitol Hill, Harrisburg), with its 272-foot dome and more than 600 rooms, stood in for the United States Capitol.

Dogma

(1999). Matt Damon, Ben Affleck. Pilgrimage to New Jersey is necessary to prevent extinction of civilization in late 20th century.

Pittsburgh International Airport plays the fictional General Mitchell Airport. The movie was shot almost entirely in Pittsburgh, whose locations played those in Chicago, Milwaukee and New Jersey. Locations included St. Paul's Cathedral (Fifth Avenue and Craig Street, Oakland); the Grand Concourse of the Steel Building (600 Grant Street); the Eckerds on Banksville Road; and the Franklin Inn Mexican Restaurant (2313 Rochester Road, Franklin Park).

Dressed to Kill

(1980). Angie Dickinson, Michael Caine. Hooker and murdered woman's son team up to trap psychokiller.

Dickinson indulges in an erotic game of cat-and-mouse at the Metropolitan Museum of Art (1000 Fifth Avenue at 82nd Street, New York City), which was used for the exterior shots. The interior sequences were filmed at the Philadelphia Museum of Art (Benjamin Franklin Parkway at 26th Street), opened in 1876. Also in New York, call-girl Nancy Allen leaves a client behind in the Sheraton New York Hotel (811 Seventh Avenue) before she is chased into the subway; Caine's basement psychiatric office is at 162 East 70th Street.

Fallen

(1998). Denzel Washington, John Goodman. Host body of fallen dark angel is executed, and its demon comes back to haunt arresting detective.

Although the Eastern State Penitentiary (22nd Street and Fairmount Avenues) and City Hall (Broad and Market streets at Penn Plaza) make appearances, the film utilizes lesser known Philadelphia landmarks. Geno's Steaks (9th and Passyunk Avenue), an historic purveyor of Philadelphia cheesesteaks, is prominently featured in night scenes.

The Fish That Saved Pittsburgh

(1979). Julius Erving, Jonathan Winters. Woeful basketball team gets help from psychic.

The movie was filmed mostly in Pittsburgh's north side; the basketball scenes were staged at the Pittsburgh Civic Arena (1 Mario Lemiuex Place).

Flashdance

(1983). Jennifer Beals, Michael Nouri. Woman dreams of giving up welding job for ballet school.

Beals dances through the Hall of Sculpture at the Carnegie (4400 Forbes Avenue), a cultural complex in the heart of the university area.

Girl Interrupted

(1999). Winona Ryder, Angelina Jolie. Seemingly normal girl ends up in a mental institution after a failed suicide attempt.

Ryder is hospitalized at the Harrisburg State Hospital (Cameron and McClay streets). Built in 1853, the historic asylum is open by appointment. The river scenes were shot along the Susquehanna River at the 5-mile Riverfront Park in Harrisburg. The ice cream scenes were filmed at Eckel's Drug Store (36 East Main Street, Mechanicsburg). Other buildings along Main Street between Arch and Market streets were used for the movie.

Hairspray

(1988). Rikki Lake, Sonny Bono. Television teen dance show gets integrated in the 1960s.

Dorney Park (3830 Dorney Park Road off Hamilton Boulevard, Allentown) portrayed the Tilted Acres amusement park. Of Dorney Park's five rollercoasters, two are vintage wooden coasters, and the Dentzel carousel dates to 1921.

Innocent Blood

(1992). Anne Parrillaud, Robert Loggia. Vampire stalks the streets of Pittsburgh, never feeding on the innocent.

Anthony LaPaglia finally kills Loggia at Liberty Avenue near Market Square; earlier Pittsburgh locations included the Melody Lounge, which played a Mob hangout, and Shadyside Gas in Squirrel Hill.

Just the Way You Are

(1984). Kristy McNichols, Michael Ontkean. Woman with crippled leg dons a fake cast at a ski resort to find love.

Shot mostly in Europe, McNichol does board a bus in front of the Gallery shopping center in Philadelphia at Market and 9th streets.

King Pin

(1996). Woody Harrelson, Randy Quaid. Crippled bowling champion tries to convince his Amish protégé to join the pro tour.

The early bowling scenes were staged at the Forward Lanes (5844 Forward Avenue, Pittsburgh), in the 4th floor of a brick warehouse. The final million-dollar winner-take-all bowling match between Bill Murray and Harrelson was filmed at the National Bowling Stadium in Reno, Nevada. The largest bowling center in the United States, it cost $43 million to build in 1994.

Lorenzo's Oil

(1992). Susan Sarandon, Nick Nolte. Parents start working on cure for rare disease afflicting their son after the medical establishment forsakes them.

Pittsburgh portrayed Washington DC in the movie; Sarandon's

house is actually a facade built between two existing homes on Dickson Avenue in Ben Avon, a Pittsburgh suburb. Nolte and Sarandon discuss their son's case with Peter Ustinov after an opera performance at the Carnegie Music Hall (4400 Forbes Avenue).

Major League II

(1994). Tom Berenger, Charlie Sheen. Players again battle owner and other teams for World Series championship.

Riverside Stadium in Harrisburg (City Island in the Susquehanna River) was used for the spring training home of the Cleveland Indians in Winter Haven. Camden Yards in Baltimore, Maryland, stood in for Cleveland's Jacobs Field.

Mannequin

(1987). Andrew McCarthy, Kim Cattrall. Artist falls in love with store mannequin he has created.

The store dummies come to life in both this movie and the sequel in John Wanamaker's (now Lord & Taylor) at 13th and Market streets in Philadelphia. The department store, with its celebrated pipe organ and familiar baroque bronze eagle, opened in 1861. McCarthy visits his girlfriend in the Dorchester Apartments on Rittenhouse Square.

Mrs. Soffel

(1984). Mel Gibson, Diane Keaton. Warden's wife carries on affair with prisoner she helps to escape.

The film was shot at the Allegheny Jail (930 Second Avenue, Pittsburgh). Built in 1886, the jail was the site of the real-life incident upon which the story is based. The tower of the adjoining stone courthouse was once the tallest structure in Pittsburgh at 325 feet. The train scenes were shot on the Mid-Continent Railroad in North Freedom, Wisconsin.

Night of the Living Dead

(1968). Duane Jones, Judith O'Dea. Radiation causes recently buried corpses to rise from the grave and seek human flesh for food.

The low-budget horror classic was shot in and around Pittsburgh. The opening shot was filmed along the entrance road of the Evans City Cemetery, 30 miles north of Pittsburgh. The obelisk which O'Dea cowers behind while Russell Steiner grapples with a ghoul is the Kramer monument.

Only You

(1994). Robert Downey, Jr., Marisa Tomei. Woman leaves behind a fiancé to chase a man she believes to be her soul mate.

Although the movie was filmed mostly in Italy, there were scenes shot in Pittsburgh prior to the story moving overseas, including at the Kennywood Amusement Park (Exit 9 off I-376, West Mifflin), built in 1899 by A.W. Mellon. Tomei lived in an apartment in Shadyside at Bayard and Morewood avenues.

Philadelphia

(1993). Tom Hanks, Denzel Washington. Lawyer suffering from AIDS sues his former law firm for wrongful dismissal.

Despite its title and its location shooting, the movie doesn't show as much of the city as most, since most of the action was set indoors. The Mellon Bank Center (1735 Market Street) portrayed the exterior of the Wheeler Building, where Hanks worked as a lawyer. Across the street is the Pickwick Pharmacy where Washington fends off the advances of a gay student who incorrectly assumes that he is gay because he's defending a gay man. Washington decides to represent Hanks in the University of Pennsylvania Fine Arts Library (Walnut Street), and the courtroom scenes were filmed in Courtroom 243 at City Hall (Broad and Market streets at Penn Square). Washington picks up party food after the birth of his daughter at Famous Deli (Bainbridge Street). The Action AIDS Office was located at 1216 Arch Street, and Hanks dies at Mt. Sinai Hospital (Fourth and Reed streets).

Rocky

(1976). Sylvester Stallone, Talia Shire. Unknown working class boxer gets a chance to fight for the heavyweight championship.

Part of Stallone's training regimen involves running up the steps of the Philadelphia Art Museum (26th Street and Benjamin Franklin Parkway). A statue of Stallone as Rocky once stood here but has been moved to the Spectrum at Broad and Pattison streets.

Rocky II

(1979). Sylvester Stallone, Talia Shire. Boxer struggles with personal life after winning the world championship.

Stallone and Shire walk through Rittenhouse Square in Philadelphia and visit the Italian Market on 9th Street.

Silence of the Lambs

(1991). Jodie Foster, Anthony Hopkins. FBI cadet must befriend psychopathic killer to help capture a serial killer.

The Soldiers and Sailors Museum (4141 Fifth Avenue and Bigelow Boulevard, Pittsburgh) was transformed into the Memphis Town Hall where Hopkins is caged and interrogated by Foster. The exhibits honor the memory of veterans from all American wars and military conflicts. Foster also walks through the "bug room" in the Carnegie Museum of Natural History (4400 Forbes Avenue, Pittsburgh).

Sixth Sense

(1999). Haley Joel Osment, Bruce Willis. Boy who communicates with spirits seeks the help of a depressed child psychologist.

Among the many Philadelphia locations used were City Hall (Broad and Market streets at Penn Square); the Undine Barge Club on Boat House Row in Fairmount Park; Old St. Augustine's Church (Fourth and Vine streets); and the cobblestone streets around Head House Square. Osment's school was the Stoddart-Fleischer Middle School (13th and Green streets), and the anniversary dinner was filmed at the Striped Bass (1500 Walnut Street).

Slap Shot

(1977). Paul Newman, Michael Ontkean. Failing minor league hockey team resorts to violence on the ice to find success.

Cambria County War Memorial Arena (326 Napoleon Street) in Johnstown served as home ice for the fictional Charlestown Chiefs.

Striking Distance

(1993). Bruce Willis, Sarah Jessica Parker. Cop looks for father's killer inside the police force and is demoted to river duty.

The movie was filmed almost entirely in Pittsburgh; Willis docks his houseboat at Washington's landing on the Allegheny River, the car explosion in the opening sequence was filmed in the Armstrong Tunnel, and three police cars go airborne on Fifth Avenue in Duquesne. The River Resuce Station that Willis worked from was built atop a barge at the old River Rescue Center on Pittsburgh's south side. Another movie creation was the cabin on Duck Hollow, which was the scene of the final shoot-out.

Sudden Death

(1995). Jean Claude Van Damme, Powers Booth. Terrorists kidnap the Vice-President of the United States. The ice arena saboteurs threaten to blow up during the Stanley Cup Finals is the Pittsburgh Civic Arena (1 Mario Lemieux Place).

Taps

(1981). George C. Scott, Timothy Hutton. Cadets stage armed takeover of military academy to protect it from condominium developers.

Valley Forge Military Academy played the fictional 150-year-old, financially strapped Bunker Hill Military Academy. Prior to filming, young actors such as Hutton, Sean Penn and Tom Cruise went through a rigorous 45-day orientation to military school at Valley Forge.

Trading Places

(1983). Eddie Murphy, Dan Aykroyd. At the whim of millionaire brothers, a homeless man and successful businessman switch roles.

Filmed largely in Philadelphia, the opening scene features Murphy pretending to be a legless veteran while panhandling in Rittenhouse Square. Aykroyd's handsome home is at 2014 Delancey Street, and the First Union Building at the corner of Broad and Sansom streets played the Duke and Duke bank owned by millionaire pranksters Don Ameche and Ralph Bellamy. Murphy and Aykroyd board a New York–bound train in disguises at 30th Street Station on 30th Street.

Twelve Monkeys

(1995). Bruce Willis, Brad Pitt. Futuristic convict volunteers to be sent back in time to stop a deadly plague.

Time traveler Willis is sent too far back in the past and institutionalized as insane at a mental hospital played by the Eastern State Penitentiary (22nd Street and Fairmount Avenue, Philadelphia). The prison opened in 1829 and became one of the most influential and most copied buildings ever built in the United States, with its private cells in individual cell blocks radiating out from a central rotunda. To depict a post-apocalyptic America, footage was shot in the industrial wastelands of Philadelphia and Baltimore. A scene was shot at Garrett-Jacobs Mansion (11 West Mt. Vernon Place), the largest and most expensive townhouse ever built in Baltimore, home of Robert Garrett, president of B & O Railroad.

Two Bits

(1990). Al Pacino, Mary Elizabeth Mastrantonio. Old man makes deal with grandson before he dies.

The 2300–2400 blocks of Philadelphia's South 7th Street were transformed into the South Philadelphia of the 1930s Depression. The President's Banquet Room (2308 Snyder Avenue) plays the La Paloma Theatre, and the wedding and funeral take place at St. Gabriels Church (29th and Dickinson streets).

Unbreakable

(2000). Samuel Jackson, Bruce Willis. Mysterious stranger approaches lone survivor of train crash with a theory on his survival.

The devastating train crash takes place in Philadelphia where Willis works as a security guard at Franklin Field (33rd and South streets). Footage was also shot in the Manayunk section of the city at Pretzel Park (Cotton and Cresson streets).

Witness

(1985). Harrison Ford, Kelly McGillis. City cop goes undercover in Amish country to protect young boy who saw a murder.

Lukas Haas witnesses the murder while hiding in a restroom stall and is later interrogated by Ford at 30 Street Station (30th Street, Philadelphia). In his disguise as an Amish farmer, Ford slugs a bully while eating ice cream at the W.L. Zimmerman & Sons General Store in downtown Intercourse.

Wonder Boys

(2000). Michael Douglas, Robert Downey, Jr. English professor struggles with an unstable student, his pregnant lover and unfinished novel.

Much of the film was shot on the campus of Carnegie-Mellon, with inside scenes at Baker Hall and the College of Fine Arts. Additional footage was shot in Pittsburgh's Hill District and on the North Side.

Worth Winning

(1989). Mark Harmon, Madeleine Stowe. Man accepts challenge to secure marriage proposals from three women.

Harmon lives in Philadelphia at 322 Delancey Street and sees his three fiancées plotting their revenge at nearby Head House Square. Harmon marries at Old Swede's Church on Christian Street, organized in 1642 and the oldest congregation in Pennsylvania.

RHODE ISLAND

Amistad

(1997). Morgan Freeman, Matthew McConaughey. Slaves rebel aboard ship coming to the West Indies and are tried in America.

The leaders of the insurgents are brought to Newport for trial and placed in a jail built on Queen Anne Square in front of Trinity Church. Other locations used in Rhode Island include St. John's Church (61 Polar Street, Newport) and the State House on Smith Street in Providence. Occupied in 1900, the Charles Follen McKim–designed arch is the second largest of four unsupported marble domes in the world. Anthony Hopkins, as John Quincy Adams, argues the case at the Massachusetts State House (Beacon Street, Boston). A complete replica of the 129-foot schooner Amistad was constructed at the Mystic Seaport (Route 27, Mystic, Connecticut) for filming. The ship docks around the world but winters in the 17-acre historical area that was founded in 1929 on the site of three of the five shipyards that once lined the Mystic River.

The Betsy

(1978). Laurence Olivier, Robert Duvall. Race car driver hired to design a fuel-efficient car gets entangled in family-owned auto corporation's feuds.

Rosecliff (Bellevue Avenue, Newport), the French-style chateau built by Horace Trumbauer in 1901, served as Olivier's home. The mansion is open for tours. Auto scenes were filmed in a long-defunct American Motors Corporation assembly plant in Kenosha, Wisconsin.

The Great Gatsby

(1974). Robert Redford, Mia Farrow. Young Midwesterner observes the opulent lifestyle of his *nouveau riche* landlord.

Hammersmith Farm (Ocean Drive, Newport), built in 1887 by John W. Auchincloss (and Jacqueline Bouvier Kennedy's childhood home), was used for the exteriors of Redford's Long Island, New York, mansion. The property is open for tours during the summer. The actual kitchen of the Breakers (Ochre Point Avenue) was used in the movie. Doubling as a French hotel in Normandy was Rosecliff (Bellevue Avenue, Newport), a 1902 creation of Stanford White modeled after the Grand Triano at Versailles. Rosecliff is open for tours.

The 75-acre Aldrich Mansion in Warwick, Rhode Island, was the movie set for Brad Pitt and Anthony Hopkins in *Meet Joe Black*. (Ultima Studio, Inc.)

Meet Joe Black

(1998). Brad Pitt, Anthony Hopkins. Death takes a human form and develops earthly interests.

Most of the action takes place at Aldrich Mansion (836 Warwick Neck Avenue, Warwick). The 70-room chateau, built on 75 acres overlooking Narragansett Bay by Senator Nelson W. Aldrich, took 16 years to build before it was finished in 1912. It is open to the public for receptions and parties. In New York City, Pitt visits Hopkins in his luxurious penthouse apartment at the Pierre Hotel (E. 61st Street).

Providence

(1999–). Mike Farrell, Melina Kanakaredes. Woman returns home to practice medicine in her home town.

In the opening credits for the television series, the camera follows a taxi from the airport to Providence's East Side.

SOUTH CAROLINA

The Abyss

(1989). Ed Harris, Mary Elizabeth Mastrantonio. Civilian divers on oil rig are called on by the Navy to rescue a stricken nuclear submarine.

The movie was filmed in the half-completed Cherokee Nuclear Power Plant near Gaffney. After pouring $700 million into its construction, Duke Power abandoned the project in 1983. When planning for the film was underway, the producers heard of the Gaffney site, and after visiting, bought the facility for $3 million. Two specially designed tanks were constructed for underwater filming, including one converted from the nuclear reactor containment building that holds over seven million gallons of water and became the largest underwater set in the world. After filming, 20th Century-Fox left the set standing, but it is closed to the public.

The Big Chill

(1983). Kevin Kline, Glenn Close. Group of college friends reunite for funeral of one of their friends.

Kline and Close live at Tidalholm (1 Laurens Street, Beaufort), a home built in 1853. The early morning jogging scene, complete with banter on insider trading, was filmed along Bay Street in Beaufort.

Chasers

(1994). Tom Berenger, William McNamara. Navy men assigned to prisoner-escort duty discover their criminal is a gorgeous woman.

Berenger and McNamara slug it out at Wacky Golf (3900 Highway 17 South, Myrtle Beach), where they wreck a car on the volcano of the miniature golf course that was built for the movie). Later they visit Harold's Country Club Bar and Grill (Highway 17-A, Yemassee), located inside an old-fashioned rural service station. The denouement comes on the Old Grace Bridge.

Die Hard: With a Vengeance

(1995). Bruce Willis, Samuel Jackson. Bomber taunts super cop in New York City with game of "Simon Says".

The Grace Memorial Bridge in Charleston, South Carolina, is commandeered during the movie; the exterior of Trucker's Inn (7701 Assateague Avenue, Jessup, Maryland) plays Canada, where the helicopter lands in the ending sequence.

The Great Santini

(1979). Robert Duvall, Michael O'Keefe. Marine disciplinarian relates to family the same way he does his troops.

Many of the military scenes were filmed at the Marine Corps Air Station (Main Gate at the intersection of U. S. Highway 21 and SC 116, Beaufort). The windows of the Air Station gymnasium were blacked out for the nighttime high school basketball game scene. Duvall's home, with views of the marsh, was Tidalholm (1 Laurens Street, Beaufort). Built in 1853, spacious Beaufort-style renovations were made following the Storm of 1893, which blew the second-floor roof away. O'Keefe finds a drunken Duvall under the oak tree at "The Point" (bordered by King, Pinckney, Laurens and Short Streets in the Beaufort Historic District). The Tidalholm property is adjacent to the Laurens Street-Short Street corner of the square.

Last Dance

(1996). Sharon Stone, Rob Morrow. Young lawyer assigned to clemency case of convicted murderer grows close to her as execution date nears.

Prison scenes were filmed in the unopened state prison in Ridgeland; other locations include the Castle (411 Crave Street, Beaufort) and Hunting Island State Park (Highway 21 South).

Major League: Back to the Minors

(1998). Scott Bakula, Corbin Bernsen. Ex–major league ballplayer takes managing job down in the minor leagues.

Seven Charleston-area ballparks were used to replicate the minor league schedule of the South Carolina Buzz. College Park, built in 1907, became the "Littleville" home field of the Buzz, and is currently the practice field for Citadel baseball. Historic Mirmow Field in Orangeburg, built in 1947, was used for baseball scenes. The other ballparks utilized were the exteriors of Remley's Point (the sports complex of the College of Charleston), Collins Park (a small American Legion park in North Charleston) and the Summerville High School field (1101 Boone Hill Road, Summerville). Joe Riley Stadium (360 Fishburne Street, Charleston) provided interiors, and the Charleston Coliseum (5001 Coliseum Drive, North Charleston) doubled for the Metrodome's tunnels and locker rooms. Off the field, four sets were built in the grand ballroom of the Francis Marion Hotel, built in 1924 by famed architect W. Lee Stoddard. The final game between the Buzz and the Minnesota Twins was staged inside the Hubert H. Humphrey Metrodome (34 Kirby Puckett Drive, Minneapolis, Minnesota).

Paradise

(1991). Don Johnson, Melanie Griffith. A couple torn apart by family tragedy rekindle love through a summer guest.

Childless Johnson and Griffith live in the Plaza Apartments at 3rd and Prospect streets in Cleveland, Ohio. Elijah Wood attends private school at the Mather Mansion on Euclid Avenue there. Most of the film was shot in the tiny town of McClellanville on Highway 17 between Charleston and Georgetown. Georgetown, where many of the original buildings from the 1700s are still in use, played a fishing village named Brimley in the movie.

The Patriot

(2000). Mel Gibson, Jason Isaacs. French and Indian War hero is reluctantly drawn into the American Revolution.

The story was set and filmed across South Carolina, including Historic Brattonsville (off Highway 322) in Rock Hill. The 720-acre living history village features a block of Colonial-era homes and other structures open to the public. It was an actual Revolutionary War battle site. In Brattonsville, Hightower Hall served as the exterior and interior of Camden Plantation, and the Homestead House became the interior of Joely Richardson's house. The College of Charleston doubled for Charleston Assembly Hall, and exteriors were shot of Charleston's colorful colonial homes on Tradd Street and Meeting Street. The elaborate British party hosted by Tom Wilkinson took place at Middleton Place (4300 Ashley River Road, Charleston), featuring America's oldest landscaped gardens.

The Prince of Tides

(1991). Barbra Streisand, Nick Nolte. Psychologist probing the roots of patient's suicide attempt becomes involved with her brother.

The Bay Street Inn (601 Bay Street, Beaufort), an 1852 mansion converted into a bed-and-breakfast, played Kate Nelligan's home. Beach footage was obtained on Fripp Island (Route 21, east of Beaufort), and Manhattan apartment scenes were filmed in Beaufort Arsenal (713 Craven Street). In New York City, Streisand maintained an office at 4 East 74th Street in Manhattan, and Nolte stopped for fresh bread while jogging each day at Vesuvio Bakery (160 Prince Street). They enjoyed a romantic dinner at the Rainbow Room on the 65th Floor at 30 Rockefeller Plaza.

The Program

(1993). James Caan, Halle Berry. Young men struggle with the pressures of playing major college football.

Football scenes were filmed at Williams-Brice Stadium (701 Assembly Street) on the campus of the University of South Carolina. A controversial scene that was erased from prints of the movie after two weeks involved players lying in the intersection of Meeting and State streets, which involved copycat incidents from young teens after viewing the movie. Ironically, the sequence in the movie was inspired by actual stunts. Collegiate scenes were also filmed in Durham, North Carolina, in Duke University's Gothic Reading Room and several other campus buildings.

Rules of Engagement

(2000). Samuel Jackson, Tommy Lee Jones. Attorney defends army officer who ordered troops to fire on civilians.

The south end of Hunting Island State Park (Hwy 21) doubled for Quang Tri Province in Vietnam. A replica of the Marine Corps Base at Camp LeJeune was built at Vint Hill Farm Station in Manassas, Virginia.

Shag

(1989). Phoebe Cates, Bridget Fonda. Friends take soon-to-be-bride to the beach for a final fling in 1963.

The Pavilion on Ocean Boulevard and 9th Avenue in Myrtle Beach, a 1960s amusement complex where the dance craze of the title actually started, was the location for much of the shooting. The Pavilion was largely wiped out by Hurricane Andrew in 1992. Other locations include the Thomas Cafe (703 Front Street, Georgetown) and the Skyview Drive-In (1815 W. Palmetto, Florence).

Something to Talk About

(1995). Julia Roberts, Dennis Quaid. Husband's affair leads woman to reassess everything and everyone in her life.

Filming locations in Beaufort included the University of South Carolina-Beaufort's Performing Arts Center (801 Cateret Street) and Michael Rainey Antiques (702 Craven Street). The Dauart Plantation in Gillionsville (US Hwy 278 and SC 462) portrayed the King Farm.

Swamp Thing

(1982). Louis Jordan, Adrienne Barbeau. Mad scientist tries to create a new species by blending animals and plants.

Jordan's experiments go awry at the Audubon Swamp Garden at Magnolia Plantation (3550 Ashley River Road, Charleston). John James Audubon visited the blackwater cypress and tupelo swamp to collect specimens. The garden, which covers 60 acres, is open for tours.

The War

(1994). Kevin Costner, Elijah Wood. War vet deals with son's "war" with rival neighborhood children.

The massive oak prominent in the film, where Wood builds a tree fort, is located at the entrance to Carolina Shores at the end of Carolina Avenue, off Bruce K. Smalls Drive in the Gray's Hill area of Beaufort. A county ordinance was amended to permit the film crew to demolish and remove the road around the oak tree and to replace the pavement afterwards.

White Squall

(1996). Jeff Bridges, Caroline Goodall. Teenage boys put to sea to learn discipline.

Many locations were filmed in downtown Beaufort, including the Budget Print building (510 Carteret Street), which became a bus terminal; the Rhett House Inn (1009 Craven Street); the Chocolate Tree (507 Carteret Street); Murr's Graphic & Printing (1012 Boundary Street); and the churchyard of St. Helena's Episcopal Church (501 Church Street).

SOUTH DAKOTA

Dances with Wolves

(1990). Kevin Costner, Mary McDonnell. Civil War soldier turns his back on the military to embrace life with Sioux Indians.

The opening sequence, where Costner receives his orders at Fort Hays to travel to Fort Sedgewick, was filmed on a private ranch east of Rapid City. Two of the movie's sets, the major's house and the blacksmith shop, have been moved to this tourist spot, known as the Fort Hays Film Set (four miles south of Rapid City). The Sage Creek Wilderness Area in the Badlands National Park was the backdrop for the wagon trip through Sioux Indian country to Fort Sedgewick. The Indian winter camp was set up in Spearfish Canyon in the Black Hills National Forest; the exact spot of the final scene where Costner and McDonnell leave the tribe was once marked by signs, but they have long since succumbed to souvenir-hunters.

North by Northwest

(1959). Cary Grant, Eva Marie Saint. Man is mistaken for a spy and leads a chase across the country.

Grant is kidnapped from the lobby of the Plaza Hotel (Fifth Avenue and Central Park South, New York City); afterward he is taken to James Mason's estate at Old Westbury Gardens (71 Old Westbury Road, Old Westbury, New York). In Chicago, Grant bribes a porter for his uniform at Union Station and tracks Saint to her hotel room in the Ambassador East (1301 North State Parkway). Grant meets Leo G. Carroll at Midway Airport before flying to Rapid City, South Dakota. Although the famous scene at Mount Rushmore was filmed at the Shrine of Democracy from a distance, the close-ups of the characters running down the faces was filmed on a set at MGM.

Thunderheart

(1992). Val Kilmer, Sam Shepherd. FBI agent is sent to investigate a murder on an Indian Reservation.

Kilmer pokes around Pine Ridge Indian Reservation in the wilderness of the Badlands to solve his case.

TENNESSEE

Cast Away

(2000). Tom Hanks, Helen Hunt. Workaholic supervisor is stranded for four years on a deserted island.

Hanks worked as a Federal Express executive out of the company headquarters at 942 South Shady Grove Road in Memphis.

The Client

(1994). Susan Sarandon, Tommy Lee Jones. Boy carries Mafia secret away from lawyer's suicide.

Brad Renfro witnesses the mob lawyer's suicide in John F. Kennedy Park (4575 Raleigh–La Grange Road, Memphis). Other Memphis locations include Sarandon's office in the Sterick Building (9 North Third Street); the Memphis County Courthouse (140 Adams Avenue), where Jones tries to force Renfro to testify; the Criminal Justice Center (201 Poplar Avenue), where Renfro is locked up for a night; and the Arcade Hotel (540 South Main Street), where Renfro's life is endangered.

Coal Miner's Daughter

(1980). Sissy Spacek, Tommy Lee Jones. Trail from poverty to fame for country singer Loretta Lynn.

Spacek performs in the Ryman Auditorium (116 5th Avenue North, Nashville), the former home of the Grand Ole Opry. Opened in 1892 as a revival church, the Ryman was renovated a century later and can be viewed through self-guided tours.

A Family Thing

(1996). Robert Duvall, James Earl Jones. White rural Southerner finds his real mother was a black woman and sets out to find his half-brother.

Ernestine and Hazel's, an old whorehouse turned nightclub on South Main Street at Calhoun Street in Memphis, takes a brief starring role.

Finding Graceland

(1998). Harvey Keitel, Jonathan Schaech. Man making pilgrimage to Graceland picks up a hitchhiker claiming to be Elvis Presley.

Seeking to shoot their movie in the Graceland mansion (3764 Elvis Presley Boulevard, Memphis), producers sent the script to Priscilla Presley for approval. She liked it so much she not only granted permission but became a financial backer of the project. Keitel and Schaech pick up Bridget Fonda, playing a Marilyn Monroe impersonator, at the Grand Casino (13615 Old Highway 61 North, Tunica, Mississippi).

The Firm

(1993). Tom Cruise, Jeanne Tripplehorn. Young lawyer starts dream job with law firm that isn't quite what it seemed.

While attending school at Harvard University in Massachusetts, Cruise waiters at the Abbey in South Boston and runs in front of the Trinity Church and into the Copley Plaza Hotel on Copley Square. When Cruise goes to Memphis to work, he is feted at a rooftop party at the Peabody Hotel (149 Union Avenue); the exterior of his new firm, Bendini, Lambert and Locke, is played by the Union Planters Building (Front and Madison streets). Cruise is first approached by FBI agent Ed Harris at the Blues City Cafe (138 Beale Street) and meets Holly Hunter to plan a way out of the firm at the Front Street Deli (77 Front Street). The cemetery where lawyers who challenge the firm end up is the Elmwood Cemetery at 824 Dudley Avenue in Memphis.

Great Balls of Fire

(1989). Dennis Quaid, Winona Ryder. The story of the unconventional lifestyle of pioneer rock and roller Jerry Lee Lewis.

Quaid shuttles Ryder to and from school at Bruce Elementary School (1206 Carr Road, Memphis). Scenes were also shot at Sun Studio (706 Union Street), the recording studio made famous by Elvis Presley, Lewis, Carl Perkins, Roy Orbison, Johnny Cash and others. Guided tours are available, and visitors can even make their own recordings. Scenes of this biopic were also shot at Lewis' actual childhood home in Marion, Arkansas (93 Military Road).

The Green Mile

(1999). Tom Hanks, David Morse. Prison guards in the 1930s supervise a man on death row with a gift for healing.

The story begins with flashbacks from a nursing home played by Flat Top Manor near Blowing Rock, North Carolina, at Milepost 284 of the Blue Ridge Parkway. The graceful estate with the commanding views was built by Moses Cone, the "Denim King." The empty Tennessee State Penitentiary (Centennial Boulevard, Nashville) stood in for the Cold Mountain prison in Louisiana. The low, one-story building next to the administration building was used for filming.

Mystery Train

(1989). Steve Buscemi, Nicoletta Braschi. Three sets of foreigners seek America from a base in a sleazy Memphis hotel.

The Arcade Hotel (540 South Main Street, Memphis) stars as the hotel where the characters stay. The rooms have no televisions and are barely furnished, but every room features a portrait of Elvis Presley.

Nashville

(1975). Ned Beatty, David Arkin. The lives of various people in the country music business intersect.

The climax of the movie takes place in Centennial Park (West End Avenue, Nashville) at the replica of the Parthenon on the Acropolis in Athens, Greece. The full-size reproduction is the only such model in the world.

October Sky

(1999). Jake Gyllenhaal, Chris Cooper. High school boys in 1957 build rockets while their small town smirks.

The town of Coalwood, West Virginia, the setting of the true story, disappeared when the mine was closed in 1965. The main set of the coalmining town was built in Petros, even constructing a fake mine with a 125-foot wrought-iron mining tipple. Businesses and homes were shot in Oliver Springs; the 1900 brick Sienknecht Store on Main Street became the Olga Coal Company store. Downtown Knoxville stood in for

Sun Studio in Memphis, Tennessee, where many a legendary recording career began, was a movie set in *Great Balls of Fire*, the movie biography of Jerry Lee Lewis.

1950s Indianapolis as the setting for the National Science Competition, and the characters visit the Tennessee Theatre at 604 South Gay Street.

The People vs. Larry Flynt

(1996). Woody Harrelson, Courtney Love. Lowbrow pornography publisher turns into crusader for free speech.

Memphis stood in for 1960s Columbus, Ohio, including the elegant Peabody Memphis (149 Union Avenue), with a fountain in the lobby where ducks march to and from the penthouse. The first trial was staged in Courthouse Square, Oxford, Mississippi, and later the Supreme Court was recreated in a 1929 Memphis train terminal.

The Rainmaker

(1997). Matt Damon, Danny DeVito. Idealistic young lawyer and cynical partner take on powerful law firm representing crooked insurance company.

Cleveland, Ohio's, landmark Terminal Tower (127 Public Square on the southwest corner) serves as headquarters for the insurance company sued by Matt Damon. The statue out front is of Moses Cleveland, founder of the city. The trial takes place at Shelby County Courthouse (140 Adams Avenue, Memphis). Other Memphis locations include the Pinch Historic District where Memphis was founded in 1819; Court Square; and the Las Savell jewelry store in the stone building at 61 S. McLean Boulevard.

The Thing Called Love

(1993). River Phoenix, Samantha Mathis. Friendship and rivalry among young singer-songwriters in the country music business.

Phoenix and Mathis belt out country tunes at the Bluebird Cafe (4104 Hillsboro Pike, Nashville).

Wag the Dog

(1997). Robert DeNiro, Dustin Hoffman. Political spin doctor convinces Hollywood producer to fabricate a war to deflect public attention from Presidential sex scandal.

A small part of this political satire was filmed in Nashville, in Riverfront Park (First Avenue and Broadway) from the bridge to downtown.

TEXAS

Ace Ventura: When Nature Calls

(1995). Jim Carrey, Ian McNeice. Pet detective investigates the disappearance of a rare white bat in Africa.

777 Ranch, a 15,000-acre wildlife and adventure park in Hondo, Texas, with open, grassy savannas and varied herds of grazing animals, doubled for the African villages of Wachati and Wachootoo; the two sets are still in place. In South Carolina, the Botany Bay Plantation on Edisto Island near Charleston, a nature and game preserve, offered lush, dense, tropical vegetation, as well as rivers and a salt marsh with tall brown grass, to duplicate the African jungle. The Cherokee Plantation (5109 Combahee Road, Yemassee, South Carolina), featuring a Georgian manor house and manicured lawns, served as the exterior of the British Consulate in Bonai.

All the Pretty Horses

(2000). Matt Damon, Henry Thomas. Texas drifter heads for Mexico in search of better times after mother sells the family ranch.

In Texas, Damon's Ruby Ranch was portrayed by the Hill Ranch in Helotes, an 1850s stone hacienda. Other shooting locations included the Gallagher's Ranch (two miles southwest of the junction of Park Road 37 and State Highway 16, in far northeastern Medina County), the oldest dude ranch in Texas. The spread was named for civil engineer Peter Gallagher, who was commissioned in 1833 to find a location for a Mexican supply depot on San Geronimo Creek. San Antonio locations included the Scottish Rite Cathedral (308 Avenue E. at 4th Street) and the Cadillac Bar and Grill (212 South Flores). Damon is shot in a gunfight at the Charles R Ranch south of Las Vegas, New Mexico. Damon is returned from a Mexican jail to the New Mexico Prison in Santa Fe, which has stood empty since 1980.

Any Given Sunday

(1999). Al Pacino, Cameron Diaz. Woman owner tries to prove herself in the macho world of professional football.

The Sharks play their home games at the Orange Bowl in Miami, Florida, and the climactic playoff game takes place in Texas Stadium (2401 E. Airport Freeway, Irving).

Apollo 13

(1995). Tom Hanks, Gary Sinese. Story of astronauts and ground crew averting disaster on a mission to the moon.

Shot in the Johnson Space Center (1601 NASA Road, Houston), the zero gravity scenes were staged aboard the "Vomit Comet," an old Boeing 707 modified at Ellington Field. Space Center Houston, the official Visitor Center, is open to visitors.

Arlington Road

(1999). Jeff Bridges, Timothy Robbins. Widower of FBI agent killed in an anti-terrorist operation suspects his new neighbors might be terrorists.

Bridges is a professor at the University of Houston (4800 Calhoun Road), which substitutes for Georgetown University in Washington DC. The car chase was filmed partially on Allen parkway through downtown Houston, and the batting cage scene was filmed near Houston Baptist University.

The Bad News Bears Break Training

(1977). William Devane, Clifton James. Star of misfit team travels to Houston for an exhibition game and to make amends with estranged father.

In Houston, the big game is played at the world's first domed stadium, the Astrodome (8400 Kirby Drive). Tours are available. Additional scenes were shot in Bayland park at Bissonet and Hillcroft.

The Best Little Whorehouse in Texas

(1982). Burt Reynolds, Dolly Parton. Sheriff—and regular patron—fights to keep whorehouse open when it is targeted by a TV evangelist.

Parton's Chicken Ranch was portrayed by a century-old farmhouse in Pflugerville, and the mythical Lanville County Courthouse was played by the Lavaca County Courthouse (Courthouse Square, corner of Main and 3rd streets, Hallettsville).

Big Green

(1995). Steve Guttenberg, Olivia d'Abo. Misfit kids bring pride to depressed Texas town on soccer field.

The big concluding soccer game was staged in Austin's Zilker Park, off Barton Springs Road (FM 2444). Bordering Town Lake, the 389-acre park's centerpiece is Barton Springs, a spring-fed 1,000-foot-long swimming pool

The Bad News Bears baseball team play their big game in Houston's Astrodome in *The Bad News Bears Break Training*.

with a constant temperature of 68 degrees.

Bonnie and Clyde

(1967). Warren Beatty, Faye Dunaway. Violent bank-robbing couple become folk heroes in the Midwest during the Depression.

The movie was filmed on location across Texas, and some of the banks appearing in the film were robbed in real-life by Bonnie Parker and Clyde Barrow. One was the Ponder State Bank, now a preserved historic site in Ponder on FM 156. The Ponder bank was robbed by an associate of Clyde Barrow's, but it had actually failed the week before. Another was the Farmers and Merchants Bank on the town square of Pilot Point.

Born on the Fourth of July

(1989). Tom Cruise, Caroline Kava. Gung-ho Marine paralyzed in Vietnam becomes anti-war activist.

Part of Dallas was transformed into 1957 Massapequa, New York, and later made over again to shoot a 4th of July parade along South Edgefield Avenue in 1969. Cruise's high school was portrayed by the Margaret B. Henderson Elementary School (2200 Edgefield Street, Edgefield) and wrestling matches were filmed at Justin Kimball High School (3605 South Westmoreland, Dallas).

Boys Don't Cry

(1999). Hilary Swank, Chloe Sevigny. Teen girl tries to live her life as a boy.

Small Texas towns surrounding Dallas substituted for Falls City, Nebraska; the courthouse scene was shot at the Hunt County Courthouse (2500 Lee Street, Greenville). The building dates to 1929.

Brewster McCloud

(1970). Bud Cort, Sally Kellerman. Boy dreams of taking flight inside the Astrodome.

Scenes of the Astrodome (8400 Kirby Drive) include footage from when the "8th Wonder of the World" was new; it is open for tours. Other Houston filming locations include Buffalo Bayou Park along Allen Parkway, and Houston Zoological Park (1513 N. MacGregor Drive), home to more than 5,000 animals.

Cloak and Dagger

(1984). Dabney Coleman, Henry Thomas. Imagination-prone boy becomes involved in murder and espionage, but no one believes him.

Thomas is chased by spies through San Antonio's River Walk and confronts his pursuers at the Japanese Sunken Gardens in Breckenridge Park; his imaginary spy adventure occurred at the Tower Life Building (310 South Saint Mary's). The pep rally was staged at Thomas Jefferson High School (723 Donaldson, San Antonio).

Dallas

(1978–1991). Larry Hagman, Patrick Duffy. Saga of a Texas oil family.

Southfork Ranch (3700 Hogge Street, Parker), the setting for the long-running television series, is one of Texas' most popular tourist destinations. More than a half-million people each year take the tour of the working ranch featuring Texas longhorns and American paint horses.

Dancer, Texas Pop 81

(1998). Breckin Mayer, Peter Facinelli. Four of the five members of a high school graduation class make plans to leave small town.

The Jefferson Davis County Courthouse (1149 Pearl Avenue, Beaumont), made of pressed cement bricks and limestone, doubled as the Dancer High School. Other scenes were filmed in Alpine, nestled in the Texas Alps, and along Front Street in Ft. Davis in the heart of the Davis Mountains.

Dazed and Confused

(1993). Jason Landon, Lauren Adams. Suburban Texas teens on the last day of high school in 1976.

Bedichek Middle School (6800 Bill Hughes Road, Austin) played the Robert E. Lee High School; the burger joint where the waitresses bring food to the car was the Top-Notch (7525 Burnet Road, Austin).

Dr. T and the Women

(2000). Richard Gere, Helen Hunt. Popular Texas gynecologist is besieged by the women in his life.

Scenes were shot at Dealey Plaza in downtown Dallas and at the upscale North Park Center Mall (Northwest

The Ewing Ranch House at Southfork, a working ranch outside Dallas, was used in the popular television series *Dallas* and is one of the top tourist destinations in Texas. (Southfork)

Highway at I-75, Dallas), one of more than 600 shopping centers in Dallas.

8 Seconds

(1993). Luke Perry, Stephen Baldwin. The life of bull-riding legend Lane Frost.

Rodeo sequences were filmed around Texas, including at the Bluebonnet Palace (I-35 North and Parkway, Selma) and at the Super bull competition in Del Rio. Also featured was the Floore Country Store (14664 Bandera Road, San Antonio).

Fandango

(1985). Kevin Costner, Judd Nelson. Five college buddies take a road trip to Mexico before entering the real world.

The stunts where airplanes land on the expressway were filmed at the Utica exit on the Broken Arrow Expressway (Highway 51) in Tulsa, Oklahoma. The road trip also features a stop at the ruins of the Presidio mansion in Marfa.

Father Hood

(1992). Patrick Swayze, Halle Berry. Small-time crook hooks up with two kids on the road.

Filmed partly on location in San Antonio, the movie also shot a sequence at Cascade Caverns (226 Cascade Caverns Road, Bodine), where the group escapes through the oldest show cave in Texas. The Tyrannosaurus Rex prop from the film is still at the show cave, which opened in 1933.

Flesh and Bone

(1993). Meg Ryan, Dennis Quaid. Young boy who witnesses his father killing a family grows up to meet the girl who was spared during the slaughter.

The Victorian farmhouse where Julia McNeal and Ron Kuhlman were murdered was located in Hutto on Farm-to-Market Road 685. The exterior was cosmetically aged 30 years during the movie with mud and fake shingles.

The Getaway

(1972). Steve McQueen, Ali MacGraw. Sheriff coerces parolee into robbing another bank.

The chase sequence was filmed along the San Antonio River Walk. Other Texas locations included the town of Fabens, where the shotgun is taken and the police car is shot, and New Braunfels, the site of the veterinarian's office.

Giant

(1956). James Dean, Elizabeth Taylor. Two generations of life inside a Texas ranch family.

The ruins of the Presidio mansion, which played Little Rialta Ranch still stand on the Ryan Ranch in Marfa. The crumbling mass of wood has been untouched since filming crews left in 1955, save for pieces of the dilapidated set taken as souvenirs by James Dean fans. The windmill that was framed by the "Little Rialta"

The windmill framed by the "Little Rialta" ranch sign in *Giant* can be seen on the Ryan Ranch from Highway 90 west of Marfa. Kevin Costner and Judd Nelson also visited here in *Fandango*.

entrance sign can be seen on Highway 90, 12 miles west of town.

Heartbreak Hotel

(1988). David Keith, Tuesday Weld. Teenager kidnaps Elvis Presley in 1972 to take him home to his lonely divorced mother.

The town of Taylor played Ohio, where the story takes place. The Green Pastures Restaurant (811 West Live Oak Street, Austin) played the inn owned by Weld. Concert footage was obtained at Palmer Auditorium (400 31st at Riverside, Austin).

Hellfighters

(1968). John Wayne, Katharine Ross. Roustabouts fight oil well fires.

The oil rig in the opening scene is in Baytown on Evergreen Road; much of the location filming took place in the Goose Creek Oilfield, the first offshore drilling site in Galveston Bay.

Home Fries

(1998). Drew Barrymore, Luke Wilson. Pregnant woman falls for the stepson of the deceased father of her baby.

The orange-and-turquoise Burger-Matic where most of the action takes place was specially constructed on an isolated stretch of the main highway near Bastrop. A 1913 Prairie-style home located in Bastrop's historic district served as Catharine O'Hara's house, and a long-abandoned house in Coupland was transformed into Shelley Duvall's house.

Hope Floats

(1998). Sandra Bullock, Harry Connick, Jr. Woman returns to hometown after husband's affair is revealed on national television.

The movie was filmed mostly in Smithville, where Bullock was three-time Corn Queen.

JFK

(1991). Kevin Costner, Sissy Spacek. New Orleans lawyer investigates possible conspiracy in the assassination of John Kennedy.

Director Oliver Stone was able to obtain permission to film the movie exactly where the assassination of John Kennedy occurred in Dallas. The motorcade was filmed in Dealey Plaza, and the School Book Depository Building (now the Dallas County Administration Building at 411 Elm Street) was returned to its original look. Trees were even shorn of 30 years of growth for the filming. Other historic Dallas locations appearing in the film include the Texas Theater (231 West Jefferson Street), where Gary Oldman (as Lee Harvey Oswald) is taken into custody and the Old Dallas City Jail, where Brian Doyle Murray (as Jack Ruby) shoots Oswald. The Parkland Hospital where Kennedy is pronounced dead was portrayed by St. Joseph's Hospital (5909 Harry Hines Boulevard). Costner is in Louisiana at the Napoleon House (500 Chartres Street, New Orleans) when he learns about the death of the President. A confrontation with John Candy, playing an unscrupulous lawyer, occurs at Antoine's (713–717 Rue St. Louis, New Orleans). One interior scene was filmed at the Louisiana State Penitentiary in Angola.

Johnny Be Good

(1988). Anthony Michael Hall, Robert Downey, Jr. High school football hotshot must decide between game and a girl.

Some of the locations used in San Antonio were Cambridge Elementary School (1001 Townsend Road), which played Jefferson High School; Alamo Heights High School (6900 Broadway); and the Olmos Pharmacy (3902 McCullough Street), where the fountain scene was filmed.

The Last Picture Show

(1971). Ben Johnson, Cloris Leachman. The suffocating life of a small Texas town in the 1950s.

The burned-out remains of the Royal Theater in Archer City at 115 East Main Street, which played the fictional Thalia, were a big tourist attraction after the release of the movie. The Royal Theater was restored and reopened in 2000. Walking tours of both *The Last Picture Show* and *Texasville* filming locations are available.

Leap of Faith

(1992). Steve Martin, Debra Winger. Traveling faith healer tries to work his tricks to charm a small-town waitress.

Much of the location shooting was accomplished in downtown Plainview, including the Quik Lunch Cafe at 108 East Seventh Street. The town is named for its magnificent view of the surrounding wide open spaces. The town of Groom, which features a 190-foot-tall Cross of Our Lord Jesus Christ visible for 20 miles, became the fictional Rustwater, Kansas, where Martin erected his revival tent.

The Legend of Billy Jean

(1985). Helen Slater, Keith Gordon. Brother and sister unjustly accused of crime flee police and become teen cult heroes.

A featured set in the movie is the Kleberg County Courthouse (end of Kleberg Avenue, Kingsville). The courthouse was used for both interior and exterior shots.

Logan's Run

(1976). Michael York, Richard Jordan. In post-apocalyptic 2274, survivors are sealed in domed city where everyone must be killed at age 30 to maintain population balance.

The headquarters of the Sandmen, the organization in charge of carrying out the decree, was at the Zale International Building (901 West Walnut Hill Lane, Irving). Most of the futuristic city scenes were filmed at Dallas Market Center (2015 Center Boulevard, Dallas). Additional scenes were shot at the Fort Worth Water Gardens' hydro-galvanic power system at 1502 Commerce Street, and at the now-closed Oz Restaurant and Night Club (5818 LBJ Freeway, Dallas), which played the Love Shop.

Lone Star

(1996). Chris Cooper, Matthew McConaughey. Unearthed skeleton sets lawman on a case entwined with his legendary sheriff-father.

The movie was filmed largely in Eagle Pass, 150 miles southwest of San Antonio on the Mexican border; many of the flashback scenes to 1957 were filmed in Bog O's Roadhouse, a shell of a building that was once Caesar's Ballroom. The showdown between McConaughey and Kris Kristofferson takes place here. The pivotal scenes that take place at a drive-in were shot at a specially constructed set on a nearby abandoned radar base. The shots of the Rio Grande River were taken near the International Bridge and Commercial Street. Also featured was the Maverick County Courthouse (West Main Street, Eagle Pass), built in 1885.

Lonesome Dove

(1989). Robert Duvall, Tommy Lee Jones. Two ex–Texas rangers set out to move cattle from Texas to Montana.

Driving along the arid, remote stretch of Route 170 through southwest Texas, what appears to be a Spanish ghost town seems west of the small town of Lajitas. In fact, the dozen or so adobe buildings are the remains of a movie set built for the Spanish film *Contrabando* in 1955. The collection of homes, church and store have been used for such productions as *Streets of Laredo* (William Holden, Macdonald Carey) and *Buffalo Girls* (Anjelica Huston, Melanie

Built for the Spanish movie *Contrabando* in 1955, the abandoned Mexican village set on the Rio Grande River west of Lajitas has been used in several other productions.

Griffith), and was one of many Texas and New Mexico locations used in the filming of *Lonesome Dove*. So remote is the area that the set can be explored without restriction by anyone willing to stop the car. The interiors of the buildings belie their hardscrabble exterior appearance; the church even contains a screen where moviemakers could review "dailies" shot that afternoon.

Lost Angels

(1989). Donald Sutherland, Adam Horowitz. Troubled teen unjustly sent to mental hospital is befriended by sympathetic doctor.

Interiors of the San Antonio State Hospital (6711 S. New Braunfels Avenue, San Antonio) were used to portray Sutherland's hospital. Also filmed in San Antonio were scenes along Zarzamora Street and at the Crossroads Mall (4522 Fredericksburg Road) in northwest San Antonio.

Michael

(1996). John Travolta, Andie MacDowell. Big city reporters discover that reports of an angel living in Iowa are true.

The somewhat-less-than-angelic Travolta dances with two ladies and brawls with regulars at Toms, portrayed by the Gruene Hall (Gruene and Hunter roads, Austin). Established in 1880, Gruene Hall is the oldest honky tonk in Texas. Also featured is the Fayette County Courthouse (Main Street, LaGrange), a three-story blue sandstone Romanesque Revival structure built in 1891.

Midway

(1976). Charlton Heston, Henry Fonda. Dramatization of the pivotal battle in the Pacific Theater during World War II.

The *USS Lexington* (2914 North Shoreline Boulevard, Corpus Christi) played all seven aircraft carriers—three American and four Japanese—in the recreation of the battle. The ship, commissioned in 1943, was mistakenly reported sunk four times during World War II and earned the nickname "The Blue Ghost" from the Japanese for its blue paint.

Miss Congeniality

(2000). Sandra Bullock, Michael Caine. FBI agent goes undercover in beauty pageant to thwart the bombing of the event.

Austin locations used in the movie include the Starbucks at Sixth and Congress, and the Cue Lounge (409 Colorado Street). Filming also took place in San Antonio at Alamo Plaza.

Nadine

(1987). Jeff Bridges, Kim Basinger. Hairdresser seeking divorce witnesses a murder while trying to retrieve nude pictures of herself.

The movie was filmed extensively on 6th Street in Austin, which was made to look like it was 1954, and in San Antonio's King William Historic District.

Gruene Hall, the oldest honky tonk in Texas, played Tom's, where John Travolta danced and brawled in *Michael*.

Necessary Roughness

(1991). Scott Bakula, Robert Loggia. College football team on probation must field a team of actual students.

Fouts Field at the University of North Texas in Denton portrayed the home field of the fictitious Texas State University Fighting Armadillos. The fight scene was staged at Billy Bob's Texas in Fort Worth's Historic Stockyards, off Stockyard Boulevard and Exchange Street.

Newton Boys

(1998). Matthew McConaughey, Ethan Hawke. Real-life saga of Texas brothers who robbed 80 banks and trains across the country from 1914 to 1924.

Texas towns played host to some of the 80 World War I-era banks robbed by the real-life Newton brothers throughout the Midwest and Canada. San Antonio was made to look like the early 1900s in places such as Toronto, Chicago and Omaha, Nebraska. Locations used included Peacock Alley, the Menger Hotel (204 Alamo Plaza), the St. Anthony Hotel (300 East Travis) and the Koehler House (1300 San Pedro Avenue). A 1916 train robbery that led to the capture of the Newton boys was staged aboard Engine No. 786 on the Hill Country Flyer of the Austin Texas Steam Railroad, running between Cedar Park and Liberty Hill (US 183).

Pearl Harbor

(2001). Ben Affleck, Alec Baldwin. Love story played out against the drama of World War II.

Every Japanese aircraft carrier was eventually destroyed in World War II, so the *USS Lexington* (2914 North Shoreline Boulevard, Corpus Christi) doubles for a Japanese carrier. The *Lexington*, which was at sea during the attack on Pearl Harbor, is now a museum, and self-guided tours are available.

Pee Wee's Big Adventure

(1985). Paul Reubens, Elizabeth Daily. Childish man scours the country in search of his stolen bicycle.

Reubens heads for the Alamo to look for his bicycle in the basement and does Tequila Dance at the Wheel Inn (50900 Seminole Drive, Cabazon, California), featuring two immense concrete dinosaurs—Dinny, a brontosaurus, and Rex, a tyrannosaurus.

A Perfect World

(1993). Clint Eastwood, Kevin Costner. Escaped convict bonds with boy he has kidnapped.

Costner escapes from Huntsville State Penitentiary in Walker county and kidnaps J.T. Lowther on Columbus Street in Austin. The town of Martindale plays the fictional Noodle, where Costner robs the Friendly's dry goods store on Main Street. Costner and Lowther stop to eat at the defunct Mack's Squat and Gobble Barbeque at 4010 Farm-to-Market Road 2673 in Canyon Lake. The shaded barbecue spot remains.

Powder

(1995). Sean Patrick Flanery, Mary Steenburgen. Albino boy in small town seems to possess special powers.

Featured in the movie is the Wharton County Courthouse (103 S. Fulton Street, Wharton), which is currently being restored to its original 1888 Second Empire design.

Reality Bites

(1994). Winona Ryder, Ethan Hawke. Young woman struggles with choice between a bohemian life and conventional work world.

Shooting took place in Houston; there are extensive shots of the skyline, and action takes place in Tranquility Park (Rusk, Bagby, Smith and Walker streets). Five towers resembling rockets rise from a 32-level fountain and decorative reflecting pool.

Robocop 2

(1990). Peter Weller, Thomas Rosales, Jr. A corrupt businessman sets out to dismantle the cyborg law enforcer.

The setting of fictional New Detroit moved from Dallas to Houston for the sequel. The OCP offices were set up in the Cullen Center (1600 Smith); the abandoned Jefferson Davis Hospital on Allen Parkway became an illegal drug factory, and Weller shoots it out with his mechanical antagonist at the George R. Brown Convention

Kevin Costner paid a visit to this now-abandoned barbecue restaurant in Canyon Lake, Texas, while on the run in *A Perfect World*.

Center (1001 Avenue of the Americas), which played the Civic Centrum.

Rush

(1991). Jason Patric, Jennifer Jason Leigh. Two small-town cops get addicted to the drug world they are trying to infiltrate.

Playing a starring role is the Swinging Door (3818 FM359, La Porte), a restaurant and dance hall 25 miles from Houston.

Rushmore

(1998). Jason Schwartzsman, Bill Murray. High school impresario battles mentor for affections of his teacher.

Rushmore Academy is portrayed by St. Johns School (2401 Claremont Lane, Houston) and the public school where Schwartzsman is forced to attend after his expulsion from Rushmore was played by Lamar High School (3325 Westheimer Road, Houston). The scene where he finally accepts Sara Tanaka's friendship was filmed in the parking lot of Delmar Stadium (2020 Magnum Road, Houston).

Selena

(1997). Jennifer Lopez, Edward James Olmos. Story of popular Tejano music star murdered by jealous employee.

The scenes of Selena Quintanilla's childhood were filmed on the beach at Corpus Christi. An outdoor concert was recreated at the Fairgrounds in Poteet, and her last big concert, at the Houston Livestock and Rodeo show in the Astrodome, was recreated in San Antonio's Alamodome (100 Montana). Other locations used in San Antonio included the River Walk at 100 Villila and the San Antonio Public Library (600 Soledad).

Sidekicks

(1992). Beau Bridges, Jonathin Brandis. Frail boy learns karate and dreams of meeting his martial-arts hero.

Brandis and Chuck Norris battle bad guys in Houston's Tranquility Park (Rusk, Bagby, Smith and Walker streets). The futuristic park honors the Apollo space program and is named for the lunar landing location of Apollo XI. Also featured is the Waterwall, a fountain at the 64-story Transco Tower (2800 Post Oak Boulevard).

Slacker

(1991). Richard Linklater, Rudy Basquez. A day in the life of social outcasts who seem unable to carry through on any plans.

The film featured coffeehouses and apartments around the west side of the University of Texas campus in Austin, in the neighborhood of 24th Street and Guadalupe.

Space Cowboys

(2000). Clint Eastwood, Tommy Lee Jones. When a retired engineer is called on to rescue a failing satellite, he insists that his equally aged former team must accompany him into space.

The movie utilized the Johnson Space Center at 1601 NASA Road in Houston for much of the space-related footage. There is a Visitor Center and tours available, and there is also an annual one-day open house of Mission Control and other restricted areas.

Spy Kids

(2001). Antonio Banderas, Kelly Preston. Top secret agents must be saved by their children.

Filming took place in Austin at the Millenium Center (Fourth and Lavaca). Also used was the Spanish mission–style Trois Estate (3612 Pearce Road) in the hills outside Austin.

Still Breathing

(1998). Brendan Fraser, Joanna Going. A dreamer and a cynic forge a bond through a wise old woman.

Fraser's puppeteer works in San Antonio, and the city did some standing in for Going's home of Los Angeles as well. Fraser's favorite place in the world is the Rose Window on the south wall of the San Jose Mission (Roosevelt Street); he tells the legend of the "Queen of Missions" to Going as they stroll on the walkway east of the chapel. The Babylon Restaurant on South Alamo Street plays the LA Coffee House where Fraser and Going meet. River scenes were filmed at the San Marcos River, the shortest river in America, which flows through the center of San Marcos. The waters are absolutely clear because the river gushes out of its headwater springs at such a tremendous rate.

The Texas Chainsaw Massacre

(1974). Marilyn Burns, Allen Danziger. A family of cannibals use power tools in rural Texas.

The cult horror film was shot in the fields near Round Rock, about thirty miles north of Austin.

Texasville

(1990). Jeff Bridges, Cybill Shepherd. Characters of *The Last Picture Show* 30 years later.

The three-story cream-colored hotel in the movie is the historic Spur Hotel (110 North Center Street, Archer). Part of the film's whorehouse was built into a wall of the meeting room in the Archer Public Library at 105 Center Street. Additional filming locations in Archer included the Dairy Queen on the south side of town and Sonny's Quick Stop, both on TX 79.

Urban Cowboy

(1980). John Travolta, Debra Winger. Young man from the country gets an education at a Houston bar.

Gilley's (2200 South Main Street, Pasadena) became world famous when Travolta rode mechanical bulls there during the movie. The club burned in 1990, but the ruins of the largest honky tonk in Texas, including the concrete foundations and Rodeo Arena, are still there. The cemetery scene was filmed in Pearland at South Park Cemetery (1310 North Main Street).

Varsity Blues

(1999). James Van Der Beek, Jon Voight. Hopes of small Texas town rest on second string quarterback who doesn't buy into coach's view of football as religion.

The town of Elgin, whose town center features 67 historic buildings erected between 1872 and 1947, became the fictitious West Canaan. The climactic game for the West Canaan Coyotes was staged before 4000 extras at Elgin High School's Wildcat Stadium.

What's Eating Gilbert Grape

(1993). Johnny Depp, Leonardo DiCaprio. Young man is saddled with responsibilities of caring for retarded younger brother and obese mother who hasn't left the house for seven years.

The town of Manor played the fictional Endora, Iowa. Also featured was the Caldwell County Courthouse (110 South Main Street, Lockhart).

Where the Heart Is

(2000). Ashley Judd, Natalie Portman. Pregnant girl lives in Wal-Mart while trying to rebuild her life.

Filming took place partly in downtown Austin on 6th Street, including Babe's Bar & Grill (208 E. 6th Street).

Popular Texas Locations

ALAMO VILLAGE

Filming is not permitted inside the Alamo Mission, which has often posed problems for moviemakers desiring to incorporate the ultimate American symbol of bravery and sacrifice into their celluloid stories. The definitive solution came in the 1950s with the construction of an exact replica 130 miles west of the original in the small town of Brackettville.

The economic fortunes of Brackettville were sagging after World War II, when mayor James Tullis "Happy" Shahan decided that Hollywood might have an answer to the region's problems. He traveled to southern California with an armful of location photos and began knocking on doors. He persuaded executives at Paramount Studios to film *Arrowhead* in Brackettville in 1951.

Then he got wind of a project involving John Wayne, who wanted to film the definitive version of the siege of the Alamo. Shahan was convinced that Brackettville was the place to film the big-budget extravaganza. He struck a deal with Wayne that he would build a town if *The Alamo* would use it as the movie set.

Some $12 million was sunk into the building of Alamo Village. As many as 400 workmen at one time swarmed across the Shahan Angus Ranch in Kinney County, six miles north of Brackettville, building

Built in the desert of West Texas for *The Alamo*, starring John Wayne, Alamo Village is a tourist attraction and an active movie set for today's stars.

200,000 square feet of permanent buildings. More than one million adobe bricks were handmade, using techniques practiced by desert craftsmen for 300 years. There are no false fronts in the town, all the buildings are fully functional. More than ten miles of pipes carry concealed electrical and telephone wires underground.

To recreate the Alamo itself, researchers scoured original plans sent to Spain by the Catholic priests who built the mission. The reproduction was meticulously pieced together in preparation for *The Alamo*, which was released in 1959. Afterward, Shahan took to promoting his western town studio to Hollywood producers himself. Over the years more than 20 films and many commercials have used Alamo Village as a shooting location. Included in the roster of Brackettville films are *Two Rode Together* (Jimmy Stewart, Richard Widmark), *Bandolero!* (Jimmy Stewart, Raquel Welch), *Barbarosa* (Willie Nelson, Jane Fonda) and *Lonesome Dove*.

Although the Alamo Village remains an active film set, it operates today mainly as a tourist attraction. Spread out in front of the famous mission are a cantina and restaurant, a trading post, an Indian store, a church, a jail, and a blacksmith shop. The village features the trappings of a western town, with stagecoaches, wagons and horses. A herd of longhorn cattle graze in the vicinity. Alamo Village is open to the public year-round.

THE STUDIOS AT LAS COLINAS

Minutes from downtown Dallas, the Studios at Los Colinas were built in 1982 with more than 72,000 square feet of production space. Featuring top-quality equipment and lighting, the studios have become a favorite for video and commercial production. Hollywood has also made good use of the state-of-the-art facilities. Such movies as *Silkwood* (Meryl Streep, Cher) and *Robocop* (Peter Weller, Nancy Allen) are among the many productions filmed here.

The Studios at Las Colinas (6301 N. O'Connor Boulevard, Irving) are open for tours daily during the week at 12:30, 2:30 and 4:00. One Saturday tour is offered at 10:30 a.m. The tour features demonstrations of special effects, behind-the-scenes visits to soundstages and movie memorabilia.

UTAH

Drive Me Crazy

(1999). Melissa Joan Hart, Adrian Grenier. When girl's dream date spurns her before a school prom, she asks her grungy neighbor to escort her.

Ogden High School (2828 Harrison Boulevard, Ogden) was used for Hart's school, and the final dance was staged in the State Capitol (350 N. Main Street on Capitol Hill, Salt Lake City). The Corinthian-style Revival building constructed of native Utah granite and Georgia marble is open for tours.

Footloose

(1984). Kevin Bacon, Lori Singer. City boy moves to small town and joins rebellion against elders who have banned rock and roll music and dancing.

The school scenes were shot at Payson High School (1050 South Main Street, Payson), and the car wash was filmed in American Fork. The drive-in restaurant where everyone dances in the parking lot is now a flower shop just north of First N. and 500 W. streets in Provo. Bacon's dance sequence was staged in the Lehi Flour Roller Mills, off I-15 in Lehi.

Galaxy Quest

(1999). Tim Allen, Sigourney Weaver. Actors in popular space travel television series are kidnapped by aliens to fight real war.

The intricately eroded rock formations of Goblin Valley State Park (Temple Mountain Road off Route 24, Green River) served as the setting for the surface of the alien planet Thermia. The rounded stones are so secluded in central Utah that they were not discovered by settlers until the 1920s. The Galaxy Quest convention was filmed at the Hollywood Palladium.

Jeremiah Johnson

(1972). Robert Redford, Will Geer. Mountain man living a solitary existence endures vendetta by Indians.

Producers of *Galaxy Quest* found the otherworldly rock formations of Goblin Valley State Park in central Utah perfect to depict the alien planet of Thermia.

The mountain setting was near Park City in the Sundance Resort and also in the nearby Uinta National Forest on Mt. Timpanogas (Utah Highway 92).

The Outlaw Josey Wales

((1976). Clint Eastwood, Sandra Locke. Farmer turns vigilante after Union soldiers murder his family.

Part of the filming took place several miles east of Kanab, UT, on US 89 in a parking area and side gravel road heading north, leading to the old townsite of Pahreah. Old Pahreah was settled in 1870, but by the 1930s it was completely abandoned, frequent floods having driven people away. A western town movie set was built here, and several movies were filmed in the valley, including *The Outlaw Josie Wales*. The movie set was destroyed by flooding a couple years ago, but there are a few remnants of the pioneer community still visible.

Three O'Clock High

(1987). Casey Siemaszko, Richard Tyson. Teen nerd tries to avoid scheduled fight with school tough guy.

School scenes were played out at Ogden High School (2828 Harrison Boulevard, Ogden).

Popular Utah Locations

KANAB

In 1924 Tom Mix, Hollywood's first great Western star, came to southwestern Utah to film *Deadwood Coach* amidst the Vermillion Cliffs in Johnson Canyon near the old Mormon settlement of Kanab. Over the next few decades, so many movie productions followed that Kanab came to be known informally as "Little Hollywood."

Kanab proved especially popular as a site for filming television series. Ronald Reagan filmed most of his *Death Valley Days* in the area. In Angel Canyon many episodes of *The Lone Ranger* (Clayton Moore, Jay Silverheels), *The Adventures of Rin Tin Tin* (Lee Aaker, Joe Sawyer), and *The Six Million Dollar Man* (Lee Majors, Lindsay Wagner) were filmed.

Kanab was also home to the longest running drama in television history: *Gunsmoke* (James Arness, Amanda Blake). The set for the series still stands as the Johnson Canyon Movie Set, including such familiar Dodge City landmarks as the Longbranch Saloon and Doc's office. The Johnson Canyon Movie Set is open to the public year round for guided tours.

MOAB

After introducing the cinematic world to Monument Valley and filming four pictures there, director John Ford went looking for another desert location in 1949 for his upcoming *Wagon Master*, to star Ben Johnson and Ward Bond. He drove north and arrived in the town of Moab, where he was shown the Professor Valley and the Fisher Towers along Route 128 on the Colorado

Susan Sarandon drives her Thunderbird convertible down the Shafer Trail and over the cliff to avoid police apprehension in *Thelma and Louise* in Canyonlands National Park in Utah.

River. Ford indeed shot *Wagon Master* in the Professor Valley and brought moviegoers to an area John Wayne thought defined the West. More than 50 feature films would be shot on location around Moab in the next 50 years.

Landmarks from *Wagon Master* include the cathedral-like Fisher Towers, which can be reached by trail in the Colorado River Recreation Area, and the Colorado River, where Bond and Johnson probed for a suitable water crossing, just upstream from the Fisher Towers. Other films that shot along the Colorado River in this area include *Rio Grande* (John Wayne, Ben Johnson), *Ten Who Dared* (Brian Keith, Ben Johnson), and *Against a Crooked Sky* (Richard Boone, Stewart Petersen).

Moab is the gateway town to two National Parks, the Arches and the Canyonlands, which have been used in many motion pictures, including *Cheyenne Autumn* (Richard Widmark, Karl Malden) and *Warlock* (Henry Fonda, Richard Widmark). In Arches National Park, Jack Palance appears to Billy Crystal in the Windows arches in *City Slickers II*, and River Phoenix travels with his fellow boy scouts in the opening scenes of *Indiana Jones and the Last Crusade* along South Park Avenue. In the Canyonlands, Max Von Sydow delivers the "Sermon on the Mount" in *The Greatest Story Ever Told* while standing on a cliff facing the Green River. Since film companies must stay on paved roads in the two national parks, there is easy access to filming locations here.

The most famous movie to film in Moab is *Thelma and Louise* (Susan Sarandon, Geena Davis). Opening vistas and road scenes were shot in the nearby La Sal Mountains, and Sarandon and Davis apologetically relieve a police officer of his gun and lock him in the trunk of his patrol car at the Courthouse Towers in Arches National Park. In the famous final scene, Sarandon drives their Thunderbird convertible over the cliff in Canyonlands National Park. The exact site is off the Shafer Trail under Dead Horse Point, which can be seen from the auto tour. Shafer Trail can be accessed by four-wheel drive vehicles. Although there are wrecked automobiles in the canyon below this Dead Horse Point, they were placed there by the Bureau of Land Management to shore up the river bank. The wreckage from the movie was airlifted out of the canyon by helicopter.

VERMONT

Baby Boom

(1987). Diane Keaton, Sam Shepherd. High-powered New York business woman inherits a baby and moves to Vermont.

Keaton discovers that yuppies can't get enough of her gourmet baby food at the J.J. Hapgood general store on Main Street in Peru. In New York City, Keaton's advertising offices were in the Seagram Building (375 Park Avenue at 52nd Street); she inherits her cousin's baby and half-heartedly tries to leave it with the coatcheck girl at the Cafe Pierre (Fifth Avenue and 61st Street); and she shares an apartment with Harold Ramis at 19 East 88th Street.

Beetlejuice

(1988). Alec Baldwin, Michael Keaton. Ghosts hire a "bio-exorcist" to remove obnoxious new humans in their house.

Movie exteriors were filmed in East Corinth, but the Victorian house built for the film was torn down. Most of the interiors were shot on a sound stage in Culver City, California. Baldwin and Geena Davis wreck their car on the White River bridge in East Corinth.

Cider House Rules

(1999). Tobey Maguire, Charlize Theron. Boy raised in Maine orphanage comes of age in the 1940s.

Filming took place all over New England. The apple packing scenes, using an 1862 apple packing machine, were staged on the Scott Farm next to the Kipling House on Kipling Road in Dummerston. The train scenes were shot in the Union Railroad Station (54 Depot Street, Bellows Falls), operated by the Green Mountain Railroad. The movie train used No. 260, the oldest standard gauge passenger car still in use in New England. Sightseeing trips aboard the Green Mountain Flyer are available. In Massachusetts there were

Ventfort Hall in Lenox, Massachusetts, a Beaux Arts summer cottage built in 1893 for J. P. Morgan's sister, played the exterior of St. Cloud's orphanage in *Cider House Rules*. (Massachusetts Film Office)

sequences shot in Northampton State Mental Hospital (Route 66, Northampton), a sprawling array of 76 abandoned ramshackle buildings, and at Ventfort Hall (104 Walker Street, Lenox), a Beaux Arts summer cottage built in 1893 for J.P. Morgan's sister, which played the exterior of St. Cloud's orphanage. In Maine, the first glimpse of the sea comes at Arcadia National Park's Sand Beach, one of only three sandy beaches on the Maine coast.

Ethan Frome

(1993). Liam Neeson, Patricia Arquette. Husband falls in love with young woman hired to take care of his ailing wife.

This was filmed in and around East Peacham, including the simple white church with the dominating steeple. Another location was Thresher's Mill (north side of TH1 about ½ mile east of junction with TH7, Barnet), which dates to the 1870s.

Funny Farm

(1988). Chevy Chase, Madolyn Smith-Osborne. Writer moves to Vermont to work on novel but doesn't find peace and quiet.

The farmhouse where Chase takes up residence is in Grafton. The gazebo that is featured on the town square was specially built for the movie on the Townshend Village Green; townsfolk liked it and decided to keep it.

The Man with a Plan

(1995). Fred Tuttle, Bill Blachly. 73-year-old farmer needs money, so he runs for Vermont's lone seat in the United States House of Representatives.

In this mock documentary, septuagenarian Tuttle looks for a job "for a self-starter with no past experience" and settles on politics. He runs his campaign from his home around Tunbridge in the mountains of Orange County. Four years after the movie was released Tuttle actually did enter politics when a rich Massachusetts carpetbagger tried to win the Vermont seat. The 77-year-old Tuttle, a celebrity from the movie, defeated his Massachusetts opponent in the Republican primary and then turned over the seat to his Democratic opponent.

Me, Myself & Irene

(2000). Jim Carrey, Renee Zellweger. Man forgets medication he needs to keep personality disorder under control when he falls for a woman.

Opening sequences took place in Rhode Island: Carrey's house is on Hollusk Drive on Great Island in Narragansett, and the picnic was filmed at King's Beach in Brenton State Park (Ocean Drive, Newport). The action then moved to Vermont, where most of the filming took place. Carrey and Zellweger visit yard sales in Essex on the Kellogg Road and Mill Pond Road, and knock over a fence in Burlington's Battery Park, downtown at the foot of Pearl Street. The scene at the gas station was staged at Go-Go Gas (Susie Wilson Road, Essex), and the footbridge over the water was filmed in Middlebury. The Ben & Jerry's ice cream factory tour (Route 100, Waterbury) was also featured.

Newhart

(1982–1990). Bob Newhart, Mary Frann. Writer and wife leave New York City to buy a Vermont Inn.

The Waybury Inn (457 East Main Street, Route 125, East Middlebury), established in 1810 as a stagecoach stop in the Green Mountains and believed to be the oldest continuously operating lodging establishment in Vermont, was used as the exterior for the Stratford Inn in the television series. Interiors were shot on a Hollywood sound stage and look nothing like the interiors of the Waybury Inn.

Spitfire Grill

(1996). Ellen Burstyn, Alison Elliott. Ex-convict arrives in small Maine town to work at restaurant and start anew.

The set for the title eatery, where most of the drama unfolds, was created in the Peacham General Store in the village of Peacham. Additional scenes were shot in St. Johnsbury.

The Trouble with Harry

(1955). John Forsythe, Edmund Gwenn. A man's body found in the woods of a New England town sparks suspicions among neighbors.

Director Alfred Hitchcock used the village of Craftsbury Common, a National Historic Site, as his movie set.

What Lies Beneath

(2000). Harrison Ford, Michelle Pfeiffer. Woman tries to make contact with apparition that has started to appear after her car accident.

Ford teaches at the University of Vermont, and several scenes feature the Burlington campus and its Green. The paranormal activity takes place at Ford and Pfeiffer's home, which was specially built for the movie on the banks of Lake Champlain in DAR State Park (SR 17). Also used in the filming was the Chimney Point Bridge in West Addison between Vermont and New York.

VIRGINIA

Crazy People

(1990). Dudley Moore, Darryl Hannah. Advertising man develops ads based on truth and is sent by his boss to a mental institution to get well again.

Moore is institutionalized in Bennington Sanitarium, played by Chatham Hill, a private girl's school in Chatham. The Manhattan advertising agency where Moore and Paul Reiser work was portrayed by the Crestar Bank (310 First Street, Roanoke). Also used in Roanoke was the Grandin Theater marquee at 1310 Grandin Road.

Dirty Dancing

(1987). Patrick Swayze, Jennifer Gray. Rich girl falls in love with dancing teacher at 1960s summer resort.

Mountain Lake Hotel (Route 700, Mountain Lake) played the Kellerman Resort in New York's Catskills Mountains. Grey and her family stayed in Room 232.

First Kid

(1996). Sindbad, Brock Pierce. Secret Service agent guards the President's obnoxious son.

The shoot-out in the closing scenes was staged at the Galleria at Tysons II Mall (Route 7 and Route 123, Tyson's Corner).

The Four Seasons

(1981). Alan Alda, Carol Burnett. Three couples vacation with each other through different times of the year.

One of the vacation locales used in the movie was Kewsick Hall (701 Club Drive, Keswick), a 600-acre estate in the Shenandoah Valley.

Hannibal

(2001). Anthony Hopkins, Julianne Moore. Cannibalistic killer matches wits with a vengeful victim.

The fish market in the beginning of the story was shot in Richmond, built under the train tracks in Shockoe Bottom, near the Canal Club (1545 East Cary Street). Also in Richmond,

The Virginia Cottage at the Mountain Lake resort played a cabin in New York's Catskills in *Dirty Dancing*. (Mountain Lake)

the Old State Library on the edge of Capital Square, built in a classical modern design from 1938 to 1940, doubled as the Baltimore Mental Hospital, and Shockoe Cemetery (2nd Street) stood in for Arlington Cemetery, where the live newscast was shot. Gary Oldman's house was portrayed by the Biltmore in Asheville, North Carolina; scenes were filmed in the library and tapestry room, and deer statues were added to the porch.

Lassie

(1994). Tom Guiry, Helen Slater. Dog helps city family adapt to new life on ancestral farm.

The family farm is located in Ward's Cove at the base of the Clinch mountain range in Tazewell County. In the climactic sequence, Lassie struggles in the rapids of Sandstone Falls in New River near Hinton.

Major Payne

(1995). Rodney Barnes, Ross Bickell. Retiring soldier instills dignity in ragtag ROTC students.

The campus shots were filmed at the Miller School of Albemarle (1000 Samuel Miller Loop). Location shooting in Richmond included the clock tower at Main Street Station and the old police station on Hull Street.

My Dinner with Andre

(1981). Wallace Shawn, Andre Gregory. Two friends talk about their life experiences and philosophies over an extended meal.

The Grand Ballroom of the

Jefferson Hotel (Franklin and Adams Street, Richmond) provided the setting for Shawn and Gregory's repast. The ornate Beaux Arts hotel, built in 1895 and host to nine United States Presidents, was closed at the time of the shooting. It has since undergone a $34 million restoration. Its famed staircase in the lobby has been considered the model to the majestic stairs created at Tara in *Gone with the Wind*.

Navy Seals

(1990). Charlie Sheen, Michael Biehn. Elite commando corps stage raid on Middle Eastern terrorists.

Some of the key scenes were shot on the restricted Norfolk Navy Base, home of the world's largest naval fleet. Public locations include the Virginia Beach shoreline and the Berkeley Bridge in Norfolk, which Sheen's stunt double leaps off of. The attack sequences were filmed in Spain.

Random Hearts

(1999). Harrison Ford, Kristin Scott Thomas. Man and woman discover their loved ones were carrying on an affair after they die in a plane crash.

Various locations include the Mall in Washington DC; a wooded area at Pohick Bay in Woodridge used for a tryst between Scott Thomas and Ford; interiors and exteriors of the Reagan National Airport in Crystal City; and King Street in Richmond, where a funeral procession passed. In Miami Beach, Florida, the National Hotel, a classic art deco building at 1677 Collins Avenue, was used for courtyard and pool scenes.

Rollercoaster

(1977). George Segal, Richard Widmark. Extortionist places bombs on rollercoasters in major amusement parks.

The rollercoaster Timothy Bottoms sabotages at the beginning of the movie was "The Rocket" from the long-gone Ocean View Amusement Park in Norfolk (100 W. Ocean View Drive). The money drop sequence, in which Bottoms leads Segal throughout the park, takes place at King's Dominion (16000 Theme Parkway, Doswell). The denouement was filmed at Six Flags Magic Mountain (26101 Magic Mountain Parkway, Valencia, California), where Bottoms is thumped by the newly opened "The Revolution." Still operating, "The Revolution" is the second-oldest of the park's 15 rollercoasters.

Sommersby

(1993). Richard Gere, Jodie Foster. Civil War soldier presumed dead returns home a changed man — or an imposter.

Gere and Foster's family home was the Hidden Valley Bed and Breakfast (Hidden Valley Road, Warm Springs). Main and Washington Streets in Lexington were covered with dirt and transported back to the 1860s; Gere was hanged in a parking lot off Main Street.

Toy Soldiers

(1991). Lou Gossett, Jr., Sean Astin. Columbian terrorists have more to fear from their prep school hostages than their potential rescuers.

The post office on Alamo Square in San Antonio, Texas, became La Paz, Bolivia's, Palace of Justice, where the convicted drug smugglers kill hostages. The school held captive is the Miller School (1000 Samuel Miller Loop, Charlottesville).

True Colors

(1991). John Cusack, James Spader. Law students find friendship strained by differing ideals as they enter the real world.

Classroom scenes were filmed in Clark Hall on the University of Virginia campus in Charlottesville. A party was staged in Richmond's Historic District at Shockoe Slip in an old tobacco warehouse (Cary Street at Thirteenth Street). Skiing sequences were filmed at Big Sky Ski Resort (Highway 191, Bozeman, Montana).

What About Bob?

(1991). Bill Murray, Richard Dreyfuss. Phobic patient trails his psychiatrist on vacation.

Smith Mountain Lake became the New Hampshire resort of Lake Winnipesaukee, and Moneta played the town where Murray wins the hearts of psychiatrist Dreyfuss's family — over Dreyfuss's vociferous protestations. The vacation home was a private home on the lake, and a ¾-size model of the home was used for its exploding demise in the finale.

WASHINGTON

Assassins

(1995). Sylvester Stallone, Antonio Banderas. Veteran hitman looking to get out of the business becomes the target of a maniacal young assassin.

Stallone escapes Banderas by leaping from the Seattle Monorail, the nation's first commercial monorail system (it was built for the 1962 World's Fair). The entire trip through downtown Seattle covers nine-tenths of a mile and takes two minutes. The Monorail runs from Westlake Center terminal at 5th Avenue and Pine Street to Seattle Center. The soccer match at which Banderas threatens to shoot a player was filmed at the Georgetown Playfield in south Seattle, just north of Boeing Field.

Benny and Joon

(1993). Johnny Depp, Mary Stuart Masterson. Eccentric enters the life of a mentally limited woman cared for by a diligent older brother.

Masterson is hospitalized in a mental hospital played by St. Michael's Church (8500 North Street, Spokane), and Depp swings in front of her window here. Also in Spokane, Aidan Quinn's Benny's Auto Clinic was portrayed by Hilliard Tire (5404 North Market Street). Depp performs antics in Riverfront Park off I-90 along the Spokane River. Expo '74 was located in the 50-acre park featuring the tumbling waters of the Spokane Falls. Julianne Moore waitresses at Ferguson's Cafe (804 West Garland Avenue).

Body of Evidence

(1993). Madonna, Willem Dafoe. Woman is accused of killing her wealthy lover with too much rough sex.

Dafoe defends Madonna in the matter of the death of her paramour in the Senate chamber of the State Capitol Building (14th Street and Cherry Lane, Olympia). Built in 1927, its 287-foot dome is one of the largest in the world. The chandelier that graces the rotunda was designed by Louis Comfort Tiffany.

Cinderella Liberty

(1973). James Caan, Marsha Mason. Sailor falls in love with a hooker and becomes surrogate father to her son while on extended liberty.

The sailors spend their Cinderella Liberty, Navy slang for a pass, around First Avenue, a working seaport in Seattle. The movie provides a time capsule look at Seattle before the infusion of high tech money.

Disclosure

(1994). Michael Douglas, Demi Moore. Female executive sets out to ruin the career of her rival and former lover.

Douglas lived on Bainbridge Island and worked with Moore at the fictional software company DigiCom, whose headquarters was portrayed by the Smith Tower Building (506 Second Avenue, Seattle) in the downtown Pioneer Square district. Most of the buildings in the 30-block historic area were erected after the Great Fire of 1889.

The Fabulous Baker Boys

(1989). Jeff Bridges, Michelle Pfieffer. Small-time musicians rejuvenate their career by adding a female singer to the act.

The third floor of Mason's Furniture Store on Pioneer Square was transformed into Bridges' apartment. Other scenes were filmed around Pioneer Square, but most of the movie was shot in Los Angeles because producers were afraid of inclement weather in Washington.

The Hand That Rocks the Cradle

(1992). Rebecca DeMornay, Annabella Sciorra. Nanny is out to wreck lives of an unsuspecting couple.

DeMornay seeks her revenge in a house on the 800 block of North Yakima in the Stadium Historical District; she takes her young charge to the McGilvra Elementary School playground (1617 38th Avenue East, Seattle). The hospital scenes were staged at Tacoma General (315 Martin Luther King Jr. Way, Tacoma).

Harry and the Hendersons

(1987). John Lithgow, Melinda Dillon. Family tries to hide a Bigfoot-type creature they find on a hunting trip.

The forest scenes were filmed in the Snoqualmie National Forest near North Bend, where Bigfoot is rumored to be. Lithgow's family camps on Lake Kachess in the Wenatchee National Forest (Route 2, east of Seattle) and stops at "The Reptile Man" shop in Snohomish at the confluence of the Pilchuck and Snohomish rivers. The Reptile Man is now the Washington Serpentarium on Route 2 in Gold Bar.

Harry in Your Pocket

(1973). James Coburn, Walter Pidgeon. The adventures of a group of skilled pickpockets.

The pickpockets work the streets of Seattle, and Pidgeon can be seen liberating a wallet from a passenger boarding an electric trolley bus at the 4th and Pike Street loading stop.

I Love You to Death

(1990). Kevin Kline, Tracy Ullman. A woman unsuccessfully tries to kill philandering husband since her religion doesn't permit divorce.

Location filming across Tacoma included Bob's Java Jive (2102 South Tacoma Way), a restaurant and lounge shaped like a coffee pot and built in 1927 by designer Bert Smyser; the Elks Club (565 Broadway), which portrayed a police station; and the triangular Bostwick Building (764 Broadway), which became Joey Boca's Pizzaria where Kline worked.

Northern Exposure

(1990–1995). Rob Morrow, Janine Turner. Newly graduated doctor finds a quirky town when he moves to Alaska to satisfy the requirements of his scholarship.

The main locations for the television series were shot along a four-block stretch of Pennsylvania Avenue in Roslyn, a one-time coal boom town. Morrow's store-front office, Ruth-Anne's General Store, the Brick Tavern and the totem pole of fictional Cicely, Alaska, were shot in this town 80 miles east of Seattle.

An Officer and a Gentleman

(1982). Richard Gere, Debra Winger. Selfish recruit becomes a leader and a man at Navy Flight School.

Most of the training scenes at fictional Fort Rainier were filmed at Fort Worden State Park (200 Battery Way, Port Townsend). Lou Gossett, Jr. salutes Gere at the end of the story on the porch of the Conference Center; Gere's dorm room was number 204, and the barber shop was in number 202. The balloon hanger where Gere and Gossett fight on the mat is now the park's 1200-seat performing arts pavilion. Winger worked at the Simpson Tacoma Kraft Mill (801 Portland Avenue, Tacoma), where Gere sweeps her off her feet at the end of the movie. The Tides Inn (1807 Water Street) was where military couples went for off-base trysts, and where David Keith commits suicide.

Bob's Java Jive in Tacoma, Washington, built in 1927, made an appearance in *I Love You to Death*. (Tacoma Film Office)

Room number 10, where Gere and Winger stayed, is now known as the "Officer and a Gentleman Room."

The Parallax View

(1974). Warren Beatty, Hume Cronyn. Reporter investigates fellow journalists present during an assassination who are now dying mysteriously.

The assassination of the United States Senator that triggers the story takes place on the observation deck at the 520-foot level of the 605-foot Space Needle built for the 1962 World's Fair in Seattle.

Practical Magic

(1998). Sandra Bullock, Nicole Kidman. Two sisters are cursed by the spirit of an ancestor hanged as a witch.

Main Street in Coupeville on Whidbey Island in Puget Sound was covered with facades to play Maria's Island. The rambling New England home in the story was built in the San Juan Island National Park on San Juan Island. Also appearing is the Admiralty Head Lighthouse in Coupeville.

Prefontaine

(1997). Jared Leto, R. Lee Ermey. Story of America's top distance runner in the 1970s who died prematurely in a car crash.

Race sequences were filmed on the track of the University of Puget Sound's Baker Stadium (1500 N. Warner, Tacoma). Other track scenes were shot at the University of Washington's Husky Stadium, which was dressed to look like Munich's Olympic Stadium during the 1972 Olympics.

Say Anything

(1989). John Cusack, Ione Skye. Unambitious high school graduate pursues class valedictorian harbored by a protective father.

Cusack drives through downtown Seattle past the Westlake Center and along 45th Street, where he passes the Guild 45th Theatre, the original silent movie theater in Seattle.

Singles

(1992). Bridget Fonda, Campbell Scott. Dating life for young men and women in Seattle's progressive music scene.

Filmed all over Seattle, much of the story takes place in the five-story OK Hotel (212 Alaskan Way South), which played the Java Stop. Fonda worked here, and Matt Dillon's band, Citizen Dick, featuring members of Pearl Jam, performed here. The characters lived in an apartment building at 19th and Thomas on Capitol Hill. Dillon visits the grave of Jimi Hendrix in Greenwood Memorial Park in Renton.

The Sixth Man

(1997). Marlon Wayans, Kadeem Hardison. Star college basketball player dies and returns as ghost to help his brother replace him.

The star for the fictional Seattle Huskies works his magic around the campus of the University of Washington.

Sleepless in Seattle

(1993). Meg Ryan, Tom Hanks. Boy tries to find widowed father a date by calling a radio talk show.

The opening scene, where Rob Reiner encourages Hanks to date again, takes place while walking through Seattle's Pike Place Market (Pike Street and First Avenue), in continuous operation since 1907. Elsewhere in Seattle, Hanks and Ross Mallinger live in a houseboat on Lake Union, near Westlake Avenue, and play football on Alki Beach in West Seattle; Hanks has a date with a woman who can't stop laughing at the Dalia Lounge (1904 Fourth Avenue) and attends a New Years Eve party in the Arctic Building (Third Street and James). In Maryland, Ryan overhears waitresses discussing "sleepless in Seattle" in the Capitol Diner, played by the Hollywood Diner (Holliday and Saratoga streets, Baltimore). Her apartment is at 904 South Broadway, and she is filmed working in the offices of the *Baltimore Sun* (501 North Calvert Street). Ryan and Hanks meet for the first time at Seattle-Tacoma International Airport (State Route 99).

Snow Falling on Cedars

(1999). Ethan Hawke, Youki Kudoh. Tension builds between Japanese community and Anglo community when fisherman is found drowned in his nets after World War II.

The docks were built near an abandoned cannery in Cathlamet near the mouth of the Columbia River; Whidbey Island became the fictional island of San Pedro; and Port Townsend was the setting for the evacuation scene at the dock for internment camp.

Ten Things I Hate About You

(1999). Heath Ledger, Julia Stiles. high school girl tries to find boyfriend for her sister so she can start dating.

Padua High School was played by Stadium High School (111 North E Street, Tacoma). The French Chateau-styled building with the copper-tipped towers was begun in 1891 as the Northern Pacific Railroad Tourist Hotel, but construction was abandoned. Purchased by the Tacoma School District, each suite is now a classroom in "The Brown Castle." Also featured is the Paramount Theater (901 Pine Street, Seattle), a 1928 design by Marcus Priteca boasting crystal chandeliers, marble stonework and luxurious velvet draperies. Also shot in Seattle was the paintball fight staged in Gas Works Park.

This Boy's Life

(1993). Ellen Barkin, Leonardo DiCaprio. Memoir of mother and son traveling through western towns in the 1950s.

The main street of Concrete was dressed up to look like the 1950s, and the town liked the look so much that most of the changes were kept.

Three Fugitives

(1989). Nick Nolte, Martin Short. Robber bungles bank heist and winds up taking a recently paroled bank robber hostage.

Short botches the bank robbery to get money needed for his daughter's illness at Old Tacoma City Hall (625 Commerce Street, Tacoma), now a collection of upscale businesses. Gas Works Park on the north shore of Lake Union (2101 North Northlake Way, Seattle) played Boswell Park, where Short and Nolte duck under bushes to evade police and Sarah Rowland Doroff talks for the first time. Nolte was paroled from the McNeil Island Prison in south Puget Sound, which portrayed the Washington State Prison. The correctional facility is open for tours.

Twin Peaks

(1990–1991). Kyle MacLachlan, Michael Ontkean. Odd detective investigates murder of young woman in bizarre town.

The exterior shots of the Great Northern Hotel were provided by the Salish Lodge next to the 268-foot Snoqualmie Falls (37807 Southwest Snoqualmie–Fall City Road, Snoqualmie); interiors were shot at the Kiana Lodge (14976 Sandy Hook Road, Poulsbo). The exterior of the Colonial Inn (SR 202, Snoqualmie) was used for the Roadhouse. MacLachlan ate cherry pie and drank coffee in the Double R Diner, which was played by the Mar-t Cafe (137 West North Bend Way, North Bend).

Vision Quest

(1985). Matthew Modine, Linda Fiorentino. High school wrestler loses single-minded devotion to his sport when he meets an alluring woman.

Four high schools in Spokane provided the mosaic for the story: Joel E. Ferris High School (3020 East 37th Avenue); John R. Rogers High School (1622 East Wellesley Avenue); North Central High School (1600 North Howard); and Shadle Park

High School (4327 North Ash). Also starring in Spokane were the Big Foot Tavern (9115 N. Division), playing a nightclub; Ferguson's Cafe (804 West Garland); and Cavanaugh's Ridpath Hotel (515 West Sprague). Modine works as a waiter in this turn-of-the-century inn.

Waiting for the Light

(1990). Shirley MacLaine/Teri Garr. Former Vaudeville magician concocts a ghost and gets believing town riled up.

The three-story square brick former Colonial Hotel, now Colonial Square (701 Commerce Street, Tacoma), served as MacLaine's apartment complex. Garr worked at the Rialto Theater (301 South 9th Street), which joined the Tacoma cityscape in the 1920s.

War of the Roses

(1989). Michael Douglas, Kathleen Turner. Unhappy couple want to divorce but neither wants to leave the house, so a war begins.

The town of Coupeville on Whidbey Island played a quaint New England village in the opening scenes. Coupeville is one of Washington's oldest cities, established in 1853 to defend Puget Sound from intruders.

Wargames

(1983). Matthew Broderick, Dabney Coleman. Teenaged computer whiz is called on to stop thermonuclear war.

Anderson Island in Puget Sound played Goose Island; Broderick and Ally Sheedy take the Steliacoom Ferry to reach the island. Many exteriors were shot in western Washington state, including Boeing Field standing in for the Oregon Airport. The fictional Norad headquarters, built in the Cascade Mountains, was constructed at a cost of a million dollars, and was the most costly set ever at the time.

WEST VIRGINIA

Matewan

(1987). Chris Cooper, James Earl Jones. Labor union organizer works to end brutal treatment of coal miners at the hands of a mining company.

The movie was staged in the town of Thurmond on WV 25. Once a great railroad town, Thurmond became a ghost town in the 1920s. Now a part of New River Gorge National River, the historic Chesapeake and Ohio Railway depot serves as the park visitor center. The longest steel arch bridge in the world is located here.

Night of the Hunter

(1955). Robert Mitchum, Shelley Winters. Cellmate of man who took $10,000 for murder gets out of jail and goes looking for the hidden treasure.

The story is set in West Virginia in the 1930s, and Mitchum's murderous minstrel did time in the Gothic fortress of the West Virginia Penitentiary (818 Jefferson Avenue, Moundsville). The prison, opened in 1867 and used until 1995, is open for tours.

Reckless

(1984). Aidan Quinn, Darryl Hannah. Straight-laced co-ed looks for danger and excitement with rebellious youth from the wrong side of town.

As the film was shot largely on location in Weirton, the Weirton Steel Corporation looms throughout the movie. There were no exterior lights on the mill so hundreds of movie lights were shipped from New York to stage the night scenes. Other locations included the Millsop Community Center on Main Street, where the swimming pool sequences were shot, and Weir High School (100 Red Rider Road). The cemetery scene was filmed in Wheeling.

Sweet Dreams

(1985). Jessica Lange, Ed Harris. Story of country singing legend Patsy Cline.

The town of Martinsburg stood in for Winchester, Virginia, including the Rainbow Club on Route 340. Also featured is the Ryman Auditorium (116 5th Avenue North, Nashville, Tennessee), the original home of the Grand Ole Opry, which was transformed to its appearance in the 1950s.

WISCONSIN

American Movie: The Making of Northwestern

(1999). Mark Borchardt, Mike Schank. Independent filmmaker struggles to produce a movie his way.

Monomonee Falls performed double duty, providing the locations for both the feature and *Coven*, the horror film within a film.

Back to School

(1986). Rodney Dangerfield, Sally Kellerman. Rich businessman decides to enter college to help his floundering son stay in school.

Most of the scenes for the fictional Grand Lakes University were filmed at the University of Wisconsin in Madison. The pivotal diving scenes in the outdoor pool were filmed in Hollywood.

Damien: Omen 2

(1978). William Holden, Lee Grant. Demon-child goes to live with unsuspecting relatives.

Jonathan Scott-Taylor attends military school at the former Northwestern Military Academy in Lake Geneva. The building is now deserted but the school has survived by merging with St. Johns Military Academy and moving to Delafield.

I Love Trouble

(1994). Julia Roberts, Nick Nolte. Rival newspaper reporters mix it up romantically and professionally.

A car tries to run Nolte and Roberts down on King Street in front of the Wisconsin State Capitol in Madison. Located on Capitol Square, the white granite Roman Renaissance government building was built in 1917. Roberts swims in the nude at Devil's Lake State Park (Highway 123, Baraboo).

WYOMING

Any Which Way You Can

(1980). Clint Eastwood, Sandra Locke. Drifter and pet orangutan travel the cowtowns for a second go-round.

In this sequel, Eastwood lets Clyde the Orangutan carry the picture, set in Jackson. Featured locations include the Buckrail Lodge (110 East Karns Avenue) and the Cowboy Bar (25 N. Cache Street), which won the first post–Prohibition liquor license in Wyoming in 1937. The big final fight scene sprawls across the streets of Jackson.

The Big Trail

(1930). John Wayne, Marguerite Churchill. Man leads hundreds of settlers across the Great Plains to a new life.

The movie that marked the first speaking role for John Wayne (and is rumored to be the first time he was on a horse) was filmed in part at Dead Man's Bar, 25 miles north of Jackson on Route 89. This stretch of the Snake River earned its name for its treacherous passage to boatmen. The film was also shot near Moran.

Close Encounters of the Third Kind

(1977). Richard Dreyfuss, Teri Garr. After a man's encounter with a UFO, he questions official government reports on space travelers.

In the climactic last third of the movie the aliens land and make contact with humans at Devil's Tower National Monument, the nation's first National Monument, in northeastern Wyoming. To create the arrival of the mother ship in the film, director Steven Spielberg used Hangars 5 and 6 at Brookley Field (Old Bay Street, Mobile). Six times the size of a normal sound stage, the hangars were built to hold dirigibles at the former air force base. The night scene was created inside the hangars with hundreds of arc lights. The Brookley Industrial Complex is not open to the public, but the hangars can be viewed from beyond the gates.

Clint Eastwood and his orangutan companion Clyde visited the Cowboy Bar in Jackson, Wyoming, in *Any Which Way You Can*.

Prison

(1988). Lane Smith, Viggo Mortensen. Spirit of executed prisoner returns to seek vengeance on his one-time guard, now the warden.

The film was shot in the Wyoming Frontier Prison (500 W. Walnut Street, Rawlins). Formidably constructed in 1901 to replace the state prison in Laramie, the castle-like fortress housed an infamous collection of cattle rustlers, thieves, and murderers until 1981. The "Old Pen" has been open to the public as a museum since 1987. Included in the guided tour are visits to the cell blocks, infirmary and death house.

Rocky IV

(1985). Sylvester Stallone, Talia Shire. Boxer avenges death of a friend at the hands of Russian super fighter.

Carl Weathers and Dolph Lundgren fight in the opening sequence at the old MGM Grand, now Ballys, at 3799 Las Vegas Boulevard South in Las Vegas, Nevada. The Bridger-Teton National Forest portrayed Siberia in the film, and Stallone trained for his tussle with Lundgren by running up Rendezvous Peak. Tram rides can cover most of the ground Stallone did.

Shane

(1953). Alan Ladd, Jean Arthur. Gunfighter looking to settle down is drawn into a conflict between settlers and ranchers.

The Wyoming scenery that was as big a star in the movie as any of the players was shot in the Bridger-Teton National Forest, the largest national forest in the contiguous United States.

Arthur and Van Heflin's homestead was on Gros Ventre Road, north of Kelly on the Antelope Flats area of the Elk National Wildlife Refuge.

Spencer's Mountain

(1963). Henry Fonda, Maureen O'Hara. Homesteader promises to build his big family a new house.

When Fonda inherits a Wyoming mountain, his homestead is portrayed by the Triangle X Ranch (2 Triangle X Ranch Road, Route 89, north of Moose), an authentic dude ranch. The log church was St. John Episcopal Church (170 N. Glenwood, Jackson).

Starship Troopers

(1997). Casper Van Dien, Dina Meyer. Futuristic military does battle with 75-foot bugs.

Hell's Half Acre (40 miles northwest of Casper off U.S. 20/26) served as the primary film site for the planet Klendathu, inhabited by nasty, brain-sucking bugs. The Half-Acre is actually 300 acres of stark rock formations in the middle of Wyoming prairie, flanked by mountains and valleys.

The Vanishing

(1993). Jeff Bridges, Keifer Sutherland. Man searches for missing girlfriend for years while her abductor observes him.

Sutherland's car stalls at the 3000-foot tunnel on Highway 14/16/20, six miles west of Cody, and Sandra Bullock goes for gas. She then disappears in Washington state from the Texaco gas station, playing the Titan, at Exit 30 off I-90 (742 SW Mount Si Boulevard, North Bend). The cabin by the lake sequences were also shot in Washington at the Camp Omache boy scout camp (25600 Monroe Los Camp Road, Snohomish).

Henry Fonda inherits a Wyoming homestead in *Spencer's Mountain*, played by the Triangle X Ranch north of Moose, Wyoming, and opposite Grand Teton National Park.

APPENDIX: LOCATIONS LISTED BY TYPE

Airports

Alpena Airport, Mi.
Baltimore-Washington International Airport, Md.
Boeing Field, Wash.
Cleveland Hopkins International Airport, Ohio
Dulles National Airport, Wash.
Ephrata Airfield, Wash.
Kennedy Space Center, Fla.
Libby Airport, Mo.
Lincoln Park Airport, Colo.
Logan International Airport, Mass.
MacArthur Airport, N.Y.
McCarran Airport, Nev.
Midway Airport, Ill.
Monterey Peninsula Airport, Calif.
O'Hare Airport, Ill.
Opa-Lacka Airport, Fla.
Orlando International Airport, Fla.
Orlando Sanford Airport, Fla.
Pittsburgh International Airport, Pa.
Reagan National Airport, Wash.
Rickenbacker International Airport, Ohio
San Jose International Airport, Calif.
Santa Rosa Air Center, Calif.
Sky Harbor Airport, Ariz.
Sonoma County Airport, Calif.
Stapleton Airport, Colo.
Tom Nevers Field, Mass.

Amusement Parks

Astroland Park, N.Y.
Bowcraft Amusement Park, N.J.
Dorney Park, Pa.
Kennywood Amusement Park, Pa.
King's Dominion Amusement Park, Va.
Oaks Amusement Park, Ore.
Ocean View Amusement Park, Va.
Paramount's Great America, Calif.
Paramount's King's Island, Ohio
Paul Bunyan Amusement Center, Minn.

APPENDIX

Playland Amusement Park, Canada
Santa Cruz Boardwalk, Calif.
Six Flags Elitch Gardens, Colo.
Six Flags Magic Mountain, Calif.
The Pavilion, S.C.
Universal Studios Theme Park, Fla.

Auto and Horse Race Tracks

Atlanta Motor Speedway, Ga.
Churchill Downs, Ky.
Darlington Raceway, S.C.
Daytona International Speedway, Fla.
Hialeah Park, Fla.
Lowe's Motor Speedway, N.C.
Meadowlands Race Track, N.J.
Petaluma Speedway, Calif.
Phoenix International Raceway, Ariz.
Portland International Raceway, Ore.
Portland Meadows, Ore.
Talladega Superspeedway, Ala.
Turf Paradise Race Track, Ariz.

Ballparks, Arenas and Stadiums

3 Com Park, Calif.
Alamodome, Tex.
Astrodome, Tex.
Baker Stadium, Wash.
Bluebonnet Palace, Tex.
Bosse Field, Ind.
Burlington Athletic Stadium, N.C.
Bush Stadium, Ind.
Cambria County War Memorial Arena, Pa.
Camden Yards, Md.
Charleston Coliseum, S.C.
Charlotte Coliseum, N.C.
Cobo Arena, Mich.
College Park, Md.
Collins Park, N.Y.
Comiskey Park, Ill.
County Stadium, Wis.
Delmar Stadium, Tex.
Durham Athletic Park, N.C.
Ernie Shore Field, N.C.
Fenway Park, Mass.
Fleming Stadium, N.C.
Florida Citrus Bowl, Fla.
Fouts Field, Tex.
Franklin Field, Va.
Grayson Stadium, Ga.
Hi Corbett Field, Ariz.
Hubert H. Humphrey Metrodome, Minn.
Huntingburg Stadium, Ind.
Husky Stadium, Wash.
Jack Ruhr Stadium, Minn.
Joe Riley Stadium, S.C.
Joe Robbie Stadium, Fla.
Kiel Auditorium, Miss.
Knute Rockne Stadium, Ind.
Lamar Porter Field, Ark.
Louisiana Superdome, La.
Luther Williams Field, Ga.
Madison Square Garden, N.Y.
Mile High Stadium, Colo.
Mirmow Field, S.C.
Mumford Stadium, La.
Network Associates Coliseum, Calif.
Orange Bowl, Fla.
Philadelphia Arena, Pa.
Pittsburgh Civic Arena, Pa.
Point Stadium, Pa.
PSI Net Stadium, Md.
Rickwood Field, Ala.
Riverside Stadium, Pa.
San Jose Arena, Calif.
Shea Stadium, N.Y.
Spec-Martin Stadium, Fla.
The Spectrum, Pa.
Sun Devil Stadium, Ariz.
Texas Stadium, Tex.
Tiger Stadium, Mich.
Tinker Field, Fla.
US Cellular Arena, Wis.
Veterans Stadium, Pa.
War Memorial Stadium, Ark.
Whittier Field, Maine
Williams-Brice Stadium, S.C.
World War Memorial Stadium, N.C.
Wrigley Field, Ill.
Yankee Stadium, N.Y.

LOCATIONS LISTED BY TYPE

Bowling Alleys and Billiard Parlors

Country Club Bowling, N.J.
Forward Lanes, Pa.
National Bowling Stadium, Nev.
North Center Bowling Alleys, Ill.
Recckio's Lanes, N.Y.
St. Paul's Billiards, Ill.
Windy City Bowling Alley, Ill.

Businesses

A.M. Grove General Store, Md.
Admiral Drive-In, Okla.
Adobe Drug, Calif.
All-American Sports Park, Nev.
American Can Company, Md.
American Motors Corporation, Wis.
Andy's Tire and Service Center, N.J.
Anguilla Gallery, Conn.
Auto Recyclers, N.J.
Ben & Jerry's, Vt.
Bloomingdale's, N.Y.
Brookley Industrial Complex, Wyo.
Budget Print, S.C.
Cammareri Brothers Bakery, N.Y.
Cape Ann Anchor & Forge Company, N.H.
Carmen's House of Flowers, D.C.
Cascade Caverns, Texas
Center Block, N. Mex.
Chapel of the Bells, Nev.
Checker Motor Company, Mich.
Cheese Board Bakery, Calif.
Cherokee Nuclear Power Plant, S.C.
Chicago Board of Trade, Ill.
Chocolate Tree, S.C.
City Lights, Calif.
Coliseum Ballroom, Fla.
Contra-Costa Newspapers, Calif.
Crestar Bank, Va.
Daily News Building, N.Y.
Dairy Queen—Archer, Tex.
Dover Garage, N.Y.
Eastern Market, D.C.
Eckel's Drug Store, Pa.
Elsa's Gowns, N.Y.
Enchanted Forrest, Ark.
Eye Care Center, Ill.
Famous Deli, Pa.
FAO Schwarz, N.J.
Farmers and Merchants Bank, Tex.
Federal Express—Memphis, Tenn.
Floore Country Store, Tex.
Friendly's Dry Goods, Tex.
Fulton Cotton and Bag Mill, Ga.
Fulton Street Market, Ill.
Fun Wash, Ark.
Genoa Country Store, Nev.
Gilbert & Bennett Wire Mill, Conn.
Go-Go Gas, Vt.
Gold's Scrapyard, N.Y.
Golden Lamb, N.Y.
Good Deals on Wheels, Nev.
Groove Jet, N.C.
Guss's Pickle Stand, N.Y.
Halles Department Store, Ohio
Happy Donuts, Calif.
Harry Winston Jewelers, N.Y.
Hilliard Tire, Wash.
Home Depot—Phoenix, Ariz.
Hooper's Market, Mass.
House of Hirsch, Fla.
The Ice House, N.C.
Italian Market, Pa.
J.J. Hapgood General Store, Vt.
Jacks Music, N.J.
John Breuner Company, Calif.
John Wanamaker's, Pa.
Johnson's Corner, Mo.
Kelmscott Bookstore, Md.
Kronk Gym, La.
L.L. Lanier & Sons Tupelo Honey, Fla.
Lambda Bookstore, D.C.
Las Savell, Tenn.
Lehi Flour Roller Mills, Utah
Leon's Food Mart, Nebr.
Love Saves The Day, N.Y.
Macy's, N.Y.
Marin Art and Garden Center, Calif.
Marshall Field, Ill.
Marshallan Company, Ohio

APPENDIX

Martha Washington Bakery, Mich.
Mason's Furniture Store, Wash.
Maud Frizon Shoe Store, N.Y.
Maya Schaper Cheese and Antiques, N.Y.
McMullen's Soda Fountain, Calif.
Mel's Drive-In, Calif.
Miami Herald, Fla.
Michael Rainey Antiques, S.C.
Midcity Bank, Ill.
Mollye's Market, N.C.
Murr's Graphic & Printing, S.C.
New Hope Ice Arena, Minn.
Nieman Marcus-San Francisco, Calif.
Nob Hill Pharmacy, Oreg.
North Beach Video, Calif.
Nubest and Company Salon, N.Y.
Oakland Tribune, Calif.
Ocean Ice Palace, N.J.
Olmos Pharmacy, Tex.
Orca Bay Trading Post, Ala.
Pageant Book and Print Shop, N.Y.
Parade Ice Arena, Minn.
Park Wedding Chapel, Nev.
Parkers Western Wear, Nev.
Parkside Candy Shoppe, N.Y.
Peacham General Store, Vt.
Phar-Mor Grocery — Rio Rancho, N.M.
Pickwick Pharmacy, Pa.
Pike Place Market, Wash.
Ponder State Bank, Tex.
Quick Stop and RST Video, N.J.
Ralph Lauren Store, N.Y.
Ray's Bait Shop, La.
Riggs National Bank, D.C.
Ruth-Anne's General Store, Wash.
St. Louis Bread Company, Ill.
Schlumberger Gallery, Calif.
Shadyside Gas, Pa.
Shakespeare and Company, N.Y.
Silver Bells Wedding Chapel, Nev.
Simpson Tacoma Kraft Mill, Wash.
Skyview Drive-In, S.C.
Sonny's Quick Stop, Tex.
Sotheby's, N.Y.
South of the Border, S.C.
Spratt Music, Pa.
Staglin Family Vineyard, Calif.
Starbucks — Austin, Tex.
Strand Bookstore, N.Y.
Sun Studio, Tenn.
Tastee Freeze — Tulsa, Okla.
Thresher's Mill, Vt.
Tiffany & Company, N.Y.
Tony Mart's, N.J.
Tower Records — Manhattan, N.Y.
Vaughn Tobacco Warehouses, Ky.
Vesuvio Bakery, N.Y.
Village Ice Cream Parlor, N.Y.
W.L. Zimmerman & Sons General Store, Pa.
Wacky Golf, S.C.
Washington Post Building, D.C.
Washington Serpentarium, Wash.
Waterbury Brass Company, Conn.
Weirton Steel Corporation, W.V.
Weitz, Weitz and Coleman Booksellers, N.Y.
West Side Market, Ohio
WQED-TV, Pa.
Yaskawa Electric America, Ill.

Casinos

The Aladdin, Nev.
Bally's Casino, Nev.
Binion's Horseshoe, Nev.
Caesar's Palace, Nev.
Circus Circus, Nev.
Crowne Plaza Las Vegas, Nev.
Desert Inn, Nev.
Dunes, Nev.
Eldorado Hotel and Casino, Nev.
Flamingo Hilton, Nev.
Four Jacks Casino, Nev.
Fremont Hotel and Casino, Nev.
Grand Casino, Miss.
Hard Rock Hotel and Casino, Nev.
Harold's Place, Nev.
Harrah's — Reno, Nev.
John Aseuaga's Nugget, Nev.
Las Vegas Hilton, Nev.
The Luxor, Nev.
Mandalay Bay, Nev.
Mapes Casino, Nev.

The Mirage, Nev.
Pioneer Club, Nev.
River Palms, Nev.
Riverside Casino, Nev.
Riviera Hotel and Casino, Nev.
Sahara Hotel & Casino, Nev.
Sands—Atlantic City, N.J.
Sands Hotel and Casino, Nev.
Stardust Hotel and Casino, Nev.
Tropicana Hotel and Casino, Nev.
Trump Taj Mahal, N.J.

Cemeteries

Allegheny Cemetery, Pa.
Blue Hill Cemetery, Mass.
Bohemian National Cemetery, Ill.
Bonaventure Cemetery, Ga.
Calvary Cemetery, N.Y.
Cedar Hill Cemetery, Miss.
Elmwood Cemetery, Tenn.
Evans City Cemetery, Pa.
Evergreen Cemetery, Nev.
Greenwood Memorial Park, Wash.
Grove Street Cemetery, Conn.
Lafayette Cemetery No. 1, La.
Laurel Grove Cemetery, Ga.
Maplewood Cemetery, Ky.
Moffett Cemetery, Kans.
St. Louis Cemetery #1, La.
Shockoe Cemetery, Va.
South Park Cemetery, Tex.

Churches

Ascension St. Agnes Church, D.C.
Black River Presbyterian Church, N.C.
Cathedral of Our Lady of Peace, Hawaii
Christ Episcopal Church, Ga.
Church of the Good Shepherd, Md.
Dahlgren Chapel, D.C.
Glencoe Union Church, Ill.
Highland Lake Congregational Church, Colo.
Holy Trinity Church, N.Y.
Memorial Lutheran Church, Minn.
Mission San Francisco de Asis, Calif.
Mission San Juan Bautista, Calif.
Mount Carmel Catholic Church, Ill.
Old Swede's Church, Pa.
Old Trinity Church, Mass.
Our Lady of Good Voyage Church, Mass.
Our Lady of Grace Church, N.Y.
Plymouth Baptist Church, Ill.
Riverside Memorial Chapel, N.Y.
St. Anne's Church, Md.
St. Anne's Convent, Ky.
St. Augustine's Church, Pa.
St. Bartholomew's Church, N.Y.
St. Gabriel's Church, Pa.
St. Helena's Episcopal Church, S.C.
St. John Episcopal Church, Wy.
St. John's Basilica, Minn.
St. John's Church, R.I.
St. Joseph's Catholic Church, Tex.
St. Louis Cathedral, La.
St. Lucy's Church, N.J.
St. Martin de Tours Church, La.
St. Mary of the Angels Church, Ill.
St. Mary's Church, Fla.
St. Michael's Church, Md.
Saint Paul Methodist Church, Md.
St. Paul's Cathedral, Pa.
St. Paul's Catholic Church, Calif.
St. Theodosius Russian Orthodox Cathedral, Ohio
St. Thomas Aquinas Church, Nev.
St. Vincent DePaul Church, Ill.
Saints Peter and Paul Church, Calif.
San Jose Mission, Tex.
Scottish Rite Cathedral, Tex.
Swedenborgian Church, Calif.
Trinity Church—Boston, Mass.
Trinity Church—Newport, R.I.
Winnetka Congregational Church, Ill.

Colleges

Agnes Scott University, Ga.
Berry College, Ga.

APPENDIX

Bowdoin College, La.
Bridgewater State College, Mass.
Broward Community College, Fla.
Butler University, Ind.
Carnegie-Mellon University, Pa.
Case Western University, Ohio
College of Charleston, S.C.
College of Santa Fe, N.M.
Duke University, N.C.
Georgetown University, D.C.
Harvard University, Mass.
Hebrew Union College, Ohio
Holy Cross College of Notre Dame, Ind.
Houston Baptist University, Tex.
Hunter College, N.Y.
Indiana University, Ind.
Jefferson College, Miss.
Louisiana State University, La.
Loyola University, Ill.
Merritt College, Calif.
Miami University, Fla.
Monmouth College, N.Y.
New York University, N.Y.
Northwestern University, Ill.
Notre Dame University, Ind.
Ohio State University, Ohio
Penn State University, Pa.
Princeton University, N.J.
Rutgers Law School, N.Y.
St. Joseph's College, Ind.
Savannah State University, Ga.
Smith College, Mass.
Southeastern Louisiana University, La.
Southern University, La.
Stanford University, Calif.
Stetson University, Fla.
Swarthmore College, Pa.
Tufts University, Mass.
Tulane University, La.
Union College, N.Y.
United States Naval Academy, D.C.
University of Arizona, Ariz.
University of California-Berkeley, Calif.
University of Chicago, Ill.
University of Cincinnati, Ohio
University of Florida, Fla.
University of Houston, Tex.
University of Kansas, Ks.
University of Maryland, Md.
University of Minnesota, Minn.
University of Mississippi, Miss.
University of Nebraska, Nebr.
University of North Texas, Tex.
University of Oregon, Oreg.
University of Pacific, Wash.
University of Puget Sound, Wash.
University of Texas, Tex.
University of Vermont, Vt.
University of Virginia, Va.
University of Washington, Wash.
University of Wisconsin, Wisc.
Upsala College, N.J.
Valencia Community College East, Fla.
Wake Forest University, N.C.

Farms & Ranches

Charles R Ranch, N.M.
Cowboy Morning Figure 3 Ranch, N.M.
Gallagher's Ranch, Tex.
Hancock Fruit Farm, Ind.
Hill Ranch, Tex.
Lazy E Ranch, Okla.
Long's Pea Patch Farm, La.
777 Ranch, Tex.
Southfork Ranch, Tex.
Triangle X Ranch, Wyo.

Golf Courses

Kiawah Island — Ocean Course, S.C.
Par Golf, N.C.
Rolling Hills Golf & Tennis Club, N.C.
Tubac Golf Resort, Ariz.

Government Buildings

Agriculture Building, Calif.

LOCATIONS LISTED BY TYPE

Anson County Courthouse, N.C.
Arkansas Health Center, Ark.
Atascadero City Hall, Calif.
Baltimore County Courthouse, Md.
Barstow Courthouse, Calif.
Caldwell County Courthouse, Tex.
Chambers County Courthouse, Ala.
Chicago City Hall, Ill.
City/County Building — Pittsburgh, Pa.
Clarence Mitchell Courthouse, Nev.
Clark County Courthouse, Nev.
Colorado Springs Administration Building, Colo.
Criminal Justice Center, Tenn.
Dallas County Administration Building, Tex.
Department of Employment Services Building, D.C.
Duval County Courthouse, Fla.
East Feliciana Parish Courthouse, La.
Fayette County Courthouse, Tex.
Federal Hall, N.Y.
Frank Murphy Hall of Justice, Mich.
Fresno City Hall, Calif.
Graves County Courthouse, Ky.
Group Health Administration Building, N.Y.
Hartley Dodge Memorial Building, N.J.
Hinds County Courthouse, Miss.
Housing and Urban Development Building, D.C.
Hunt County Courthouse, Tex.
Interstate Commerce Commission Building, Fla.
Jackson County Courthouse, Mo.
Jasper County Courthouse, Ga.
Jefferson Davis County Courthouse, Tex.
Kleberg County Courthouse, Tex.
Lafayette Police Station, La.
Lavaca County Courthouse, Tex.
Los Alamos National Laboratories, Tex.
Louisiana State Capitol, La.
Madison County Courthouse, Miss.
Marin County Civic Center, Calif.
Massachusetts State House, Mass.
Maverick County Courthouse, Tex.
Maxwell Precinct Station, Ill.
Memphis County Courthouse, Tenn.
Menlo Park City Hall, Calif.
National Center for Atmospheric Research, Colo.
New York County Supreme Court, N.Y.
Newton County Courthouse, Ga.
9th Precinct Police Station, N.Y.
Norwich City Hall, Conn.
Old Tacoma City Hall, Wash.
Old Wilmington Light Infantry Armory, N.C.
Olde Brokerage, Mich.
Orlando City Hall, Fla.
Ouray County Courthouse, Colo.
Palace of Governors, N.M.
Pennsylvania State Capitol, Pa.
Pentagon, D.C.
Philadelphia City Hall, Pa.
Phoenix Courthouse, Ariz.
Plantation City Hall, Fla.
Portland City Hall, Ore.
Redwood City Hall of Justice, Ark.
Reno Post Office, Nev.
Rhode Island State House, R.I.
St. Louis City Hall, Mo.
San Francisco City Hall, Calif.
San Francisco Department of Public Health, Calif.
Shelby County Courthouse, Tenn.
Sonoma Community Center, Calif.
South County Courthouse, Fla.
Suffolk County Courthouse, Mass.
Supreme Court Building, N.Y.
Treasury Building, D.C.
Tweed Courthouse, N.Y.
United Nations, N.Y.
United States Capitol, D.C.
United States Depart of Energy's Argonne National Laboratory, Ill.
Utah State Capitol, Utah
Veterans Memorial Building, Calif.
Virginia Capitol, Va.
War Memorial Building, Calif.
Washington State Capitol, Wash.
Washoe County Courthouse, Nev.
Wharton County Courthouse, Tex.
William F. Brennan Courthouse, N.J.

APPENDIX

Winnipeg City Hall, Minn.
Wisconsin State Capitol, Wisc.

Historic Homes

Afton Villa Gardens, La.
Airlie Gardens, N.C.
Aldrich Mansion, R.I.
Armstrong Estate, Calif.
Ashland-Belle Helene Plantation, La.
Bellamy Mansion, N.C.
Belvedere Castle, N.Y.
Biltmore Estate, N.C.
Borden House, Ark.
Botany Bay Plantation, S.C.
Breakers, R.I.
Ca' d'Zan, Fla.
Cantigny, Ga.
The Castle, D.C.
Castle Hill, N.Y.
Chandler Estate, Maine
Chateau-sur-Mer, Mass.
Cherokee Plantation, S.C.
Cuneo Estate and Gardens, Ill.
Dauart Plantation, S.C.
Destrehan Plantation, La.
Dunsmuir House and Gardens, Calif.
Eden State Gardens and Museum, Fla.
Ehrman Mansion, Calif.
Ernest Hemingway Home and Museum, Fla.
Filoli, Calif.
Flat Top Manor, N.C.
Fleur de Lac, Nev.
Gallier Hall, La.
Garrett-Jacobs Mansion, Pa.
Germaine Wells Mansion, La.
Goodwood House, Minn.
Graceland, Tenn.
H. Cornell Wilson House, D.C.
Hammersmith Farm, R.I.
Hempstead House, N.Y.
Hermann-Grima House, La.
Hightower Hall, S.C.
Houmas House Plantation, La.
Iolani Palace, Hawaii

Kenan House, N.C.
Keswick Hall, Va.
Kipling House, Vt.
Krebs-Peterson House, La.
Lemp Mansion, Mo.
Mabel Dodge Luhan House, N.M.
Mableton Mansion, Calif.
Magnolia Plantation, S.C.
Mather Mansion, S.C.
Middleton Place, S.C.
Mohonk Mountain House, N.C.
Myrtle Grove Plantation, Ga.
North Carolina Governor's Mansion, N.C.
Oak Alley Plantation, La.
Oaklawn Manor, La.
Old Westbury Gardens, N.Y.
Orton Plantation, N.C.
Owens-Thomas House, Ga.
Pontalba Buildings, La.
Presidio Mansion, Tex.
Pyle House, N.H.
Rose Court Mansion, Calif.
Rosecliff, R.I.
Shades Plantation, La.
Tidalholm, S.C.
Trois Estate, Tex.
Vanderbilt Museum, N.Y.
Ventfort Hall, Vt.
Vizcaya Museum and Gardens, Fla.
Walker-Plant House, Ala.
William W. Kimball Residence, Ill.
Wise House, N.C.
Wolf House, Calif.
Wormsloe, Ga.

Hospitals

Agnews Developmental Center, Calif.
Children's Hospital — Baltimore, Md.
Dosher Memorial Hospital, N.C.
Elmhurst General Hospital, N.Y.
Harrisburg State Hospital, Pa.
Illinois Masonic Hospital, Ill.
Jefferson Davis Hospital, Tex.
Lawrence Memorial Hospital, Kans.
Lincoln General Hospital, Nebr.

Los Medanos Hospital, Calif.
Marc Island Naval Hospital, Calif.
Metropolitan State Hospital, Mass.
Michael Reese Hospital and Medical Center, Ill.
Mt. Sinai Hospital, Pa.
Needham-Glover Hospital, Mass.
Northampton State Mental Hospital, Vt.
Northwestern Memorial Hospital, Ill.
Oregon State Mental Hospital, Ore.
Our Lady of the Lake Hospital, La.
St. Ann's Hospital, Ill.
St. Elizabeth's Hospital, D.C.
St. Joseph's Hospital, Ind.
St. Mary's Hospital, Miss.
San Antonio State Hospital, Tex.
San Francisco General, Calif.
Tacoma General Hospital, Wash.
University of Illinois-Chicago Hospital, Ill.
Wishard Memorial Hospital, Ind.

Hotels and Motels

Ambassador East, S.D.
Arcade Hotel, Tenn.
Ashby Bed and Breakfast, Md.
Bancroft Hotel, Calif.
Bay Street Inn, S.C.
Big 8 Motel — El Reno, Nev.
Biltmore Hotel, N.C.
Blackstone Hotel, Ill.
Blair House Inn, Calif.
Boca Raton Resort Hotel and Club, La.
Buckrail Lodge, Wyo.
Cal-Neva Lodge Resort, Nev.
Cathedral Hill Hotel. Calif.
Chicago Hilton and Towers, Ill.
Clairmount Motor Inn, Ohio
Clarion Hotel, Md.
Colonial Inn, Wash.
Column's Hotel, La.
Copley Plaza Hotel, Mass.
Days Inn Uptown, N.C.
The Drake, Ill.
Don Ce Sar Beach Resort, Fla.
Eden House Hotel, Fla.
Eden Roc Resort and Spa, Fla.
Edison Walthall Hotel, Miss.
El Rancho Motel, Ill.
El Tovar Hotel, Ariz.
Essex House, N.Y.
Fairfield Hills Hospital, N.Y.
Fontainebleu Hilton Resort and Spa, Fla.
Francis Marion Hotel, S.C.
Golden Lamb Inn, Ohio
Goldfield Hotel, Nev.
Governor Hotel, Ore.
Grand Hotel, Mich.
Griggs House, Md.
Hay-Adams Hotel, D.C.
Heritage House, Calif.
Hermosa Inn, Ariz.
Hidden Valley Bed and Breakfast, Va.
Hillier Hotel, N.C.
Hilton Hotel — Manhattan, N.Y.
Holiday Inn-San Francisco, Calif.
Hotel 17, N.Y.
Hotel Dominico, N.Y.
Hotel Monte Vista, Ariz.
Hotel Washington, D.C.
Hurley Mountain Inn, N.Y.
Hyatt Regency, Calif.
Inn of Lincoln, Nebr.
Inn on the Cliffs, Hawaii
Jefferson Hotel, Va.
Kennedy Hotel, Calif.
Kiana Lodge, Wash.
Koehler House, Tex.
La Castaneda Hotel, Nev.
La Fonda Hotel, N.M.
Landmark Hotel, Nev.
Lido Beach Hotel, N.Y.
The Lodge of Pebble Beach, Fla.
Lord Jeffrey Inn, Mass.
Mauna Lani Hotel, Hawaii
Mayflower Hotel on the Park, N.Y.
Menger Hotel, Tex.
Meridien Hotel, N.Y.
Midland Hotel, Kans.
Mirror Lake Resort, Idaho
Mountain Lake Hotel, N.Y.
Napoleon House, La.

National Hotel, Fla.
Ocean Hacienda Inn, Fla.
OK Hotel, Mont.
Omni Ambassador Hotel, Ill.
Omni Shoreham Hotel, D.C.
Peabody Hotel, Tenn.
Pegleg Inn, N.H.
Peninsula Hotel, N.Y.
Peppermill Inn, Nev.
Phoenix Park Hotel, D.C.
Pierre Hotel, N.Y.
Plaza Hotel, N.Y.
Raintree Inn Bed and Breakfast, Ky.
Rhett House Inn, S.C.
Rice Hope Plantation, S.C.
Ridpath Hotel, Wash.
Ritz Hotel — Manhattan, N.Y.
Royal Host Motel, Colo.
St. Anthony Hotel, Tex.
St. Charles Hotel, Mo.
St. Regis Hotel, N.Y.
Salish Lodge, Wash.
San Francisco Hilton, Calif.
Sheraton New York Hotel, N.Y.
Sherry Netherland Hotel, N.Y.
Spur Hotel, Tex.
Stanford Inn, Fla.
Tallahassee Motor Lodge, Fla.
Thunder Bay Inn, Mich.
Tides Inn, Wash.
Timberline Lodge, Ore.
Waldorf Astoria, N.Y.
Watergate Hotel, D.C.
Waybury Inn, Vt.
Willard Intercontinental Hotel, D.C.
York House, Tenn.

Libraries

Archer Public Library, Tex.
Blackstone Library, R.I.
Carnegie Library — Santa Rosa, Calif.
Detroit Public Library, Mich.
George Peabody Library, Md.
Morgan Library, N.Y.
Northbrook Public Library, Ill.
Old State Library, D.C.
Pasadena Public Library, Tex.
Porter Memorial Library, Ga.
Reagan Library, D.C.
San Antonio Public Library, Tex.
University of Pennsylvania Fine Arts Library, Pa.
Widener Library, Mass.

Lighthouses

Admiralty Head Lighthouse, Wash.
Big Bay Point Lighthouse, Mich.
Brant Point Lighthouse, Mass.
Gayhead Lighthouse, Mass.
Marshall Point Lighthouse, Maine
Point Arena Lighthouse, Calif.
Round Island Lighthouse, Mich.
Yaquina Head Lighthouse, R.I.

Military Bases

Camp Blanding, Fla.
Coast Guard Training Center, Calif.
Craig Field, Ala.
Fort Jackson, S.C.
Fort Knox, Ky.
Fort Sill, Okla.
Hamilton Air Force Base, Calif.
Mare Island, Calif.
Marine Corps Air Station — Beaufort, S.C.

Museums

American Museum of Natural History, N.Y.
B & O Railroad Museum, Md.
Baltimore Museum of Art, Md.
Carnegie Mellon Institute, N.Y.
Carnegie Museum of Natural History, Pa.
Cleveland Museum of Natural History, Ohio

255 LOCATIONS LISTED BY TYPE

Columbus Center of Science and Industry, Ohio
Field Museum, Wis.
Johnson Space Center, Tex.
Knox Mill Museum, Maine
Las Vegas Neon Museum, Nev.
Liberace Museum, Nev.
Maine Maritime Museum, Maine
Metropolitan Museum of Art, N.Y.
Museum of Science and Industry, D.C.
Mystic Seaport, Conn.
National Baseball Hall of Fame, N.Y.
National Design Museum, N.Y.
National Museum of the American Indian, N.Y.
Oregon Trail Museum, Oreg.
Orlando Science Center, Fla.
Palace of Fine Arts, Calif.
Philadelphia Museum of Art, Pa.
Pima Air Museum, Ariz.
Railway Museum of Greater Cincinnati, Ohio
Randall Davey Audubon Center, N.M.
Ringling Circus Museum, Fla.
Smithsonian Institution, D.C.
Solomon R. Guggenheim Museum, Pa.
United States Space and Rocket Center, Ala.
Walters Art Gallery, Md.

Chesapeake & Ohio Canal Historical Park, Ohio
Devil's Tower National Monument, Wyo.
Elk National Wildlife Refuge, Wyo.
Glen Canyon National Recreation Area, Ariz.
Golden Gate National Recreation Area, Calif.
Grand Canyon National Park, Ariz.
Jefferson Memorial, D.C.
John Day Fossil Beds National Monument, Ore.
Lake Powell National Recreation Area, Ariz.
Lincoln Memorial, D.C.
Mount Rushmore National Monument, S.D.
National Tropical Botanical Garden, Hawaii
Neonatal National Forest, N.C.
Rock Creek Park, D.C.
San Juan Island National Park, Wash.
Sawtooth National Recreation Area, Idaho
Snoqualmie National Forest, Wash.
Statue of Liberty, N.Y.
Uinta National Forest, Utah
Washington Monument, D.C.
Wenatchee National Forest, Wash.
White Sands National Monument, N.M.

National Parks and Monuments

Arcadia National Park, Maine
Badlands National Park, S.D.
Bent's Old Fort National Historic Site, Colo.
Black Hills National Forest, S.D.
Bridger-Teton National Forest, Wyo.
Canyon de Chelly National Monument, N.M.
Canyonlands National Park, Utah
Carlsbad Caverns National Park, N.M.
Cascades National Park, Ohio

Office Buildings

Atlas Building, N.Y.
Bank America Building, Calif.
Bostwick Building, N.Y.
Brill Building, N.Y.
Chemical Bank Building, N.Y.
Chicago Sun Times Building, Ill.
Chrysler Building, N.Y.
Cullen Center, Tex.
Cyberdyn Systems Building, Calif.
Dante Building, Calif.
Empire State Building, N.Y.
First Union Building, Pa.

APPENDIX

General Motors Building, Mich.
HarperCollins Building, N.Y.
Leo Burnett Building, Ill.
Marriott Renaissance Center, Mich.
Mellon Bank Center, Pa.
Merchandise Mart, Ill.
Metropolitan Life Building, N.Y.
MGM Building, N.Y.
MONY Building, N.Y.
Nations Bank Corporate Center, N.C.
RR Donnelly Building, Ill.
Seagram Building, N.Y.
Smith Tower Building, Wash.
Sterick Building, Tenn.
Tech Mart Building, Calif.
Terminal Tower, Ohio
Tower Life Building, Tex.
Transco Tower, Tex.
Union Planters Building, Tenn.
United States Steel Building, Pa.
Wheeler Building, Pa.
World Financial Center, N.Y.
World Trade Center, N.Y.

Prisons

Alcatraz Island, Calif.
Allegheny Jail, Pa.
Anamosa State Penitentiary, Iowa
Arrendale Correctional Institution, Ga.
Eastern State Penitentiary, Pa.
Georgia State Prison, Ga.
Holmesburg Prison, Pa.
Huntsville State Penitentiary, Tex.
Joliet Correctional Institution, Ill.
Louisiana State Penitentiary, La.
McNeil Island Prison, Wash.
Montana Territorial Prison, Mont.
Nevada State Penetentiary, Nev.
Ohio State Reformatory, Ohio
Parchman Penitentiary, Miss.
Stateville Correctional Facility, N.M.
Tennessee State Penitentiary, Tenn.
West Virginia Penitentiary, W.V.
Wyoming Frontier Prison, Wyo.

Railroad Stations

30th Street Station, Pa.
Chesapeake & Ohio Railway depot, W.V.
Flagstaff train station, Ariz.
Glenwood Springs Train Depot, Colo.
Grand Central Station, N.Y.
Hamlet train station, N.C.
Niles railroad depot, Mich.
Old Frisco Depot, Calif.
Santa Rosa Railroad Depot, Calif.
South Dayton train depot, Ohio
Two Harbor Depot, Minn.
Union Station — Chicago, Ill.
Union Station — Denver, Colo.
Union Station — St. Louis, Mo.
Union Terminal — Cincinnati, Ohio

Railroads

Alaska Railroad, Ala.
Arkansas & Missouri Railroad, Ark.
Austin Texas Steam Railroad, Tex.
Central Montana Railroad, Mont.
Cumbres and Toltec Scenic Railroad, Colo.
Denver & Rio Grande Railroad, Colo.
Durango & Silverton Railroad, Colo.
Green Mountain Railroad, Vt.
Magma Arizona Railroad, Ariz.
Mid-Continent Railroad, Wisc.
Sierra Railroad, Wisc.
Virginia & Truckee Railroad, Va.

Restaurants and Bars

The Abbey, Mass.
Alice Restaurant, Wyo.
Alice's Restaurant, Mass.
American Fish Company, N.C.
Antoine's, La.
Argentine Grill, D.C.
Arnold's Bar & Grill, Ohio

LOCATIONS LISTED BY TYPE

Babe's Bar & Grill, Tex.
Babylon Restaurant, Tex.
Barbetta, N.Y.
The Bayou, La.
Belvedere Condominiums, Md.
Bendix Diner, N.J.
Bento Restaurant, Ill.
Big Foot Tavern, Wash.
Bix Restaurant, Calif.
Bluebird Cafe, Tenn.
Blues City Cafe, Tenn.
Bob's Diner, N.J.
Bob's Java Jive, Wash.
Bog O's Roadhouse, Tex.
Brennan's Restaurant, Tex.
Brick Tavern, Wash.
Budlows, Md.
Bull & Finch Pub, Mass.
Cadillac Bar and Grill, Tex.
Cafe Budapest, Mass.
Cafe Cheneville, Calif.
Cafe des Artistes, N.Y.
Cafe Elysian, N.Y.
Cafe Jake's, Fla.
Cafe Lalo, N.Y.
Cafe Lautrec, Va.
Cafe Piaf, N.C.
Cafe Pierre, N.Y.
Cafe Reggio, N.Y.
Canal Club, Va.
Canton Tea Garden, Neb.
Carnegie Deli, N.Y.
Castrelo Restaurant, N.J.
Charlie Trotter's Restaurant
Chuck E Cheese — Altamonte Springs, Fla.
Chumley's, N.Y.
Club Berlin, N.Y.
Cowboy Bar, Wyo.
Cowgirl Hall of Fame, N.Y.
Coyote Ugly, N.Y.
Crab Claw, Md.
Crab Shack, S.C.
Crow's Nest, Mass.
Dalia Lounge, Wash.
Denny's-Buena Park, Calif.
Denny's-Mechanicsburg, Calif.
Depot Bar and Grill, Minn.
Desiree Supper Club, Fla.
Dick's Cafe, Utah
Dixie Brewery, La.
Dixie Grill, N.C.
Dojo Restaurant, N.Y.
Dom Ivana, Calif.
Dot and Etta's Shrimp Hut, La.
Doyle's Cafe, Mass.
Duff's, Mo.
Duly's Coney Island, Mich.
Elaine's, N.Y.
Elbow Room, Fla.
Elysian Cafe, N.J.
Emerald Pub, N.Y.
Ernestine & Hazel's, Tenn.
Euclid Tavern, Ohio
Ferguson's Cafe, Wash.
First Avenue, Wash.
Fitzgerald's, Ill.
Fitzgerald's Club, Nev.
Fog Diner, Calif.
Franklin Inn Mexican Restaurant, Pa.
Front Street Deli, Tenn.
Geno's Steaks, Pa.
Gilley's, Tex.
Gray's Papaya, N.Y.
Grecian Corner, N.C.
The Green Mill, N.Y.
Green Pastures Restaurant, Tex.
Gruene Hall, Tex.
Gus's Place, N.Y.
Halt Time Rec. Bar, Minn.
Harold's Country Club Bar and Grill, R.I.
Hey Hey Club, Mo.
Hieronymous Seafood Restaurant, N.C.
Hollywood Diner, Md.
Horn & Hardart's Automat, N.Y.
Inner Harbor Concert Hall, Md.
Iridium Jazz Club, N.Y.
Jackson Brewery, La.
Jim's Coffee Shop and Bakery, Minn.
Kay's Restaurant, Nebr.
Kelly's, Ill.
Kendall's Famous Burgers, Ariz.
Kernville Steak and Seafood, Oreg.
King of Clubs Bar, Minn.
Knickerbocker Bar & Grill, N.Y.
Loeb Boathouse Cafe, N.Y.

APPENDIX

Lumber Jack Tavern, Mich.
Mack's Squat and Gobble Barbecue, Tex.
Mad Greek Cafe, Calif.
Maple Leaf Bar, La.
Maple Leaf Coffee Shop, N.J.
Mar-t Cafe, Wash.
McNear's Restaurant, Ark.
Melody Lounge, Pa.
Meow Mix, N.Y.
Mezzogiorno, N.Y.
Mia's Restaurant, Nev.
Mickey's Diner, Minn.
Millie's Chili Bar, Calif.
Miss Albany Diner, N.Y.
Moose's Restaurant, Calif.
Mori Restaurant, N.Y.
Mother's, Ill.
Murphy's Soup & Salad, Ariz.
The Muscoot, N.Y.
Mystic Pizza, Conn.
Nate's Deli, Ill.
Northeast Corner, N.Y.
Ocean Grill, N.Y.
Old Ebitt Grill, D.C.
Old Main Street Saloon, Calif.
Oz Restaurant and Night Club, Tex.
Palace Bar, Ariz.
Pete's Bubble Room, Fla.
Piccolo Angelo, N.Y.
Pompilios Restaurant, R.I.
Port Charlie's Restaurant, N.C.
President's Banquet Room, Pa.
Prudente's Italian Deli, N.Y.
Pump Room, Ill.
Quik Lunch Cafe, Tex.
Rainbo Cafe, Calif.
Rainbo Club, Ill.
Rainbow Club, Tenn.
Rainbow Room, N.Y.
Raoul's Restaurant Francais, N.Y.
Raw Bar's Palm Room, N.C.
Rawhide 2 Country and Western Bar, Calif.
Reata Pass Steakhouse, Ariz.
Restaurant Provence, N.Y.
River Diner, N.Y.
River Rat Tap, Oreg.
Roadside Diner, La.

Russian Tea Room, N.Y.
Sandbar and Grill, Calif.
Sardine Factory Restaurant, Calif.
Satin Dolls, N.J.
Sequoia, D.C.
Sharky's Beach Bar, Fla.
Silver Skillet, Ga.
Snarley's Tavern, Calif.
Sophie Kay's Restaurant, Fla.
Spinnaker, Fla.
Squeeze, Fla.
Stenger Cafe, Ohio
Striped Bass, Pa.
Swinging Door, Tex.
Tavern on the Green, N.Y.
Thomas Cafe, S.C.
Thuderbirds, Fla.
Tic Toc Diner, N.J.
Tides Restaurant, Calif.
Tiffany Diner, N.Y.
Tom's Pizza, S.C.
Tom's Restaurant, N.Y.
Top-Notch, Tex.
Tosca Cafe, Calif.
Trucker's Inn, Md.
The 21 Club, N.Y.
Twin Anchors Restaurant, Ill.
Warehouse Nightclub, Ohio
Werner's, Md.
Wheel Inn, Calif.
Whistle Stop Cafe, Ga.
White Knight Cafe, Mo.
Wild Horse Saloon, Ohio
Woody's L Street Tavern, Mass.
Yvonne's Diner, N.J.
Zanzibar, Colo.
Zeezee Gardens, La.

Schools

Alamo Heights High School, Tex.
Arlington High School, Minn.
Bennett High School, N.Y.
Berry Middle School, Ohio
Bixby High School, Okla.
Broken Arrow High School, Okla.
Brookline High School, Mass.

Bruce Elementary School, Tenn.
Cambridge Elementary School, Tex.
Centennial School, Nev.
Chatham Hill, N.Y.
Christie School, Oreg.
Coronado High School, Ariz.
The Dalton School, N.Y.
Dreyfoos School of the Arts, Fla.
East Boston High School, Mass.
Eastside High School, N.J.
Eastview High School, Minn.
Egg Harbor Township High School, N.J.
Elgin High School, Tex.
Emma Willard School, N.Y.
Etowah High School, Ga.
Falcon Heights Elementary School, Minn.
Frankfort Senior High School, Ind.
Glenbard High School, Ill.
Glenbrook North High School, Ill.
Grant High School, Ore.
Greater Johnstown High School, Pa.
Groveland Park Elementary School, Minn.
Hamilton High School, Ohio
Haven Middle School, Ill.
Henry W. Grady High School, Ga.
Holy Redeemer High School, Mich.
Horace Mann High School, N.Y.
International Studies Academy, Calif.
Joel E. Ferris High School, Wash.
John Marshall High School, Calif.
John R. Rogers High School, Wash.
Justin Kimball High School, Tex.
Kaley Elementary School, Fla.
Kent Denver School, Calif.
Kilgour Elementary School, Ohio
Knightstown Academy, Ind.
Lake Forest Academy, Ill.
Lamar High School, Tex.
Lane Technical School, Ill.
Liberty Junior High School, Miss.
Liberty-Union High School, Md.
Libertyville High School, Ill.
Lincoln High School, Ore.
Louise McGehee School, La.
Maine North High School, Ill.
Margaret B. Henderson Elementary School, Tex.
Massie School, Ga.
McGilvra Elementary School, Wash.
Memorial Middle School, Nev.
Middlesex School, Mass.
Millbrook School, N.Y.
Miller School of Albemarle, Va.
Montclair High School, N.J.
New City School, Mo.
New Hanover High School, N.C.
New Trier Township High School, Ill.
New Trier West High School, Ill.
New Utretcht High School, N.Y.
Niles East High School, Ill.
North Central High School, Wash.
Northgate High School, Calif.
Northwestern Military Academy, Wisc.
Oakland Technical High School, Calif.
Ogden High School, Utah
Payson High School, Utah
Percy Julian Junior High School, Ill.
Petaluma High School, Calif.
Pompton Lakes High School, N.J.
Potter Schoolhouse, Calif.
Robert E. Lee High School, Tex.
Ross School, Calif.
St. Mary's Academy, Calif.
St. John's School, Tex.
St. Johns Military Academy, Wisc.
St. Rita High School, Ill.
Santa Rosa High School, Calif.
Saugus High School, Calif.
Scottsdale High School, Ariz.
Shadle Park High School, Wash.
Snow Hill High School, Md.
Sprayberry High School, Ga.
Stadium High School, Wash.
Stoddart-Fleischer Middle School, Pa.
Suffern High School, N.Y.
Summerville High School, S.C.
Summit County High School, Calif.
Tahoe Lake Elementary School, Nev.
Thomas Jefferson High School, Tex.
Towson High School, Md.
Tucson High School, Ariz.
Valley Forge Military Academy, Pa.
Washington Park Elementary School, N.Y.
Wayzata West Junior High School, Minn.

APPENDIX

Weir High School, W.V.
Wilbur Wright Elementary School, N.C.
William E. Tolman High School, Mass.
Worcester Academy, Pa.

Ships

USS Alabama, Ala.
USS Lexington, Tex.
USS Navajo, Calif.
USS North Carolina, N.C.

Shopping Centers

Bayfair Mall, Calif.
Bridgewater Commons Mall, N.J.
Cermak Plaza Shopping Center, Ill.
Crossroads Mall, Tex.
Dallas Market Center, Tex.
Dealey Plaza, Tex.
Dixie Square Shopping Center, Ill.
Eden Prairie Center, Minn.
The Galleria at Tysons II Mall, Va.
The Gallery, Pa.
Independence Shopping Mall, N.C.
Kensington Mall, Okla.
Mall of America, Minn.
Metrocenter Mall, Ariz.
Monroeville Mall, Pa.
Navy Pier, Ill.
North Park Center Mall, Tex.
Northbrook Court Shopping Center, Ill.
Roland Park Shopping Center, Md.
Sanford Plaza, Fla.
South Gate Plaza, Fla.
Southland Mall, Calif.
Stamford Town Center, N.Y.
Stanford Shopping Center, Calif.
Tucson Mall, Ariz.
Westlake Center, Wash.

Ski Resorts

Big Sky Ski Resort, Mont.
Breckinridge, Colo.
Copper Mountain Resort, Colo.
Ski-Wheelers Lodge, N.H.
Sugar Bowl Ski Resort, Calif.
Sundance Resort, Utah

State and Local Parks

Bahia Honda State Park, Fla.
Battery Park, N.Y.
Bidwell Park, Calif.
Bill Baggs State Park, Fla.
Breckinridge Park, Colo.
Brenton State Park, R.I.
Buffalo Bayou Park, Tex.
Carolina Beach State Park, N.C.
Centennial Park, Tenn.
Central Park, N.Y.
Central Park — Mansfield, Ohio
Chimney Rock Park, N.C.
Chugach State Park, Ala.
Columbia State Park, Calif.
DAR State Park, Vt.
Devil's Lake State Park, Wisc.
Devou Park, Ohio
Elysian Park, N.Y.
Eno River State Park, N.C.
Fairmount Park, Pa.
Fenton Lake State Park, N.M.
Forest River Park, Mass.
Fort Worden State Park, Wash.
Fuji Park, Nev.
Garrapatta State Beach, Calif.
Gas Works Park, Wash.
Goblin Valley State Park, Utah
Gooseberry Falls State Park, Minn.
Grant Park, Ill.
Harry P. Leu Botanical Gardens, Fla.
Hell's Half Acre, Wyo.
Henry Cowell Redwoods State Park, Calif.
Hunting Island Park, S.C.
Hunting Island State Park, S.C.

LOCATIONS LISTED BY TYPE

Island Beach State Park, Pa.
Jerediah Smith Redwoods State Park, Calif.
John F. Kennedy Park, Calif.
Joseph Sylva State Beach, Mass.
Lava Tree State Monument, Hawaii
Lincoln Park, Ill.
Meteor Crater, Ariz.
Moose Lake State Park, Minn.
Morningside Park, Fla.
Oleta River State Recreational Park, Fla.
Palisades Interstate Park, N.J.
Patapsco State Park, Md.
Patuxent River Park, Md.
Piatt Park, Ohio
Planting Fields Arboretum, N.Y.
Prairie Grove Battlefield State Park, Ark.
Pretzel Park, Pa.
Rice Park, Minn.
Rittenhouse Square, Pa.
Riverfront Park — Harrisburg, Pa.
Riverfront Park — Nashville, Tenn.
St. Andrew's State recreation Area, Fla.
Sands Point Preserve, N.Y.
Saratoga Spa State Park, Mont.
Stinson Beach State Park, Calif.
Sutro Park, Calif.
Tallulah Falls State Park, Tenn.
Tettegouche State Park, Minn.
Tranquility Park, Tex.
Valley of Fire State Park, Nev.
Victory Park, N.J.
Wakulla Springs State Park, Fla.
Washington Park, N.Y.
Washington Square Park, N.Y.
Washoe Lake State Park, Nev.
Wekiwa Springs State Park, Fla.
Zilker Park, Tex.

Theaters

Academy of Music, Pa.
Belasco Theater, N.Y.
Biograph Theater, Ill.
Carnegie Hall, N.Y.
Carnegie Music Hall — Pittsburgh, Pa.
Chicago Theater, Ill.
Cocoa Village Playhouse, Fla.
Colonial Theater — Philadelphia, Pa.
Colonial Theater — Phoenixville, Pa.
Columbia Theater, La.
Cort Theater, N.Y.
Ed Sullivan Theater, N.Y.
Eisenhower Auditorium, Pa.
Everett Theater, Del.
Ferndale Repertory Theater, Calif.
Fox Theater, Calif.
Fox Warfield Theater, La.
Grandin Theater, Va.
Great Auditorium, N.J.
Guild 45th Theatre, Wash.
Heinz Hall for the Performing Arts, Pa.
Hippodrome Performing Arts Center, Md.
Hollywood Palladium, Utah
King's Opera House, Ark.
Lincoln Center, N.Y.
Lucas Theater for the Arts, S.C.
Majestic Theatre, N.Y.
Moreland Movie Theater, Wisc.
Murphy Theater, N.C.
Mystic Theater, Calif.
Palmer Auditorium, Tex.
Paramount Theater, Wash.
Performing Arts Center of the North Carolina School of Arts, N.C.
Playhouse Theater, N.C.
Plymouth Theatre, N.Y.
Polynesian Cultural Center, Hawaii
Rialto Theater, Ill.
Roxy Theater — Northampton, Pa.
Royal Theater, Tex.
Ryman Auditorium, Tenn.
Senator Theater, Pa.
Severance Hall, Ohio
Sheldon Concert Hall, Mo.
State Theater, Mich.
Steppenwolf Theater, Ill.
Tennessee Theatre, Tenn.
Tercentuary Theater, Mass.
Texas Theater, Tex.
Thalia, N.Y.
Thalian Hall, N.C.
University of South Carolina-Beaufort's Performing Arts Center, S.C.

Wang Center for the Performing Arts, Mass.
War Memorial Opera House, Calif.
Warner Theater, D.C.
Woodstock Opera House, Ill.

Houston Zoological Park, Tex.
Lincoln Park Zoo, Ill.
Monterey Bay Aquarium, Calif.
New England Aquarium, Mass.
North Carolina Aquarium, N.C.
Oakland Zoo, Calif.
Steinhart Aquarium, Calif.

Zoos & Aquariums

Audubon Zoo, La.
Central Park Zoo, N.Y.

ACTOR AND DIRECTOR INDEX

Aaker, Lee 225
Abraham, F. Murray 133
Ackland, Josh 120
Adams, Brooke 24, 126, 145
Adams, Joey Lauren 140
Adams, Julie 55
Adams, Lauren 210
Affleck, Ben 68, 109, 120, 140, 191, 218
Aiken, Liam 169
Albert, Eddie 71
Albert, Shari 151
Alda, Alan 32, 173, 230
Alexander, Jace 88
Alexander, Jason 16, 142, 167
Allen, Joan 35, 93
Allen, Karen 10, 31, 112, 166
Allen, Mikki 165
Allen, Nancy 190, 191, 223
Allen, Penelope 153
Allen, Tim 103–104, 224
Allen, Woody 30, 42, 45, 143, 149, 150, 152, 157, 160, 161, 162, 172
Alley, Kirstie 103–104
Altman, Robert 125
Alvarado, Trini 169
Ameche, Don 54, 56, 137, 195
Anderson, Jeff 140
Anderson, Loni 5, 43
Anderson, Michael 132

Andrews, David 130
Ann-Margret 119, 138
Anspach, Susan 30
Anwar, Gabrielle 154–155, 166
Archer, Anne 105
Arkin, Alan 3, 4
Arkin, David 205
Armstrong, Bess 83
Arness, James 225
Arnott, David 55
Arquette, David 32, 73
Arquette, Patricia 117–118, 228
Arquette, Rosanna 139, 148, 152–153
Arthur, Jean 13, 52, 242–243
Asner, Ed 98, 120
Astin, Mackenzie 119
Astin, Sean 89, 232
Autry, Gene 39
Avital, Mili 81
Aykroyd, Dan 32, 60, 77, 137, 155–156, 195

Babcock, Barbara 80
Bacall, Lauren 19, 136, 157
Bacon, Kevin 26, 39, 46, 65, 85, 86, 104, 112, 124, 183, 224
Baker, Joe Don 162
Baker, Kathy 190

Bakula, Scott 200, 217
Baldwin, A. Michael 29
Baldwin, Adam 82
Baldwin, Alec 51, 84, 110, 113, 123, 218, 227
Baldwin, Stephen 210
Baldwin, William 56
Balgobin, Jennifer 130
Bancroft, Anne 57, 59
Banderas, Antonio 136, 220, 233
Banes, Lisa 151
Banks, Tyra 140
Barbeau, Adrienne 202
Barkin, Ellen 95–96, 118, 166, 238
Barnes, Rodney 231
Barr, Roseanne 167
Barry, Raymond 82
Barrymore, Drew 32, 82, 140, 153, 178, 213
Barrymore, Lionel 107
Basinger, Kim 72, 216
Basquez, Rudy 220
Bassett, Angela 11, 160
Bates, Kathy 64, 68, 134
Beals, Jennifer 191–192
Beatty, Ned 89, 205
Beatty, Warren 23, 159, 169, 209, 236
Bedalia, Bonnie 41
Begley, Ed, Jr. 167

ACTOR AND DIRECTOR INDEX

Bellamy, Ralph 195
Belushi, James 30, 63, 75, 78, 84, 175–176
Belushi, John 77, 185
Belzer, Richard 147
Benadaret, Bea 29
Benedict, Nick 99
Bening, Annette 48, 159, 165
Benson, Robby 124
Berenger, Tom 9, 76, 141, 168, 188, 193, 199
Bergen, Candice 63, 165–166
Bergen, Patrick 177
Bergman, Ingrid 8
Berkley, Elizabeth 136
Berle, Milton 54
Bernsen, Corbin 200
Berry, Halle 201, 211
Bickell, Ross 231
Biehn, Michael 232
Billingsley, Peter 180
Bisset, Jacqueline 78, 165–166
Blachly, Bill 228
Black, Jack 80
Blades, Ruben 146
Blair, Linda 50
Blake, Amanda 225
Blake, Robert 92
Bloom, Claire 107
Bogart, Humphrey 8, 19, 37
Bogosian, Eric 44
Bond, Ward 225–226
Bono, Sonny 192
Boone, Pat 116
Boone, Richard 226
Booth, Powers 195
Borchardt, Mark 240
Borgnine, Ernest 39, 125
Bosco, Philip 82
Bosley, Tom 26
Bottoms, Timothy 111–112, 232
Bowen, Julie 141
Bowie, David 146
Boyd, Bill 39
Boyle, Peter 18, 153
Bracco, Lorraine 63, 143, 186
Bradford, Jesse 125
Bradford, Richard 146
Bradley, Doug 175
Braff, Zach 160
Brandauer, Klaus Maria 7
Brandis, Jonathin 220
Brando, Marlon 142, 155, 156
Braschi, Nicoletta 205
Brazzi, Rosanno 74
Brennan, Walter 43

Brewton, Maria 75
Bridges, Beau 220
Bridges, Jeff 10, 20, 35, 94, 107, 127, 154, 158, 202, 208, 216, 221, 234, 243
Bridges, Lloyd 37
Broderick, Matthew 13, 14, 69, 70, 78, 128, 148, 155, 156, 239
Brody, Adrien 104
Brolin, James 23, 139
Brooks, Albert 49, 134
Brooks, Avery 112
Brooks, Mel 23
Brosnan, Pierce 75
Brown, Blair 182
Brown, Bryan 151
Brumley, Wilford 54
Buchanan, Edgar 29
Bujold, Genevieve 101
Bullock, Sandra 27, 68, 72, 87, 124, 213, 216, 236, 243
Burke, Delta 14
Burnett, Carol 139, 230
Burns, Edward 151
Burns, George 135
Burns, Marilyn 221
Burress, Hedy 186
Burstyn, Ellen 32, 50, 190, 229
Burton, Richard 5, 114
Buscemi, Steve 43, 118, 189, 205
Busey, Gary 85, 118, 177, 184
Byrne, Anne 160
Byrne, Gabriel 99, 131

Caan, James 50, 88, 132, 134, 156, 157, 161, 181, 201, 234
Caesar, Adolph 14
Cage, Nicolas 10, 29, 31, 104, 130–131, 132, 133, 141, 142, 143, 161, 184, 189
Cagney, James 165
Caine, Michael 6, 98, 157, 191, 216
Campbell, Glen 44
Campbell, Neve 32, 73
Candy, John 83–84, 86, 213
Capra, Frank, Jr. 178
Capshaw, Kate 5, 23, 59, 142
Cara, Irene 154
Cardenelli, Linda 42
Carey, Macdonald 215
Carlson, Richard 55
Carradine, David 14
Carradine, Keith 100

Carradine, Robert 10
Carrey, Jim 41, 53, 64, 160, 207, 229
Carroll, Beeson 174
Carroll, Leo G. 203
Carter, Dixie 14
Cartwright, Veronica 24
Carvey, Dana 87
Cassavetes, John 166
Cates, Phoebe 202
Cattrall, Kim 150, 193
Cavanaugh, Thomas 141
Cazale, John 132, 180
Channing, Stockard 168
Charbonneau, Patricia 131
Charles, Frances 37
Chase, Chevy 10, 13, 21, 42, 54, 137, 147, 228
Cher 110, 114, 161, 223
Chin, Joey 158
Chin, Tsai 25
Chinh, Kieu 25
Chism, Glenda 60
Chlumsky, Anna 60
Christie, Julie 23, 29
Christopher, Dennis 88
Christy, Kevin 82
Churchill, Marguerite 241
Clark, Fred 157
Clift, Montgomery 94
Clooney, George 11, 37, 99, 112, 124
Close, Glenn 92, 123, 144, 154, 162, 199
Coburn, James 235
Coleman, Dabney 210, 239
Collet, Christopher 160–161
Connery, Sean 31, 58, 59, 86, 145
Connick, Harry, Jr. 213
Connolly, Walter 91
Conte, Richard 156
Cooper, Alice 87
Cooper, Chris 180, 205, 215, 239
Cooper, Gary 23, 37
Corsaut, Aneta 189
Cort, Bud 22, 210
Cosby, Bill 151
Costner, Kevin 11, 40, 52, 86, 91, 101–102, 129–130, 173, 202, 203, 211, 212, 213, 218, 219
Cotten, Joseph 32
Cox, Courteney 53
Cox, Ronny 181
Crawford, Cindy 56

ACTOR AND DIRECTOR INDEX

Crenna, Richard 37
Crewson, Wendy 138
Cromwell, James 69
Cronyn, Hume 236
Crowe, Russell 24
Crudup, Billy 145
Cruise, Tom 8, 9, 51, 78, 84–85, 94, 98, 151, 189, 195, 204, 209
Crystal, Billy 62, 147, 149, 171, 226
Culkin, Macauley 22, 60, 80, 138, 176
Culkin, Quinn 138
Culp, Robert 129
Curreri, Lee 154
Curtis, Jamie Lee 21, 64
Curtis, Tony 169
Cusack, Joan 27, 28, 141
Cusack, John 9, 34, 72, 80, 88, 111, 115, 130–131, 151, 233, 236

d'Abo, Olivia 208
Dafoe, Willem 4, 124, 147, 234
Dailey, Dan 130
Daily, Elizabeth 218
Dalton, Timothy 60
Daly, Tim 114
Damon, Matt 71, 109, 112, 143, 191, 206, 207
Danes, Claire 116
D'Angelo, Beverly 10, 42, 137
Dangerfield, Rodney 42, 54, 240
Daniels, Jeff 41, 63, 128, 173
Danner, Blythe 102
Danson, Ted 22, 25, 109, 170
Danza, Tony 17
Danziger, Allen 221
Darby, Kim 44
Davi, Robert 60
Davidovich, Lolita 31, 96
Davis, Bette 33, 98
Davis, Brad 112
Davis, Geena 89, 146–147, 159, 164, 227
Davis, Hope 26, 111
Davis, Mac 33
Davis, Milton, Jr. 17
Davis, Phyllis 137
Dawber, Pam 42, 43
Day-Lewis, Daniel 148, 175
Dean, James 212
Dean, Loren 26
DeHavilland, Olivia 16, 98

DeLaurentis, Dino 178
Del Rio, Dolores 97
DeMille, Cecil B. 37
DeMornay, Rebecca 84–85, 138, 144, 234
Dempsey, Patrick 8
DeNiro, Robert 46, 54, 76, 81, 86, 95, 115, 130, 149, 150, 156, 165, 170, 180, 187, 207
Dennehy, Brian 116
Dennis, Sandy 163
Depardieu, Gerard 157
Depp, Johnny 56, 140, 221, 233
Dern, Bruce 45, 54
Dern, Laura 74, 176
Devane, William 208
DeVito, Danny 25, 45, 106, 115, 116, 144, 147, 160, 170, 206
Diaz, Cameron 63, 208
DiCaprio, Leonardo 221, 238
Dick, Andy 184
Dickinson, Angie 191
Dillon, Matt 65, 92, 184, 186, 237
Dillon, Melinda 53, 234
Dobson, Kevin 158
Doe, John 136
Doherty, Shannen 120
Donahue, Heather 103
D'Onofrio, Vincent 138
Donovan, Ted 71
Doolittle, John 135
Doroff, Sarah Rowland 238
Douglas, Kirk 13
Douglas, Michael 17, 21, 48, 154, 163, 171, 196, 234, 239
Downey, Robert, Jr. 22, 49, 104, 106, 164, 193, 196, 214
Drew, Roland 97
Dreyfuss, Richard 16, 59, 106, 127, 129, 156, 182, 187, 233, 241
Driver, Minnie 84, 88, 115
Duchovny, David 84
Duff, Howard 161–162
Duffy, Patrick 210
Dukakis, Olympia 190
Duke, Patty 46, 122, 163
Dukes, David 177
Dummar, Melvin 134
Dunaway, Faye 162, 170, 189, 209
Dunn, Moses 167
Dunne, Griffin 148

Dunst, Kirsten 50, 118
Durning, Charles 116, 170
Dussault, Nancy 34
Duvall, Robert 8, 50, 65, 109, 132, 162, 163, 176, 197, 199–200, 204, 215
Duvall, Shelley 188, 213

Eastwood, Clint 8, 13, 20, 30, 32, 34, 35, 41, 51, 75, 90, 95, 101, 102, 132, 135–136, 188, 218, 220, 225, 241, 242
Eastwood, Kyle 132
Eden, Barbara 181
Edwards, Anthony 10, 78
Edwards, Luke 119
Edwards, Penny 37
Eichhorn, Lisa 125
Eikenberry, Jill 149, 157
Elfman, Jenna 20
Elliott, Alison 229
Elliott, Sam 45, 57, 89
Embry, Ethan 67
Emje, David 190
Erbe, Kathryn 86, 120
Ermey, R. Lee 236
Erving, Julius 191
Estevez, Emilio 68, 77, 120, 129
Eythe, William 157

Facinelli, Peter 210
Farnsworth, Richard 92
Farrell, Mike 198
Farrell, Terry 175
Farrow, Mia 149, 150, 157, 162, 164–165, 166, 172, 197
Faureau, Jon 137
Feldman, Corey 174
Fenn, Sherilyn 66
Field, Sally 4, 10, 26, 53, 100, 168
Field, Todd 62
Fiennes, Joseph 57
Finney, Albert 20, 32, 99, 106, 139
Fiorentino, Linda 238
Fishburne, Laurence 59, 158, 167
Fisher, Carrie 171
Fitzgerald, Barry 161–162
Flanders, Ed 51
Flanery, Sean Patrick 218
Fletcher, Louise 187
Flint, Sam 37
Flockhart, Calista 106

ACTOR AND DIRECTOR INDEX

Flowers, Jim 14, 15
Flynn, Errol 16
Flynn Boyle, Lara 76, 189
Fonda, Bridget 142, 167, 176, 202, 204, 237
Fonda, Henry 13, 42, 139, 188, 216, 226, 243
Fonda, Jane 45, 46, 98, 131, 150, 223
Fonda, Peter 64, 97, 179
Force, Ken 190
Ford, Harrison 23, 31, 37, 79, 105, 116, 145, 165, 172, 180, 196, 230, 232
Ford, John 12, 225–226
Ford, Paul 111
Forrest, Frederic 19
Forsythe, John 229
Forsythe, William 10, 123
Foster, Jodie 143, 144–145, 170, 176, 181–182, 194, 232
Fox, Michael J. 55–56, 150, 154–155, 159, 181
Frann, Mary 229
Franz, Dennis 163
Fraser, Brendan 17, 21, 112, 114, 220
Freeman, Morgan 10, 50, 67, 77, 142, 175, 183, 197
Frobe, Gert 58
Fuchs, Leo 102
Furlong, Edward 189
Furst, Stephen 153

Gable, Clark 134
Gallagher, Peter 87, 113
Gallo, Vincent 151
Gandolfini, James 143
Garber, Victor 154
Garcia, Andy 36, 43, 79–80, 158
Garner, James 9, 10, 52
Garofolo, Janeane 126
Garr, Teri 59, 148, 239, 241
Gaynor, Mitzi 74
Gazzara, Ben 114–115
Gedrick, Jason 136
Geer, Will 224
Gellar, Sarah Michelle 175
Gere, Richard 51, 84, 105, 152, 210, 232, 235–236
Getty, Estelle 33
Gibson, Mel 9, 21, 59, 101, 134, 165, 193, 201
Gifford, Jack 55
Gilsis, Jessalyn 107
Gish, Annabeth 45

Givens, Robin 183
Gleason, Jackie 33, 83
Glenn, Scott 31, 147, 184, 188
Glover, Danny 8, 17, 47, 59, 134, 174
Going, Joanna 220
Goldberg, Whoopi 25–26, 103, 136–137, 140, 155, 174
Goldblum, Jeff 24, 27
Golden, Norman D., II 55
Goldwyn, Tony 155
Goodall, Caroline 202
Gooding, Cuba 59, 187
Goodman, John 10, 48, 60, 76, 127, 191
Gordon, Eva 102
Gordon, Keith 214
Gordon, Ruth 22, 166
Gordon-Levitt, Joseph 17
Gorney, Karen Lynn 166
Gossett, Lou, Jr. 30, 127, 232, 235
Gould, Elliott 181
Grable, Betty 157
Graf, David 61
Granger, Stewart 145
Grant, Cary 37, 148, 203
Grant, David Marshall 40
Grant, Hugh 27, 161
Grant, Lee 240
Gray, Jennifer 230
Green, Kerri 81
Greene, Lorne 130
Gregory, Andre 231–232
Grenier, Adrian 223
Grier, Pam 75
Griffith, Andy 14, 175
Griffith, Melanie 27, 48, 63, 150, 172, 182, 200, 215–216
Grodin, Charles 115, 158, 182
Guardino, Harry 19
Guier, Adam 99
Guiry, Tom 231
Guthrie, Arlo 106
Guttenberg, Steve 103, 170, 208
Gwenn, Edmund 161, 229
Gyllenhaal, Jake 205

Haas, Lukas 196
Hackman, Gene 4, 19, 50, 52, 83, 89, 102, 105, 123, 124
Hagerty, Julie 134
Hagman, Larry 210
Haim, Corey 25, 81, 174, 177

Hall, Anthony Michael 85, 87, 214
Hall, Arsenio 151
Hamill, Mark 31, 37
Hamilton, George 65
Hamilton, Linda 34, 75, 175
Hancock, John 89
Hanks, Tom 35, 68, 83, 89, 139, 150, 168–169, 172, 194, 203, 205, 208, 237
Hann-Byrd, Adam 181–182
Hannah, Darryl 159, 168–169, 230, 240
Harden, Marcia Gay 20
Hardin, Ty 61
Hardison, Kadeem 237
Harmon, Mark 143–144, 196–197
Harper, Valerie 120
Harrell, Rebecca 89
Harrelson, Woody 60–61, 133, 136, 145, 146, 192, 206
Harris, Ed 31, 64, 182, 199, 204, 240
Harris, Julie 56
Harris, Neil Patrick 103
Harris, Richard 65
Harrold, Kathryn 176
Harry, Jackee 42
Hart, Dolores 65
Hart, Melissa Joan 223
Hauer, Rutger 129, 162
Hawke, Ethan 7, 21, 48, 58, 59, 217, 218, 237
Hawn, Goldie 21, 55, 88, 109, 111, 154
Hawthorne, Nigel 125
Hayden, Russell 37
Hayek, Salma 131
Hayworth, Rita 27
Headly, Glenne 162, 187
Hedison, David 60
Hedren, Tippi 18
Hedya, Dan 144
Heflin, Van 243
Hemingway, Mariel 60, 160, 188
Henry, Justin 85, 159
Hepburn, Audrey 150
Hepburn, Katharine 139
Herrmann, Edward 5, 176
Hershey, Barbara 14, 89, 157
Heston, Charlton 59, 216
Hewitt, Jennifer Love 175
Hickey, William 164
Hines, Gregory 62, 116, 152, 182–183

ACTOR AND DIRECTOR INDEX

Hirsch, Judd 170
Hitchcock, Alfred 23, 32
Hoffman, Dustin 22, 27, 48, 79–80, 94, 159, 161, 170, 173, 207
Hoffman, Elizabeth 75
Hoffman, Philip Seymour 111
Hogan, Hulk 43
Hogan, Paul 152
Holden, William 13, 162, 215, 240
Holliday, Judy 158
Holm, Celeste 130
Holmes, Katie 174
Hopkins, Anthony 59, 176, 194, 197, 198, 198, 230
Hopper, Dennis 41, 97, 118, 173
Horovitz, Adam 136, 216
Horse, Michael 147
Hoskins, Bob 110
Houseman, John 111–112
Houston, Whitney 11, 129–130
Howard, Arliss 105
Howard, John 91
Howard, Ron 16
Howell, C. Thomas 146, 184
Hudson, Bill 187
Hudson, Ernie 145, 174, 177
Hudson, Rock 101
Hughes, Sterling 40
Hunt, Bonnie 84, 138
Hunt, Helen 135, 160, 185, 203, 210
Hunter, Holly 10, 46, 49, 104, 124, 127, 204
Hunter, Jeffrey 13
Huppert, Isabelle 103
Hurley, Elizabeth 17, 129
Hurt, Mary Beth 55
Hurt, William 49, 54, 125, 143, 153
Huston, Angelica 9, 16, 152, 215
Hutton, Timothy 118, 189, 195
Hyser, Joyce 9
Irving, Amy 152

Isaacs, Jason 201
Ives, Burl 181
Ivey, Judith 37

Jackson, Anne 56
Jackson, Janet 30
Jackson, Michael 171–172
Jackson, Samuel 82, 159, 167, 196, 199, 201
Jackson, Victoria 185
Jagger, Mick 68
James, Clifton 208
James, Clinton 150
Jason Leigh, Jennifer 106, 125, 167, 219
Jett, Joan 181
Johansen, Peter 151
Johnson, Ben 100, 214, 225–226
Johnson, Don 11, 200
Jolie, Angelina 186, 192
Jones, Duane 193
Jones, James Earl 65, 91, 151, 204, 239
Jones, Tommy Lee 3, 5, 79, 83, 86–87, 96, 107, 201, 204, 215, 220
Jordan, Louis 202
Jordan, Richard 214
Judd, Ashley 62, 62, 96–97, 175, 221
Julia, Raul 16
Jump, Gordon 183

Kahn, Madelaine 23
Kanakaredes, Melina 198
Kaplan, Gabe 171
Katsulas, Andreas 168
Kaufman, Andy 160
Kava, Caroline 209
Kavner, Julie 137, 164
Kazan, Elia 169
Keaton, Diane 30, 32, 42, 149, 154, 160, 174, 179, 193, 227
Keaton, Michael 24, 27, 146–147, 153, 163, 190, 227
Keitel, Harvey 115, 140, 204
Keith, Brian 28, 33, 226
Keith, David 178, 213, 235
Kellerman, Sally 210, 240
Kelley, De Forest 6
Kelly, Daniel Hugh 19
Kelly, Grace 23
Kelly, Jean Louisa 86
Kennedy, Arthur 147
Kerr, Deborah 74, 145, 148
Kidder, Margot 139, 169
Kidman, Nicole 110, 173, 236
Kilmer, Val 19, 72, 147, 203
King, Adrienne 141
Kinney, Terry 3
Kinski, Nastassja 96, 170

Kirby, Bruno 155
Klein, Chris 119
Kline, Kevin 8, 49, 66, 66, 106, 141, 147, 168, 199, 235
Knight, Ted 34
Kotero, Apollonia 122
Kotto, Yaphet 98, 104, 115
Kozlowski, Linda 152
Krabbe, Jeroen 152
Kristofferson, Kris 63, 93, 127, 179, 215
Kudoh, Youki 237
Kudrow, Lisa 25
Kuhlman, Ron 212
Kurtz, Swoosie 88

Ladd, Alan 242
Ladd, Diane 190
Lake, Rikki 192
Lancaster, Burt 13, 74, 136, 169
Landau, Martin 152
Landon, Jason 210
Landon, Michael 130
Lane, Diane 24, 52, 124, 152, 176
Lange, Jessica 3, 97, 105, 158, 170, 174, 179, 240
Langella, Frank 174
Lansbury, Angela 26, 73
LaPaglia, Anthony 192
LaSalle, Eriq 78
Latzen, Ellen Hamilton 154
Laughlin, Tom 7
Law, Jude 21
Lawford, Peter 158
Lawrence, Martin 25, 53
Leachman, Cloris 89, 177, 214
LeBrock, Kelly 37, 87
Ledger, Heath 237–238
Lee, Brandon 174
Lee, Jason 140
Leibman, Rob 4
LeMat, Paul 17, 134
Lemmon, Jack 52, 119, 158, 163
Leonard, Joshua 103
Leoni, Tea 141
Leto, Jared 236
Lewis, Jerry 54, 131
Lewis, Juliette 54, 70, 146
Lincoln, Elmo 101
Lindo, Delroy 5
Linklater, Richard 220
Liotta, Ray 57, 125, 156
Lithgow, John 23, 31, 40, 106, 128, 160, 234–235

ACTOR AND DIRECTOR INDEX   268

Little, Cleavon 44
Lloyd, Christopher 129, 153
Lloyd, Emily 94
Locke, Sandra 3, 8, 13, 34, 41, 225, 241
Loggia, Robert 135, 139, 192, 217
Lohan, Lindsay 28
London, Daniel 28
Long, Nia 26, 81
Long, Shelley 109
Lopez, Jennifer 36, 99, 219
Lord, Jack 74
Loren, Sophia 119
Louis-Dreyfuss, Julia 142
Love, Courtney 206
Lowe, Rob 14, 15, 75, 78, 105, 135
Lowther, J.T. 218
Lundgren, Dolph 242
Lynch, Kelly 78, 186
Lynch, Richard 70
Lyon, Sue 93

MacDonald, Bruce 139
MacDowell, Andie 79, 100, 157, 158, 216
MacLachlan, Kyle 136, 238
MacLaine, Shirley 95, 104, 128, 239
MacNicol, Peter 168
Macy, William 113, 118
Madigan, Amy 91
Madison, Guy 131
Madonna 152–153, 234
Maguire, Tobey 126, 227
Majors, Lee 225
Makepeace, Chris 82
Malden, Karl 142, 226
Malik, Art 64
Malkovich, John 51
Malone, Jena 169
Manheim, Camryn 112
Mann, Leslie 21
Mantegna, Joe 76, 137, 149, 166
Margolyes, Miriam 148
Marin, Cheech 62
Marisa Tomei 72, 122, 163, 193
Markey, Enid 101
Marshall, Garry 89
Martin, Dean 13, 135
Martin, Steve 13, 26, 61, 83–84, 109, 111, 112, 214
Marvin, Lee 45, 73, 136, 188
Mason, James 114, 203

Mason, Marsha 156, 234
Masterson, Mary Stuart 233
Mastrantonio, Mary Elizabeth 19, 196, 199
Matheson, Tim 126, 185
Mathis, Samantha 207
Matlin, Marlee 187
Matthau, Walter 119, 164
Mature, Victor 13
Mayer, Breckin 210
Mazar, Debi 182
McArthur, James 74
McBride, Chi 107
McCarthy, Andrew 78, 92, 177, 180–181, 193
McComb, Heather 162
McConaughey, Matthew 20, 36, 124, 144–145, 197, 215, 217
McDermott, Dylan 112
McDonnell, Mary 88, 203
McDormand, Frances 118
McDowell, Malcolm 34, 96
McGavin, Darren 180
McGhee, Brownie 95
McGillis, Kelly 76, 196
McGlone, Mike 151
McGoohan, Patrick 20
McGovern, Elizabeth 85, 103, 165
McGowan, Rose 32
McGraw, Ali 110, 212
McKean, Michael 55
McKeon, Doug 182
McNamara, William 199
McNeal, Julia 212
McNichols, Kristy 192
McNiece, Ian 207
McQueen, Steve 9, 18, 34, 81, 189, 212
Meyer, Dina 243
Midler, Bette 45, 109, 154, 169
Miles, Sylvia 161
Milland, Ray 57, 58
Miller, Jason 50
Miller, Penelope Ann 84, 123
Mills, Hayley 28
Minnelli, Liza 113, 149
Mitchum, Robert 239–240
Mix, Tom 39, 225
Modine, Matthew 27, 60, 189, 238–239
Monroe, Marilyn 7, 43, 134, 157
Montalban, Ricardo 74
Moore, Clayton 225

Moore, Demi 57–58, 75, 132–133, 142, 155, 173, 234
Moore, Dudley 149, 170–171, 230
Moore, Julianne 27, 102, 123, 230, 234
Moore, Mary Tyler 83, 120
Moore, Michael 116
Moore, Robert 113
Moore, Roger 36, 98
Moranis, Rick 26, 132, 155
Moriarty, Cathy 60, 165
Moriarty, Michael 46, 75, 149
Morita, Pat 111
Morrow, Rob 200, 235
Morse, David 205
Mortensen, Viggo 242
Mostel, Zero 164
Mulroney, Dermot 82
Murphy, Eddie 17, 25, 151, 191, 195
Murphy, Michael 160
Murray, Bill 79, 81, 95, 126, 155–156, 164, 166, 192, 219, 233
Murray, Brian Doyle 213
Murray, Don 7
Myers, Mike 33, 87, 129

Neal, Patricia 14, 49
Neeson, Liam 83, 176, 228
Neill, Sam 74
Nelligan, Kate 172, 201
Nelson, Craig T. 189
Nelson, Judd 77, 105, 211, 212
Nelson, Willie 223
Neuwirth, Bebe 104
Newhart, Bob 229
Newman, Barry 44
Newman, Paul 34, 40, 53, 78, 80, 85, 90, 96, 97, 99, 114, 126, 163, 188, 195
Nicholas, Thomas Ian 85
Nicholson, Jack 51, 92, 97, 114, 115, 128, 157, 158, 164, 172, 187–188
Nimoy, Leonard 6, 33
Nolan, Lloyd 157, 181
Nolte, Nick 18, 45, 54, 88, 94, 177, 183, 192–193, 201, 238, 241
Norris, Chuck 70, 220
Northern, Jeremy 27
Norton, Edward 84, 143, 153
Nouri, Michael 191
Novak, Kim 23, 35–36, 131
Nuyen, France 25

ACTOR AND DIRECTOR INDEX

O'Brien, Edmund 40
O'Connor, Carroll 70
O'Connor, Glynnis 124
O'Dea, Judith 193
O'Donnell, Chris 17, 123, 166
O'Halloran, Brian 140
O'Hara, Maureen 28, 83, 161, 243
O'Keefe, Michael 199–200
Oldman, Gary 180, 213, 231
Olin, Lena 116
Oliver, Barrett 55
Oliver, Michael 61
Olivier, Laurence 197
Olmos, Edward James 219
O'Neal, Ryan 36, 93, 110
O'Neal, Tatum 93
O'Neill, Ed 67, 82
Ontkean, Michael 103, 192, 195, 238
O'Quinn, Terry 129
Orbach, Jerry 159
Osment, Haley Joel 194–195
O'Sullivan, Maureen 111
O'Toole, Annette 118

Pacino, Al 24, 55, 102, 132, 140, 153, 156, 166, 167, 196, 208
Page, Geraldine 95
Palance, Jack 147, 226
Palmer, Betsy 141
Paltrow, Gwynneth 58, 163
Pare, Michael 141
Parker, Mary Louise 140
Parker, Sarah Jessica 109, 195
Parks, Michael 100
Parrillaud, Anne 192
Parton, Dolly 86, 100, 208
Patric, Jason 25, 219
Patton, Will 72
Paxton, Bill 14, 122
Payne, John 161
Peck, Gregory 45
Penn, Sean 21, 96, 195
Peppard, George 150
Perabo, Piper 140
Perkins, Elizabeth 104, 139
Perry, Luke 210
Perry, Matthew 131
Pesci, Joe 72, 80, 114
Pescow, Donna 166
Peters, Bernadette 135
Petersen, Stewart 226
Peterson, Amanda 8
Petty, Lori 186–187

Pfeiffer, Michelle 60, 64, 113, 148, 172, 179, 230, 234
Philips, Lee 102
Phillips, Mackenzie 17
Phoenix, Joaquin 24
Phoenix, River 187, 207, 226
Pickford, Mary 30
Pidgeon, Walter 235
Pierce, Brock 230
Pinteuro, Danny 19
Piscopo, Joe 144
Pitt, Brad 70, 98, 99, 127–128, 131, 195–196, 198, 198
Platt, Oliver 131
Pleasence, Donald 125
Plummer, Amanda 154
Plummer, Christopher 153, 172
Poitier, Sidney 81, 168
Polito, Jon 99
Pollack, Kevin 51
Pollack, Sydney 170
Pollan, Tracy 136
Pomeranc, Max 166–167
Porizkova, Paulina 104
Portman, Natalie 221
Prentiss, Paula 46
Presley, Elvis 73, 138
Presley, Priscilla 204
Preston, Kelly 24, 25, 220
Preston, Robert 9
Price, Vincent 56
Prince 122
Pryor, Nicholas 98
Pryor, Richard 85, 114
Pullman, Bill 87, 185
Purl, Linda 175

Quaid, Dennis 28, 65, 88, 95–96, 97, 101, 202, 205, 212
Quaid, Randy 192
Questel, Mae 162
Quinlan, Kathleen 19, 103
Quinn, Aidan 76–77, 153, 233, 240
Quinn, Patricia 106

Ramis, Harold 95, 143–144, 156, 227
Rampling, Charlotte 143
Randolph, John 167
Rapaport, Michael 161
Rashad, Phylicia 151
Redford, Robert 18, 32–33, 40, 48, 64, 85, 127, 131, 132–133, 150, 159, 162, 170, 171, 197, 224

Redgrave, Vanessa 107
Reeve, Christopher 107, 116–117, 117, 169
Reeves, Keanu 7, 55, 77, 105, 187
Reinhold, Judge 87
Reiser, Paul 160, 230
Remar, James 152
Remick, Lee 114
Renfro, Brad 204
Renni, Michael 49
Reno, Jean 156
Renzi, Maggie 139
Reubens, Paul 218
Reuhl, Mercedes 60, 182
Reunifier, Brad 183
Reynolds, Burt 5, 55, 63, 66, 71–72, 185, 208
Ricci, Christina 16, 151
Richardson, Joely 84
Richardson, Miranda 125
Richardson, Patricia 64
Richter, Jason James 186–187
Rickman, Alan 190
Riegert, Peter 152
Ringwald, Molly 85, 164, 173, 180–181
Ritter, John 61, 142
Robards, Jason 92, 120, 134
Robbins, Tim 80, 141–142, 183, 190, 208
Roberts, Eric 6, 62
Roberts, Julia 20, 45, 52–53, 79, 82, 105, 153, 169, 177, 179, 202, 241
Roberts, Tanya 36
Roberts, Tony 30
Robertson, Cliff 61, 107, 170
Rogers, Mimi 168
Rogers, Roy 37, 39
Rohner, Clayton 9
Rollins, Howard 14, 70, 165
Romano, Andy 31
Rooney, Mickey 27, 56, 128
Rosales, Thomas, Jr. 218
Ross, Diana 171–172
Ross, Katherine 22, 40, 45, 46, 213
Rossellini, Isabella 20, 173
Roundtree, Richard 167
Rourke, Mickey 95, 103, 147
Rowlands, Gena 94
Ruck, Alan 78
Rudd, Paul 120
Russell, Kurt 11, 18, 37, 60, 76, 125, 146, 147, 183

ACTOR AND DIRECTOR INDEX   270

Russell, Theresa 73
Russo, Rene 11, 16, 27, 51, 165
Ryan, Meg 36, 84, 136, 141–142, 148, 171, 172, 212, 237
Ryan, Robert 5
Ryder, Winona 56, 110, 192, 205, 218

Saget, Bob 21
Saint, Eva Marie 142, 203
San Giacomo, Laura 100
Sand, Julian 66
Sandler, Adam 64
Sandy, Gary 183
Sarandon, Susan 96, 126, 169, 173, 192–193, 204, 226, 227
Savage, Fred 87
Savalas, Telly 158–159
Sawyer, Joe 225
Scacchi, Greta 188
Schaech, Jonathan 204
Schallert, William 163
Schank, Mike 240
Schneider, Roy 109
Schroeder, Rick 163
Schwartzsman, Jason 219
Schwarzenegger, Arnold 25, 34, 50, 64, 84, 119, 147, 176
Schwimmer, David 81
Sciorra, Annabella 234
Scorcese, Martin 14
Scott, Campbell 112, 237
Scott, George C. 29, 51, 93, 195
Scott-Taylor, Jonathan 240
Scott Thomas, Kristin 127, 232
Seagal, Steven 4, 5, 6, 44, 75, 93
Seale, Douglas 56
Secor, Kyle 104
Sedgwick, Kyra 30
Segal, George 232
Segal, Katey 82
Seinfeld, Jerry 167
Selleck, Tom 45, 56, 104, 133, 170
Sellica, Connie 23
Sevigny, Chloe 209
Seymour, Jane 116, 117
Shakur, Tupac 30
Shatner, William 6, 33, 137
Shaver, Helen 131
Shaw, Robert 54, 109
Shawn, Wallace 231–232
Sheedy, Ally 83, 135, 239

Sheen, Charlie 9, 32, 171, 193, 232
Sheffer, Craig 127–128
Shelton, Marley 122
Shepherd, Cybill 49, 170, 221
Shepherd, Sam 31, 203, 227
Shields, Brooke 100
Shire, Talia 194, 242
Shore, Pauly 184
Short, Martin 238
Shue, Elisabeth 22, 60, 75, 76, 133, 151, 168
Siemaszko, Casey 185, 225
Silverheels, Jay 225
Silverman, Jonathan 177
Simon, Paul 182
Sinatra, Frank 27, 95, 135
Sinbad 119, 230
Sinese, Gary 68, 143, 208
Singer, Lori 224
Sizemore, Tom 61, 84
Skye, Ione 145, 236
Slater, Christian 7, 26, 31, 88, 98, 117–118, 122
Slater, Helen 214, 231
Smith, Bubba 61
Smith, Kevin 140
Smith, Lane 191, 242
Smith, Maggie 136
Smith, Will 50, 53, 71, 147, 168
Smith-Osborne, Madolyn 228
Snider, Dee 42
Snipes, Wesley 51, 61, 86–87, 128–129
Sobieski, Leelee 119
Sokoloff, Marla 122
Sorvino, Mira 161
Sorvino, Paul 156
Spacek, Sissy 92, 106, 174, 179, 204, 213
Spacey, Kevin 66, 66, 72, 82, 119, 135
Spader, James 37, 100, 126, 233
Spano, Vincent 139, 144, 180
Spielberg, Steven 241
Spilsbury, Klinton 147
Stallone, Sylvester 33, 37, 40, 63, 135, 140, 162, 183, 194, 233, 242
Stamos, John 21
Stamp, Terrance 159
Stapleton, Maureen 164
Starrett, Charles 37

Steenburgen, Mary 61, 124, 134, 182, 218
Steiger, Rod 81
Steiner, Russell 193
Stern, Daniel 80
Stewart, Catherine Mary 182
Stewart, Jimmy 35–36, 52, 59, 114, 147, 223
Stewart, Patrick 137
Stiles, Julia 237–238
Stiller, Ben 63
Stitch, Elaine 55
Stockwell, Dean 60
Stone, Sharon 17, 63, 94, 130, 200
Stowe, Madeleine 69, 76, 77, 175, 196
Strassman, Marcia 132, 171
Streep, Meryl 90, 90, 112, 142–143, 146, 157, 158, 159, 167, 168, 223
Streisand, Barbra 36, 171, 201
Strode, Woody 13
Sutherland, Donald 24, 31, 83, 116, 168, 216
Sutherland, Kiefer 41, 79, 125, 136, 145, 150, 243
Swank, Hilary 111, 209
Swayze, Patrick 83, 128–129, 146, 155, 211, 230
Sweeney, D.B. 187

Tanaka, Sara 219
Tandy, Jessica 67, 68
Tate, Larenz 81
Tate, Sharon 46
Taylor, Delores 7
Taylor, Elizabeth 27, 94, 114, 212
Taylor, Rod 18
Tenney, Jon 17
Thal, Eric 31
Theron, Charlize 227
Thomas, Henry 207, 210
Thomas, Richard 122
Thompson, Emma 25
Thompson, Lea 5
Thornberry, Bill 29
Thornton, Billy Bob 14, 23, 53, 122
Thurman, Uma 118, 186
Tilly, Meg 3, 184
Todd, Beverly 142
Tomita, Tamlyn 25, 186
Torn, Rip 146
Tracy, Spencer 24, 39, 107, 128

ACTOR AND DIRECTOR INDEX

Travanti, Daniel J. 80
Travis, Nancy 33
Travolta, John 7, 25, 30, 69, 109, 166, 190, 216, 217, 221
Trevor, Claire 12
Tripplehorn, Jeanne 204
Tucker, Forrest 147
Turner, Janine 235
Turner, Kathleen 29, 54, 101, 105–106, 129, 164, 239
Turner, Lana 102
Turtutto, Jon 124
Tuttle, Fred 228–229
Tyler, Liv 24
Tyson, Richard 225

Ullman, Tracy 235
Ulrich, Skeet 126
Underwood, Blair 59
Urich, Robert 112, 137
Ustinov, Peter 193

Valentino, Rudolph 37
Vance, Courtney B. 123
Van Cleef, Lee 125
Van Damme, Jean Claude 195
Van Der Beck, James 174, 221
Van Dien, Casper 243
Varney, Jim 56
Vartan, Michael 82
Vaughn, Robert 18
Vaughn, Vince 137
Vidal, Christina 159
Villechaize, Herve 74
Voight, Jon 6, 66, 67, 67, 161, 221
Von Sydow, Max 132, 133, 226

Wagner, Lindsay 225
Wahlberg, Mark 11, 37, 112
Waits, Tom 158
Walken, Christopher 13, 43, 127, 158
Walker, Clint 187
Walker, Jessica 30
Wallach, Eli 81
Walsh, J.T. 18
Ward, Fred 39
Warden, Jack 11, 102, 151
Warner, David 34
Warner, Julie 31, 55
Warren, Linda 111
Washington, Denzel 52, 69, 72, 160, 191, 194
Waterston, Sam 105–106, 127, 159
Wayans, Marlon 237
Wayne, John 12, 13, 42, 44, 45, 73, 101, 136, 147, 213, 222, 222, 226, 241
Weathers, Carl 242
Weaver, Sigourney 49, 153, 155, 156, 224
Weber, Steven 114
Welch, Racquel 223
Weld, Tuesday 213
Weller, Peter 218, 223
Welles, Orson 99
Whitaker, Forest 182–183
Whitton, Margaret 101
Widmark, Richard 223, 226, 232
Wiest, Dianne 157, 182
Wilder, Gene 37, 85, 164
Wilkinson, Tom 201
Williams, Billy Dee 65, 88, 162
Williams, Jo Beth 92, 183
Williams, Michelle 50

Williams, Robin 20, 24, 26, 28, 42, 43, 48, 109, 110, 138, 144, 154
Williams, Vanessa 167
Willis, Bruce 41, 51, 53, 93, 142, 150, 163, 194, 195, 196, 199
Wilson, Luke 213
Wilson, Scott 92
Wilson, Try 10
Winfrey, Oprah 47, 47
Winger, Debra 18, 45, 65, 73, 76, 128, 159, 214, 221, 235–236
Winningham, Mare 35
Winter, Alex 7
Winters, Jonathan 24, 191
Winters, Shelley 239
Witherspoon, Reese 120, 128
Wood, Elijah 123, 138, 142, 200, 202
Wood, Natalie 13, 129, 169
Woods, James 35, 86, 123, 127
Woodward, Joanne 90, 97, 99, 126
Workman, Jimmy 16
Wright, Robin 68, 101
Wright, Teresa 32
Wuhl, Robert 3
Wyman, Jane 30

Yankovic, Al 185
Yasbeck, Amy 61
Yoakam, Dwight 14
York, Michael 214

Zellweger, Renee 9, 10, 17, 142–143, 229
Zorin, Max 36
Zuniga, Daphne 34

MOVIE AND TELEVISION SHOW INDEX

About Last Night 75
Above the Law 75
Absence of Malice 53
Absolute Power 102
The Abyss 199
Ace Ventura: Pet Detective 53
Ace Ventura: When Nature Calls 207
Addams Family Values 16
Addicted to Love 148
Adventures in Babysitting 75–76
Adventures of Huck Finn 123
The Adventures of Rin Tin Tin 225
Adventures of Robin Hood 16
The Adventures of Rocky and Bullwinkle 16
An Affair to Remember 148
After Hours 148
Against a Crooked Sky 226
The Age of Innocence 148
Air Force One 180
The Alamo 222–223
Alice 149
Alice's Restaurant 106
All the President's Men 48
All the Pretty Horses 207–208
All the Right Moves 189

Ally McBeal 106–107
Always 127
American Flyers 40
American Graffiti 16–17
American Movie: The Making of Northwestern 240
American President 48
Amistad 197
The Amityville Horror 139
Analyze This 149
Anatomy of a Murder 114–115
And God Created Woman 144
And Justice for All 102
Angel Heart 95
Angels in the Outfield 17
Animal Factory 189
Animal House 185
Annie 139
Annie Hall 149
Another Stakeout 129
Any Given Sunday 208
Any Which Way You Can 241, 242
The Apartment
Apollo 13 208
Arizona 13
Arlington Road 208
Armageddon 53
Arrowhead 222
Arthur 149

Article 99 125
Assassins 233
Austin Powers: International Man of Mystery 129
Avalon 102–103

The Babe 76
Baby Boom 227
Baby Geniuses 129
Baby It's You 139
Baby's Day Out 76
The Bachelor 17
Back to School 240
Backdraft 76
Bad Boys 53–54
Bad Day at Black Rock 39
Bad News Bears Break Training 208, 209
Bandolero! 223
Bang the Drum Slowly 149
Barbarosa 223
Barefoot in the Park 150
Basic Instinct 17
Beau Geste 37
Beautiful Girls 118
Bedazzled 17
The Bedroom Window 103
Beetlejuice 227
The Beguiled 95
The Bellboy 54
Beloved 47–48
Benny and Joon 233–234

MOVIE AND TELEVISION INDEX

The Best Little Whorehouse in Texas 208
Betrayed 76
The Betsy 197
Betsy's Wedding 173
Beverly Hills Cop 3 17–18
Big 139
The Big Brass Ring 125
The Big Chill 199
The Big Easy 95–96
Big Green 208–209
The Big Trail 241
Bill and Ted's Excellent Adventure 7
Billy Bathgate 173
Billy Jack 7
Biloxi Blues 13–14
The Bingo Long Traveling All Stars and Motor Kings 65
The Birds 18
Birdy 189
Birth of a Nation 37
Black Sunday 54
Black Widow 73
The Blair Witch Project 103
Blaze 96
Blind Fury 129
Blink 76–77
The Blob 189–190
Blow Out 190
Blown Away 107, 108
Blue Chips 88
Blue Collar 115
Blue Hawaii 73
Blue Sky 3
Blue Velvet 173
The Blues Brothers 77
Bob and Carol and Ted and Alice 129
Bob Roberts 190
Body Heat 54
Body of Evidence 234
Body Snatchers 3
The Bodyguard 129–130
Bonanza 130
The Bonfire of the Vanities 150
Bonnie and Clyde 209
Born on the Fourth of July 209
Born Yesterday 48
Boston Public 107
The Bostonians 107
Boxcar Bertha 14
Boxing Helena 66
Boys Don't Cry 209–210

Boys on the Side 140
Boys Town 128
Breakdown 18
Breakfast at Tiffanys 150
Breakfast Club 77
Breaking Away 88
Breaking In 185–186
Brewster Mccloud 210
Brian's Song 88
Bridges of Madison County 90–91
Bright Lights, Big City 150
Broadcast News 49
Broadway Danny Rose 150
Broken Arrow 7
Brothers McMullen 151
Buffalo Girls 215
Buffalo 66 151
Bull Durham 173
Bullets Over Broadway 151
Bullitt 18
Bus Stop 7
Butch Cassidy and the Sundance Kid 40
The Butcher's Wife 173–174

Caddyshack 54
Call of the North 37
The Candidate 18
Cannery Row 18–19
Can't Buy Me Love 8
Cape Fear 54
Captains Courageous 107
Casablanca 8
Casino 130
Cast Away 203
Cat Ballou 45
Cat People 96
The Cemetery Club 190
Chain Reaction 77–78
The Chamber 123
Chances Are 49
Charly 107
Chasers 199
Chasing Amy 140
Cheers 109
Cherry 200 130
Cheyenne Autumn 226
Chicken Every Sunday 130
Chisum 147
A Christmas Story 180
Cider House Rules 227–228
Cinderella Liberty 234
City of Hope 180
City Slickers 147
City Slickers II 226
A Civil Action 109

Clara's Heart 103
Class 78
Class Action 18
Clean and Sober 190
Clerks 140
The Client 204
Cliffhanger 40
Cloak and Dagger 210
Close Encounters of the Third Kind 241
Coal Miner's Daughter 204
Cobb 3
Cocktail 151
Cocoon 54
Cocoon: The Return 54–55
The Color of Money 78
The Color Purple 174
Come See the Paradise 186
Coming to America 151
Con Air 130–131
Conagher 45
Consenting Adults 66
Contact 144–145
Contrabando 215
The Conversation 19
Cookie's Fortune 123
Cool World 131
Cop and a Half 55
Cop Land 140
Cosby 151
The Cotton Club 152
The Cowboy Way 145
The Cowboys 45
Coyote Ugly 140
Crazy People 230
Creature from the Black Lagoon 55
Crimes and Misdemeanors 152
Crimes of the Heart 174, 179
Crisscross 55
Crocodile Dundee 152
Crocodile Dundee II 152
Crossing Delancey 152
The Crow 174
Cujo 19
Curly Sue 78

Dallas 210, 211
Damien: Omen 2 240–241
Dancer, Texas Pop 81 210
Dances with Wolves 203
Dante's Peak 75
Dark Passage 19
D.A.R.Y.L. 55
Dave 49
Dawn of the Dead 190

MOVIE AND TELEVISION INDEX 274

Dawson's Creek 174, 179
The Day After 92
The Day the Earth Stood Still 49–50
Days of Thunder 8
Dazed and Confused 210
Dead Man Walking 96
Dead Poets Society 48
Deadwood Coach 225
Death Valley Days 225
Deep Impact 50
The Deer Hunter 180
Deliverance 66–67, 67
Denver and Rio Grande 40–41
Desert Hearts 131
Designing Women 14
Desperately Seeking Susan 152–153
Devil's Advocate 55
Dick 50
Die Hard II 41
Die Hard with a Vengeance 199
Diggstown 127
Diner 103
Dirty Dancing 230, 231
Dirty Harry 19
Disclosure 234
The Distinguished Gentleman 191
Doc Hollywood 55–56
Dr. T and the Women 210–211
Dog Day Afternoon 153
Dogma 191
Donnie Brasco 140–141
Donovan's Reef 73
The Doors 19–20
Double Jeopardy 96–97
Dream a Little Dream 174
The Dream Team 153
Dressed to Kill 191
Drive Me Crazy 223–224
Driving Miss Daisy 67
Drop Dead Gorgeous 118
The Drowning Pool 97
Drugstore Cowboy 186
Dumb and Dumber 41
Dutch 67

Easy Rider 97
Ed 141
Ed TV 20
Eddie 174
Eddie and the Cruisers 141
Edward Scissorhands 56

8 Seconds 211
Eight Men Out 88
Election 128
Electric Horseman 131
Enemy of the State 50
ER 78
Eraser 50
Erin Brockovich 20
Ernest Saves Christmas 56, 57
Escape from Alcatraz 20
Escape from New York 125
Ethan Frome 228
Evangeline 97
Even Cowgirls Get the Blues 186
Every Which Way But Loose 41
Everybody Wins 45
Everybody's All-American 97–98
Everyone Says I Love You 153
The Exorcist 50–51
The Exorcist III 51
Eyewitness 153–154

Fabulous Baker Boys 234
A Face in the Crowd 14–15
Fair Game 56
Fallen 191
Fame 154
Family Man 141
A Family Thing 204
Fandango 211
Fantasy Island 74
Fargo 118
Fatal Attraction 154
Father Hood 211
Fearless 20
Ferris Bueller's Day Off 78–79
A Few Good Men 51
Field of Dreams 91
Finding Graceland 204
Fire Down Below 93
Firestarter 178
The Firm 204–205
First Kid 230
The First of May 56
The First Wives Club 154
The Fish That Saved Pittsburgh 191
The Fisher King 154
Five Against the House 131
Flashback 41–42
Flashdance 191–192
Flatliners 79

Flesh and Bone 212
Flim Flam Man 93
Flubber 20
Folks 56–57
Foolin' Around 118
Fools Rush In 131
Footloose 224
For Love or Money 154–155
For Richer or Poorer 103–104
Forces of Nature 68
Forever Mine 57
Forever Young 21
Forrest Gump 68
Fort Apache 13
Foul Play 21
The Four Seasons 230
Fox Fire 186
Frank and Jesse 15
Free Willy 186–187
Freejack 68
Fresh Horses 180–181
The Freshman 155
Friday the 13th 141
Fried Green Tomatoes 68–69
Frogs 57, 58
From Here to Eternity 74
The Fugitive 79
Full House 21
Funny Bones 131
Funny Farm 228

Galaxy Quest 224
The Game 21
Gas Food Lodging 145
Gattaca 21
The Gauntlet 8
The General's Daughter 69
George of the Jungle 21–22
The Getaway 212
Getting Even with Dad 21
Ghost 155
Ghostbusters 155
Ghostbusters II 155–156
Ghosts of Mississippi 123
GI Jane 57–58
Giant 212–213
Girl Interrupted 192
Glory 69–70
The Godfather 156
The Godfather Part II 132
Godzilla 156
Goldfinger 58
The Good Son 138
Good Will Hunting 109, 110
The Goodbye Girl 156
Goodfellas 156

MOVIE AND TELEVISION INDEX

The Graduate 22
Grand Canyon 8–9
Great Balls of Fire 205, 206
Great Expectations 58–59
The Great Gatsby 197
The Great Santini 199–200
The Greatest Show on Earth 59
The Greatest Story Ever Told 132, 133, 226
Green Card 157
Green Fields of Wyoming 181
The Green Mile 205
The Grifters 9
The Groove Tube 147
Grosse Pointe Blank 115
Groundhog Day 79
Grumpier Old Men 119
Grumpy Old Men 119
Guarding Tess 104
The Gun in Betty Lou's Handbag 123
Gunfight at the OK Corral 13
The Gunfighter 39
Gunga Din 39
Gunsmoke 225

Hairspray 192
The Hand That Rocks the Cradle 234
Hannah and Her Sisters 157
Hannibal 230–231
Hard Rain 88–89
Harold and Maude 21
Harper Valley PTA 181
Harry and the Hendersons 234–235
Harry and Walter Go to New York 181
Harry in Your Pocket 235
Hawaii Five-O 74
He Said/She Said 104
Hear No Evil 187
Heart and Souls 22
The Heart Is a Lonely Hunter 3–4
Heartbreak Hotel 213
Heartburn 157
Heaven Can Wait 23
Heaven's Gate 127
Hellfighters 213
Hellraiser III: Hell on Earth 175
Her Alibi 104
Here on Earth 119
Hero 79–80
Hide in Plain Sight 157

High Anxiety 23
High Fidelity 80
High Noon 23
Hill Street Blues 80
Hi-Lo Country 145
Hocus Pocus 109
Hoffa 115
Home Alone 80
Home Alone II: Lost in New York 80
Home for the Holidays 104
Home Fries 213
Homegrown 23
Homicide: Life on the Street 104
Honey, I Blew Up the Kid 132
Honeymoon in Vegas 132
Honky Tonk Man 132
Hoosiers 89
Hope Floats 213
The Horse Whisperer 127
Hotel 23
The House on 92nd Street 157
Housesitter 109
How the West Was Won 39, 42
How to Marry a Millionaire 157–158
The Hudsucker Proxy 80–81
The Hunter 81
Hurry Sundown 98
Hush Hush Sweet Charlotte 98
Hysterical 187

I Know What You Did Last Summer 175
I Love Trouble 241
I Love You to Death 235, 236
Ice Palace 5–6
In and Out 141
In Cold Blood 92
In Country 93–94
In the Army Now 184
In the Heat of the Night (movie) 81
In the Heat of the Night (TV) 70, 71
In the Line of Fire 51
Indecent Proposal 132–133
Indiana Jones and the Last Crusade 145, 226
Indiana Jones and the Temple of Doom 23

Innocent Blood 192
An Innocent Man 133
The Insider 24
Instinct 59
Interview with a Vampire 98, 99
Invasion of the Body Snatchers 24
Invasion USA 70
Inventing the Abbotts 24
IQ 141–142
Iron Will 119
Ironweed 158
It Could Happen to You 142
It Should Happen to You 158
It's a Mad Mad Mad World 24

Jack 24
Jack Frost 24–25
Jackal 51
Jaws 109–110
Jeremiah Johnson 224–225
Jerry Maguire 9
JFK 213–214
Jingle All the Way 119
Johnny Be Good 214
The Joy Luck Club 25
Jumanji 138
Junior 25
Junior Bonner 9
Jurassic Park 74
Just Cause 59
Just One of the Guys 9
Just the Ticket 158
Just the Way You Are 192

Kalifornia 70–71
Kansas 92
Kansas City 125
King Kong 158
King of New York 158
King of the Hill 125
King Pin 192
King Solomon's Mines 145–146
Kiss the Girls 175
Kissing a Fool 81
Kojak 158–159
Kramer Vs. Kramer 159

Ladybugs 42
Larger Than Life 126
Lassie 231
Last Dance 200
The Last of the Mohicans 175

MOVIE AND TELEVISION INDEX

The Last Picture Show 214, 221
Law and Order 159
A League of Their Own 89
Lean on Me 142
Leap of Faith 214
Leaving Las Vegas 133–134
Legal Eagles 159
The Legend of Bagger Vance 71
The Legend of Billy Jean 214
The Legend of the Lone Ranger 147
Let It Ride 59
Lethal Weapon III 59
Lethal Weapon 4 134
Liberty Heights 104–105
License to Kill 60
Life 25
The Life and Assassination of the Kingfish 98
Life with Mikey 159
Light of Day 181
Little Big League 120
Little Man Tate 181–182
Live and Let Die 98–99
Logan's Run 214
The Lone Ranger 39, 225
Lone Star 215
Lonesome Dove 215–216, 223
The Long Hot Summer 99
The Long Kiss Goodnight 159
The Longest Yard 71–72
Lorenzo's Oil 192–193
Lost Angels 216
The Lost Boys 25
Lost in America 134
Lost in Yonkers 182
Love Affair 159
Love Jones 81
Love Potion Number 9 72
Love Story 110
Lucas 81
Lucky Numbers 25

Mad About You 160
Mad Dog and Glory 81–82
Made in America 25–26
Major League 9
Major League — Back to the Minors 200
Major League II 193
Major Payne 231
Malcolm X 160
Malice 110
Mallrats 120
Man from Laramie 147
Man on the Moon 160
The Man Who Fell to Earth 146
The Man with a Plan 228–229
The Man Without a Face 101
Manhattan 160
Manhattan Murder Mystery 160
The Manhattan Project 160–161
Mannequin 193
Married to the Mob 60
Married ... with Children 82
Mars Attacks! 92
Mary Tyler Moore 120
Matewan 239
Matinee 60
Matlock 175
Maverick 9
Me Myself and Irene 229
Mean Season 60
Meet Joe Black 198
Melvin and Howard 134
Men Don't Leave 105
Men of Honor 187
Mercury Rising 51
Mermaids 110–111
Message in a Bottle 101–102
Michael 216, 217
Mickey Blue Eyes 161
Midnight Cowboy 161
Midnight in the Garden of Good and Evil 72
Midnight Run 115–116
Midway 216
Mighty Aphrodite 161
The Mighty 94
The Mighty Ducks 120
The Mighty Ducks II 120
The Milagro Beanfield War 146
Milk Money 182
Miller's Crossing 99
Miracle on 34th Street 161
Mischief 182
Misery 134
The Misfits 134–135
Miss Congeniality 216
Miss Firecracker 124
Mississippi Burning 4, 124
Mr. and Mrs. Bridge 126
Mr. Destiny 175
Mr. Holland's Opus 187
Mr. Smith Goes to Washington 52
Moonstruck 161
Mork and Mindy 42, 43
Mortal Thoughts 142
Movie Index
Mrs. Doubtfire 26
Mrs. Soffel 193
Mumford 26
Murder at 1600 52
Murder in the First 26
Murder, She Wrote 26
Murphy's Romance 10
My Best Friend's Wedding 82
My Blue Heaven 26–27, 28
My Bodyguard 82
My Cousin Vinny 72
My Darling Clementine 13
My Dinner with Andre 231–232
My Dog Skip 124
My Fellow Americans 52
My Girl 60
My Heroes Have Always Been Cowboys 184
My Own Private Idaho 187
My Summer Story 182
Mystery Train 205
Mystic Pizza 45
Myth of Fingerprints 102

Nadine 216
The Naked City 161–162
Nashville 205
National Lampoon's Christmas Vacation 42
National Lampoon's Vacation 10
National Velvet 27
The Natural 162
Natural Born Killers 146
Navy Seals 232
Necessary Roughness 217
The Negotiator 82
Nell 176
The Net 27
Network 162
Never Been Kissed 82
Never Too Late 111
New Port South 82
New York Stories 162
Newhart 229
Newton Boys 217
The Next Karate Kid 111
Next of Kin 83
Next Stop Wonderland 111

277 MOVIE AND TELEVISION INDEX

Night of the Hunter 239–240
Night of the Living Dead 193
Nighthawks 162–163
Nine Months 27
No Way Out 52
Nobody's Fool 163
Norma Rae 4–5
North 142
North By Northwest 203
North of the Great Divide 37
Northern Exposure 235
Nothing in Common 83
Nurse Betty 10
NYPD Blue 163

O Brother Where Art Thou 124
Ocean's Eleven 135
October Sky 205–206
Ode to Billie Joe 124
An Officer and a Gentleman 235
Oh God You Devil 135
On Deadly Ground 6
On Golden Pond 139
On the Waterfront 142
One Crazy Summer 111
One Flew Over the Cuckoo's Nest 187–188
One Trick Pony 182
One True Thing 142–143
Only the Lonely 83
Only You 193
Ordinary People 83
Other People's Money 45
Out of Sight 99–100
The Out of Towners 111, 163
Outbreak 27
Outlaw Josie Wales 13, 225
The Outsiders 184
Over the Top 135
Overnight Delivery 120
Oxford Blues 135

Pacific Heights 27
The Package 83
Paint Your Wagon 188
Pal Joey 27–28
Pale Rider 75
Palmetto 60–61
The Paper 163
The Paper Chase 111–112
Paper Moon 93
Paradise 200
The Parallax View 236
The Parent Trap 28

Parenthood 61
Passenger 57 61
Patch Adams 28–29
The Patriot 201
Patriot Games 105
The Patty Duke Show 163–164
Pay It Forward 135
Pearl Harbor 218
Pee Wee's Big Adventure 218
Peggy Sue Got Married 29
Pelican Brief 52–53
Penitentiary 91
The People Vs. Larry Flynt 206
A Perfect Murder 163
The Perfect Storm 112, 113
A Perfect World 218, 219
Personal Best 188
Petticoat Junction 29
Petulia 29
Peyton Place 102
Phantasm 29
Phenomenon 30
Philadelphia 194
The Pick-Up Artist 164
Pink Cadillac 135–136
The Pistol: Birth of a Legend 100
Planes, Trains and Automobiles 83–84
Play It Again Sam 30
Play It to the Bone 136
Play Misty for Me 30
Plaza Suite 164
Poetic Justice 30
Police Academy 5: Assignment in Miami Beach 61
Polish Wedding 116
Pollyanna 30
Powder 218
Practical Magic 236
The Practice 112
Prancer 89
Prefontaine 236
Prelude to a Kiss 84
Presumed Innocent 116
Pretty Baby 100
Primal Fear 84
The Prince of Tides 201
The Principal 30
Prison 242
Prizzi's Honor 164
Problem Child 61
The Producers 164
The Professionals 136
The Program 201

Promised Land 136
Providence 198
PT 109 61
Pump Up the Volume 31
The Puppet Masters 31
Purple Rain 122

Quick Change 164

Radio Days 164–165
A Rage in Harlem 182–183
Raging Bull 165
Ragtime 165
Raiders of the Lost Ark 31
Rain Man 94
The Rainmaker 206
Raintree County 94
Raising Arizona 10
Raising Cain 31
Rambling Rose 176
Rambo III 37
Rancho Deluxe 127
Random Hearts 232
Ransom 165
Rat Patrol 37
Raw Deal 176
The Real McCoy 72
Reality Bites 218
Reckless 240
Red Dawn 146
Red Heat 84
Regarding Henry 165
The Relic 84
Remember the Titans 72–73
Renaissance Man 116
The Replacements 105
Return of the Jedi 31, 37
Return of the Secaucus Seven 139
Return to Me 84
Revenge of the Nerds 10
Rich and Famous 165–166
Richie Rich 176
Ride with the Devil 126
The Right Stuff 31
Rio Bravo 13
Rio Grande 226
Risky Business 84–85
A River Runs Through It 127–128
The River Wild 112
The Road to Wellville 176–177
Roadside Prophets 136
Robocop 223
Robocop 2 218–219
The Rock 31–32

MOVIE AND TELEVISION INDEX

Rocky 194
Rocky II 194
Rocky IV 242
Roger and Me 116
Rollercoaster 232
The Rookie 32
Rookie of the Year 85
The Rosary Murders 116
Rosemary's Baby 166
Rounders 143
The Royal Mounted Patrol 37
Ruby in Paradise 62
Rude Awakening 62
Rudy 89
Rules of Engagement 201
Rumble Fish 184
Runaway Bride 105
Runaway Train 6
Running Scared 62–63
Rush 219
Rushmore 219

The Sacketts 45
Sahara 37
St. Elmo's Fire 105
Same Time, Next Year 32
Saturday Night Fever 166
Savage Bees 100
Say Anything 236
Scenes from a Mall 45–46
Scent of a Woman 166
School Ties 112
Scream 32
Scream 2 73
Scrooged 166
Sea of Love 166
The Searchers 12–13
Searching for Bobby Fischer 166–167
Seinfeld 167
Selena 219–220
Semi-Tough 63
Sergeant Rutledge 13
Serial Mom 105–106
Serpico 167
Sex Lies and Videotape 100
Shadow of a Doubt 32
Shaft 167
Shaft Returns 167
Shag 202
Shane 242–243
Shattered 188
The Shawshank Redemption 183
She-Devil 167
She Wore a Yellow Ribbon 13

She's Having a Baby 85
The Shiek 37
The Shining 188
Shoot the Moon 32
The Shootist 136
Showgirls 136
Sidekicks 220
Silence of the Lambs 194
Silent Fall 106
Silkwood 146, 223
Silver Bullet 177
Silver Streak 85
Silverado 147
Simpatico 94
A Simple Plan 122
Single White Female 167
Singles 237
Sister Act 136–137
Six Degrees of Separation 168
The Six Million Dollar Man 225
Sixteen Candles 85
The Sixth Man 237
Sixth Sense 194–195
Slacker 220
Slap Shot 195
Sleeper 42
Sleepers 46
Sleeping with the Enemy 177, 179
Sleepless in Seattle 237
Sling Blade 15–16
A Small Circle of Friends 112
Snake Eyes 143
Sneakers 32–33
Snow Falling on Cedars 237
So I Married an Axe Murderer 33
A Soldier's Story 16
Some Came Running 95
Someone to Watch Over Me 168
Something About Mary 63
Something to Talk About 202
Something Wild 63
Sometimes a Great Notion 188
Sometimes They Come Back 126
Somewhere in Time 116–117
Sommersby 232
Sophie's Choice 168
The Sopranos 143
Soul of the Game 5
South Pacific 74
Space Camp 5

Space Cowboys 220
Spanish Prisoner 112
The Specialist 63
Speechless 146–147
Spencer's Mountain 243
Spenser: For Hire 112–113
Spies 177, 179
Spitfire Grill 229
Splash 168–169
Splendor in the Grass 169
Spy Kids 220
Stagecoach 12
Stanley and Iris 46
Star Trek: Generations 137
Star Trek IV: the Voyage Home 33
Star Trek VI: the Undiscovered Country 6–7
Stardust Memories 143
Stargate 37
Starman 10–11
Starship Troopers 243
State and Main 113
Stealing Home 143–144
Steel Magnolias 100
Stella 169
Stepford Wives 46
Stepmom 169
Stick 63
Still Breathing 220–221
The Sting 85–86
Sting II 33
Stir of Echoes 86
Stop! Or My Mom Will Shoot 33
Storm Center 33–34
Straight Story 92
Straight Talk 86
Strangeland 42–43
Streets of Laredo 215
Striking Distance 195
Stripes 95
Stroker Ace 5
Sudden Death 195
Sudden Impact 34
Sugar and Spice 122
Superman 169
The Sure Thing 34
Swamp Thing 202
Sweet Dreams 240
The Sweet Smell of Success 169
Swingers 137

Tango and Cash 183
Taps 195
Tarzan 101

279 MOVIE AND TELEVISION INDEX

Taxi 170
Taxi Driver 170
Teachers 183
Tell Me That You Love Me, Junie Moon 113
Telling Lies in America 183
The Temp 189
Ten Things I Hate About You 237–238
Ten Who Dared 226
Terminator 2: Judgment Day 34
Terms of Endearment 128
Tex 184–185
The Texas Chainsaw Massacre 221
Texasville 221
Thelma and Louise 226, 227
The Thing Called Love 207
Things Change 137
Things to Do in Denver When You're Dead 43
This Boy's Life 238
This Is My Life 137
Three Amigos 13
Three Days of the Condor 170
Three Fugitives 238
Three Kings 11
Three Men and a Baby 170
Three Ninjas: High Noon at Mega Mountain 43
Three O'clock High 225
Thunderheart 203
A Ticket to Tomahawk 43–44
Tightrope 101
Time After Time 34
A Time to Kill 124
Tin Cup 11
Tin Men 106
To Gillian on Her 37th Birthday 113, 179
To Wong Foo, Thanks for Everything, Julie Newmar 128–129
Too Close for Comfort 34
Tootsie 170
Towering Inferno 34–35
Toy Soldiers 232–233
Traces of Red 63
Trading Places 195
Trail of the Lonesome 37
Tremors 39
The Trouble with Harry 229
True Colors 233
True Crime 35

True Grit 44
True Lies 64
True Romance 117–118
Truman Show 64
Tucker: A Man and His Dream 35
Turner and Hooch 35
Twelve Monkeys 195–196
Twin Peaks 238
Twins 147
Twister 185
Two Bits 196
Two Rode Together 223

Uhf 185
Ulee's Gold 64
Unbreakable 196
Uncle Buck 86
The Undefeated 101
Under Siege 4, 5
Under Siege 2 44
Under Western Stars 39
Undercover Blues 101
Unfaithfully Yours 170–171
Untamed Heart 122
The Untouchables 86
Up Close and Personal 64
Urban Cowboy 221
U.S. Marshals 86–87
Used Cars 11

Valley of the Dolls 46
The Vanishing 243
Vanishing Point 44
Varsity Blues 221
Vega$ 137
Vegas Vacation 137–138
The Verdict 114
Vertigo 35–36
Vice Versa 87
A View to a Kill 36
Violets Are Blue 106
Vision Quest 238–239
Viva Las Vegas 138

Wag the Dog 207
Wagon Master 225–226
Waiting for the Light 239
Waiting to Exhale 11, 12
Wall Street 171
The War 202
War of the Roses 239
Wargames 239
Warlock 226
Washington Square 106
Waterboy 64–65
The Way We Were 171

Wayne's World 87
The Wedding Planner 36
Weeds 177
Weekend at Bernie's 177, 179
Weird Science 87
Welcome Back Kotter 171
What About Bob? 233
What Lies Beneath 230
What's Eating Gilbert Grape 221
What's Up Doc? 36
When a Man Loves a Woman 36
When Harry Met Sally 171
Where the Boys Are 65
Where the Heart Is 221
While You Were Sleeping 87–88
White Fang 6, 7
White Palace 126
White Sands 147
White Squall 202
Who's Afraid of Virginia Woolf? 114
Wild Things 65
Wild Wild West 147
Wildcats 88
Wilder Napalm 65
Wings 114
The Winner 138
Winning 90
Wise Guys 144
The Witches of Eastwick 114
With Honors 114
Witness 196
The Wiz 171–172
WKRP in Cincinnati 183–184
Wolf 172
The Woman in Red 37
Woman Wanted 46–47
Wonder Boys 196
Wooly Boys 179
Working Girl 172
The World According to Garp 144
Worth Winning 196–197
Wrestling Ernest Hemingway 65
Wyatt Earp 147

You'll Like My Mother 121, 122
You've Got Mail 172
Yukon Gold 37

Zelig 172